to my chinese friend Cecil on occasion of his birthday [illegible]

7.04.88

[illegible]

Neue dänische Architektur

Tobias Faber

Neue dänische Architektur

Verlag Gerd Hatje Stuttgart

Übersetzung ins Englische und Deutsche von E. Rockwell

Contents

Inhalt

In 1926, an exhibition of modern Danish architecture, held in Berlin, showed the works of a number of prominent younger Danish architects who, in years to come, were destined to become the leading architects of their country: Ivar Bentsen, Kaj Gottlob, Kay Fisker, Kaare Klint, Steen Eiler Rasmussen and the landscape gardener G.N. Brandt. The reviews in the Berlin press brought almost identical descriptions, though the appraisals were partly highly flattering, partly somewhat disparaging. The critics referred to "a sober objectivity in the modern spirit", "an unaffected but self-confident simplicity", "houses which grow naturally out of the landscape"; they wrote about "the architects' lack of keenness to experiment", but also about "an avoidance of architectural licentiousness", and finally about "a strict and sure taste", which some of the critics found "cold right to the innermost heart" whilst others regarded it as "salutary like an old and timeless tradition". In the early 1920s, Danish architecture was dominated by a simplified, formal neo-classicism, which coincided with efforts of sober social and functional purport. The appraisals in the Berlin press are however applicable to essential aspects of older as well as modern Danish architecture.

Denmark has not always been such a small country as it is now; architecturally, however, it has always been a province which has not been able to make any decisive contribution to the general development of architecture. Denmark has always derived its inspirations from abroad. On the other hand, Danish builders and architects have always been critical of new trends and have tried to adapt the impulses received from abroad to Danish conditions and habits, Danish climate and landscape and to the crafts tradition of the country. Danish architecture is marked by an evolutionary development without major excesses, but also without epoch-making architectural monuments. Right up to our time, Danish architecture has been influenced by a functional tradition which had dominated large parts of building activities, with close relation to the crafts and to the materials in common use; timber and brick. The different stylistic periods followed each other in smooth transition with buildings which were felt to be variations on the theme of the "Danish House" rather than outstanding examples for contemporary international architectural styles. Danish architecture is therefore apt to make a sober impression in a romantic age, and a romantic impression in periods with a more rational outlock.

In the, at one time, wooded country with few deposits of natural stone, the most valuable architectural heritage from the Middle Ages is represented by some 2000 well-preserved village churches built throughout the country during the 12th and 13th centuries (Fig.1). They are simple, mighty buildings of granite or limestone with naves and choirs covered by steep saddle-roofs (Fig. 2). Despite conversions and additions of belfries, porches and vaults dur-

1. Vraa Church, Vendsyssel, Jutland. Typical Danish village church with Romanesque nave and choir of hewn ashlar and Gothic belfry with rough-cast walls.

1. Vraa-Kirche in Vendsyssel, Jütland. Typische dänische Dorfkirche mit romanischem Schiff und Chor aus behauenen Steinquadern und gemauertem, weißverputzten gotischen Turm.

2. Børglumkloster, Vendsyssel, Jutland, 12th to 15th century. Abbey church and manor house, converted around 1750 by architect Laurids de Thurah.

2. Børglum-Kloster in Vendsyssel, Jütland, 12. bis 15. Jahrhundert. Klosterkirche und Herrenhof, um 1750 vom Architekten Laurids de Thurah umgebaut.

Einleitung

Im Jahr 1926 fand in Berlin eine Ausstellung neuerer dänischer Architektur statt. Sie zeigte die Arbeiten einer Reihe hervorragender jüngerer dänischer Architekten, die in den folgenden Jahrzehnten eine führende Stellung einnehmen sollten: Ivar Bentsen, Kaj Gottlob, Kay Fisker, Kaare Klint, Steen Eiler Rasmussen und Gartenarchitekt G.N. Brandt. In den Berliner Tageszeitungen wurden die ausgestellten Arbeiten fast gleichartig beschrieben, wenn auch die subjektiven Urteile teils äußerst schmeichelhaft, teils abschätzig ausfielen. Die Kritiker sprachen von »einer nüchternen Sachlichkeit im Zeichen der Zeit«, von »einer unaffektierten, jedoch selbstbewußten Einfachheit«, von »Häusern, die auf natürliche Weise aus der Landschaft herauswachsen«, von »einer mangelnden Lust zum Experimentieren seitens der Architekten«, jedoch gleichzeitig auch von »einer Vermeidung architektonischer Ausschweifungen«, und schließlich von »einem strengen und sicheren Geschmack«, den einige Kritiken als »kalt bis an die Herzwurzeln« und andere als »wohltuend wie eine alte, zeitlose Überlieferung« empfanden. Die dänische Architektur war zu Anfang der zwanziger Jahre von einem vereinfachten, formellen Neoklassizismus geprägt, der mit einem Streben nach nüchterner, sozial orientierter und funktionsbezogener Artikulation zusammenfiel. Die in Berlin ausgesprochenen Urteile treffen jedoch auf wesentliche Züge sowohl der älteren als auch der neueren dänischen Baukunst zu.

3. Lynderup Manor, North-Jutland, 1556. Half-timbered two-storey manor house.

3. Lynderupgård in Nord-Jütland, 1556. Zweigeschossiger Herrenhof in Fachwerkbauweise.

Gebietsmäßig war Dänemark nicht immer ein so kleines Land wie es jetzt ist; architektonisch war es jedoch seit jeher eine Provinz, die zur allgemeinen architektonischen Entwicklung keinen ausschlaggebenden Beitrag leisten konnte. Dänemark hat seine Impulse stets aus dem Ausland geholt. Andererseits standen dänische Baumeister und Architekten schon immer allen neuen Strömungen kritisch gegenüber und versuchten, die von außen empfangenen Impulse der dänischen Lebensweise, den dänischen Sitten, dem dänischen Klima, der dänischen Landschaft und der handwerklichen Überlieferung des Landes anzupassen. Die dänische Architektur ist daher durch eine stetige Entwicklung ohne große Schwingungen gekennzeichnet, die allerdings auch keine markanten architektonischen Denkmäler zu schaffen vermochte. Bis in die neueste Zeit hat sich in der dänischen Baukunst eine funktionell orientierte Tradition geltend gemacht, die auf große Teile der Bautätigkeit einen entscheidenden Einfluß ausübte, wobei die handwerkliche Überlieferung in der Bauweise und in der Verwendung der allgemein üblichen Baustoffe – Holz und Ziegel – sehr wichtig genommen wurde. Die verschiedenen Stilperioden gingen ohne scharfe Zäsuren ineinander über und hinterließen Bauwerke, die nicht so sehr als ausgeprägte Beispiele internationaler Architekturstile, sondern eher als Variationen zum Thema des »dänischen Hauses« empfunden werden. Dänische Architektur kann daher in einem romantischen Zeitalter nüchtern und in einer mehr rational eingestellten Zeit romantisch wirken.

In dem ursprünglich waldreichen, jedoch an Naturstein armen Land besteht das wertvollste architektonische Erbgut des Mittelalters aus etwa zweitausend gut erhaltenen Dorfkirchen, die im 12. und 13. Jahrhundert überall im Lande errichtet wurden (Abb.1). Es sind einfache, kraftvolle Gebäude aus Granit oder Kalkstein mit Kirchenschiffen und Chören, die von steilen Satteldächern überragt werden (Abb.2). Trotz der späteren Umbauten und der Hinzufügung von Türmen, Vorbauten und Wölbungen während der Gotik haben diese Kirchenbauten innen wie außen als Dominanten der dänischen Landschaft eine Note einfacher, ausdrucksvoller Kraft bewahrt.

Abgesehen vom Kirchenbau war bis ins 19. Jahrhundert das Holz der allgemein gebräuchliche Baustoff und das Fachwerk die vorherrschende Bauweise, sowohl auf dem Lande (Abb. 3) als auch in den Städten. Durch die regelmäßige Unterteilung der Fachwerkbauten wurde dem Wohnhausbau eine natürliche Ordnung gegeben, die sich mit wenigen Variationen zu einem maßgetreuen, vereinheitlichten Bausystem entwickelte (Abb.4). Der Bauherr konnte beim Handwerksmeister ein Haus mit soundsoviel Fächern und mit einem, zwei oder drei Geschossen bestellen, und wußte dann, was er zu erwarten hatte. Seit dem Ende des 18. Jahrhunderts wurden die Fachwerkbauten mehr und mehr von Ziegelbauten abgelöst, während gleichzeitig die Strohdächer in den Städten durch Ziegeldächer ersetzt wurden. Die regelmäßige Unterteilung der Fachwerkbauten blieb jedoch auch bei den Ziegelhäusern in dem regelmäßigen Rhythmus von Pfeilern und Fenstern erhalten. Dazu kam noch, daß Einfachheit, Ordnung, Präzision und das natürliche Proportionsgefühl der

ing the Gothic period, these church buildings have preserved a simple and expressive strength both in their interiors and externally as dominant features in the Danish landscape.
Apart from churches, timber used to be the material most generally employed, and half-timbering used to be the dominating construction method right up to the 19th century, both in the country (Fig. 3) and in town. The regular bay partition of the half-timbered house bestowed on the house a natural orderliness which was developed into a module-governed, standardised building system with but few variations (Fig. 4). The client was able to place his order with the master builder for a house with so many bays and with one, two or three floors, and he then knew what to expect. From the end of the 18th century onwards, half-timbering came to be gradually superseded by brick buildings whilst, at the same time, the thatched roofs in the towns were replaced by tiled roofs. But the bay partition inherited from half-timbering was continued in the brick house through the regular rhythm of piers and windows. This development was also favoured by the fact that the simplicity, orderliness, precision and natural proportioning of the half-timbering tradition were in keeping with the classicistic architectural ideal of the time (Fig. 5). All the simple, oil-painted brick houses in the towns and the beautiful half-timbered farm houses in the country with their black-tarred timber and white-washed infilling panels were the result of an extensive building activity in a period of economic progress and became the models for the anonymous building activities which continued through most of the 19th century. Later, more important Danish architects sought inspiration from the anonymous, rhythmically partitioned, simple brick house and tried to improve and refine its sterling qualities: the prismatic shapes, the simple, well-solved details, and the fine quality inherent in the traditional materials.
Since the turn of this century, the Danish architects' renewed cultivation of the unpretentious and functional house has kindled an interest in solving simple functional tasks which the builder was previously able to solve without the aid of an architect. During the 1920s and 30s, this became particularly manifest in high-quality low-rent housing. There were, however, also a number of Danish architects who cut loose from this tradition or played on the theme in a highly personal and less restrained manner. But the special *cachet* which, in spite of all this, is apparent in Danish architecture, and the general architectural quality which has been characteristic for important sections of Danish building activities, are due to an unbroken and close association with a functional, craft-dominated building tradition and its simple architectural expressions.

The main currents of modern architectural history have made only modest impacts on contemporary Danish architecture. Impulses from the Chicago School and Sullivan were, at the beginning of this century, solely taken up by Anton Rosen. Art Nouveau merely managed to make an appearance in Denmark through Thorvald Bindesbøll's highly personal efforts in the field of arts and crafts and through Georg Jensen's silverware, before the movement was abandoned in other European countries. No Danes took part in the heated debates which took place, across national boundaries, during the years around the first World War between Italian Futurists, Russian Constructivists, French Cubists and Dutch partisans of "De Stijl". And the Bauhaus was first mentioned in the Danish architectural journal "Arkitekten" ten years after the school was opened – and when Gropius had already left.
It was only during the years 1926 to 1928, that Danish architects were seriously awakened from their cultivation of neo-classicist and traditional qualities by the journal "Kritisk Revy" which declaimed against the neo-classicist formalism and keenly propagated a simple and natural mode of design related to the great social events of the time. It is, however, characteristic that the editor, Poul Henningsen, who was an architect himself and the creator of the PH lamp, was just as disdainful of the outwardly modernistic forms of expression within the many 'isms' as he was of the formalism of neo-classicism.
It was via Sweden through the great housing exhibition in Stockholm in 1930, and in particular through Gunnar Asplund's talented and inspiring framework for the exhibition, that functionalism in its wider sense came to be applied to actual building activities in Denmark. At the same time, too, Le Corbusier's architecture and ideas, propagated in his own emphatic publications, assumed great importance for Danish architects. And at the time when the great nations from whom the modernistic school had essentially emanated found themselves in the throes of a reaction which also comprised architecture, it was Denmark in conjunction with the other Scandinavian countries as well as the Netherlands, Switzerland and Czechoslovakia who offered a refuge for the ideal of functionalism. Architecturally, the small countries may not have initiated any essential innovation during these years; but they made a significant contribution through stabilising the conquests made by others and through en-

4. Typical Danish four-winged farm building from about 1800, built in half-timbering with white-washed mudwalls and thatched roofs.

4. Typischer dänischer Bauernhof mit vier Flügeln aus der Zeit um 1800, in Fachwerkbauweise mit weißgekalkten Lehmfüllungen und Strohdächern.

5. Vestergade, Copenhagen. Neo-classicistic mansions dating back to approx. 1800. Oldest part of the city with medievally curved streets.

5. Vestergade in Kopenhagen. Neoklassizistische Bürgerhäuser, um 1800 errichtet. Ältester Teil der Stadt mit mittelalterlich gekrümmten Straßenführungen.

überlieferten Fachwerkbauweise mit dem klassizistischen Architekturideal sehr im Einklang standen (Abb.5). All die einfachen, mit Ölfarbe gestrichenen Backsteinhäuser der dänischen Städte und die schönen Fachwerkbauten der Gutshöfe auf dem Lande mit ihren schwarzgeteerten Holzkonstruktionen und weißgekalkten Füllwänden waren das Ergebnis einer umfassenden Bautätigkeit in einer Zeit des wirtschaftlichen Aufschwungs. Sie gaben das Vorbild für das anonyme Bauen ab, das den größten Teil des 19. Jahrhunderts hindurch fortgesetzt wurde. Später haben sich viele bedeutende dänische Architekten von dem anonymen, regelmäßig unterteilten, einfachen Backsteinhaus inspirieren lassen und danach gestrebt, dessen gediegene Eigenschaften weiter zu verbessern und zu verfeinern: die prismatischen Hauptformen, die einfachen, gut gelösten Details und die schöne Materialwirkung der traditionellen Baustoffe.
Seit der Jahrhundertwende hat die erneute Beschäftigung der dänischen Architekten mit dem prunklosen, funktionsbestimmten Haus das Interesse an der Lösung einfacher, vorwiegend funktionaler Aufgaben aufleben lassen, die früher vom Handwerker ohne Mitarbeit eines Architekten bewältigt wurden. In den zwanziger und dreißiger Jahren machte sich dies in besonders hohem Grade im qualitätsbetonten sozialen Wohnungsbau bemerkbar. Es gab jedoch auch einige dänische Architekten, die sich von dieser Tradition lösten oder das Thema in höchst persönlicher und freier Weise behandelten. Davon abgesehen sind die besondere Note, die im dänischen Bauwesen zu finden ist, und die hohe architektonische Qualität, die wesentliche Teile der Bautätigkeit kennzeichnet, zweifellos auf die ständige und enge Verbindung mit einer funktionell und handwerklich betonten Bauüberlieferung und ihre einfache architektonische Ausdrucksweise zurückzuführen.

Die Hauptströmungen der modernen Architekturgeschichte haben in der dänischen Architektur des zwanzigsten Jahrhunderts nur einen bescheidenen Widerhall gefunden. Anregungen von der Chicago-Schule und Sullivan wurden zu Anfang des Jahrhunderts lediglich von Anton Rosen weiterverfolgt. L'Art Nouveau konnte sich in Dänemark nur in den stark persönlich betonten kunstgewerblichen Arbeiten von Thorvald Bindesbøll und in den Silberwaren von Georg Jensen durchsetzen, bevor sie im übrigen Europa in Vergessenheit geriet. An den hitzigen Debatten, die in den Jahren um den ersten Weltkrieg über die Ländergrenzen hinweg zwischen italienischen Futuristen, russischen Konstruktivisten, französischen Kubisten und holländischen Stijl-Anhängern geführt wurden, nahmen keine Dänen teil. Selbst das Bauhaus wurde in der dänischen Architekturzeitschrift »Arkitekten« erst zehn Jahre nach seiner Eröffnung besprochen, und zwar zu einem Zeitpunkt, als Gropius die Schule längst verlassen hatte.
In den Jahren 1926 bis 1928 wurden die dänischen Architekten ernstlich aus ihrer etwas einseitigen Pflege neoklassizistischer und traditioneller Werte durch die Zeitschrift »Kritisk Revy« herausgerissen, die gegen den neoklassizistischen Formalismus wetterte und für eine einfache und natürliche Gestaltung in enger Beziehung zu den großen Sozialaufgaben der Gegenwart plädierte. Es ist jedoch charakteristisch, daß der Herausgeber Poul Henningsen, der selbst Architekt war und die »PH-Lampe« entworfen hatte, ebenso stark gegen die nach außen hin modernistischen Ausdrucksformen innerhalb der vielen Ismen anging wie gegen den Formalismus des Neoklassizismus.
Den Anstoß für die praktische Anwendung des Funktionalismus im weiteren Sinne brachte die große Wohnausstellung von 1930 in Stockholm und besonders der von Gunnar Asplund in ebenso begabter wie inspirierender Weise geschaffene Rahmen für diese Ausstellung. Gleichzeitig gewannen auch Le Corbusiers Architektur und die in seinen Schriften vertretenen Gedanken für dänische Architekten besondere Bedeutung. Dänemark entwickelte sich zusammen mit den übrigen nordischen Ländern und gemeinsam mit Holland, der Schweiz und der Tschechoslowakei zu einer Freistätte für die Ideale des Funktionalismus – und das zu einem Zeitpunkt, als die großen Nationen, aus denen ursprünglich ein wesentlicher Teil des modernen Gedankengutes gekommen war, auch auf architektonischem Gebiet bereits von der Reaktion erfaßt wurden. In architektonischer Beziehung mögen die kleinen Länder in diesen Jahren zwar kaum eine wesentliche Neuerung gebracht haben; doch leisteten sie einen bedeutenden Einsatz dadurch, daß sie die Eroberungen anderer stabilisierten und den funktionalistischen Bauten eine handwerkliche Qualität gaben, die von den vielen technischen Fehlern frei war, wie sie die von den Vorkämpfern errichteten Häuser kennzeichneten.
Die ersten größeren, unzweifelhaft funktionalistischen Bauten in Dänemark waren das Ergebnis einer Gemeinschaftsarbeit unter Leitung des Stadtbaumeisters Poul Holsøe. Dieser hatte einen Kreis begabter Architekten um sich versammelt, die entweder – wie F.C. Lund,

dowing the functionalistic houses with a high standard of workmanship free from the many technical shortcomings which characterised so many of the houses of the pioneers.
It was a collectively organised drawing office under the direction of Copenhagen's City Architect Poul Holsøe which carried out the first major distinctly functionalistic building schemes. Holsøe had gathered a circle of gifted architects who either, like F.C. Lund, Johan Pedersen, Tage Rue, Curt Bie, Ib Lunding and later Hans Christian Hansen, came to exert a decisive influence on municipal building activities in subsequent decades or, like Arne Jacobsen and Flemming Lassen, later broke out and created their own sphere of work. Among the first internationally inspired works of the City Architect were the Brønshøj Water Tower, erected in untreated reinforced concrete (1930), and the buildings of the Copenhagen Meat Market (1931–34) with their white-painted cubic blocks rising over a framework structure of reinforced concrete. It was Mogens Lassen who introduced, in the 1930s, reinforced concrete houses of the Le Corbusier type and built, in 1937, the first block of flats in Denmark with a reinforced concrete framework and bearing crosswalls (Systemhuset, Ordrup). Vilhelm Lauritzen became a fine exponent of the ideas of functionalism in their application to new, contemporary tasks such as the airport building (1937) and Broadcasting House (1937–45, Fig.11) in Copenhagen. Hans Hansen built, in 1936–39, the KB Sports Hall whilst Kaj Gottlob created high-standard elementary schools in the form of concentrated three-storey buildings surrounding an assembly hall. Frits Schlegel became the first Danish protagonist of reinforced concrete construction in the Perret style, with the Mariebjerg Crematorium (Fig. 9) as his finest work. Edvard Thomsen built the indoor swimming pool at the State Gymnastics Institute (1940, Fig.10). Finally, the young Arne Jacobsen became, as the architect for the Bellevue group of buildings at Klampenborg with lido, theatre and restaurant (1930–37), a pioneer of a new architecture. Later he built – in collaboration with Erik Møller and Flemming Lassen, respectively – the town halls at Århus and Søllerød which can be regarded as the climax of the progressive architecture of the 1930s, before the Second World War and the resulting shortages of materials gave rise to a reaction against functionalism and to an enforced return to the general use of conventional Danish building methods.
But even for those architects who, during the 1930s, felt most closely associated with the functional Danish tradition, the impulses from functionalism held a positive inspiration. This applied, not least, to the erection of the most important monumental buildings of the 1930s, the University at Århus (page 131). In 1930, Kay Fisker, C.F. Møller and Povl Stegmann were awarded the First Prize in an architectural competition for a project which showed the many institutions of the University placed in isolated, self-contained buildings informally arranged in a park. This arrangement, which has been adhered to for all the intermittent extensions of the University up to this day, was entirely in keeping with the ideals of functionalism. Both in plan and in size, it was possible to design each institution individually in accordance with functional requirements. In the architectural design of the individual buildings, the tradition of the Danish house was followed in a characteristic manner. All buildings are erected in yellow brick in a strict prismatic shape with a roof pitch of 30°. The first of the buildings, viz. that of the Chemico-Physical Institute completed in 1933, is still the architecturally strongest. But C.F. Møller has, with great skill, continued the further extension of the University after Stegmann and Fisker had departed in 1938 and 1942, respectively. The interplay between the buildings and the landscaped park on the undulating ground reveals in the finest manner an essential aspect of Danish architecture.
Already in the neo-classicistic housing schemes of the 1920s, the leading personality of functional tradition, Kay Fisker, pioneered the efforts to endow this important part of building activities with a high standard of dwelling culture and architectural quality. Inspired, not least, by modern German housing construction, he broke away in the 1930s from the classicistic facade design with its formal repetition of identical windows, and adopted a greater differentiation with large picture windows and balconies. With his Vestersøhus in Copenhagen (1935, Fig. 8), he created the Danish prototype for a red-brick block of flats with a firm rhythm of projecting bays alternating with semi-recessed balconies. With their Bakkehusene (Fig.7), Ivar Bentsen and Thorkild Henningsen had, in 1922–23, introduced the terrace house in Denmark as a continuation of the traditional form of dwelling in Danish provincial towns with rows of streets composed of identical one-family houses with back-gardens. In all their sobriety, Bakkehusene can still be regarded as some of the best Danish dwelling environments of modern times. In the early 1930s, Bentsen followed a good functional precept by setting up a co-operative bureau of architects which assumed responsibility for the erection of the first part-type housing estate in Denmark (Blidah, 1932–34). With their Storgården block of flats (1935), Povl Baumann and Knud Hansen helped to raise Danish

6. Police Headquarters, Copenhagen, 1918–24. Architects: Hack Kampmann, Hans Jørgen and Christian Kampmann, Aage Rafn, Holger Jacobsen and Anton Frederiksen.

6. Polizeipräsidium in Kopenhagen, 1918–24. Architekten: Hack Kampmann, Hans Jørgen und Christian Kampmann, Aage Rafn, Holger Jacobsen und Anton Frederiksen.

7. Bakkehuset, Copenhagen, 1922. First modern Danish terrace house estate. Architects: Ivar Bentsen and Thorkild Henningsen.

7. Bakkehuset, Kopenhagen, 1922. Die ersten neueren dänischen Reihenhausbauten. Architekten: Ivar Bentsen und Thorkild Henningsen.

8. Vestersøhus, Copenhagen. Block of flats, 1935 to 1939. Architects: Kay Fisker and C.F. Møller.

8. Vestersøhus, Kopenhagen, ein in den Jahren 1935–39 errichteter Wohnblock. Architekten: Kay Fisker und C.F. Møller.

Johan Pedersen, Tage Rue, Curt Bie, Ib Lunding und später Hans Christian Hansen – die Bautätigkeit des Kopenhagener Stadtbauamtes in den nachfolgenden Jahrzehnten maßgeblich beeinflußten oder – wie Arne Jacobsen und Flemming Lassen – später ihre eigenen Wege gingen und sich ihr eigenes Tätigkeitsfeld schufen. Zu den ersten international inspirierten Arbeiten des Stadtbaumeisters gehören der roh belassene Stahlbetonbau des Wasserturms in Brønshøj (1930) sowie der Kopenhagener Viehhof (1931–34), dessen weißgestrichene kubische Blöcke sich über einer Stahlbeton-Skelettkonstruktion erhoben. Mogens Lassen war es, der als erster in den dreißiger Jahren die von Le Corbusier beeinflußten Stahlbeton-Villenbauten einführte und 1937 in Ordrup das »Systemhaus«, einen mehrgeschossigen Wohnblock mit Stahlbetonskelett und tragenden Querwänden, errichtete. Vilhelm Lauritzen erwies sich als ein hervorragender Verfechter der Gedanken des Funktionalismus in neuen Gegenwartsaufgaben wie dem Kopenhagener Flughafengebäude (1937) und Funkhaus (1937–45, Abb. 11). Hans Hansen baute in den Jahren 1936–39 die Sporthalle des Kopenhagener Sportklubs KB; Kaj Gottlob errichtete gute Volksschulbauten als dreigeschossige Zentralanlagen um eine durchgehende Aula herum. Frits Schlegel wurde zum dänischen Vertreter einer von Perret inspirierten Stahlbetonbauweise, die im Mariebjerg-Krematorium (Abb. 9) ihren schönsten Ausdruck fand. Edvard Thomsen baute 1940 die Schwimmhalle im Staatlichen Gymnastikinstitut (Abb. 10). Schließlich wurde der junge Arne Jacobsen als Architekt der Bellevue-Anlage in Klampenborg mit Freibad, Theater und Restaurant (1930–37) zum Vorkämpfer einer neuen Architektur. Später baute er in Zusammenarbeit mit Erik Møller beziehungsweise Flemming Lassen die beiden Rathäuser in Århus und Søllerød, die als Schlußsteine der fortschrittlichen Baukunst der dreißiger Jahre angesehen werden können, bevor der zweite Weltkrieg und die damit verbundenen Einschränkungen in der Baustoffwahl eine Reaktion gegen den Funktionalismus und eine notgedrungene Rückkehr zu einer allgemeinen Verwendung herkömmlicher dänischer Baumethoden auslösten.

Jedoch bedeuteten auch für diejenigen Architekten, die sich in den dreißiger Jahren der funktionellen dänischen Tradition am meisten verbunden fühlten, die vom Funktionalismus herrührenden Anregungen eine positive Eingebung. Das traf nicht zuletzt auch auf die bedeutendsten Monumentalbauten dieses Jahrzehnts zu: auf die Universität in Århus (Seite 131). Im Jahr 1930 wurde Kay Fisker, C.F Møller und Povl Stegmann der erste Preis in einem Architektenwettbewerb für ein Projekt zuerkannt, demzufolge die vielen Institute der Universität in selbständigen, zwanglos in einem Park gruppierten Gebäuden untergebracht werden sollten. Diese Anordnung, an der bei den ständigen Erweiterungen der Universität bis zum heutigen Tag festgehalten wurde, stand völlig mit den Idealen des Funktionalismus im Einklang. Jedes Gebäude konnte in bezug auf Grundriß und Größe den funktionellen Bedürfnissen individuell angepaßt werden. Bei der architektonischen Gestaltung der einzelnen Bauten wurde der Tradition des dänischen Hausbaus in selbstbewußter Weise Folge geleistet. Alle Gebäude sind aus gelbem Backstein in disziplinierter prismatischer Form mit einer Dachneigung von 30° errichtet. Das als erstes fertiggestellte Chemisch-physikalische

9. Mariebjerg Crematorium, 1937. Architect: Frits Schlegel.

9. Mariebjerg-Krematorium, 1937. Architekt: Frits Schlegel.

housing construction to an international level in keeping with the most advanced high-quality housing standards of the time. Kaare Klint's most important contribution was in furniture design; but he also pursued the architectural ideals of his father, Jensen Klint, from the latter's Grundtvig Church to the Bethlehem Church (1937) which, with its exquisite workmanship, came to represent a fine and personal interpretation of old Danish church building tradition. Finally, Erik Møller and Flemming Lassen were able to show, with their library at Nyborg in the Island of Funen (1938–40, Fig.12), how it was possible to solve the task of building a public institution functionalistically in an unassuming and natural manner by creating two low, single-storey brick buildings.
The war years, 1940–45, signified a period of stagnation in Danish architecture. Building activities were greatly restricted, and the shortage of materials precluded the use of iron in building construction. One had to be content with Danish brick and traditional building methods. This development was, however, beneficial to low-rise housing. The architects took up the design of open-plan houses and were able to create good and inexpensive types of dwellings to supersede the many unattractive bungalows with high basements which had been erected throughout the country during the 1930s without the assistance of architects. The new buildings became simple, single-wing houses with a roof pitch of 30°. Variations of terrace houses were developed in the form of chain houses composed of single-storey or two-storey house types. A simple fresh and untraditional scheme from that period is Viggo Møller-Jensen's group of studio houses at Utterslev, designed for painters and sculptors. With their prismatic shapes, rough-cast walls, asbestos cement roofs and tarred miniature roofs on balconies and fences, these houses create an unpretentious yet charming milieu for the daily life of the artists.
The long period of stagnation, isolation and enforced utility architecture tended to stifle the imagination and new, progressive ideas; yet it had some value in giving the architects time to let the ideals of functionalism settle. Activities were more concentrated on indoor work from which the Danish arts and crafts and especially furniture design were able to benefit. Even for some time after the war, it was still necessary to put up with serious shortages of materials, and it was first some way into the 1950s that the architects were again free to propose more advanced methods of construction and new materials in natural economic competition with conventional ones.

10. Indoor swimming pool at the State Gymnastics Institute, Copenhagen, 1940. Architect: Edvard Thomsen.

10. Schwimmhalle im Staatlichen Gymnastikinstitut, Kopenhagen, 1940. Architekt: Edvard Thomsen.

Especially among younger architects, the war-time isolation had created a tremendous demand for new impulses from abroad. Just after the war, it was the United States of America who provided the great source of inspiration. Interest was first of all centred on Frank Lloyd Wright and his dynamic concept of architecture. Departing from Wright's own sentiment-inspired, dynamic architecture with its organic structure and spatial relation between house and landscape, Jørn Utzon became through a number of competition projects a vital centre for the effort of finding new architectural expressions in association with the use of new materials and construction methods. These efforts also gave rise to a renewed interest in primitive architecture and in the natural harmony here encountered between construction and material, and between house and landscape. It was found that the architectural problems of modern times had, in many respects, greater affinity with simple, anonymous houses than with more complicated types of buildings. Apart from the organic-dynamic architecture, there appeared, around 1950, tendencies in the direction of a more static, logical-classic concept of architecture as it was reflected in Mies van der Rohe's designs. One tried to find general solutions and a degree of absolute beauty through rules of proportioning and clarified structural systems where the advantages of mass production and machine precision could be utilised. A revival of the De Stijl and Bauhaus ideas also led to the desire to harmonise architecture with scientific development and new human comprehension. In the centre of these efforts was Erik Christian Sørensen. Together with the theoretical discussion of architectural principles, there was also a demand for scientific building research in order to elucidate the situation of the Danish tradition of craftsmanship in relation to the forthcoming industrialisation of building construction. During the first decade after the war, orthodox building methods and materials were still economically superior to the less orthodox systems so that there was good reason for many Danish architects to continue in promoting the most valuable aspects of Danish building tradition based on craftsmanship. The discussion between modernists and traditionalists was, in those years, apt to be keen; yet there was no real conflict between the partisans of the different concepts, nor was there any major conflict between the Danish architectural training at the Academy of Arts and certain more progressive efforts. Danish moderation prevailed. Even the more sentimentally inclined ar-

11. State Broadcasting House, Concert Hall, Copenhagen, 1937–45. Architect: Vilhelm Lauritzen.

11. Konzertsaal im Staatlichen Rundfunkhaus, Kopenhagen, 1937–45. Architekt: Vilhelm Lauritzen.

12. Public Library, Nyborg, 1938–40. Architects: Flemming Lassen and Erik Møller.

12. Öffentliche Bibliothek in Nyborg, 1938–40. Architekten: Flemming Lassen und Erik Møller.

Institut aus dem Jahr 1933, macht architektonisch gesehen immer noch den stärksten Eindruck; doch hat C.F. Møller es verstanden, nach dem Ausscheiden Stegmanns (1938) und Fiskers (1942) den Ausbau der Universität mit großer Tüchtigkeit weiterzuführen. Das Zusammenspiel zwischen den Gebäuden und der Parklandschaft in dem hügeligen Gelände zeigt auf schönste Weise einen wesentlichen Grundzug der dänischen Architektur.
Schon im neoklassizistischen Wohnbau der zwanziger Jahre war die führende Persönlichkeit der funktionellen Überlieferung, Kay Fisker, dafür eingetreten, diese wichtige Sparte des Bauwesens sowohl ausstattungsmäßig als auch architektonisch möglichst hochwertig zu gestalten. Nicht zuletzt vom neueren deutschen Wohnungsbau inspiriert, machte sich Fisker in den dreißiger Jahren von der klassizistischen Fassadengestaltung mit ihrer formelhaften Wiederholung gleichartiger Fenster zugunsten einer größeren Differenzierung mit großen Aussichtsfenstern und Balkonen frei. Mit dem Vestersøhus (Abb. 8) in Kopenhagen schuf er 1935 das dänische Vorbild eines Wohnblocks mit Balkons und Erker, einen Bau aus rotem Backstein mit einer stark rhythmisierten Fassade, bei der sich vorgeschobene Erker mit halb zurückliegenden Balkonen abwechselten. Mit den sogenannten Bakkehusene (Abb. 7) hatten Ivar Bentsen und Thorkild Henningsen in den Jahren 1922–23 das Reihenhaus weiterentwickelt, wobei sie die traditionelle Wohnform der dänischen Provinzstädte mit ihren Straßenreihen gleichartiger Einfamilienhäuser und Hintergärten fortführten. Bei all ihrer Nüchternheit können die Bakkehusene immer noch als eines der besten dänischen Wohnmilieus der Neuzeit angesehen werden. Zu Anfang der dreißiger Jahre richtete Bentsen, übrigens unter Befolgung funktionalistischer Regeln, zusammen mit Henningsen ein gemeinschaftliches Architekturbüro ein, das für den Bau der ersten dänischen Parksiedlung – Blidah – in den Jahren 1932–34 verantwortlich war. Povl Baumann und Knud Hansen trugen mit ihrem Wohnblock Storgården (1935) dazu bei, dem dänischen Wohnungsbau einen internationalen Ruf als einem der fortschrittlichsten und am meisten qualitätsbetonten aller Länder zu verschaffen. Kaare Klints bedeutendster Beitrag lag auf dem Gebiet der Möbelkunst; er führte aber auch die architektonischen Ideale seines Vaters Jensen Klint, des Erbauers der Grundtvigskirche, mit dem Bau der Bethlehemskirche (1937) weiter, die in ihrer hervorragenden handwerklichen Ausführung eine gelungene und persönliche Interpretation der alten dänischen Kirchenbautradition darstellt. Schließlich bewiesen Erik Møller und Flemming Lassen mit ihrer Volksbibliothek für Nyborg (1938–40, Abb. 12) auf der Insel Fünen, wie sich die Bauaufgabe eines öffentlichen Institutes auf funktionalistischer Grundlage ganz unprätentiös in Form von zwei niedrigen, eingeschossigen Backsteinbauten lösen läßt.
Die Kriegsjahre 1940–45 brachten einen Stillstand in der Entwicklung der dänischen Architektur. Die Bautätigkeit war stark eingeschränkt, und die Baustoffknappheit schloß die Verwendung von Eisen aus. Man mußte sich mit dänischem Backstein und traditionellen Bauweisen begnügen. Das kam jedoch dem Wohnungs-Flachbau zugute. Die Architekten beschäftigten sich mit dem eingeschossigen Haus und schufen gute und billige Typen, welche die vielen unschönen Bungalows mit hohem Keller ablösten, die in den dreißiger Jahren ohne das Mitwirken von Architekten überall im Lande errichtet worden waren. Es handelte sich um einfache, einflügelige Bauten mit Ziegeldächern von 30°. Ferner entstanden Variationen von Reihenhäusern in Gestalt von Häuserketten, die sich aus ein- oder zweigeschossigen Einfamilienhäusern zusammensetzten. Ein frischer, untraditioneller Bau aus dieser Zeit war Viggo Møller-Jensens Atelierhaus in Utterslev, das für Maler und Bildhauer bestimmt war. Mit prismatischen Bauformen, verputzten Wänden, Eternitdächern sowie geteerten Kleindächern über Balkonen und Zäunen wurde ein unprätentiöser und ansprechender Rahmen für das tägliche Leben der Künstler geschaffen.
Die lange Periode des Stillstands, der Isolierung und der erzwungenen architektonischen Askese unterdrückte Phantasie und fortschrittliche Ideen; doch hatte auch diese Zeit ihr Gutes, indem sie den Architekten Gelegenheit bot, die Ideale des Funktionalismus zu verarbeiten. Je weniger es zu bauen gab, desto mehr konzentrierte man sich auf den Innenraum, was besonders dem dänischen Kunstgewerbe, und hier wiederum besonders dem Möbelbau zugute kam. Die Materialknappheit hielt noch einige Jahre nach dem Krieg an, und erst in den fünfziger Jahren konnten die Architekten wieder fortschrittlichere Bauweisen und neue Baustoffe in natürlichem wirtschaftlichen Wettbewerb mit den traditionellen Materialien zum Vorschlag bringen.

Die Isolierung während des Krieges hatte besonders bei den jüngeren Architekten ein starkes Bedürfnis ausgelöst, neue Impulse von außen hereinzuholen. Unmittelbar nach dem Kriege galten die Vereinigten Staaten als die große Quelle der Inspiration. Das Interesse

13. Søndergardsparken, Bagsværd, 1950. Housing estate layout plan. Architects: Poul Ernst Hoff & Bennet Windinge.

13. Søndergardsparken, Bagsværd, 1950. Lageplanmodell der Wohnsiedlung. Architekten: Poul Ernst Hoff & Bennet Windinge.

chitects showed a certain Appollonian self-restraint whilst, on the other hand, some of the more formally inclined architects produced organically derived details and fine human features. It goes without saying that the most important architects could not help giving their works a personal note. It is, however, noteworthy that also after the war, the best Danish architecture was created by many different architects and that it is their works as a whole rather than in isolation which revealed the strength of modern Danish architecture. It is characteristic of the efforts made in the 1950s and early 1960s that it is mainly for tasks not primarily based on unorthodox and rational production methods that Danish architects were at their best. This applies to small-house construction as well as to schools, public institutions and administration buildings. With these tasks, the architects were able to work in the manner which can be regarded as traditional in the best sense, where function, construction and design are treated as equivalent components and where they were able to rely on well-designed standard units as well as on high-quality workmanship with orthodox constructions and materials.

After the war, it was housing construction which first came into its own again and in this field, it was the non-profit-making housing associations which, acting as clients, resumed the progressive social approach of the 1930s. Aided by favourable conditions for Government loans, it became a natural solution to undertake the large-scale planning of major housing schemes where the individual buildings could be placed more ideally in relation to each other and in relation to joint open spaces and collective service facilities. Under Erling Knudsen's management, the association known as "Dansk Almennyttigt Boligbyggeri" took the lead and erected, in 1950, the Søndergårdsparken estate at Bagsværd with Poul Ernst Hoff & Bennet Windinge as architects (Figs. 13, 14). Grouped around a large common open space were semi-detached bungalows, one-and-a-half-storey high terrace houses, as well as shopping centre, crêche, kindergarten and spare-time centre. Here, the advantages of the small house were combined with the possibilities for collective services inherent in the large housing scheme. It was necessary to use conventional materials, and the buildings were erected in yellow brick with white-washed window rebates. Even to-day, this estate can still be regarded as one of the most attractive residential districts in the country. In the block of service flats known as Høje Søborg (1951), the same association and architects were able to provide single people and working couples with good housing conditions in flats which, though relatively small, had the benefit of numerous service facilities. With their Carlsro scheme at Rødovre (1950–55), the association continued their progressive line with a mixed housing scheme of low terrace houses for families with children and a tower block with flats for single people; here, the collective services were even more sophisticated. In this scheme the architects were Mogens Jacobsen, Alex Poulsen, Magnus Stephensen and Knud Thorball.
In 1945, an architectural competition was held to obtain plans for the development of one of Copenhagen's highest sites, Bellahøj (page 76), which offers a view over the whole of the

wandte sich in erster Linie Frank Lloyd Wright und seiner dynamischen Architekturauffassung zu. Ausgehend von Wrights eigener, gefühlsbetonter dynamischer Architektur mit ihrer organischen Struktur und räumlichen Beziehung zwischen Haus und Landschaft wurde Jørn Utzon zum Mittelpunkt für die Bestrebungen, denen es darum ging, in Verbindung mit neuen Baustoffen und Bauweisen einen neuen architektonischen Ausdruck zu finden. Diese Bestrebungen, die bei Utzon das Ergebnis einer Reihe von Wettbewerbsentwürfen waren, führten auch zu einem erneuten Interesse an primitiver Architektur und an dem natürlichen Einklang, der hier zwischen Bauweise und Baustoff und zwischen Haus und Landschaft zu finden ist. Man fand, daß die Probleme der Gegenwart in vielerlei Hinsicht eher mit Anregungen aus der einfachen anonymen Architektur als mit komplizierteren Bauformen zu lösen waren. Daneben zeigten sich um 1950 herum aber auch Tendenzen, die auf eine mehr statische, logisch-klassische Architekturauffassung abzielten, wie sie in Mies van der Rohes Bauten zum Ausdruck kam. Man versuchte hier, allgemein verbindlichen Lösungen und einem absoluten Schönheitsbegriff durch Proportionsregeln und rationale Bauweisen näherzukommen, bei denen industrielle Fertigungsmethoden und die Genauigkeit der maschinellen Herstellung ausgenutzt werden konnten. Ein Wiederaufflackern der Stijl- und Bauhaus-Ideen führte ferner zu dem Bestreben, die Architektur mit der wissenschaftlichen Entwicklung und neuen menschlichen Erkenntnissen in Einklang zu bringen. Im Zentrum dieser Bestrebungen stand Erik Christian Sørensen. Gleichzeitig mit der architekturtheoretischen Debatte wandte man sich auch der wissenschaftlichen Bauforschung zu, um die dänische Handwerkstradition zu analysieren und sich auf die kommende Industrialisierung des Bauwesens einzustellen. Im ersten Jahrzehnt nach dem Kriege waren die herkömmlichen Bauweisen und Baustoffe den weniger traditionellen Systemen wirtschaftlich noch überlegen, so daß viele dänische Architekten mit gutem Grund danach strebten, die wertvollsten Wesenszüge der dänischen Bautradition auf handwerklicher Basis fortzusetzen. Die Debatte zwischen Modernisten und Traditionalisten konnte damals recht hitzig werden, doch kam es zu keinem ausgesprochenen Konflikt zwischen den Verfechtern der verschiedenen Richtungen, wie sich auch die dänische Architektenausbildung auf der Kunstakademie den fortschrittlicheren Bestrebungen nicht widersetzte. Der dänische Wesenszug des Maßhaltens machte sich weiterhin geltend. Selbst die mehr gefühlsbetonten Architekten zeigten apollinische Selbstbeherrschung, während umgekehrt die Arbeiten der mehr formell eingestellten Architekten organisch bestimmte Detaillösungen und ausgeprägte humane Züge aufwiesen. Die bedeutendsten Architekten ließen sich selbstverständlich nicht davon abhalten, ihren Arbeiten einen persönlichen Stempel aufzudrücken. Es ist jedoch auffallend, daß auch in der Nachkriegszeit die besten Beispiele dänischer Architektur von einer Vielzahl verschiedener Architekten geschaffen wurden, und daß ihre Arbeiten eher im Ganzen als im Einzelnen die Stärke der zeitgenössischen dänischen Baukunst repräsentieren. Für die Bauvorhaben der fünfziger Jahre und zu Anfang der sechziger Jahre ist es typisch, daß die dänischen Architekten ihre Höchstleistungen vor allem auf solchen Gebieten zeigten, bei denen nicht von vornherein eine untraditionelle, rationelle Produktionsmethode voraus-

14. Søndergardsparken, Bagsværd. Housing estate. One-family house and kindergarten. Architects: Poul Ernst Hoff & Bennet Windinge.

14. Søndergårdsparken, Bagsværd. Wohnsiedlung. Einfamilienhaus und Kinderheim. Architekten: Poul Ernst Hoff & Bennet Windinge.

town. The prize-winning design was adopted for the erection, during the years 1950 to 1956, of 28 tower blocks which were placed informally in a parkland area. Certain overall directives were laid down for the joint application of unorthodox building methods with prefabricated concrete units; but the detailed design work was left to different architectural firms. With its closely spaced tower blocks, the Bellahøj estate may appear to be fairly massive; it has become a landmark in Copenhagen's skyline. Among the major park-type housing schemes of the first post-war years, the Voldparken estate in Copenhagen (Fig.15) is mainly distinguished by the section which Kay Fisker designed in 1949–51, consisting of fully enclosed blocks of flats with three to seven storeys erected in yellow brick, with continuous balconies and hipped asbestos cement roofs. Eske Kristensen's Bredalspark (1953) is distinguished by its thoroughly considered floor plans and its attractive garden space. Good dwelling conditions with high architectural qualities were created with conventional building materials in the later park-type housing schemes with two or three storeys such as Eva and Nils Koppel's Søllerød Park (1953–55, page 78), Palle Suenson's Skolepark (1955) and Nærumvænge (1950–59) as well as Henning Jensen's & Torben Valeur's Eskemosegård (1958–59, page 84). The advance in dwelling standards experienced around 1950 was maintained but no vital innovations were added. Size and layout of the dwelling units do not differ greatly from those types which, during the 1930s, signified a decisive improvement in dwelling standards. Progress in the sphere of major housing schemes began to stagnate in the mid-1950s. The activities of the housing associations were hampered by reductions in government subsidies while design work became more difficult as a result of restrictive government regulations, inter alia those prescribing the use of unorthodox building methods with a high incidence of unskilled labour with a view to obtaining a high output of dwelling units at low costs. For a time, the architects as a group lost interest in this important section of building activities and turned to other tasks. The great challenge inherent in finding an architectural solution for fully developed industrialised housing construction was, for the time being, ignored by most Danish architects.

In the sphere of individual house design, inspiration had been derived from Wright's rich spatial art, from the material-romantic timber houses of the Greene brothers and later Bay Region architects, and from the exposed architecture and open plan solutions sponsored by the Japanese as well as by Mies van der Rohe. One tried to break away from the rectangular type of houses with the 30° roof pitch and separate rooms universally encountered during the years of restrictions. The aim was to find more differentiated plans with intimate contact between house and garden and with adaptation to the surrounding land. Harald Plum's and Mogens Lassen's house at Jægersborg (1954, page 38) provides a good example. By adopting the built-up roof, it became possible to use flat roofs which would stand up to the Danish climate and which permitted greater flexibility in designing the plan. With his own house at Hellebæk (1952, page 34), Jørn Utzon introduced the open into Denmark. The house consists of a single large room, divided by light, partly movable partitions into different sections assigned to different functions whilst large windows on the south side provide contact with garden and terraces. On the north side, the house is enclosed by a tight wall of yellow brick. In 1955, Erik Christian Sørensen expanded, for his own house (page 44), the possibilities of the open plan within a strict structural principle with exposed, black-tarred timber columns and beams. The T-shaped plan shows a finely proportioned and well-differentiated concatenation of rooms with fine relations between the different functional sections and the protected outdoor sitting areas assigned to them. Clearly inspired by Japanese examples, Halldor Gunnløgsson consistently adopted the principle of the structurally exposed spatial architecture in his own house at Rungsted (1958, page 46). The main qualities of this house with its strictly formal design must be seen in its lucid simplification and spatial relationship between house and furniture as well as in the contact with the coast of the Sound in the east and with a protected garden space in the west. Houses built by architects for their own use are of course more indicative of the architects' ideals than of general dwelling standards. But these architectural ideals are highly infectious to building activities at large. Knud Peter Harboe's house (1959, page 52) provides a good example for the further sophistication of architectural principles as applied to a good family dwelling. Danes are closely attached to their homes, and there is a tradition for members of the family to regard the design of the home as something vital to them. Many people aim at giving their home a personal note, and it has been general practice to surround oneself both with new and old furniture and objects of which one is fond. "Home comfort" is often mentioned as a specifically Danish concept, in the positive as well as in the negative sense. In Børge Mogensen's own house (page 54),

15. Voldparken, Copenhagen. Housing estate, 1949–51. Architect: Kay Fisker.

15. Voldparken, Kopenhagen. Wohnsiedlung, 1949–51. Architekt: Kay Fisker.

gesetzt wird. Dies gilt ebenso für den Bau individueller Einfamilienhäuser wie für Schulen, Behördenbauten und Verwaltungsgebäude. Bei diesen Aufgaben konnten die Architekten ihren Beruf auf der Grundlage einer bewährten Tradition ausüben und Funktion, Bauweise und Gestaltung als gleichwertige Entwurfsbestandteile behandeln, wobei sie sich, sowohl sorgfältig durchgearbeitete Standardelemente als auch gute handwerkliche Arbeit in herkömmlichen Bauweisen und Baustoffen zunutze zu machen wußten.

Nach dem Krieg war es der Wohnungsbau, der zuerst wieder in Gang kam, und hier wiederum waren es die gemeinnützigen Wohnbaugesellschaften, die als Bauherren die fortschrittliche soziale Linie der dreißiger Jahre weiterführten. Aus den günstigen Bedingungen für staatliche Anleihen ergab sich als natürliche Folge die Möglichkeit, Bauvorhaben in größeren Einheiten zu planen, wobei die einzelnen Gebäude günstiger eingeordnet und mit gemeinschaftlichen Grünflächen und Dienstleistungsanlagen verbunden werden konnten. Unter der Leitung von Erling Knudsen entwickelte sich die »Dansk Almennyttigt Boligbyggeri« zur führenden Wohnbaugesellschaft, die 1950 mit Poul Ernst Hoff und Bennet Windinge als Architekten die Siedlung Søndergårdsparken in Bagsværd errichtete (Abb. 13, 14). Um eine große gemeinschaftliche Grünanlage herum gruppieren sich die eingeschossigen, paarweise zusammengebauten Einfamilienhäuser und 1½-geschossige Reihenhäuser sowie Einkaufszentrum, Kindergarten und Freizeiteinrichtungen. Hier wurden die Vorteile des frei stehenden Einfamilienhauses mit den Möglichkeiten vereint, die ein großes Bauvorhaben durch kollektiv genutzte Einrichtungen bieten kann. Man war zur Verwendung traditioneller Baustoffe gezwungen: die Häuser sind aus gelbem Backstein mit weißgeschlämmten Fenstereinfassungen errichtet. Trotzdem kann die Siedlung heute noch als eines der ansprechendsten Wohngebiete des Landes gelten. Das Kollektivhaus Høje Søborg, das im Jahr 1951 von derselben Wohnbaugesellschaft und den gleichen Architekten errichtet wurde, bot ledigen Mietern und berufstätigen Ehepaaren gute Wohnmöglichkeiten in Apartments, die zwar verhältnismäßig klein waren, aber die Vorteile zahlreicher, gemeinschaftlich benutzter Serviceeinrichtungen boten. Mit der Siedlung Carlsro in Rødovre (1950–55) setzte die gleiche Gesellschaft ihr fortschrittliches Konzept fort in einer gemischten Bebauung aus niedrigen Reihenhäusern für kinderreiche Familien und einem Hochhaus mit Wohnungen für Ledige bei weiterem Ausbau der Gemeinschaftsdienste. In diesem Fall waren Mogens Jacobsen, Alex Poulsen, Magnus Stephensen und Knud Thorball die verantwortlichen Architekten.

Im Jahr 1945 wurde ein Architektenwettbewerb für die Bebauung eines der höchstgelegenen Stadtteile Kopenhagens – Bellahøj (Seite 76) – ausgeschrieben, von wo aus sich eine Aussicht über die ganze Stadt bietet. Der mit dem ersten Preis bedachte Bebauungsplan konnte in den Jahren 1950–56 durch die Errichtung von 28 Hochhäusern verwirklicht werden, die zwanglos in einem Park angeordnet sind. Gewisse Richtlinien für eine einheitliche, untraditionelle Bauweise mit vorgefertigten Betonelementen waren vorgeschrieben, während die Entwurfsarbeit im übrigen den verschiedenen Architekturbüros überlassen blieb. Die Bebauung mit ihren dicht beieinander stehenden Hochhäusern mag recht massiv erscheinen; ihre Silhouette ist jedoch ein Wahrzeichen der Stadt geworden. Unter größeren Parksiedlungen der ersten Nachkriegsjahre hebt sich die Voldparken-Anlage in Kopenhagen hauptsächlich durch den Teil hervor, in dem Kay Fisker zwischen 1949 und 1951 aneinandergereihte drei- bis siebengeschossige Wohnblöcke aus gelbem Backstein mit durchgehenden Balkonen und Walmdächern aus Eternit erbaute (Abb. 15). Eske Kristensens Bredalspark aus dem Jahre 1953 zeichnet sich durch sorgfältig durchgearbeitete Grundrisse und schöne Gartenräume aus. Gute Wohnbedingungen und qualitätvolle Architektur wurden auch in später errichteten, zwei- bis dreigeschossigen Parksiedlungen unter Anwendung herkömmlicher Baustoffe geschaffen, so zum Beispiel von Eva und Nils Koppel (Søllerød Park, 1953–55, Seite 78), Palle Suenson (Skolepark, 1955, und Nærumvænge, 1950–59) sowie Henning Jensen und Torben Valeur (Eskemosegård, 1958–59, Seite 84). Zu den Fortschritten, die im Wohnungsbau um 1950 herum erzielt worden waren, kamen später keine wesentlichen Neuerungen mehr hinzu. Bei genauerer Betrachtung unterscheiden sich die einzelnen Wohnungen in Größe und Grundriß nur wenig von den Typen, die in den dreißiger Jahren eine entscheidende Verbesserung des Wohnungsbaus bedeuteten. Mitte der fünfziger Jahre stagnierte die Entwicklung auf dem Gebiet der Großsiedlungen immer mehr. Die Tätigkeit der Wohnbaugesellschaften wurde durch Einschränkung der staatlichen Finanzierungshilfe gehemmt; gleichzeitig komplizierte sich die Entwurfsarbeit durch einschränkende Regierungseingriffe, unter anderem durch die Auflage, an Stelle traditioneller Bauweisen moderne Methoden anzuwenden, bei denen im wesentlichen ungelernte Arbeitskräfte eingesetzt werden

the formal framework has receded into the background, and a robust design of house and furniture enables the members of the family to make the most of their home, individually as well as jointly. For the Middelboe House at Holte (1953, page 36), Utzon used a building method with prefabricated units of reinforced concrete and wood which indicated certain possibilities for the industrial production of small houses. This particular house, however, was never reproduced. Later, the question of the standard type house was taken up for thorough examination, inter alia by the Danish Association of Architects. To-day, when about 60 per cent. of all new Danish housing consists of small houses, a large number of more or less industrially produced standard houses have been built though these have not yet reached a particularly noteworthy standard of architectural quality.
The design of summer houses has often appealed to the architects' imagination and passion for experiments and has been, especially in the 1930s, the proving ground for ideas which were later adopted for permanently occupied houses. During the last decades, the two-dwellings principle has become more and more widespread in Denmark, and there has also been a growing tendency to give the summer house the same high standard of equipment as the winter dwelling. Large as well as very small summer cottages have grown up along all the coasts of Denmark. In order to obviate an excessive sprawl of cheap summer cottages, work has been carried out in recent years on integrally designed schemes for major summer house colonies. Claus Bremer's holiday colony at Blokhus is a good example. Among the most interesting individually designed summer houses of the post-war period, which invite to a simple and relaxed mode of living in close contact with the surrounding nature, are Vilhelm Wohlert's little guesthouse with collapsible outer walls for Niels Bohr (1957, page 56), Nils Fagerholt's simplified wooden box at Blåmunkene (page 60), and Erik Korshagen's house at Rørvig (page 58) which is dominated by a large overhung thatched roof.
The terrace house, which combines many of the advantages of the small house with those of a rational and space-saving type of housing, has continued to be a popular form of dwelling also after the war. The architects have endeavoured to vary the theme, e.g., by creating protected outdoor sitting areas, ensuring a higher degree of privacy. In his characteristic Søholm scheme at Klampenborg (1950–55, page 62), Arne Jacobsen created differentiated dwellings with fine spatial qualities.
The single-storey court-house provides good possibilities for a family life with a high degree of privacy and with close relations between the rooms of the house and the common open space which also provides protection against the blustery Danish climate. Jørn Utzon's Kingohusene near Elsinore (1958, page 65) became Denmark's first major housing estate wholly consisting of court-houses. The undulating ground inspired him to adopt a type of housing with informally curved rows of houses, enabling each house to make the most of its specific location, orientation and view on to the common open space. Erected with conventional building materials and building methods, this housing estate can be regarded as one of the most economic schemes of our time. The brick walls, varying in height, serve to hold the estate together as a richly varied unit. Later, Utzon built the Fredensborghusene (page 68) where similar court-houses are grouped around a community centre with banqueting rooms and restaurant, making the most of an exceptionally attractive view across a typically Danish landscape with fields and woods. In recent years, numerous court-house estates have been erected throughout the country both in conventional materials and by newer building methods.

The standard of modern Danish architecture has been greatly influenced by competitions. For nearly a century, the potentialities of a great number of major public tasks have been elucidated through public competition, and the architects of the country had to give of their best in order to procure for themselves the most interesting tasks. Numerous idea competitions have been held partly in order to deal with concrete tasks and partly in order to obtain basic solutions for the design of, e.g., new types of dwellings or institutions. The competitions have also been important to very young architects for whom the contest on equal terms with the paragons of their profession has been of high educational value, and who were at the same time enabled to create a name for themselves through being placed among the prize winners.
Architectural competitions have had a special impact on school design. The authorities as well as educationalists and architects have endeavoured to obtain the best possible conditions for the teaching of school children and have consistently looked for new pedagogical and architectural possibilities. During the war, the first competition projects were concerned with bungalow type schools with a view to creating the friendliest possible milieu and linking

konnten. Auf diese Weise sollte eine billige Massenherstellung von Wohnungen gefördert werden. Eine Zeitlang verlor daraufhin die Mehrzahl der Architekten das Interesse an diesem bedeutenden Gebiet des Bauwesens und zog es vor, sich anderen Aufgaben zuzuwenden. Die große Herausforderung, eine architektonisch qualitätvolle Lösung für den industrialisierten Wohnungsbau zu finden, wurde von den meisten dänischen Architekten vorläufig ignoriert.

Was den Bau von individuellen Einfamilienhäusern anbelangt, so holten sich die dänischen Architekten manche Anregungen aus der reichen Raumkunst von F.L. Wright, aus den materialromantischen Holzhäusern der Brüder Greene und späterer kalifornischer Architekten, und aus der – sowohl von den Japanern als auch von Mies van der Rohe vertretenen – strukturellen Architektur mit offenen Grundrissen. Man wollte sich von dem rechtwinkligen Haustyp mit 30°-Dachneigung und abgeschlossenen Zimmern freimachen, wie er in den Jahren der Einschränkung allgemein angewandt worden war. Statt dessen strebte man nach differenzierteren Grundrißlösungen mit intimer Verbindung zwischen Haus und Garten unter Anpassung an das umgebende Gelände. Harald Plums und Mogens Lassens Haus in Jægersborg aus dem Jahr 1954 (Seite 38) bildet dafür ein gutes Beispiel. Mit dem Prinzip des Preßdachs wurde es möglich, auf eine auch im dänischen Klima zu verantwortende Weise Flachdächer zu bauen, die eine bessere Möglichkeit für eine freie Grundrißlösung boten. Mit seinem eigenen Haus in Hellebæk (Seite 34) führte Jørn Utzon im Jahr 1952 den offenen Grundriß in Dänemark ein. Das Haus besteht aus einem einzigen großen Raum, der durch leichte, zum Teil verschiebbare Trennwände in verschiedene funktionsbestimmte Raumabschnitte unterteilt ist, während die großen Glasflächen auf der Südseite die Innenräume mit dem Garten und den Terrassen verbinden. Nach Norden zu ist das Haus durch eine fensterlose Wand aus gelbem Backstein abgeschlossen. Im Jahr 1955 erweiterte Erik Christian Sørensen in seinem eigenen Haus (Seite 44) die Möglichkeiten des offenen Grundrisses, unter strenger Beachtung einer Konstruktion aus sichtbaren, schwarzgebeizten Holzstützen und -trägern. Der T-förmige Grundriß zeigt eine wohlproportionierte und differenzierte Anordnung der Räume mit guten Beziehungen zwischen den einzelnen Funktionsabschnitten und den geschützten Freiräumen. Deutlich von Japan inspiriert, führte Halldor Gunnløgsson 1958 bei seinem eigenen Haus in Rungsted (Seite 46) die Architektur des fließenden Raumes und der sichtbaren Konstruktion höchst konsequent weiter. Die Qualität dieses streng formell entworfenen Hauses zeigt sich in seiner ausgewogenen Vereinfachung, in der räumlichen Beziehung zwischen Haus und Inneneinrichtung sowie in der engen Verbindung mit der Øresundküste im Osten und dem abgeschlossenen Gartenraum im Westen. Häuser, die von Architekten für ihren eigenen Bedarf gebaut werden, spiegeln natürlich eher die Ideale ihres Bauherrn als den allgemeinen Stand des Wohnungswesens wider. Aber diese Architektenideale wirken äußerst ansteckend. Knud Peter Harboes Haus (Seite 52) aus dem Jahr 1959 bietet ein gutes Beispiel dafür, wie Prinzipien der Architekturhäuser auf eine Familienwohnung übertragen werden können. Die Dänen sind mit ihrem Heim eng verwachsen, und seine Gestaltung wird von den Familienmitgliedern traditionsgemäß sehr wichtig genommen. Viele bemühen sich, ihrem Haus eine persönliche Note zu geben, und es ist üblich, sich mit neuen und alten Möbeln und Gegenständen zu umgeben, die man gern hat. »Häusliche Gemütlichkeit« wird oft sowohl im positiven als auch im negativen Sinne als ein spezifisch dänischer Begriff hervorgehoben. Beim eigenen Haus des Entwerfers Børge Mogensen (Seite 54) ist der formelle Rahmen in den Hintergrund getreten, und eine robuste Gestaltung des Hauses und seiner Möblierung gestattet es den Bewohnern, sich sowohl individuell als auch gesellig voll zu entfalten. Bei seinem Haus Middelboe in Holte (Seite 36) wandte Utzon 1953 eine Bauweise mit vorgefertigten Elementen aus Stahlbeton und Holz an, die gewisse Möglichkeiten für die Serienherstellung von Einfamilienhäusern aufzeigte. Allerdings wurden nie weitere Häuser dieser Art gebaut. Später machte unter anderen der Landesverband dänischer Architekten das Typenhaus zum Gegenstand eingehender Untersuchungen. Heute, wo etwa 60 Prozent aller neuen Wohnungen in Dänemark aus Einfamilienhäusern bestehen, gibt es eine große Anzahl mehr oder minder industriell hergestellter Typenhäuser; allerdings haben diese präfabrizierten Bauten bisher keine besondere architektonische Qualität erreicht.
Der Bau von Ferienhäusern hat oft die Phantasie und Experimentierlust der Architekten angeregt und bildete besonders in den dreißiger Jahren ein Versuchsfeld für Ideen, die später auf ganzjährig benutzte Häuser angewandt wurden. In den letzten Jahrzehnten hat das Zweiwohnungsprinzip in Dänemark mehr und mehr Anklang gefunden, und es besteht eine wachsende Tendenz, die Sommerwohnung ebenso hochwertig auszustatten wie die Haupt-

the individual classrooms directly with the surrounding gardens. Among the best elementary schools of the bungalow type is Arne Jacobsen's Munkegårds School at Gentofte (page 98). Its design is based on a distinct principle: self-contained units, each consisting of two twinned standard classrooms associated with their own individually designed atrium, are surrounded by crosswise corridors. The scheme is distinguished by a thorough treatment of details and a fine harmony between building and furniture. With his Nyager School at Rødovre (1965, page 113), Arne Jacobsen varied the theme of a close link between classrooms and courtyards by applying the centre corridor principle. At the Vangebo School at Søllerød (1957–60, page 106), designed by architects Brüel, Bornebusch, Selchau and Henning Larsen, each single classroom constitutes a selfcontained bungalow with its own garden court, whilst low corridors provide the inter-connections with the other sections of the school. With its coarse yellow walls and tarred or red-stained woodwork, the school has been given a robust character and should be able to stand up to wear and tear and to the somewhat rough treatment on the part of the children. An informal and expressive architectural treatment is the characteristic of Hanssted School (page 103), built in 1954–58 by Copenhagen's City Architect F.C. Lund and Hans Christian Hansen. Here, the standard classrooms are combined in groups of four forming two-storey units which are centred on one staircase and are easily identifiable by the children. The building materials are yellow brick, untreated or stained wood, and asbestos-cement cladding for parapets and roofs. Even more robust and strict in its character is Kay Fisker's Voldparken School (1951–57, page 96) which consists of a low building for small children and a three-storey wing for the older children. The different blocks of the group are impressively integrated by large asbestos-cement roofs. Henning Larsen's Klostermarken School at Roskilde (1965, page 120) is distinguished by the vestibule-cum-corridor which follows the sloping ground and merges the different parts of the school. Here, a building method using precast reinforced concrete units has been applied. All the elementary schools erected so far have adhered to the principle of standard classes with identical classrooms where each child has a permanently allocated desk. It is expected, however, that further competitions due to be held shortly will produce new types of schools with greater facilities for a flexible adaptation to different teaching methods.
As far as the latest secondary schools are concerned, the principle of the standard classroom has been abandoned. The grammar schools at Grenå (page 110) and Køge (page 116), designed by Johan Richter and Arne Gravers (1964) and by Salli Besiakov and Nils Andersen (1965), respectively, are both based on the principle of individually shaped specialised classrooms to which the pupils go for one lesson at a time. At Grenå, the classrooms face outwards towards large terraces with a free view over the landscape, turning their backs to the joint foyer and assembly hall in the centre of the group. At Køge, the plan shows a higher degree of differentiation, permitting the addition of new classrooms without affecting the overall plan. Both schools, built in red and yellow brick, respectively, are composed into sculptural units dominated by the centrally placed assembly hall blocks.
The so-called "High School" was originally a specifically Danish invention. Here, young school-leavers meet voluntarily for shorter or longer courses in general cultural subjects. The students live at the school. In a competition for a Workers' High School near Elsinore (page 123), Jørn Utzon pioneered a new type of High School where all the students' rooms are concentrated in a tower block whilst all the teaching premises are grouped around an internal courtyard on an artificially created platform. The project was never realised, but the main principle was adopted by Viggo Møller-Jensen and Tyge Arnfred in their design for the High School at Herning (1962, page 124). However, they did not seek the same sculptural effect as in Utzon's project. The tower block at Herning, with its light and bright facade cladding of aluminium contrasting with the low and rather heavy-looking school buildings proper, forms an impressive dominant in the flat landscape.
Right up to his death in 1965, Kay Fisker came to be regarded as this country's most important interpreter and developer of functional Danish tradition. This applies to his housing schemes and schools as well as to his building for the Mothers' Help Organisation in Copenhagen (1955, page 92). Placed in the midst of an older residential district, the building is distinguished by the lucidity shown in form and proportions and by the attractiveness of the yellow brick walls. The same qualities are encountered in Fisker's last work which was only completed after his death: the Danish Academy in Rome.
Harmony of house and landscape has been one of the foremost aims in designing Louisiana Museum (page 140) which occupies a very attractive site, studded with large, old trees, high above the coast of the Sound in North Zealand. The museum is the outcome of an exemplary co-operation between an idealistic client, Knud W. Jensen, and the architects Jørgen Bo and

wohnung. Große und ganz kleine Sommerhäuser sind an allen Küsten Dänemarks aus dem Boden geschossen. Um einer Überwucherung des Küstengebiets mit billigen Sommerhütten entgegenzutreten, hat man sich in den letzten Jahren mit Projekten für größere, einheitlich geplante Sommerhauskolonien befaßt. Claus Bremers Ferienkolonie bei Blokhus bietet dafür ein gutes Beispiel. Unter den interessantesten Sommerhäusern der Nachkriegszeit, die zu einem einfachen und entspannten Leben in der Natur einladen, sind zu nennen Vilhelm Wohlerts kleines Gästehaus für Niels Bohr (1957, Seite 56), mit seiner Klapp- und Faltwand, Nils Fagerholts einfache Holzkiste in Blåmunkene (Seite 60) und Erik Korshagens Haus in Rørvig (Seite 58), das von einem großen, auskragenden Strohdach überragt wird.
Das Reihenhaus, das wesentliche Vorteile des Einfamilienhauses mit einer rationellen und raumsparenden Bauform vereint, erwies sich nach dem Krieg als ein beliebter Wohnungstyp. Die Architekten waren bestrebt, das Thema dadurch zu variieren, daß sie geschützte Freiflächen schufen, die nicht von den Nachbarhäusern aus eingesehen werden können. In seiner charaktervollen Søholm-Siedlung in Klampenborg (Seite 62) aus den Jahren 1950 bis 1955 hat Arne Jacobsen differenzierte Wohnungen mit hervorragenden räumlichen Qualitäten geschaffen.
Das eingeschossige Hofhaus bietet besonders gute Voraussetzungen für ein ungestörtes, gegen jeden Einblick abgeschirmtes Familienleben und für enge Beziehungen zwischen dem Hausinneren und dem gemeinschaftlich benutzten Hofraum, der gleichzeitig gegen das windige dänische Klima Schutz bietet. Im Jahr 1958 errichtete Jørn Utzon mit seinen Kingohusene bei Helsingør (Seite 65) die erste größere Hofhausanlage in Dänemark. Ein hügeliges Gelände legte eine Gesamtanlage mit zwanglos angeordneten Hausreihen nahe, die ein Höchstmaß von Möglichkeiten bieten, bei jedem einzelnen Haus die Vorteile seiner besonderen Lage mit der Orientierung und Aussicht auf die gemeinsamen Grünflächen voll auszunutzen. Die Siedlung wurde mit herkömmlichen Baustoffen und Bauweisen erbaut und erwies sich als eine der billigsten Wohnbaulösungen der Gegenwart. Verschieden hohe Backsteinmauern verbinden die einzelnen Bauten zu einer reich variierten Einheit. Utzon errichtete später eine weitere Siedlung, Fredensborghusene (Seite 68), wo ähnliche Hofhäuser um ein Gemeinschaftszentrum mit Klublokalen und Restaurant gruppiert sind, die einen besonders schönen Ausblick über eine typisch dänische Landschaft mit Feldern und Wäldern haben. In den letzten Jahren sind überall im Lande zahlreiche Hofhaussiedlungen aus herkömmlichen Baustoffen oder nach neuen Bauweisen errichtet worden.

Die Qualität der neueren dänischen Baukunst wurde in einem hohen Grad durch Architekturwettbewerbe beeinflußt. Seit fast einem Jahrhundert hat man versucht, einen sehr erheblichen Teil der großen öffentlichen Bauaufgaben durch offene Wettbewerbe zu klären, und dänische Architekten mußten ihr Bestes leisten, um sich die interessantesten Aufträge zu sichern. Zahlreiche Ideenwettbewerbe wurden veranstaltet, um entweder konkrete Wettbewerbsprojekte oder aber grundsätzliche Lösungsvorschläge, etwa für die Gestaltung neuer Typen von Wohnungs- oder Verwaltungsbauten, zu erhalten. Die Wettbewerbe waren auch für die jüngeren Architekten von Bedeutung, als Möglichkeit, sich unter gleichen Bedingungen mit erfahrenen Kollegen zu messen und als Gelegenheit, durch prämierte Entwürfe einen Namen zu bekommen.
Besondere Bedeutung hatten die Wettbewerbe für den Schulbau. Sowohl die Behörden als auch die Pädagogen und Architekten waren bestrebt, die besten Bedingungen für die Erziehung der Kinder zu schaffen und ständig neue pädagogische und architektonische Lösungen zu entwickeln. Während des Krieges befaßten sich die ersten Wettbewerbsprojekte mit eingeschossigen Schulanlagen, bei denen es gelang, den Bauten einen besonders freundlichen Charakter zu geben und die einzelnen Klassenräume mit den anschließenden Gartenflächen in direkte Verbindung zu bringen. Zu den besten eingeschossigen Volksschulanlagen gehört Arne Jacobsens Munkegårds-Schule in Gentofte (Seite 98). Der Plan dieser Anlage folgt einem klar ersichtlichen Prinzip: Selbständige Einheiten, die aus zwei zusammengebauten Normalklassen mit einem dazugehörigen, individuell ausgestalteten Hofraum bestehen, werden von quer laufenden Korridoren umschlossen. Der Komplex zeichnet sich durch gründliche Durcharbeitung und ausgewogene Übereinstimmung zwischen Gebäude und Inventar aus. Im Jahr 1965 hat Arne Jacobsen in seiner Nyager-Schule in Rødovre (Seite 113) das Thema eines engen Verzahnens von Klassenzimmern und angeschlossenen Hofräumen durch die Verwendung von Mittelkorridoren abgewandelt. In der Vangebo-Schule in Søllerød (Seite 106), die 1957–60 von den Architekten Brüel, Bornebusch, Selchau und Henning Larsen erbaut wurde, bildet jedes Klassenzimmer ein selbständiges »Haus« mit zugehörigem Gartenhof, das durch niedrige Korridore mit den übrigen Abteilun-

Vilhelm Wohlert. The buildings are modestly retracted from the large open space of the park; but through their large windows, they take in all the beauty of the park – a feature which has also come in for criticism as it detracts from the concentration on the works of art displayed inside. The museum is designed for periodically changed displays of its own collection of modern art and of major international travelling exhibitions. With its white-washed walls inside as well as outside, its deliberately exposed timber beams, overhanging flat roofs, large windows and brown-red floor tiles, the building plays with great virtuosity on structural shapes and materials which have found wide-spread acceptance in Danish post-war architecture.

In 1957, Jørn Utzon was awarded the First Prize in the international competition for the Opera House in Sydney, and two years later, he left Denmark in order to concentrate on this monumental task. He left behind a number of unrealised projects such as the one for the Birkehøj housing estate at Elsinore (Fig.16) which, in compositional harmony with the Højstrup High School already mentioned, was meant to be placed on a terraced platform surrounding a hill-top in a wood-skirted plain. Both projects were abandoned, and the tasks assigned to other architects. Regrettably, Denmark has therefore, as yet, no major works of Utzon's except the court-house estates near Elsinore and Fredensborg. In 1963, while resident in Sydney, he prepared a project for a museum at Silkeborg (page 144) on the initiative of the painter Asger Jorn. In this project the greater part of the building is buried below ground in a kind of magic pit where the visitors, walking on spiral ramps, will be able to observe the works of art on display. Here, Utzon is seen to be one of the country's most original architectural talents, free from allegiance to any Danish tradition. The project is one of the few examples of international expressionism which has otherwise not found much support in Denmark. F.C. Lund's and Hans Christian Hansen's Ringbo hospital at Bagsværd (page 94) with its circular layout plan and boldly designed roofs represents one of the latest Danish building schemes which come closest to expressionist ideals.

Erik Christian Sørensen has consistently pursued the idea of simple expression for a spatial-constructive architecture from his own house to the data processing centre designed in 1962 (page 182). Later, he worked with projects for the Roskilde Ring housing scheme and a musium for the Viking boats. The project for Roskilde Ring (Fig. 17) shows an unusual way of utilising a gravel pit: each of the standard houses, placed on the slopes, consists of a square four-storey building with two two-storey maisonettes, and is assembled by a simple method from precast reinforced concrete units. The Viking Museum (page 146) is at present under construction at the shores of Roskilde Fjord where the ships were recently discovered. It is a simple concrete building with a clearly apparent distinction between supporting and supported parts, and with side-lighting as well as top-lighting for the interiors.

Vilhelm Lauritzen, who in the 1930s became one of the strongest protagonists of international functionalism, was able to develop his functionalistic ideals still further when, in 1957–60, in collaboration with younger partners, he designed the passenger building at Copenhagen's airport at Kastrup (page 196). The interior is a large hall which, with its galleries on different

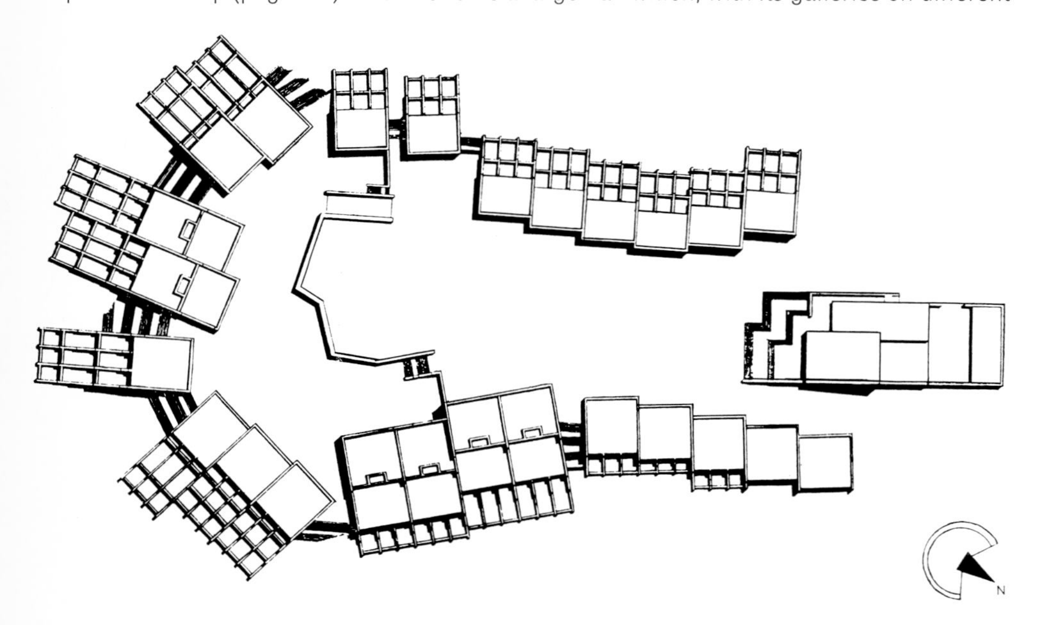

16. Birkehøj, Elsinore. Project for housing estate, 1963. Architect: Jørn Utzon.

16. Birkehøj, Helsingør. Entwurf einer Wohnsiedlung, 1963. Architekt: Jørn Utzon.

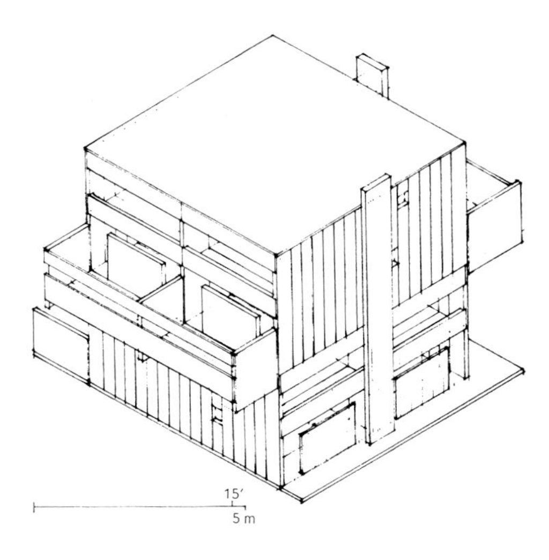

17. Roskilde Ring. Project for housing estate, 1963. Four-storey unit containing two two-storey maisonettes. Architect: Erik Christian Sørensen.

17. Roskilde Ring. Entwurf einer Wohnsiedlung, 1963. Viergeschossige Hauseinheit mit zwei übereinander angeordneten zweigeschossigen Wohnungen. Architekt: Erik Christian Sørensen.

gen der Schule verbunden ist. Mit ihren groben gelben Mauern und ihrer geteerten oder rot gebeizten Holzkonstruktion erhielt diese Schule einen besonders robusten Charakter, mit dem sie auch einer etwas rauhen Behandlung durch die Schulkinder auf lange Jahre standhalten dürfte. Eine freie und ausdrucksvolle architektonische Entfaltung kennzeichnet die Hanssted-Schule (Seite 103), die in den Jahren 1954–58 vom Kopenhagener Stadtarchitekten F. C. Lund und Hans Christian Hansen gebaut wurde. Hier liegen die Normalklassen zu viert auf zwei Geschossen verteilt um ein Treppenhaus herum, so daß sich eine für die Kinder übersichtliche Einheit ergibt. Noch robuster und strenger in ihrem Charakter ist Kay Fiskers Voldparken-Schule (Seite 96), die 1951–57 mit einem niedrigen Bau für die Unterstufe und einem dreigeschossigen Gebäude für größere Kinder erstellt wurde. Große Eternitdächer binden die verschiedenen Teile der Anlage zu einer ausdrucksstarken Einheit zusammen. Henning Larsens Klostermarken-Schule bei Roskilde (1965, Seite 120) zeigt als Hauptmerkmal einen der Geländeneigung folgenden Verbindungsgang, der die einzelnen Baukörper zusammenhält. Die Gebäude dieser Schule sind aus vorgefertigten Stahlbetonelementen errichtet. Bei allen bisher gebauten Volksschulen wurde am Normalklassenprinzip mit gleichartigen Klassenzimmern festgehalten, wo die Kinder ihre festen Plätze haben; es ist jedoch zu erwarten, daß kommende Wettbewerbe schon in nächster Zeit neue Schultypen bringen werden, die größere Möglichkeiten für eine elastische Anpassung an die verschiedenartigen Unterrichtsformen bieten.

Bei den höheren Schulen, die in den letzten Jahren entstanden, wurde das Normalklassenprinzip bereits verlassen. Die Gymnasien in Grenå (Johan Richter und Arne Gravers, 1964, Seite 110) und Køge (Salli Besiakov und Nils Andersen, 1965, Seite 116) sind nach dem Prinzip individuell gestalteter Fachklassen geplant, zu denen sich die Schüler für jede Unterrichtsstunde begeben müssen. In Grenå liegen die Klassenzimmer nach außen, in Verbindung mit großen Terrassen, die eine freie Aussicht über die Landschaft bieten und den Gemeinschaftsräumen, Halle und Aula, im Zentrum der Anlage den Rücken kehren. In Køge wurde ein stärker differenzierter Grundriß gewählt, wobei die Möglichkeit besteht, neue Klassenräume hinzuzufügen, ohne die Gesamtanordnung der Anlage zu verändern. Beide Schulen, die aus rotem beziehungsweise gelbem Backstein errichtet wurden, sind zu plastischen Einheiten zusammengefaßt, die von der Aula im Zentrum beherrscht werden.

Die sogenannte »Hochschule« ist ursprünglich eine typisch dänische Einrichtung. Hier treffen sich junge Leute nach ihrer eigentlichen Schulausbildung zwanglos für kürzere oder längere Kurse über allgemeine kulturelle Themen, wobei sie im Internat zusammenleben. In einem Wettbewerb für eine Arbeiterhochschule bei Helsingør (Seite 123) führte Jørn Utzon einen neuen Typ ein, bei dem alle Studentenzimmer in einem Turmhaus konzentriert sind, während sich sämtliche Unterrichtsräume auf einer künstlichen Plattform um einen Innenhof herum gruppieren. Das Projekt wurde niemals verwirklicht. Doch ist sein Hauptgedanke, der Wohnturm, bei der von Viggo Møller-Jensen und Tyge Arnfred entworfenen Hochschule in Herning (1962, Seite 124) aufgegriffen. Hier wurde jedoch nicht die gleiche plastische Gesamtwirkung angestrebt wie bei Utzons Projekt. Das Turmhaus in Herning mit seiner hellen, leichten Fassadenverkleidung aus Aluminium, die zu den übrigen, niedrigen und schwer wirkenden Schulgebäuden in kräftigem Gegensatz steht, bildet eine wirkungsvolle Dominante in der flachen Landschaft.

Bis zu seinem Tode im Jahre 1965 erwies sich Kay Fisker als der bedeutendste Vermittler und Fortführer der funktionellen dänischen Tradition. Dies trifft sowohl für seine Wohnbauten als auch für seine Schulen und sein Gebäude für die Mütterhilfe (1955, Seite 92) zu. Mitten in ein älteres Kopenhagener Wohnviertel gestellt, zeichnet sich dieses Bauwerk durch Klarheit in Form und Proportion und durch den Materialreiz der gelben Backsteinmauern aus. Die gleichen Qualitäten finden sich bei Fiskers letzter Arbeit wieder, die erst nach seinem Tode fertiggestellt wurde, bei der Dänischen Akademie in Rom.

Das Zusammenspiel zwischen Bau und Landschaft war für die Gestaltung des Louisiana-Museums (Seite 140) entscheidend, das auf einem sehr schönen Gelände mit großen alten Bäumen im Norden der Insel Seeland hoch über dem Øresund errichtet wurde. Das Museum kam durch eine vorbildliche Zusammenarbeit zwischen einem idealistischen Bauherrn, Knud W. Jensen, und den Architekten Jørgen Bo und Vilhelm Wohlert zustande. Die Bauten sind bescheiden aus der großen Grünfläche des Parks zurückgenommen; dafür holen sie durch große Fensterflächen alle Schönheiten der Parklandschaft in sich hinein – eine Tatsache, die allerdings auch kritisiert wurde, weil sie von der Betrachtung der ausgestellten Kunstwerke ablenkt. Das Museum ist für wechselnde Ausstellungen der eigenen Sammlung moderner Kunst sowie für größere internationale Wanderausstellungen bestimmt. Mit seinen innen wie außen weißgekalkten Wänden, seinen deutlich sichtbaren Holzträgern, seinen

levels and of different height, forms an integrating frame for the comings and goings of passengers.
Through his post-war works, Arne Jacobsen has become Denmark's internationally best-known architect. With his flexible and open talent and great professional skill, he has the gift of continually renewing himself through impulses from the international development of architecture. But however strong the influence from abroad may have been, his buildings have always shown his personal hallmark and at the same time, retained a typically Danish character. Jacobsen's work has covered all aspects of building activities: individual houses, schools, administration buildings, factories, blocks of flats; they even include landscape gardening and the design of furniture, silverware and china. In all these spheres, he has achieved remarkable success. Up to now, nearly all his major tasks had to be won in competitions. Each of his works is distinguished by thorough attention to detail so that each detail becomes an integral part of an artistic entity. Jacobsen has made a particularly important contribution to the design of office buildings and public institutions. In 1955, he introduced the American 'curtain wall' principle into Denmark for the headquarters building of Messrs. Jespersen & Søn (page 174). With its cantilevered reinforced concrete framework and attractively proportioned facade, this can be regarded as one of Jacobsen's best buildings. Shortly afterwards, he adopted the same structural principle for the town hall at Rødovre (page 164). Here, the office block is designed as a simple, module-governed three-storey block whilst council chamber and committee rooms are placed in a self-contained single-storey annex. In the details and in the design of stairs and furniture, Jacobsen has set his own personal stamp on this building which is otherwise much inspired by international ideas. With the S.A.S. building (page 158), which houses the Copenhagen Air Terminal as well as an hotel with restaurant, Jacobsen developed the curtain wall principle for a group of two intercalated blocks with 2 and 22 storeys, respectively. In the tower block, elegant use is made of all the possibilities inherent in the mirror effect and reflection of sun and sky. Dominating as it does the district around Copenhagen's Central Railway Station, the precisely shaped block also has a major town planning function. For Tom's Chocolate Factory, Jacobsen built, in 1961, a group of buildings (page 189) consisting of a large, low, rectangular factory hall and a three-storey office wing in compositional contrast to a group of high silos and chimneys. Jacobsen's latest major Danish project for an indoor swimming pool at Lyngby (page 154) has not yet been realised. The forceful design of this project reveals the artistic development which Jacobsen has experienced by exerting his abilities to the utmost in great international tasks such as St. Catherine's College, Oxford – a description of which would go beyond the scope of the present book.
Again as a result of public competitions, Halldor Gunnløgsson and Jørn Nielsen built the administration buildings for the Copenhagen suburb of Tårnby (page 168) and the market town of Fredericia in Jutland (page 171). Both these town halls are meticulously designed, strictly formal buildings which, in their logic and consistency, are manifestations of a classic-Apollonian approach to architecture. Tårnby Town Hall is distinguished by its layout plan with two staggered office blocks, one surrounding an open courtyard, the other surrounding a council chamber with high-level skylighting. In 1967, Gunnløgsson and Jørn Nielsen completed the erection of the wine warehouse and despatch building of Messrs. A/S Bestle (page 194), again revealing a sure touch in arranging the layout and a logical consistency in choosing the structural design.
Palle Suenson's administration building for the internationally well-known firm of F.L. Schmidt (1954–56, page 180) occupies a special position in office block architecture. The building is supported by narrow, closely spaced, deep brick piers which provide a distinct vertical partition and profilation, contrasting with the overhung flat roof above the retracted top storey. By his choice of materials, Suenson intended to endow the building with qualities which can sustain wear and which will, if anything, gain in attraction through exposure to atmospheric agents. Under the influence of Japanese and English brutalism, yet at the same time well in keeping with a provincial town in Jutland, is the building of Hammerum Herreds Savings Bank, built in 1964 by Poul Kjærgaard and partners (page 186). It is erected in reinforced concrete and its robust surfaces are left untreated both externally and internally. Especially inside the bank premises, the care for details is apparent, also in the sophisticated treatment of the materials of all the furniture and fittings, tangible or at least visible to the public. In Messrs. F.A. Thiele's optician's shop in Copenhagen (page 176), Kaare Klint and, after the latter's death, Vilhelm Wohlert have infused a fresh quality into the rather neglected task of shop design by meticulous attention to all furniture and fittings. Similar claims can be made for ships, and several Danish architects have in fact been concerned

flachen Kragdächern, seinen großen Fensterflächen und braunroten Fliesen spielt das Museum virtuos gerade jene Bauformen und Baustoffe aus, die in der dänischen Nachkriegsarchitektur so große Verbreitung gefunden haben.
Im Jahr 1957 gewann Jørn Utzon den internationalen Wettbewerb für das Opernhaus in Sydney und verließ zwei Jahre später Dänemark, um sich dieser monumentalen Aufgabe zu widmen. Er hinterließ einige unausgeführte Projekte wie die Siedlung Birkehøj bei Helsingør (Abb. 16), die im kompositionellen Zusammenspiel mit der bereits erwähnten Hochschule in Højstrup als Terrassenbau um eine Hügelkuppe inmitten einer waldumkränzten Ebene errichtet werden sollte. Beide Pläne wurden aufgegeben und die Aufgaben anderen Architekten übertragen. Leider sind daher in Dänemark außer den Hofhaus-Siedlungen bei Helsingør und Fredensborg noch keine größeren Projekte von Utzon verwirklicht worden. Im Jahr 1963 entwarf er in Sydney ein Projekt für ein Museum in Silkeborg (Seite 144) auf Veranlassung des Malers Asger Jorn. Der größte Teil des Bauwerks soll wie eine Zauberhöhle in die Erde eingelassen werden, wo die Besucher von Wendelrampen aus interessante wechselnde Raumeindrücke erleben können. Hier zeigt sich Utzon als das originellste Architektentalent des Landes, frei von jeglicher Hörigkeit gegenüber der dänischen Tradition. Das Projekt ist eines der wenigen Beispiele für den internationalen Expressionismus, der sonst in Dänemark wenig Anhang gefunden hat. F. C. Lunds und Hans Christian Hansens Ringbo- Pflegeheim in Bagsværd (Seite 94) ist mit seiner kreisrunden Grundrißanordnung und seinen kühnen Dachformen eine der neuesten dänischen Bauanlagen, die den expressionistischen Idealen am nächsten kommen.
Erik Christian Sørensen hat die einfache Ausdrucksform für eine räumlich-konstruktive Architektur von seinem eigenen Haus bis zum elektronischen Rechenzentrum (1962, Seite 182) konsequent weitergeführt. Später schuf er die Entwürfe für die Siedlung Roskilde Ring und für ein Museum für Wikingerschiffe. Das Projekt für Roskilde Ring (Abb. 17) zeigt eine originelle Ausnutzung einer Kiesgrube: Die auf die Hänge verlegte Bebauung besteht aus Grundeinheiten von quadratischen, viergeschossigen Häusern mit zwei übereinanderliegenden, zweigeschossigen Wohnungen. Jedes Haus ist nach einem einfachen Montagesystem aus vorgefertigten Stahlbetonelementen zusammengesetzt. Das Wikingermuseum (Seite 146) wird zur Zeit am Ufer des Roskilde-Fjords errichtet, wo die Schiffe vor einigen Jahren entdeckt wurden. Es ist ein einfaches Betongebäude, bei dem die tragenden und getragenen Elemente deutlich unterschieden sind und für das Innere sowohl Seitenlicht als auch Oberlicht Verwendung finden.
Vilhelm Lauritzen, der sich in den dreißiger Jahren als der stärkste Vorkämpfer für den internationalen Funktionalismus erwies, führte 1957–60 in Zusammenarbeit mit jüngeren Partnern seine funktionalistischen Vorstellungen mit dem Abfertigungsgebäude des Kopenhagener Flughafens in Kastrup (Seite 196) weiter. Das Innere besteht aus einer großen Halle, die mit ihren auf verschiedener Höhe angeordneten Balkonen das Getriebe der ankommenden und abreisenden Fluggäste zu einer räumlichen Einheit verbindet.
Seine Nachkriegsarbeiten machten Arne Jacobsen zu dem im Ausland am besten bekannten dänischen Architekten. Mit seinem anpassungsfähigen und offenen Talent und seiner großen fachlichen Tüchtigkeit hat er die Gabe, sich ständig durch Impulse aus der internationalen Architekturentwicklung zu erneuern. Aber wie stark auch der Einfluß aus dem Ausland gewesen sein mag, stets zeigt das fertige Bauwerk die ganz persönliche Handschrift Arne Jacobsens und zugleich ist es eine Lösung von typisch dänischem Charakter. Jacobsens Arbeit erstreckt sich auf alle Gebiete des Bauwesens, auf Einfamilienhäuser, Schulen, Verwaltungsgebäude, Fabriken und Wohnblöcke, außerdem umfaßt sie Gartengestaltung und Formgebung von Möbeln, Silberwaren und Porzellan. Auf jedem dieser Gebiete hat er Bemerkenswertes geleistet. Fast alle seine größeren Aufgaben mußte er sich bisher im Rahmen eines Wettbewerbs erkämpfen. Jede Arbeit zeichnet sich durch gründlichste Detailbearbeitung aus, und jedes Detail bildet einen natürlichen Bestandteil einer künstlerischen Einheit. Besonderen Einfluß hat Jacobsen auf den Bau von Bürohäusern und öffentlichen Gebäuden ausgeübt. Im Jahr 1955 führte er beim Bürogebäude der Firma Jespersen & Søn (Seite 174) den amerikanischen Curtain-wall in Dänemark ein. Mit seiner auskragenden Stahlbetonkonstruktion und der gut proportionierten Fassade ist dieser Bau eine der besten Arbeiten Jacobsens. Kurz danach wandte er das gleiche konstruktive Prinzip beim Rathaus in Rødovre (Seite 164) an. Hier wurde der Bürotrakt als einfacher, auf einem Modulsystem aufgebauter dreigeschossiger Block errichtet, während der Ratssaal und die Sitzungszimmer in einem besonderen eingeschossigen Anbau untergebracht sind. In der Detaillierung, in der Gestaltung der Treppen und dem Entwurf der Möbel hat Jacobsen diesem im übrigen sehr international inspirierten Bauwerk seinen besonderen Stempel aufgedrückt. Mit dem SAS-

with the interior design of liners. For instance, Kay Fisker worked on the design of the Bornholm ships and in recent years, Kay Kørbing has made a special contribution in this sphere, the Copenhagen–Oslo ship "Prinsesse Margrethe" (page 200) being one of his best known designs.
In international architecture, the design of churches has in recent years inspired an overwhelming, fanciful expressionism, perhaps because in an otherwise sober age characterised by conformity and industrialisation, many architects have here found an opportunity for more emotional professional activities for which they had no other outlet. This trend has also been apparent in Denmark, although symbolic expression as a whole is alien to Danish mentality and extrovert pathos is hardly a characteristic of Danish church building tradition. The most impressive of the examples, shown in the present book, for the rather extensive ecclesiastical building activities in Denmark in recent years is Vilhelm Wohlert's and Rolf Graae's Stengård Church at Gladsaxe (1963–64, page 209) with its characteristic exterior where the bell towers shoot up organically as the dominant feature in a sculptural entity of closely spaced brick-clad building blocks. The interior is dominated by red brick, and both pulpit and altar are made of the same material as part of the altar wall. Johan von Spreckelsen's Roman-Catholic church of St. Nikolaj, Hvidovre (page 206), is constructed in yellow brick, but the square nave is in a highly unorthodox way placed diagonally and covered by a slcping hyperboloid roof structure. In Inger and Johannes Exner's St. Clemens Church, Randers (1963–64, page 213), the view across the Gudenå Valley is effectively utilised as a backdrop for the altar wall. On the whole, however, it would seem that Danish architects feel more at home in tasks which can be solved on the strength of more sober and functional criteria. This applies, for instance, to Glostrup Crematorium (page 216) built in 1960 by Brüel, Bornebusch, Selchau and Henning Larsen. This building is distinguished by its clear layout plan, its simple yet impressive exterior, and the solemn interior of the cubically shaped chapel which is dominated by a skylight above the catafalque.

With many of the buildings shown in this book, conventional materials play a predominant role; but prefabricated units of different types also play their part. It is no longer a question of buildings erected by craftsmen in the traditional sense; yet Danish architects have always, in their designs, been able to rely on a high quality of workmanship, be it for example a case of workmanlike bricklaying or the choice of well-tried prefabricated units. They have thus been able, in time-honoured architectural fashion, to improve the individually designed house through refined detailed solutions and effective use of materials.
In view of the dynamic technical and economic development, it must be expected that the craftsman of the past will come to play an ever decreasing part in building activities, giving

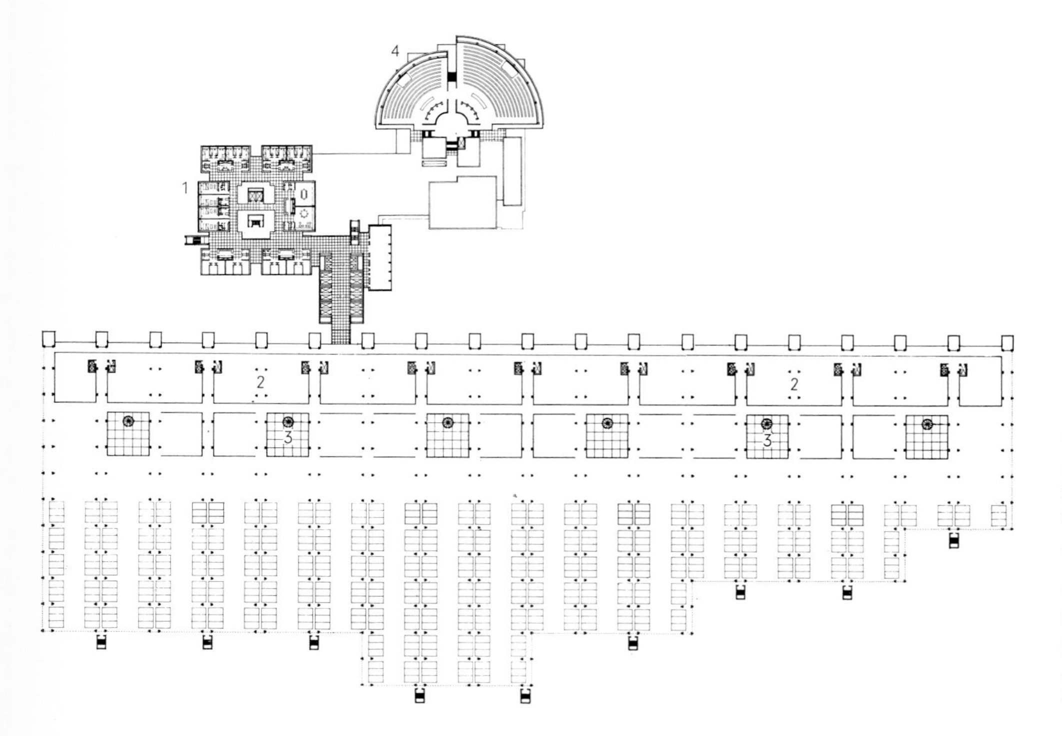

18. County Hospital at Herlev. Project, 1965. Plan. Key: 1 patients ward, 2 therapeutical department, 3 courtyards, 4 auditorium. Architects: Wilhelm Groth-Hansen, Max Brüel, Gehrdt Bornebusch, Jørgen Selchau.

18. Kreiskrankenhaus in Herlev. Projekt, 1965. Grundriß. Legende: 1 Krankenstationen, 2 Behandlungsabteilung, 3 Innenhöfe, 4 Auditorium. Architekten: Wilhelm Groth-Hansen, Max Brüel, Gehrdt Bornebusch, Jørgen Se'chau.

19. County Hospital at Herlev. Model photograph. Architects: Wilhelm Groth-Hansen, Max Brüel, Gehrdt Bornebusch, Jørgen Selchau.
20. County Hospital at Herlev. Therapeutical department, module unit of 15×15 metres with surrounding corridors and installation galleries. Architects: Wilhelm Groth-Hansen, Max Brüel, Gehrdt Bornebusch, Jørgen Selchau.

19. Kreiskrankenhaus in Herlev. Modellansicht. Architekten: Wilhelm Groth-Hansen, Max Brüel, Gehrdt Bornebusch, Jørgen Selchau.
20. Kreiskrankenhaus in Herlev. Behandlungsabteilung, Moduleinheit 15×15 m mit umschließenden Fluren und Installationskanälen. Architekten: Wilhelm Groth-Hansen, Max Brüel, Gehrdt Bornebusch, Jørgen Selchau.

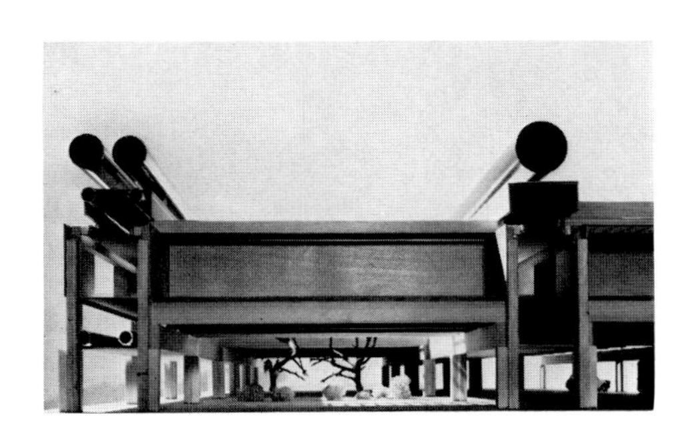

Gebäude (Seite 158), das sowohl das Empfangszentrum der Fluggesellschaft als auch ein Hotel mit Restaurant enthält, übertrug Jacobsen das Curtain-wall-System auf eine Anlage von zwei ineinander geschobenen Blöcken mit zwei beziehungsweise zweiundzwanzig Geschossen. Bei dem Hochhausblock sind auf elegante Weise alle Möglichkeiten genutzt, die sich aus der Spiegelung und aus den Reflexen von Sonnenlicht und Himmel ergeben. Da das Bauwerk das ganze Stadtviertel um den Kopenhagener Hauptbahnhof beherrscht, hat der präzise gestaltete Turmblock eine große städtebauliche Bedeutung. Für Toms Schokoladenfabrik (Seite 189) baute Jacobsen im Jahre 1961 eine Anlage, die aus einer großen, niedrigen, rechteckigen Fabrikhalle und einem dreigeschossigen Bürobau besteht, gegen die eine Gruppe hoher Silobauten und Schornsteine kompositionell in Gegensatz gebracht ist. Das neueste größere Projekt für Dänemark ist die Schwimmhalle in Lyngby (Seite 154), die bisher noch nicht gebaut wurde. Die charaktervolle Gestaltung dieses Entwurfs zeigt, wie weit Jacobsens künstlerische Entwicklung durch das äußerste Anspannen seiner Begabung bei internationalen Aufgaben, wie dem St. Catherine College in Oxford, beeinflußt worden ist, dessen Behandlung allerdings über den Rahmen dieses Buches hinausgeht.
Halldor Gunnløgsson hat zusammen mit Jørn Nielsen als Ergebnis von offenen Wettbewerben die städtischen Verwaltungsgebäude im Kopenhagener Vorort Tårnby (Seite 168) und in Fredericia in Jütland (Seite 171) gebaut. Beides sind sorgfältig durchgearbeitete, streng formelle Bauwerke, die in ihrer Logik und Konsequenz aus einer klassisch-apollinischen Architekturauffassung heraus entworfen wurden. Das Rathaus in Tårnby ist wegen seiner Grundrißgestaltung bemerkenswert; es handelt sich um zwei gegeneinander verschobene Bauten mit Verwaltungsbüros, die einen offenen Innenhof beziehungsweise einen Ratssaal mit hoch angeordnetem Oberlicht umschließen. Im Jahr 1965 brachten Gunnløgsson und Jørn Nielsen das Lager- und Versandgebäude der Weinhandlung A/S Bestle (Seite 194) zum Abschluß, eine Aufgabe, die wiederum von sicherem Gefühl für die richtige Disposition und von einem ausgeprägten Sinn für die ausgefeilte, logische Konstruktion zeugt.
Palle Suensons Verwaltungsgebäude für die Weltfirma F. L. Schmidt (1954–56, Seite 180) nimmt innerhalb des Bürohausbaus eine Sonderstellung ein. Das Haus ruht auf eng nebeneinandergestellten, tiefen Mauerpfeilern; das gibt dem Bau eine markante Vertikalteilung und Profilierung, die mit dem stark auskragenden Dach über dem zurückgesetzten Dachgeschoß kontrastiert. Durch die Auswahl gediegener Baustoffe wollte Suenson dem Bau Qualitäten verleihen, die ein Altern vertragen und durch den Einfluß der Witterung nur noch an Schönheit gewinnen. Unter dem Einfluß brutalistischer Ideen aus Japan und England stehend, aber zugleich auch der kleinen Provinzstadt in Jütland gut angepaßt, ist die von Poul Kjærgaard und Partnern im Jahre 1964 erbaute Hammerum Herreds Sparkasse (Seite 186). Der Bau wurde in Stahlbeton errichtet, dessen rauhe Oberfläche sowohl innen als auch außen

way to thoroughly developed industrial assembly systems. In this field, the development has already gone a long way, and due to the initiative of Danish engineers and contractors, Denmark has developed a technically advanced, though not yet architecturally refined, production of concrete units which are exported to many countries on a large scale. One might therefore view with some misgivings the apparent lack of interest for the reality of a new age and the continued, almost escapist cultivation of traditional craftsmanship which are typical for so many of the best Danish architectural works of the post-war period. It might even be feared that Danish architecture as such might perish together with the artisans. However, certain major works and projects of recent years have shown that leading Danish architects have seriously taken up the challenge inherent in the new production methods and in the complete industrialisation of building activities. As far as housing is concerned, this applies to two large, completely different housing schemes, viz. Høje Gladsaxe and Albertslund.
At Høje Gladsaxe, the architectural firms Hoff & Windinge, Juul Møller & Agertoft and Alex Poulsen have jointly worked out a comprehensive project for a completely industrialised housing scheme with 2000 dwelling units (page 88). Considerations for production and assembly methods have had an important influence on the design of layout and floor plans. The dwelling units are spread over five oblong 16-storey blocks and a number of nine and four storey blocks; in addition, there are a school, a shopping centre and other joint facilities. One might criticise the somewhat rigid design and the suitability of the multi-storey blocks for families with children. The houses might also be criticised for lacking the refined architectural qualities typical of the individually designed buildings described in the present book. But the attractive site on a slope affording a view over a large park and wide areas of Copenhagen is skilfully utilised, and the housing scheme is distinguished by its striking wholeness and simple expressiveness. The significance of this scheme lies first of all in the serious pioneering effort on the part of the architects which preceded the erection.
In the case of the Albertslund scheme (page 72), where the total number of dwelling units is about the same, an even greater effort was made to create a congenial residential environment and a human scale. Here, family dwellings are spread over some 1000 single-storey court-houses and 500 two-storey terrace houses, whilst about 625 smaller flats are placed in three-storey blocks. The housing density is fairly high and of urban character, and the scheme has been carried out within strict economic limits as an assembly system with prefabricated, wall-high units of rough-cast reinforced concrete and black-tarred timber. The somewhat rigid marshalling of identical buildings was governed by the cranes required for the assembly system. The desire to create a congenial human atmosphere has played an important part with the team of architects: Viggo Møller-Jensen, Tyge Arnfred, Mogens J. Pedersen, Jørn Ole Sørensen, landscape gardener Ole Nørgård and town planning consultant Knud Svensson. Vehicular and pedestrian traffic are segregated and there are, within the pedestrian area, congenial courtyards and playgrounds. The individual dwellings, each covering a floor area of approx. 430 to 1400 sq. ft., are neither particularly large nor luxuriously appointed; but all of them bear the hallmark of careful planning and a simple architectural quality which is akin to the values typical of earlier Danish building activities at large.
The dynamic development of our age is such that buildings soon become obsolete, in many cases long before they are structurally unsound. It would therefore be desirable to design them in such a way that modifications and extensions can be carried out as easily as possible so as to meet any future requirements of which we know little more than that they will occur. For the erection of the new campus buildings of Denmark's Technical University to the north of Copenhagen (page 136), architect Nils Koppel has tried to solve the problem by erecting three-storey standard buildings in isolated positions where they can be extended and adapted to changing demands by comparatively simple means. Together with those institutions which call for a more specific design, the standard buildings are concentrated in informally arranged groups within a rectangular road system, whilst a central avenue, designed in collaboration with landscape gardener Ole Nørgård, is intended to provide an architecturally dominant feature to which the different groups of buildings can be subordinated even when extensions have taken place.
Two recent schemes show promising solutions of the problem of flexibility while at the same time maintaining the overall architectural character. These schemes are the county hospital at Herlev and the University at Odense. In the Herlev scheme (Figs. 18, 19), the patients are to be accommodated in a striking 25-storey tower where each storey contains one ward with 48 beds. The therapeutical department for out-patients as well as hospital patients is placed on a single-floor platform raised on columns above a car park. This platform has top lighting and is divided into a square system of treatment sections and installation galleries (Fig. 20).

unbehandelt belassen ist. Besonders beim Innenraum findet man eine äußerst sorgfältige Detaillierung und eine Verfeinerung der Materialbehandlung für das Inventar, mit dem das Publikum in Berührung kommt. Beim Laden der Kopenhagener Firma F. A. Thiele (Seite 176) haben Kaare Klint und, nach dessen Tod, Vilhelm Wohlert in der früher architektonisch eher vernachlässigten Sparte des Ladenbaus durch sorgfältige Ausarbeitung der Inneneinrichtung einen hohen Qualitätsstand erreicht. Ähnliche Fortschritte sind bei Schiffseinrichtungen zu verzeichnen, und mehrere dänische Architekten haben sich denn auch mit der Ausgestaltung von Schiffsinterieur beschäftigt. Unter anderem wirkte Kay Fisker an der Ausstattung der Schiffe auf der Bornholmer Linie mit, und in den letzten Jahren befaßte sich Kay Kørbing besonders mit diesem Gebiet. Die Einrichtung des Kopenhagen-Oslo-Schiffs »Prinsesse Margrethe« (Seite 200) ist eine seiner bekanntesten Arbeiten.
Im Rahmen der internationalen Architektur hat der Kirchenbau in den letzten Jahren zu einem außerordentlich phantasiereichen Expressionismus Anlaß gegeben, vielleicht weil viele Architekten in einem nüchternen Zeitalter, das von Konformität und Industrialisierung beherrscht wird, hier ein geeignetes Feld für das Ausspielen von Gefühlswerten zu finden glaubten, für die sich ihnen sonst keine Auslösungsmöglichkeit bot. Diese Tendenz zeigte sich auch in Dänemark, obwohl die symbolische Ausdrucksweise im großen und ganzen der dänischen Mentalität fernliegt und äußerliches Pathos für die dänische Kirchenbautradition kaum typisch ist. Das eindrucksvollste der in diesem Buch gezeigten Beispiele für den recht umfassenden dänischen Kirchenbau der letzten Jahre ist die von Vilhelm Wohlert und Rolf Graae in den Jahren 1963–64 errichtete Stengård-Kirche in Gladsaxe (Seite 209) mit ihrem markanten Äußeren, aus dem die Glockentürme organisch als Dominante einer plastischen Gesamtanlage aus eng aneinandergestellten Backsteinbauten emporragen. Der Innenraum wird von den Farb- und Materialreizen der roten Backsteinmauern beherrscht, und das gleiche Material ist auch für Kanzel und Altar verwendet, die in die Altarwand eingebaut sind. Johan von Spreckelsens Katholische Kirche von St. Nikolaj in Hvidovre (Seite 206) ist aus gelbem Backstein errichtet; aber der quadratische Kirchenraum wurde in völlig untraditioneller Weise diagonal orientiert und mit einer schrägen, hyperbolischen Dachkonstruktion abgedeckt. In der von Inger und Johannes Exner entworfenen Sankt-Clemens-Kirche in Randers (1963–64, Seite 213) wird der Ausblick über das Gudenå-Tal in wirkungsvoller Weise als Altarwand ausgenutzt. Im großen und ganzen scheint es, als ob sich die dänischen Architekten weniger befangen und auf jeden Fall sicherer fühlen, wenn sie mit Aufgaben zu tun haben, die auf Grund nüchterner und funktionsbestimmter Gesichtspunkte zu lösen sind. Dies trifft zum Beispiel auf das Krematorium in Glostrup (Seite 216) zu, das im Jahre 1960 von Brüel, Bornebusch, Selchau und Henning Larsen errichtet wurde. Dieses Gebäude zeichnet sich durch seine klare Grundrißdisposition und sein einfaches Äußeres aus. Höhepunkt ist der feierliche Innenraum der kubisch gestalteten Kapelle, der von einem Oberlicht über dem Katafalk beherrscht wird.

Bei vielen der in diesem Band gezeigten Gebäude spielen die traditionellen Baustoffe eine vorherrschende Rolle; aber auch vorgefertigte Bauelemente der verschiedensten Art kommen in großem Umfang zur Anwendung, meist in Kombination mit den »klassischen« Materialien. Hier handelt es sich nicht mehr um ein handwerkliches Bauen im herkömmlichen Sinn; doch konnten sich die dänischen Architekten bei ihrer Entwurfsarbeit immer auf eine hochwertige Ausführung verlassen, gleichgültig ob es sich nun um gute Maurerarbeit oder um die exakte Herstellung vorgefertigter Elemente handelt. Sie waren daher imstande, nach alter Baumeistertradition das individuell gestaltete Haus durch verfeinerte Detaillösungen und Materialwirkungen zu verbessern.
Angesichts der dynamischen technischen und wirtschaftlichen Entwicklung ist zu erwarten, daß das eigentliche Handwerk immer mehr hinter den weitervervollkommneten industriellen Baumethoden zurücktreten wird. Die Entwicklung weist auf diesem Gebiet bereits große Fortschritte auf, und Dänemark hat dank der Initiative seiner Ingenieure und Unternehmer eine technisch hochstehende, wenn auch architektonisch noch nicht durchgearbeitete Massenherstellung von Betonelementen in Gang gebracht, die im großen Umfang in andere Länder ausgeführt werden. Man könnte daher mit einiger Sorge den offensichtlichen Mangel an Interesse für die Wirklichkeit einer neuen Zeit beobachten und die fast weltfremde, fortdauernde Pflege der überlieferten handwerksbetonten Werte konstatieren, die viele der besten Leistungen der dänischen Nachkriegsarchitektur charakterisieren. Ja, man könnte sogar fürchten, daß das, was man heute unter dänischer Architektur versteht, zusammen mit dem Handwerk seinem Untergang entgegen gehe. Einige große ausgeführte Arbeiten und Projekte der letzten Jahre zeigen jedoch, daß führende dänische Architekten jetzt ernsthaft

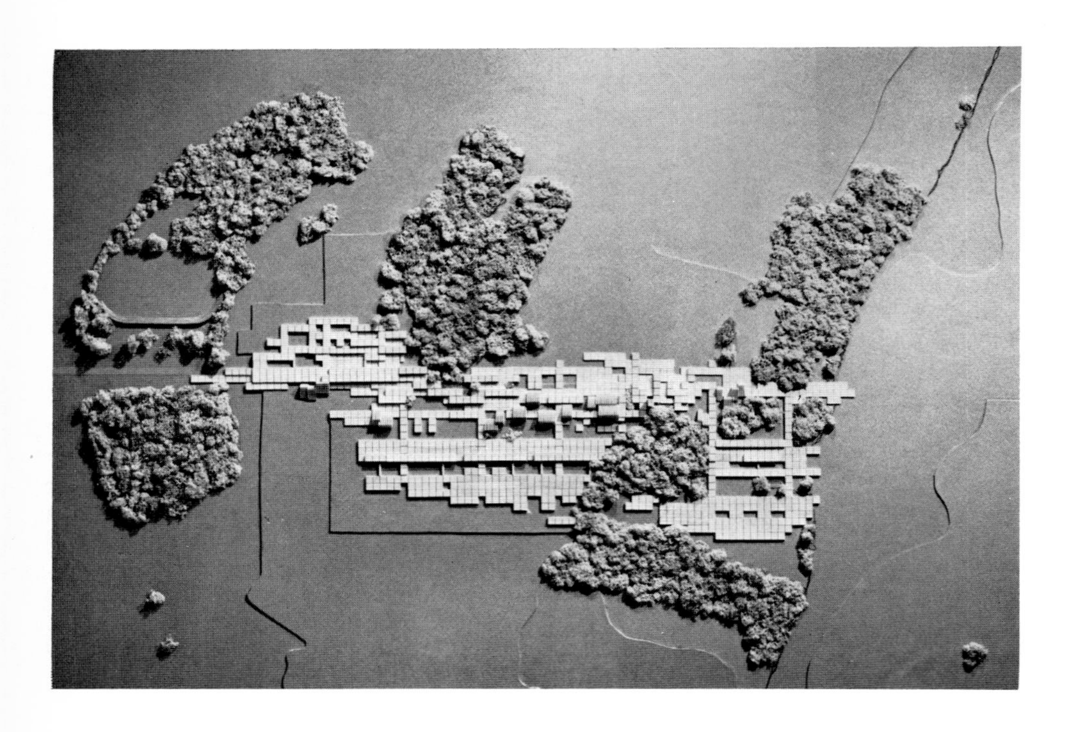

21. Odense University. Project, 1966. Site plan. Architects: Gunnar Krohn & Hartvig Rasmussen, responsible architect: Knud Holscher.

21. Universität in Odense. Projekt, 1966. Lageplan. Architekten: Gunnar Krohn & Hartvig Rasmussen, verantwortlicher Leiter Knud Holscher.

The intermediate module units of 15 × 15 metres may either accommodate a therapeutical ward unit or may be left open as a courtyard. Each unit can be subdivided by lightweight partitions so that the ward can easily be modified, or extended by yet another module unit. As part of their design work, the architects Groth-Hansen, Brüel, Bornebusch and Selchau have constructed a full-scale module unit with installations in order to check all the details which are to be repeated throughout the building.
Inspired by the felicitous result of the 1930 competition for the University at Århus, a new public competition was launched for the University at Odense in 1966 (Figs. 21–23). For, however attractive the principle of informally placing isolated buildings in a park has turned out to be at Århus, it will nowadays hardly be regarded as satisfactory for a University for approx. 6000 students, if the demand for flexible possibilities for future extensions is to be

22. Odense University. Model photograph Architects: Gunnar Krohn & Hartvig Rasmussen, responsible architect: Knud Holscher.

22. Universität in Odense. Modellphotographie. Architekten: Gunnar Krohn & Hartvig Rasmussen, verantwortlicher Leiter Knud Holscher.

23. Odense University. Schematic plan. Architects: Gunnar Krohn & Hartvig Rasmussen, responsible architect: Knud Holscher.

23. Universität in Odense. Schematischer Plan. Architekten: Gunnar Krohn & Hartvig Rasmussen, verantwortlicher Leiter Knud Holscher.

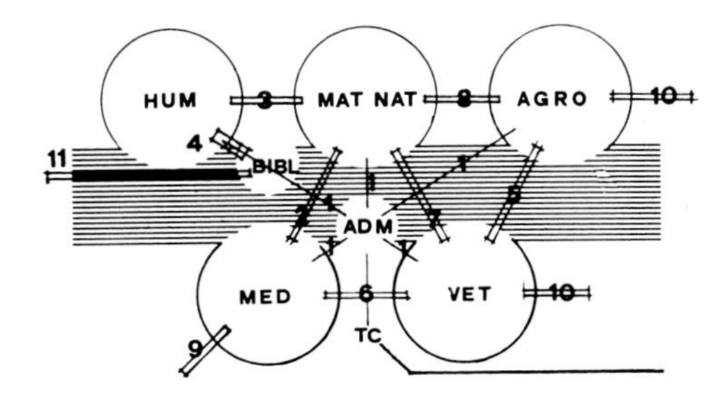

die Herausforderung angenommen haben, die hinter den neuen Herstellungsverfahren und der vollständigen Industrialisierung des Bauwesens steht. Was den Wohnungsbau anbelangt, so trifft das besonders auf zwei voneinander sehr verschiedene Wohnsiedlungen, Høje Gladsaxe und Albertslund, zu.

In Høje Gladsaxe haben die Architekturbüros Hoff & Windinge, Juul Møller & Agertoft sowie Alex Poulsen gemeinsam ein Projekt für ein völlig industrialisiertes Bauvorhaben mit 2000 Wohnungen (Seite 88) ausgearbeitet. Die Rücksichtnahme auf die Produktions- und Montageverfahren hatte einen wesentlichen Einfluß auf den Bebauungsplan und die Wohnungsgrundrisse. Die Wohnungen sind auf fünf 16geschossige Lamellenhäuser und 9- und 4-geschossige Wohnblocks verteilt, an die sich eine Schule, ein Einkaufszentrum und andere Gemeinschaftsanlagen anschließen. Man könnte die etwas starre Ausgestaltung der Wohnungen kritisieren und generell bezweifeln, ob sich ein Hochhaus als Wohnform für kinderreiche Familien eignet. Auch mag diesen Bauten die ausgefeilte architektonische Qualität fehlen, wie sie für die individuell entworfenen Bauten, die dieser Band zeigt, charakteristisch ist. Doch wurde das schöne Hanggelände, das freien Ausblick über einen Park und einen großen Teil von Kopenhagen bietet, sehr überlegt genutzt, und die Bebauung zeichnet sich durch ihren ausgeprägten, einheitlichen Charakter und ihre einfache Ausdrucksform aus. Die Bedeutung dieser Siedlung liegt vor allem in der gründlichen und zukunftsweisenden Architektenarbeit, die der Ausführung vorausging.

In Albertslund (Seite 72), wo es sich um die gleiche Anzahl von Wohnungen handelt, hat man sich noch stärker um ein angenehmes Wohnmilieu und einen menschlichen Maßstab bemüht. Hier sind die Familienwohnungen auf etwa 1000 eingeschossige Hofhäuser und mehr als 500 zweigeschossige Reihenhäuser verteilt, während etwa 625 kleinere Wohnungen in dreigeschossigen Wohnblöcken untergebracht sind. Die Bebauung hat einen verdichteten urbanen Charakter und ist innerhalb strenger wirtschaftlicher Grenzen in Montagebauweise mit vorgefertigten, wandhohen Elementen aus weißverputztem Stahlbeton und schwarzgeteertem Holz errichtet. Die etwas steif wirkende Reihung gleichartiger Häuser war durch die Kranbahnen des Montagebaus bedingt. Das Streben nach einer humanen Atmosphäre hat für die Architektengruppe, die aus Viggo Møller-Jensen, Tyge Arnfred, Mogens J. Pedersen, Jørn Ole Sørensen, Gartenarchitekt Ole Nørgård und Stadtplaner Knud Svensson besteht, eine entscheidende Rolle gespielt. Fahrverkehr und Fußgängerverkehr sind klar voneinander getrennt, und die Fußgängerflächen werden durch behagliche Hof- und Spielplätze ergänzt. Die einzelnen Wohnungen, die eine Wohnfläche von etwa 40 bis 130 m^2 bieten, sind weder besonders groß noch besonders luxuriös ausgestattet; sie zeichnen sich aber alle durch sorgfältige Planung und durch ihre unkomplizierte architektonische Qualität aus, die mit den Wertbegriffen nahe verwandt ist, wie sie früher für das Bauen in Dänemark typisch waren.

Die dynamische Entwicklung unserer Zeit bringt es auch mit sich, daß Bauwerke schnell veralten, jedenfalls noch bevor sie abgenutzt sind. Sie sollten deshalb so gebaut werden, daß Änderungen und Erweiterungen auf einfachste Weise vorgenommen werden können, sobald in der Zukunft Bedarf auftritt (von dem wir heute nicht viel mehr wissen, als daß er eines Tages entstehen wird). Bei der Errichtung der neuen Bauten für die Dänische Technische Hochschule (Seite 136) nördlich von Kopenhagen hat Nils Koppel versucht, das Problem mit frei stehenden dreigeschossigen Standardbauten zu lösen, die erweitert und mit einfachen Mitteln den verschiedensten Ansprüchen angepaßt werden können. Zusammen mit jenen Instituten und Einrichtungen, die individueller gestaltet werden müssen, sind die Standardtypen in einem rechtwinkligen Straßennetz zwanglos gruppiert, während eine durchgehende Allee, die zusammen mit dem Gartenarchitekten Ole Nørgård geschaffen wurde, die architektonische Dominante bilden soll, der sich die einzelnen Gebäudegruppen auch nach einer späteren Erweiterung zuordnen lassen.

Zwei Projekte aus den letzten Jahren zeigen vielversprechende Lösungen für flexible, erweiterungsfähige Baukomplexe, deren architektonischer Grundcharakter auch bei späteren Veränderungen gewahrt bliebe. Es handelt sich einmal um das Kreiskrankenhaus in Herlev und um die Universität in Odense. Bei dem Krankenhausprojekt (Abb. 18, 19) ist beabsichtigt, die Patienten in einem markanten 25stöckigen Hochhaus unterzubringen, in dem jedes Geschoß eine Abteilung mit 48 Betten bildet. Die Behandlungsabteilung einschließlich der Poliklinik befindet sich in einem auf Stützen über einen Parkplatz gestellten Geschoß. Diese Abteilung erhält Oberlicht und ist in ein quadratisches System von Behandlungsräumen und Korridoren mit technischen Installationen eingeteilt (Abb. 20). Die zwischen den Fluren liegenden Rasterfelder von 15 × 15 m können entweder eine Einheit der Behandlungsabteilung aufnehmen oder als Hoffläche freigelassen werden. Jede Einheit läßt sich

met. The result of the Odense competition was, in its own way, just as promising as at Århus. The First Prize was awarded to the architectural firm of Gunnar Krohn & Hartvig Rasmussen, with Knud Holscher acting as responsible architect in a team which comprised pedagogical as well as technical experts. The University buildings are placed on a sporadically wooded plain to the south of Odense, grouped around a half-a-mile long covered central avenue from which pedestrians reach all the different sections, vehicular traffic being relegated to a floor below. All along and on either side of this central axis are placed the administration building, lecture rooms, students' hostels and library. The buildings for the five Faculties of the University are so placed on either side of this axis that integration and collaboration between related Faculties is facilitated whilst the distance between the buildings is sufficient to allow for future extensions. The structural system, based on a module of 10 × 10 metres, can be varied in different ways by choosing between a side corridor and a central corridor arrangement, and between two, three and four storeys. The architectural design of the project may appear to be somewhat schematic; but it offers obvious possibilities for creating a lively and attractive University with fine correlations between teaching premises, open spaces, and the surrounding woods.

Despite their flexibility and provision for future extensions, both the Herlev scheme and the Odense scheme will be able to achieve architectural unity and a high quality of detailed design. It is by no means a law of nature that Danish architecture, when confronted with a new reality based on fully developed industrialised building methods and on demands to cater for unforeseeable future requirements, should not be able to preserve essential features of those qualities which are traditionally associated with the crafts: simple and clear expressions of the essence, function and construction of architectural work in high-quality workmanship and with due regard to the overall concept to which the architecture is required to conform. To a higher degree than ever, this is a question of careful planning in collaboration with highly qualified experts. The fact that, in future, all the components will have to be produced on an industrial scale in large numbers merely results in more exacting claims on the skill, talent and care of the architects. Jørn Utzon's work in Sydney (Fig. 24), so regrettably halted, with the prefabrication of reinforced concrete and plywood units, has shown that such work is also capable of creating new architectural expressions.

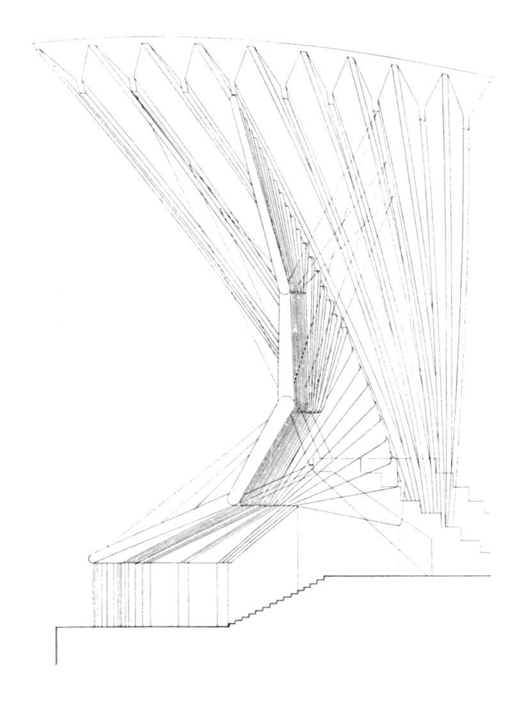

24. Opera House at Sydney, 1965. Cross-section of glass wall. Bars of prefabricated steel units. Architect: Jørn Utzon.

24. Opernhaus in Sydney, 1965. Schnitt durch die Glaswand. Sprossen aus vorgefertigten Stahlelementen. Architekt: Jørn Utzon.

durch leichte Trennwände unterteilen, so daß sie ohne großen Aufwand umgeändert oder um ein weiteres Modulfeld erweitert werden kann. Im Zuge ihrer Entwurfsarbeit ließen die Architekten Groth-Hansen, Brüel, Bornebusch und Selchau eine Moduleinheit mit allen Installationen in voller Größe bauen, um alle Einzelheiten nachprüfen zu können, die sich im ganzen Gebäude wiederholen sollen.
Angeregt durch den Erfolg, den 1930 der Wettbewerb für die Universität Århus gehabt hatte, wurde 1966 ein neuer offener Architektenwettbewerb für die Universität in Odense (Abb. 21 bis 23) ausgeschrieben. Denn so schön auch das Prinzip der zwanglos in einem Park gruppierten Bauten in Århus durchgeführt sein mag, so wenig kann dieses Schema heute zufriedenstellen, wenn man für eine Universität mit etwa 6000 Studenten flexible Erweiterungsmöglichkeiten einplanen will. Der Wettbewerb für Odense zeitigte auf seine Weise ein ebenso vielversprechendes Ergebnis wie seinerzeit Århus. Der erste Preis wurde dem Architekturbüro Gunnar Krohn & Hartwig Rasmussen zuerkannt, wobei Knud Holscher als verantwortlicher Architekt innerhalb einer Gruppe pädagogischer und technischer Sachverständiger tätig war. Die Universitätsgebäude werden auf einem ebenen, sporadisch bewaldeten Gelände südlich von Odense an einer etwa 1 km langen überdachten Achse aufgereiht, von der aus alle angeschlossenen Abteilungen auf kurzen Wegen zu Fuß zu erreichen sind, während der Fahrverkehr in ein Untergeschoß verwiesen ist. Entlang dieser Achse und auf ihre ganze Ausdehnung verteilt, werden die verschiedenen Gebäude für Verwaltung, Hörsäle, Studentenheime und Bibliothek angeordnet. Die Bauten für die fünf Fakultäten liegen zu beiden Seiten der Achse, und zwar so, daß die Verknüpfung und Zusammenarbeit der einander am engsten verwandten Studienzweige erleichtert wird, während andererseits der Abstand groß genug gehalten ist, um spätere Erweiterungen zu erlauben. Der Entwurf geht von einem Modul von 10 × 10 m aus, der in verschiedener Weise durch freie Wahl der Korridorlage (Seiten- oder Mittelkorridor) und der Bauhöhe (zwei, drei oder vier Geschosse) abgewandelt werden kann. Die architektonische Gestaltung des Projekts mag etwas schematisch anmuten; offensichtlich bietet es jedoch vielfältige Möglichkeiten, eine lebendige und schöne Universität mit ausgewogenen Beziehungen zwischen Hörsälen, Institutsräumen, Grünanlagen und umgebenden Waldungen zu schaffen.
Sowohl in Herlev als auch in Odense wird es möglich sein, trotz der erzielten Flexibilität und der Einplanung künftiger Erweiterungen einen geschlossenen architektonischen Eindruck und eine hohe Qualität des Details zu erreichen. Es ist also nicht zwangsläufig so, daß die dänische Architektur angesichts der neuen Wirklichkeit – einer Wirklichkeit, die charakterisiert ist durch voll entwickelte industrielle Baumethoden und durch die Forderung, für unvorhersehbare zukünftige Bedürfnisse heute schon Erweiterungsmöglichkeiten einzukalkulieren – wesentliche Qualitätsmerkmale preisgeben müßte, die eng mit ihrer handwerklichen Tradition verknüpft sind: der einfache und klare Ausdruck von Inhalt, Funktion und Konstruktion eines Bauwerks in einer qualitativ hochstehenden Ausführung und unter gebührender Beachtung der Gesamtsituation, der sich die Architektur einordnen soll. Mehr denn je geht es darum, in Zusammenarbeit mit hochqualifizierten Fachleuten, die vorbereitende Planung zu intensivieren. Die Tatsache, daß in Zukunft alle Elemente auf industrieller Grundlage in großer Stückzahl hergestellt werden müssen, kann die Ansprüche an die Begabung, Tüchtigkeit und Sorgfalt der Architekten nur noch erhöhen. Jørn Utzons bedauerlicherweise zum Stillstand gekommene Arbeit in Sydney (Abb. 24) hat im Hinblick auf die Vorfertigung von Stahlbeton- und Furnierholzelementen gezeigt, wie aus solchen Versuchen neue architektonische Ausdrucksmöglichkeiten entstehen können.

Jørn Utzon

Architect's own house at Hellebæk, North Zealand, 1952

With his own house at Hellebæk, Jørn Utzon introduced the open plan into Danish architecture. The house consists of a single large room which is divided by light partitions into different functional sections and is, on the north side, completely closed by a windowless wall of yellow brick. On the south side, the large windows and doors face broad terraces which are, at several levels, supported by low retaining walls against the sloping ground. The house is here shown in its original shape. In 1957, an annex with kitchen, dining room, bedroom and bathroom was added on the north-east side. To-day, the original house is mainly used for living room purposes only.

Haus des Architekten in Hellebæk im Norden der Insel Seeland, 1952

Mit seinem eigenen Haus in Hellebæk führte Jørn Utzon den offenen Grundriß im dänischen Wohnungsbau ein. Das Haus besteht aus einem einzigen großen Raum, der durch leichte Trennwände in verschiedene Funktionsabschnitte aufgeteilt und nach Norden zu durch eine fensterlose, gelbe Backsteinwand abgeschlossen ist. Auf der Südseite geht das Haus mit großen Glasfenstern und -türen in breite Terrassen über, die – in verschiedenen Höhenlagen von niedrigen Mauern abgestützt – dem fallenden Gelände folgen. Das Haus ist hier in seiner ursprünglichen Form gezeigt. Im Jahre 1957 wurde im Nordosten ein Winkelbau mit Küche, Eßzimmer, Schlafzimmer und Bad angefügt. Das ursprüngliche Haus enthält heute im wesentlichen nur Wohnräume.

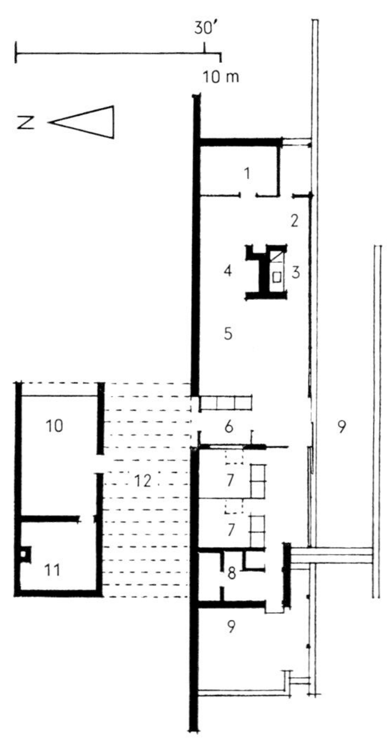

1. The house, seen from the drive. The entrance door is hidden in the otherwise closed north wall below a pergola which connects the house with the garage.
2. Plan. Key: 1 study, 2 dining area, 3 kitchen zone, 4 fireplace, 5 living area, 6 entrance, 7 bedroom, 8 bathroom, 9 terrace, 10 garage, 11 heating plant, 12 pergola.
3. The brick core in the centre of the living room contains an open fireplace facing the sitting room zone and, on the sunny south side, the kitchen installations facing the kitchen and dining zones.
4. Living room. The projecting partitions as well as the doors consist of Oregon Pine boards screwed to frames so that walls and doors have an identical appearance. North wall and ceiling have a similar cladding. The walls are separated from ceiling and floor by wooden battens, painted black.
5. South side with the large windows and doors facing the terraces. Posts and rafters are treated with black aniline dye. The bargeboard is of aluminium.

1. Ansicht von der Zufahrt her. Die Eingangstür ist in der sonst völlig geschlossenen Nordwand unter einer Pergola versteckt, die das Haus mit der Garage verbindet.
2. Grundriß. Legende: 1 Arbeitszimmer, 2 Eßplatz, 3 Küche, 4 Kaminzone, 5 Wohnbereich, 6 Eingang, 7 Schlafzimmer, 8 Badezimmer, 9 Terrasse, 10 Garage, 11 Heizung, 12 Pergola.
3. Der frei stehende Backsteinblock im Wohnraum enthält auf der Nordseite einen offenen Kamin und auf der Südseite die Einbauten der Küchenzone.
4. Wohnbereich. Die frei stehenden Wände und die Türen bestehen aus auf Rahmen aufgeschraubten Brettern aus Oregon Pine, so daß Wände und Türen gleich aussehen. Nordwand und Decke haben eine ähnliche Verkleidung. Von Decke und Fußboden sind die Wände durch schwarz gestrichene Holzleisten abgesetzt.
5. Die Südseite mit den großen Fenstern und Schiebetüren, die sich auf die Terrassen öffnen. Stützen und Sparren sind mit schwarzer Anilinfarbe behandelt. Die Traufkante besteht aus Aluminium.

Jørn Utzon

1. West side of the house with the large windows facing the lake.

1. Westseite des Hauses mit den großen Fensterflächen zum See hin.

House Middelboe at Holte near Copenhagen, 1953
The house is situated on marshy ground by the shore of a lake (Furesø) at the mouth of a canal which, during the summer, carries a heavy traffic of small pleasure craft. In order to protect the living room against the ground mist at nightfall and against view from passers-by, and in order to offer the residents a view across the lake, the house is raised one storey above ground. The ground floor merely contains hall, cloakroom and boiler room whilst the remainder of the covered space is used as car port and bicycle shed and for outdoor pastimes. Reinforced concrete posts and beams are painted black, the floor boards red, whilst both the external and internal boarding are left in natural wood colour.

Haus Middelboe in Holte bei Kopenhagen, 1953
Das Haus steht am Furesø in sumpfigem Gelände am Auslauf eines Kanals, der im Sommer sehr viel mit kleinen Booten befahren wird. Um den eigentlichen Wohnbereich dem niedrigen Abendnebel und dem Einblick von Passanten zu entziehen und gleichzeitig den Bewohnern eine Aussicht über den See zu bieten, sind die Wohnräume um Geschoßhöhe über das Gelände angehoben. Nur Diele, Garderobe und Heizung liegen zu ebener Erde, wobei jedoch der übrige Raum unter dem Haus als gedeckter Abstellplatz für Kraftwagen und Fahrräder sowie als Spielfläche ausgenutzt ist. Die Stahlbetonstützen und -balken sind schwarz gestrichen, die Deckenbretter rot, die äußere und innere Holzverkleidung ist in Naturfarbe belassen.

2. The walls on the east side are covered with boarding in which the bedroom windows form slits from floor to ceiling.
3. Plans of first floor and ground floor. Key: 1 car port, 2 boat house, 3 living room zone with veranda, 4 dining area, 5 bedrooms.
4. View from the living room zone towards the island kitchen table and the built-in installation core with open fireplace. Internal walls and ceilings have been given the same treatment and colour scheme as the outer walls.

2. Die Wände auf der Ostseite sind mit Brettern verkleidet, in denen die Schlafzimmerfenster vom Fußboden bis zur Decke durchgehende Schlitze bilden.
3. Grundrisse des Obergeschosses und Erdgeschosses. Legende: 1 Wageneinstellplatz, 2 Bootsabstellplatz, 3 Wohnbereich mit Veranda, 4 Eßplatz, 5 Schlafzimmer.
4. Innenansicht vom Wohnbereich her auf den frei stehenden Küchenblock und den eingebauten Installationskern mit offenem Kamin. Innenwände und Decken haben die gleiche Behandlung und Farbe wie die Außenwände.

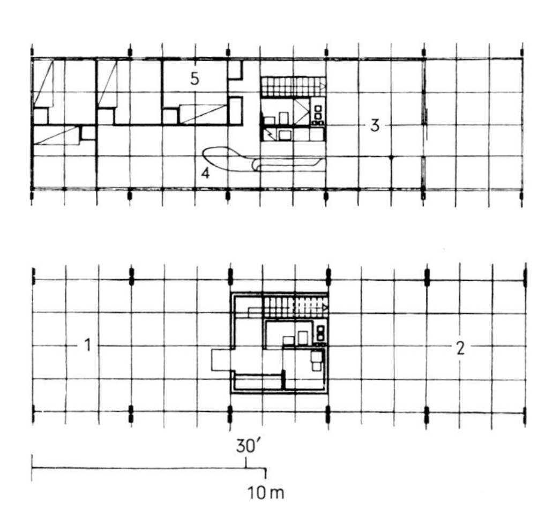

5. For this house, a simple building method with prefabricated posts and beams of reinforced concrete has been used; but the same method could also, with advantage, have been adopted for the erection of a greater number of houses. The posts are driven into the ground whilst the beams are supported and held together merely by their own weight.

5. Bei diesem Haus wurde ein einfaches Bauverfahren mit vorgefertigten Stahlbetonstützen und -trägern angewandt, das auch bei einer größeren Anzahl von Einfamilienhäusern wirtschaftlich eingesetzt werden könnte. Die Stützen sind in den Baugrund eingerammt, während die Balken ausschließlich durch ihr Eigengewicht getragen und zusammengehalten werden.

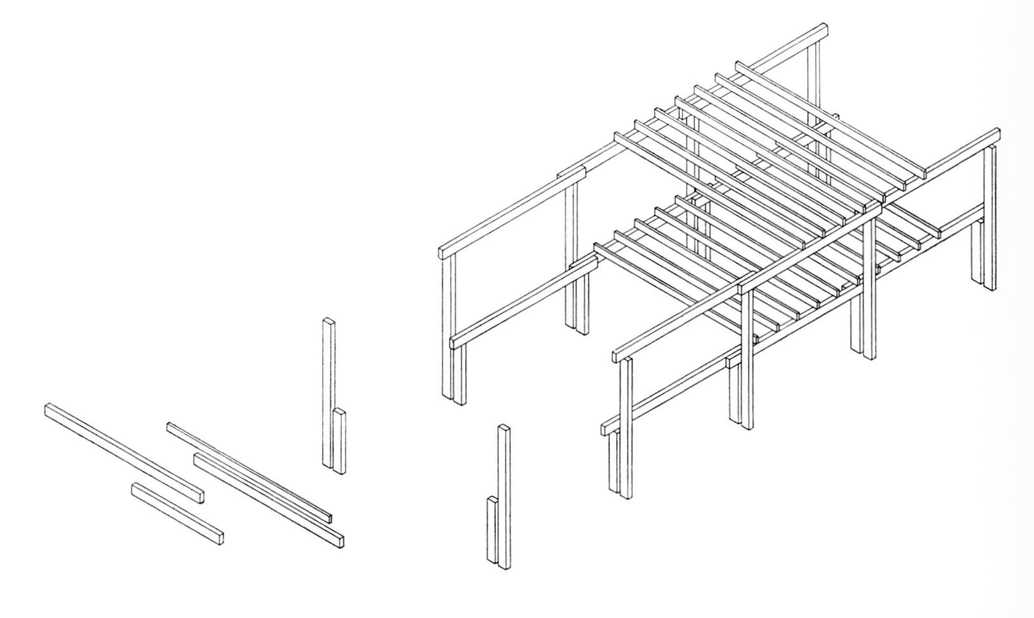

Harald Plum + Mogens Lassen

House at Soløsevej, Jægersborg near Copenhagen, 1954

The house stands on a southern slope with a view across a moor which has been converted into a public park. By staggering the levels in accordance with the slope, all the three main zones of the house can enjoy sun and view. On the top level, closest to the drive, is the dwelling proper, where kitchen, dining area and sitting area are in open connection with each other and with a special scullery. The two lower levels are taken up by a study and a large weaving shop, respectively. The house is erected in light-weight concrete and has a tiled roof.

Haus am Soløsevej in Jægersborg bei Kopenhagen, 1954

Das Haus steht auf einem Südhang mit Aussicht über eine Moorlandschaft, die in eine öffentliche Grünanlage umgestaltet ist. Das Gebäude ist dem Gelände treppenartig angepaßt, so daß alle drei Hauptzonen des Hauses Sonne und Aussicht haben. Die eigentliche Wohnung liegt auf der obersten Ebene in der Nähe der Zufahrt. Küche, Eßplatz und Wohnbereich stehen in offener Verbindung miteinander und mit einem besonderen Hauswirtschaftsraum. Auf den beiden unteren Ebenen befinden sich ein Arbeitszimmer beziehungsweise eine große Webstube. Das Haus ist aus Leichtbetonblöcken errichtet und hat ein Ziegeldach.

1. South side of the house with the screen wall protecting the large terrace in front of the living room.

1. Südansicht des Hauses mit der Schirmmauer vor der großen Terrasse des Wohnbereichs.

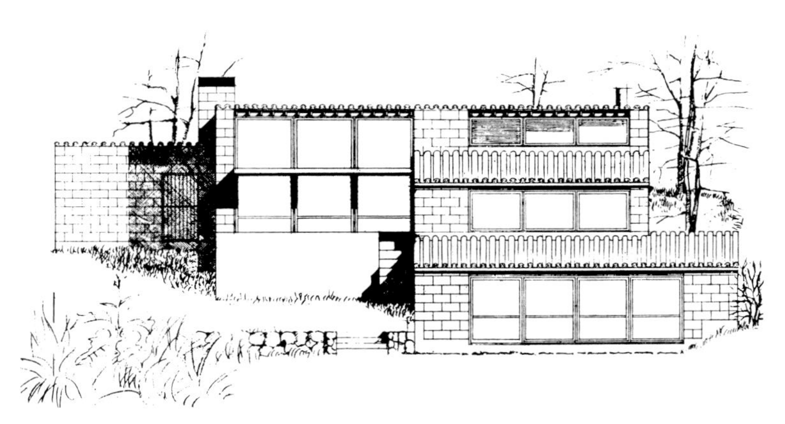

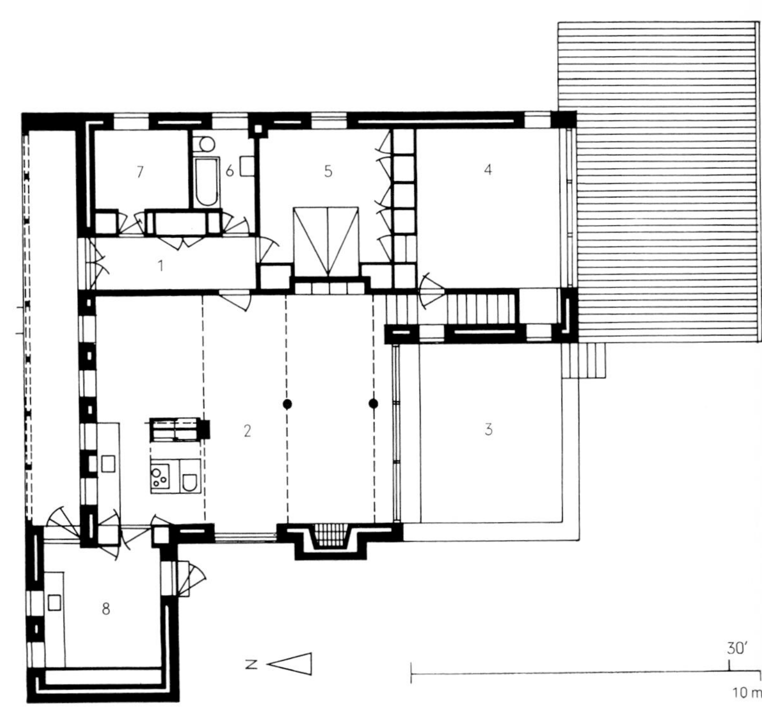

2. South terrace in front of the living room. The bedroom receives daylight through narrow windows above the roof of the study; the latter, in its turn, enjoys sunlight and view through windows above the roof of the weaving shop.
3. Living room zone with the open connection between sitting zone, dining area and kitchen. Meals are prepared on the tiled island-type cooker. The bearing timber structure as well as the ceiling boards are left untreated.
4. South elevation.
5. West elevation.
6. Ground floor plan. Key: 1 hall, 2 living room with kitchen zone, 3 terrace, 4 study, 5 bedroom, 6 bathroom and W.C., 7 guest room, 8 scullery.

2. Die Südterrasse vor dem Wohnbereich. Der Schlafraum hat ein schmales Fensterband über dem Dach des Arbeitszimmers, das seinerseits Sonne und Aussicht durch die Fenster über dem Dach der Webstube erhält.
3. Der Wohnbereich mit offener Verbindung zwischen Sitzzone, Eßplatz und Küche. Das Essen wird auf dem frei stehenden, gekachelten Herd vorbereitet. Die tragende Holzkonstruktion und die Holzverschalung der Decken sind unbehandelt belassen.
4. Ansicht der Südseite.
5. Ansicht der Westseite.
6. Grundriß des Erdgeschosses. Legende: 1 Diele, 2 Wohn- und Küchenbereich, 3 Terrasse, 4 Arbeitszimmer, 5 Schlafraum, 6 Bad und WC, 7 Gastzimmer, 8 Hauswirtschaftsraum.

1. The drawing office, added in 1962, seen from South-West.
2. Plan. Key: 1 entrance, 2 dining area, 3 living zone, 4 kitchen, 5 boiler room, 6 study, 7 bedroom, 8 bedroom, 9 drawing office.
3. On the west and south side, the windows and doors of both living and dining area open up towards covered terraces. The sculpture in the foreground is the work of the sculptor Tycho Clemmensen.
4. Living area with large windows facing the wall-screened west terrace.
5. Sitting and dining areas are in open connection with each other. The sitting room is dominated by the large fireplace. Apart from brick and timber, the indoor materials include coconut matting for the floor and bright oxhide as a covering for chairs and sofas.

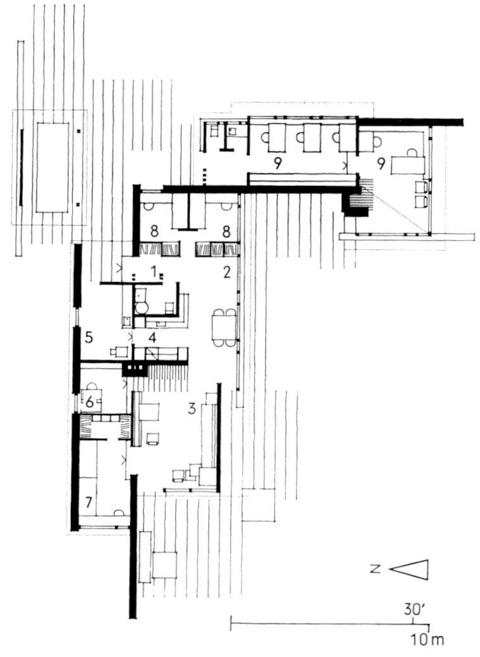

Bertel Udsen

Architect's own house at Hjortekjær near Copenhagen, 1956, Extension 1962
A combined home and workplace where the construction and external shape of the house have been decisively governed by the arrangement and mutual connection of the different zones. Special attention has been paid to the integration of interiors and exteriors. High quality has been achieved through the unorthodox use of conventional materials: yellow brick and brown-stained timber.

Haus des Architekten in Hjortekjær bei Kopenhagen, 1956, Anbau 1962
Bei dieser Kombination von Wohnhaus und Arbeitsstätte sind Konstruktion und äußere Gestaltung des Gebäudes entscheidend durch die Anordnung und gegenseitige Verbindung der verschiedenen Zonen bestimmt. Mit besonderer Sorgfalt wurde die Verzahnung von Innen- und Außenräumen behandelt. Durch die unorthodoxe Verwendung herkömmlicher Baustoffe (gelber Backstein und braun imprägniertes Holz) ergab sich eine sehr qualitätvolle Materialbehandlung.

1. Das im Jahre 1962 angebaute Architektenbüro, von Südwesten gesehen.
2. Grundriß. Legende: 1 Eingang, 2 Eßplatz, 3 Wohnbereich, 4 Küche, 5 Heizung, 6 Arbeitszimmer, 7 Schlafzimmer, 8 Schlafzimmer, 9 Architektenbüro.
3. Nach Westen und Süden öffnen sich die Fenster und Türen des Wohnbereiches und des Eßplatzes auf große teils überdeckte Freisitzplätze. Die Holzskulptur im Vordergrund wurde von dem Bildhauer Tycho Clemmensen geschaffen.
4. Der Wohnbereich mit seinem großen Westfenster, das sich auf den von Mauern beschützten Freisitzplatz öffnet.
5. Wohnbereich und Eßplatz stehen miteinander in offener Verbindung. Der Wohnbereich wird von dem großen Kamin beherrscht. Außer Ziegeln und Holz sind im Innern des Hauses Kokosmatten für die Fußböden und helle Rindlederbezüge für Stühle und Sofas verwendet.

Erik Chr. Sørensen

Villa Østerstrand at Vedbæk near Copenhagen, 1953
The T-shaped plan is governed by the narrow east-to-west orientated site. The house is projected onto the edge of a coastal escarpment so that both dining area and sitting room can enjoy the view across the east terrace on the Sound whilst the sitting room can also enjoy the afternoon sun from a large garden terrace. The upper floor contains all the bedrooms and is designed like a wooden box which rests on a reinforced concrete slab supported by steel columns. The ground floor walls are thus non-bearing and can be given a maximum of glass frontage.

Villa Østerstrand in Vedbæk bei Kopenhagen, 1953
Der T-förmige Grundriß ist durch die geringe Breite des sich von Osten nach Westen erstreckenden Grundstücks bedingt. Das Haus ist an den Rand eines Abhanges vorgeschoben, so daß Eßplatz und Wohnbereich über die Ostterrasse Aussicht über den Sund bieten, während der Wohnbereich gleichzeitig Nachmittagssonne über eine große Gartenterrasse erhält. Das Obergeschoß enthält alle Schlafzimmer und ist wie eine Holzkiste gestaltet, die auf einer von Stahlstützen getragenen Stahlbetonplatte ruht. Die Außenwände des Erdgeschosses haben daher keine tragende Funktion, so daß ein Höchstmaß von Fensterfläche möglich ist.

1. The house seen from the seaside slope, with the east terrace on the left and the special annex with the ancillary rooms on the right, which, together with the main building and a connection passage, surrounds a forecourt.
2. West side of the house, with the forecourt on the left and the sitting room terrace on the right. Above the sitting room is a sun terrace, connected to the bedrooms. The upper floor has a cladding of brown-stained deal boards.

1. Die dem Øresund zugekehrte Hangseite, mit der Ostterrasse (links) und dem Anbau mit den Nebenräumen (rechts), der mit dem Hauptbau und einem Verbindungsgang zusammen einen Vorhof umschließt.
2. Westseite des Hauses mit dem Vorhof (links) und der Wohnterrasse (rechts). Über dem Wohnbereich befindet sich eine Sonnenterrasse, die mit zwei Schlafzimmern in Verbindung steht. Das Obergeschoß hat eine Verschalung aus braun imprägniertem Kiefernholz.

3. Forecourt and hall. The continuous bar above the entrance door determines the top levels of all doors, cupboards and ground floor curtains.
4. Plans of second floor and ground floor. Key: 1 forecourt, 2 hall, 3 kitchen, 4 dining area, 5 living room, 6 study, 7 west terrace, 8 east terrace, 9 garage, 10 laundry, 11 wine cellar, 12 maid's room, 13 bedroom, 14 guest room, 15 linen room, 16 dressing room, 17 sun terrace.
5. Hall, with stairs leading to the upper floor. The close relationship between interiors and exteriors is emphasised by the use of identical stone paving.

3. Der Vorhof mit Einblick in die Diele. Die horizontal über der Eingangstür verlaufende Fenstersprosse legt die Höhe aller Türen und Schränke sowie aller Vorhänge im Erdgeschoß fest.
4. Grundrisse des Obergeschosses und Erdgeschosses. Legende: 1 Vorhof, 2 Diele, 3 Küche, 4 Eßplatz, 5 Wohnbereich, 6 Arbeitszimmer, 7 Gartenterrasse, 8 Ostterrasse, 9 Garage, 10 Waschraum, 11 Weinkeller, 12 Mädchenzimmer, 13 Schlafzimmer, 14 Gastzimmer, 15 Wäschekammer, 16 Ankleidezimmer, 17 Sonnenterrasse.
5. Die Diele mit der Treppe zum Obergeschoß. Die Zusammengehörigkeit von Innen- und Außenräumen ist durch die Wahl eines durchgehenden Fußbodenbelages aus Natursteinen hervorgehoben.

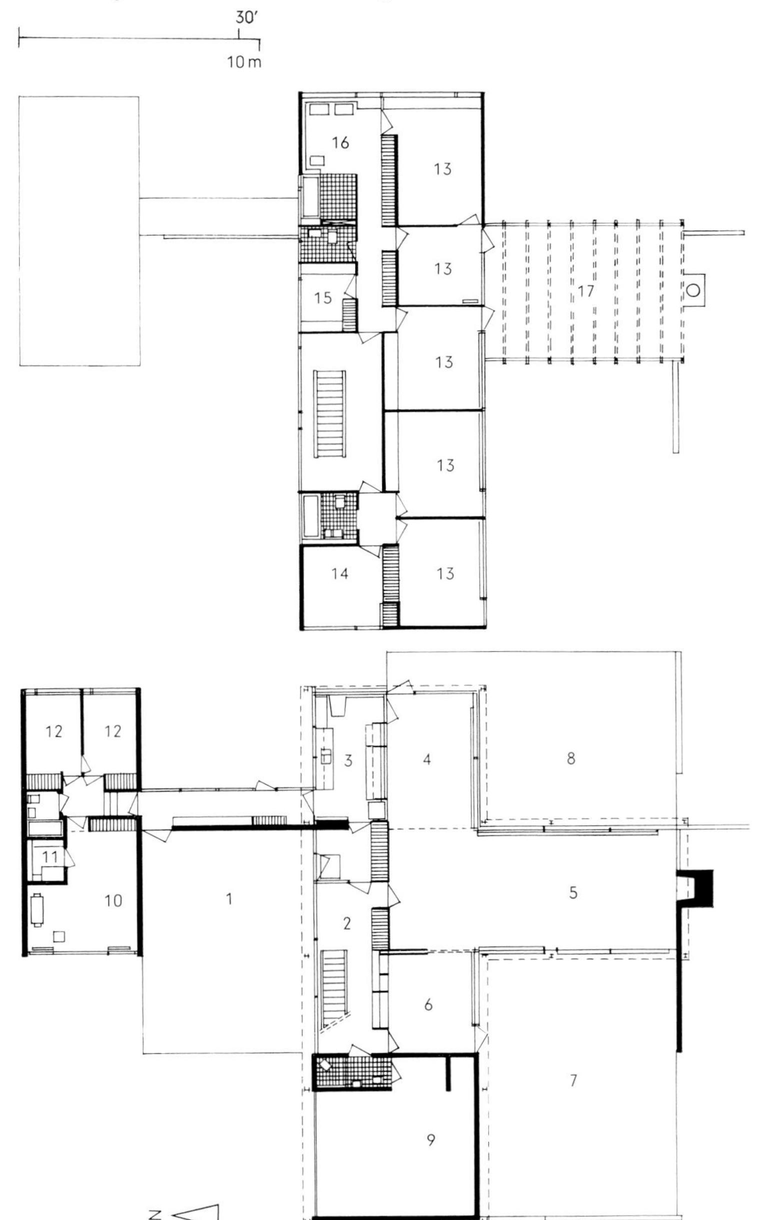

Erik Chr. Sørensen

Architect's own house at Smutvej, Jægersborg near Copenhagen, 1955

A simple structural principle of timber columns and beams dominates the architectural expression of this house which, with its skilfully differentiated plan, is designed with a sure touch for proper proportions between the different sections and for their precise integration with the associated outdoor spaces. The drawing office is accessible from the forecourt whilst the architect's own office has its own private terrace on the west side. The sitting room is attractively linked with the garden space on the south side, and both parents and children have suitable outdoor spaces in direct connection with their bedrooms and playing rooms, respectively. Outside the kitchen is a special outdoor dining area. Columns, beams and external boarding are treated with dark-brown Solignum.

Haus des Architekten am Smutvej in Jægersborg bei Kopenhagen, 1955

Ein einfaches Konstruktionsprinzip von Holzstützen und -trägern beherrscht den architektonischen Eindruck dieses Hauses, dessen geschickt unterteilter Grundriß mit sicherem Gefühl für die Proportionierung der einzelnen Zonen und ihres Zusammenhanges mit den anschließenden Freiräumen entworfen ist. Das Zeichenbüro steht mit dem Vorhof in Verbindung; das Arbeitszimmer des Architekten hat zusätzlich eine eigene private Terrasse auf der Westseite. Der Wohnraum geht nach Süden unmittelbar in den Garten über, und den Eltern- und Kinderschlafzimmern sind ebenfalls direkt erreichbare Freiflächen zugeordnet. Vor der Küche befindet sich ein besonderer Eßplatz im Freien. Stützen, Träger und Außenverschalung sind mit dunkelbraunem Solignum behandelt.

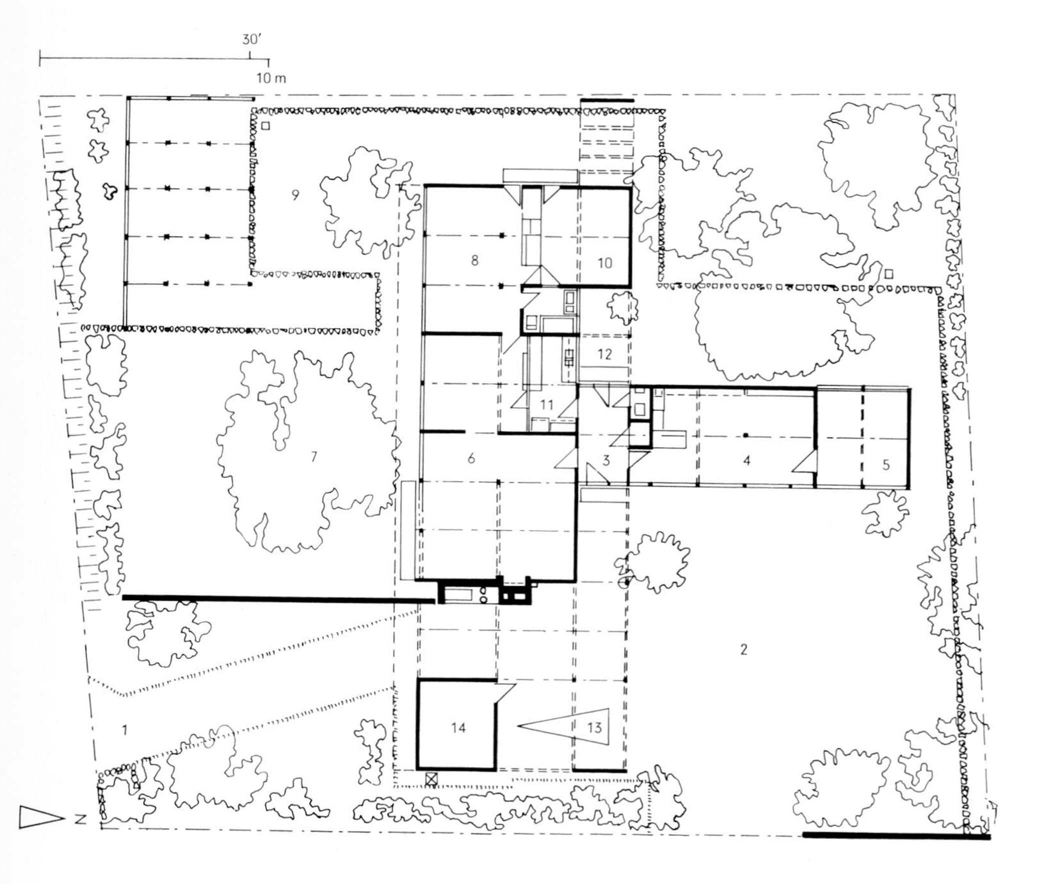

1. Plan. Key: 1 access from the road, 2 forecourt, 3 entrance, 4 drawing office, 5 architect's study, 6 living room, 7 outdoor living area, 8 children's bedroom, 9 children's playground, 10 master bedroom, 11 kitchen, 12 outdoor dining area, 13 car port, 14 bicycles, etc.

1. Grundriß. Legende: 1 Zugang von der Straße, 2 Vorhof, 3 Eingang, 4 Zeichenbüro, 5 Arbeitszimmer des Architekten, 6 Wohnraum, 7 Wohngarten, 8 Kinderschlafzimmer, 9 Kinderspielplatz, 10 Elternschlafzimmer, 11 Küche, 12 Eßplatz im Freien, 13 Wageneinstellplatz, 14 Abstellraum für Fahrräder usw.

2. Access from the south with a glimpse of the forecourt-cum-car-park. The yellow brick wall protects the privacy of the sitting room garden.
3. Sitting room with its associated garden area. The large windows are protected by eaves of 1 metre width.
4. The sitting room walls are covered with untreated deal boards, the ceiling with plasterboard, and the floor with Opdal stone flags.

2. Zufahrt von Süden mit Durchblick in den Vorhof (Parkplatz). Die gelbe Backsteinmauer schützt den Wohngarten gegen Einblick von außen.
3. Der Wohnbereich des Hauses mit dem dazugehörigen Garten. Die großen Fenster sind durch das 1 m weit auskragende Dach geschützt.
4. Die Wohnraumwände sind mit unbehandelten Kiefernholzbrettern verschalt, während die Decke mit Gipsplatten verkleidet und der Fußboden mit Opdal-Fliesen belegt ist.

Halldor Gunnløgsson

Architect's own house at Rungsted Strandvej near Copenhagen, 1958

The house straddles a narrow east-west orientated site on the shore of the Sound. The large windows on the east side of the rectangular building face the Sound, whilst the west side windows face a terraced garden. Between the windowless walls along the short sides, the structure consisting of wooden posts and beams is raised logically and consistently on a 2 × 2 metres module. The house is occupied by a couple whose children no longer live at home, and consists of two rooms with kitchen and bathroom. Despite the formal strictness of the structure, the different functions of the dwelling are attractively differentiated in well-proportioned zones within the open plan. Refined effects obtained from the materials, in conjunction with Poul Kjærholm's furniture, contribute to the high standard of interior design. The woodwork is dark-stained, inner walls as well as doors and windows are black-varnished and silk-polished, the flooring is of bright-grey Swedish marble.

1. The narrow terrace on the east side of the house, with a view across the Sound. The terrace is built up from salt-impregnated boards; all the other woodwork is dark-stained.

1. Die schmale Terrasse auf der Ostseite des Hauses bietet eine weite Aussicht über den Øresund. Die Terrasse besteht aus salzimprägnierten Brettern, die übrige Holzkonstruktion ist dunkel imprägniert.

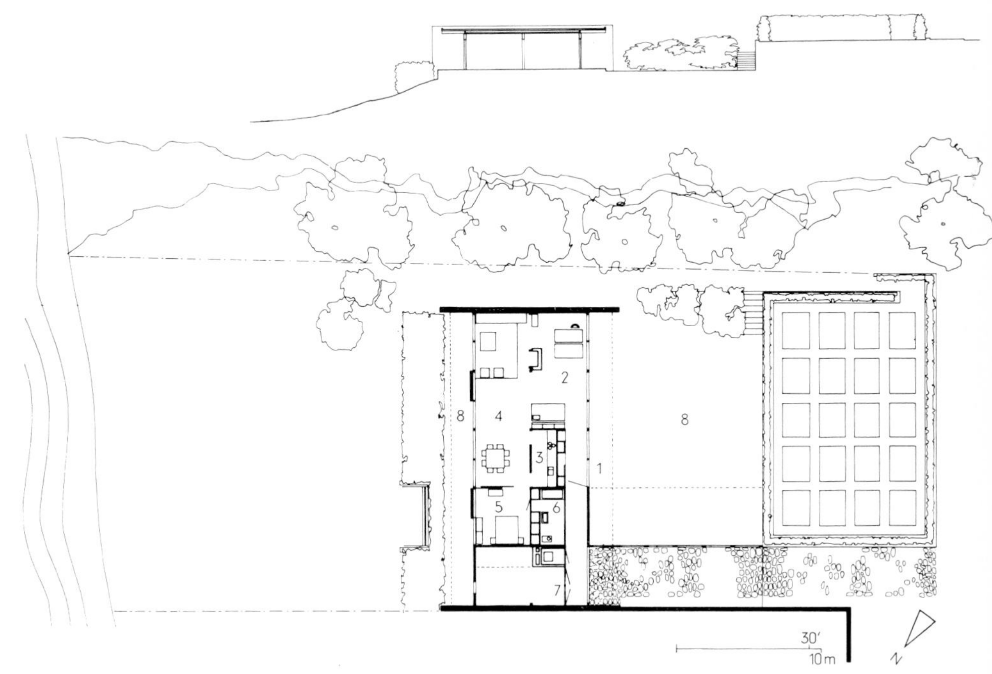

Halldor Gunnløgsson

Haus des Architekten am Strandvej in Rungsted bei Kopenhagen, 1958

Dieses Haus mit seinem einfachen, rechteckigen Grundriß steht quer auf einem schmalen, sich vom Westen nach Osten zum Øresund erstreckenden Grundstück. Die großen Fensterflächen auf der Ostseite eröffnen die Aussicht über den Sund, während sich die Westfenster dem terrassenförmigen abgetreppten Garten zuwenden. Zwischen den fenster- und türenlosen Seitenwänden ist die Konstruktion in logischer und konsequenter Weise auf einem Raster von 2 × 2 m aus Holzstützen und -trägern errichtet. Das Haus wird von einem Ehepaar bewohnt, dessen Kinder nicht mehr zu Hause leben; deshalb genügen zwei Räume mit Küche und Bad. Trotz der formellen Strenge der Konstruktion sind die verschiedenen Wohnfunktionen in wohlproportionierten Bereichen innerhalb des offenen Grundrisses differenziert. Sorgfältig abgestufte Materialwirkungen tragen zusammen mit Poul Kjærholms Möbeln zu der hohen architektonischen Qualität des Interieurs bei. Die Holzkonstruktion ist dunkel gebeizt, die Innenwände sowie Türen und Fensterrahmen sind schwarz lackiert und seidenmatt behandelt, der Fußboden besteht aus hellgrauem schwedischen Marmor.

2. West side with access road and entrance behind the braided fence on the left. Behind the windows on the right is the study.
3. Section and site plan. Key: 1 entrance, 2 living room, 3 kitchen, 4 dining area, 5 bedroom, 6 bathroom, 7 garage, 8 terrace.

2. Die Westseite mit der Zufahrt zur Garage hinter dem Flechtwerkzaun links. Hinter den Fenstern rechts vom Kamin befindet sich der Arbeitsplatz.
3. Schnitt und Lageplan. Legende: 1 Eingang, 2 Wohnraum, 3 Küche, 4 Eßplatz, 5 Schlafzimmer, 6 Badezimmer, 7 Garage, 8 Terrasse.

4. East side, seen from the beach at night.
5. Due to the large sliding doors, the living room can be brought into open connection with the east terrace facing the Sound (shown here) as well as with the garden on the other side.
6. Living room, seen towards the dining area, with a glimpse of the bedroom. The kitchen has top lighting and is placed behind the bright-grey sliding doors to the left of the dining area. Chairs designed by Arne Jacobsen.
7. Lounge area of the living room with Poul Kjærholm's furniture. The walls consist of black-varnished, silk-polished boards. The large windows can be covered by roller blinds.

4. Nachtansicht der Ostseite vom Strand her.
5. Durch große Schiebetüren läßt sich der Wohnbereich auf der einen Seite zu der hier gezeigten Ostterrasse und auf der anderen Seite zum Garten hin öffnen.
6. Innenansicht des Wohnraums zum Eßplatz hin mit Durchblick in das Schlafzimmer. Die Küche hat Oberlicht und liegt hinter den hellgrau gestrichenen Schiebetüren links vom Eßplatz. Die Stühle am Eßtisch sind von Arne Jacobsen entworfen.
7. Sitzgruppe im Wohnraum mit den von Poul Kjærholm entworfenen Möbeln. Die Wände bestehen aus schwarzlackierten, seidenmatt behandelten Brettern. An den großen Glasscheiben Rollvorhänge aus Jalousiestoffen.

1. South side of the house.
2. Plans of upper and ground floor. Key: 1 entrance, 2 hall with stairs, 3 bathroom and W.C., 4 boiler room, 5 kitchen with dining area, 6 children's room, 7 study, 8 kitchen elevator, 9 master bedroom, 10 living room, 11 garage, 12 workshop.

1. Ansicht des Hauses von Süden.
2. Grundrisse des Ober- und Erdgeschosses. Legende: 1 Eingang, 2 Treppenhalle, 3 Bad, WC, 4 Heizraum, 5 Küche mit Eßplatz, 6 Kinderzimmer, 7 Studio, 8 Speisenaufzug, 9 Elternschlafraum, 10 Wohnraum, 11 Garage, 12 Werkstatt.

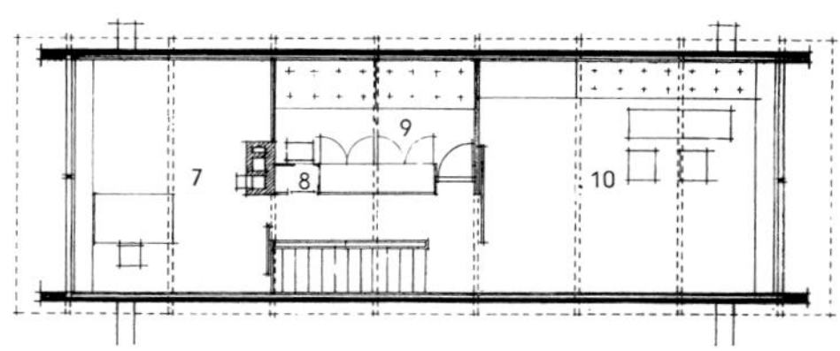

Knud Friis + Elmar Moltke Nielsen

Knud Friis' own house at Brabrand near Århus, Jutland, 1958

The design of this house has been governed by the desire to obtain a view from the high-lying ground across the Lake of Brabrand and, at the same time, an intimate contact with the garden and the edge of the woods on the eastern boundary. The ground floor contains an open-plan lounge with kitchen and dining area as well as the children's rooms in close association with the near-by woods and the enclosed garden court. On the upper floor are the master bedroom and another lounge with a view across the lake on the south side. The white-washed bearing walls of the lower floor are of brick whilst the continuous long sides of the upper floor are of concrete cast in situ, giving the appearance of beams resting on the brick walls below.

Haus Knud Friis in Brabrand bei Århus in Jütland, 1958

Der Entwurf dieses Hauses wurde durch den Wunsch bestimmt, von dem hochgelegenen Gelände aus über den benachbarten See von Brabrand sehen zu können und zugleich einen intimen Kontakt mit dem Garten und mit dem Wäldchen am Ostrand des Grundstückes zu schaffen. Im Erdgeschoß befinden sich der Gemeinschaftsraum mit Küche und Eßplatz sowie die Kinderzimmer, die mit dem Wäldchen und dem geschlossenen Gartenhof in enger Verbindung stehen. Im Obergeschoß sind 'das Elternschlafzimmer, das Studio und der Wohnraum mit Aussicht auf den See im Süden untergebracht. Die weißgekalkten tragenden Wände des Erdgeschosses bestehen aus Backstein, während die massiven Längswände des Obergeschosses aus Beton gegossen sind und konstruktiv wie Balken wirken, die auf den darunterliegenden Backsteinwänden ruhen.

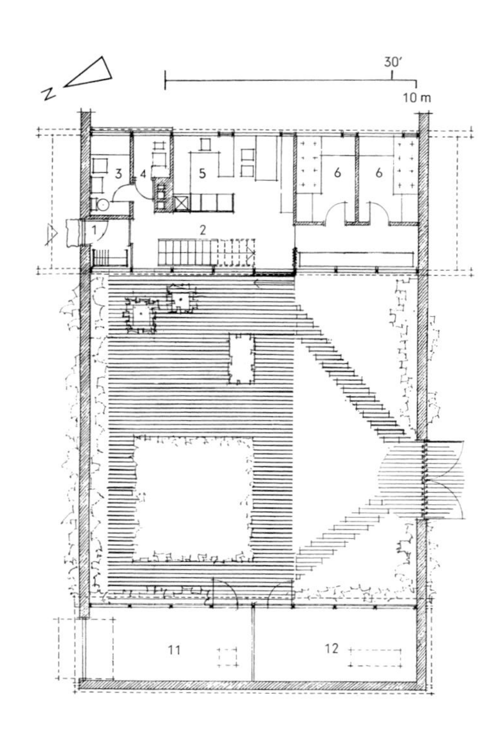

3. The courtyard is surrounded by the window front of the open-plan room in the ground floor, by the white-washed walls, and by a low annex containing garage and workshop. In the background the Lake of Brabrand.
4. The main block seen from the West, with the ground floor windows of the open-plan room and the corridor in front of the children's rooms. The top floor rooms receive additional daylight through the narrow high-level windows on the long side.
5. Top floor lounge. Wall covering of spruce boards, ceiling beams of untreated concrete, flooring of linoleum.

3. Die Umgrenzung des Gartenhofes besteht aus der Fensterfront des Gemeinschaftsraums im Erdgeschoß, aus den weißgekalkten Mauern und aus einem niedrigen Gebäude, das die Garage und eine Werkstatt enthält. Im Hintergrund der See von Brabrand.
4. Das Hauptgebäude von Westen mit den großen Fenstern des Gemeinschaftsraums und des Gangs vor den Kinderzimmern im Erdgeschoß. Die Räume im Obergeschoß erhalten zusätzliches Tageslicht durch die schmalen, hochliegenden Fensterbänder auf der Längsseite.
5. Der Wohnraum im Obergeschoß. Die Wandverschalung besteht aus Fichtenholz, die Deckenbalken aus schalungsrauhem Beton, der Fußbodenbelag aus Linoleum.

Knud Peter Harboe

Architect's own house at Skovvangen, Charlottenlund near Copenhagen, 1959
On a site by a residential road, surrounded by older houses, Harboe has built two almost identical houses, one of which is used for his own dwelling and drawing office. The transverse wing with lounge and dining area divides the site into an entrance yard with access to drawing office and car port and a private garden which, on the north side, is bordered by a narrow annex with the bedrooms. On the west side, the garden adjoins a small wood with beautiful tall trees. The house is erected in brick, scrubbed down with water and white-washed both outside and inside. The weather-exposed timber columns and beams are, like the window frames, dark-stained whilst the internal cladding is of untreated deal.

Haus des Architekten am Skovvangen in Charlottenlund bei Kopenhagen, 1959
Auf einem von älteren Wohnbauten umgebenen Grundstück an einer Villenstraße hat Harboe gleichzeitig zwei einander sehr ähnliche Häuser errichtet, von denen er eines selbst bewohnt. Auch sein Büro ist darin untergebracht. Durch den querliegenden Flügel, der den Wohnraum und Eßplatz enthält, wird das Grundstück einerseits in einen Vorhof mit dem Zugang zum Zeichenbüro und andererseits in einen abgeschirmten Wohngarten aufgeteilt, den auf der Nordseite ein schmaler Flügel mit den Schlafzimmern begrenzt. Nach Westen geht der Garten in ein kleines Gehölz mit schönen, großen Bäumen über. Die Wände sind aus Backsteinen gemauert und sowohl innen als auch außen weiß geschlämmt. Die der Witterung ausgesetzten Stützen und Träger der Holzkonstruktion sowie die Fensterrahmen erhielten eine dunkle Imprägnierung, während die Innenverschalung aus Kiefernholz unbehandelt blieb.

1. View from the west into the courtyard which is enclosed on three sides. The gentle slope of the ground is intercepted by rubble walls. Above the bedroom and living rooms, the roof is overhung, thus creating covered outdoor sitting areas. As the rooms face the courtyard, the latter becomes an additional outdoor lounge.
2. Access from the road is through an entrance yard which is enclosed by the drawing office annex and white-washed brick walls.
3. The island-type fireplace separates the dining area from the sitting room proper.
4. Plan. Key: 1 entrance, 2 living room, 3 dining area, 4 kitchen, 5 utility room, 6 maid's room, 7 W.C., 8 office, 9 master bedroom, 10 bathroom and W.C., 11 children's room, 12 guest room, 13 cupboard room, 14 boiler.
5. View from the sitting room towards west, facing the private garden. The south windows of the bedroom annex also enjoy a view onto the garden.

1. Blick von Westen in den dreiseitig umschlossenen Innenhof. Das leichte Gefälle des Grundstückes wird durch Feldsteinmauern aufgefangen. Über den Schlaf- und Wohnräumen kragt das Dach aus und bildet überdeckte Freisitzplätze. Durch die Orientierung der Räume zum Innenhof wird dieser zu einem zusätzlichen Wohnraum im Freien.
2. Von der Straße her ist das Haus durch einen Vorhof zugänglich, der von dem Zeichenbüro und den weißgekalkten Mauern umschlossen ist.
3. Der frei stehende Kamin grenzt die Sitzgruppe im Wohnbereich gegen den Eßplatz ab.
4. Grundriß. Legende: 1 Eingang, 2 Wohnraum, 3 Eßplatz, 4 Küche, 5 Hauswirtschaftsraum, 6 Mädchenzimmer, 7 WC, 8 Büro, 9 Elternschlafraum, 10 Bad und WC, 11 Kinderzimmer, 12 Gastzimmer, 13 Abstellraum, 14 Heizung.
5. Blick aus dem Wohnraum in den Gartenhof. Die nach Süden gehenden Fenster des Schlafraumflügels bieten ebenfalls Aussicht auf den Garten.

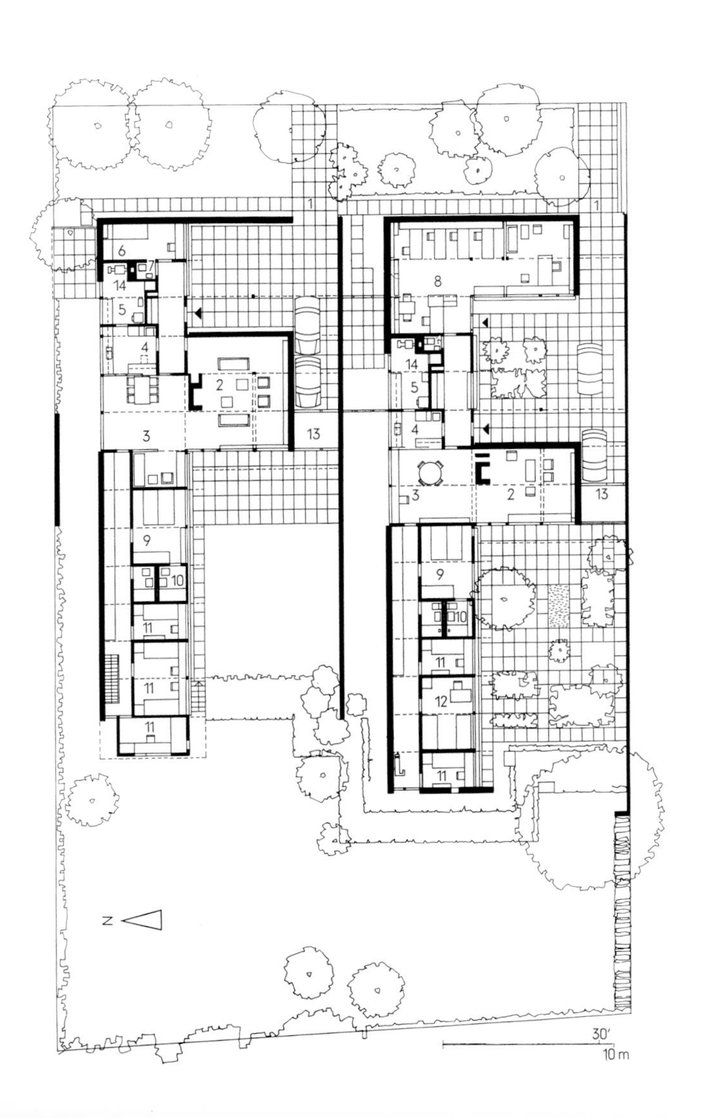
1
1
6
7
14
5
4
8
14
5
4
2
3
13
3
2
13
9
10
9
10
11
11
11
11
12
11
N
30'
10 m

Co-operating architects / Beratende Architekten: Erling Zeuthen Nielsen + Arne Karlsen

Børge Mogensen's house at Soløsevej, Gentofte, Copenhagen, 1960–64
In 1960, the furniture designer Børge Mogensen asked the architect Erling Zeuthen Nielsen to assist him with the planning of his own house which was, in 1964, extended by an open balcony on the north side and by a garden room on the south side. For this extension, Mogensen enlisted the help of architect Arne Karlsen and the landscape gardener Morten Klint. The house is situated on a northern slope so that the basement reaches full storey height on the north side where it contains a drawing office and workshop. The dwelling itself is on a single level with two large living rooms at the ends. The lounge at the north side is a quiet sitting room, whilst the dining area on the south side has an open plan so that it can also be used for all kinds of domestic activities, games and dancing. In the centre of the house are the bedrooms, designed as small cabins. Despite the modest size of the house, the many functional needs of a family home are met in an exceptionally attractive manner. The informal character of the house is emphasised by Mogensen's own furniture. The house is erected in brick. The basement walls are black-tarred, the top floor walls painted white.

Haus Børge Mogensen am Soløsevej in Gentofte bei Kopenhagen, 1960–64
Im Jahre 1960 ließ sich der Möbelarchitekt Børge Mogensen von dem Architekten Erling Zeuthen Nielsen beim Entwurf seines eigenen Hauses helfen, das er 1964 durch den Anbau eines offenen Balkons auf der Nordseite und eines Gartenzimmers auf der Südseite erweitern ließ, wobei ihn der Architekt Arne Karlsen und der Gartenarchitekt Morten Klint berieten. Das Haus steht auf einem nach Norden abfallenden Abhang, so daß im Kellergeschoß, das auf der Nordseite volle Stockwerkshöhe erreicht, ein Zeichenatelier und eine Werkstatt eingebaut werden konnten. Die eigentliche Wohnung liegt auf einer durchgehenden Ebene, mit zwei großen Wohnbereichen an den Enden. Nach Norden geht ein ruhiges Wohnzimmer, während der nach Süden gelegene Eßbereich als Gemeinschaftsraum ausgestaltet ist, der auch für Hausarbeiten, Spiel und Tanz benutzt werden kann. Die in der Mitte des Hauses zusammengefaßten Schlafräume sind nur kleine Kabinen. Trotz seiner bescheidenen Größe wird das Haus den zahlreichen Funktionen eines Familienheims in besonders gelungener Weise gerecht. Der unprätentiöse Charakter wird durch Mogensens eigene Möbel und Einbaueinheiten noch verstärkt. Das Haus ist aus Backstein errichtet. Die Kellerwände sind schwarz geteert, die Wände des Hauptgeschosses weiß gestrichen.

1. North side of the house with the covered balcony in front of the top floor lounge, added in 1964.
2. The garden court on the south side, connected with the garden room which was also added in 1964.

1. Ansicht des Hauses von Norden mit dem 1964 angebauten überdeckten Balkon vor dem Wohnraum des Hauptgeschosses.
2. Der südliche Gartenhof, der mit dem später angebauten Gartenzimmer in Verbindung steht.

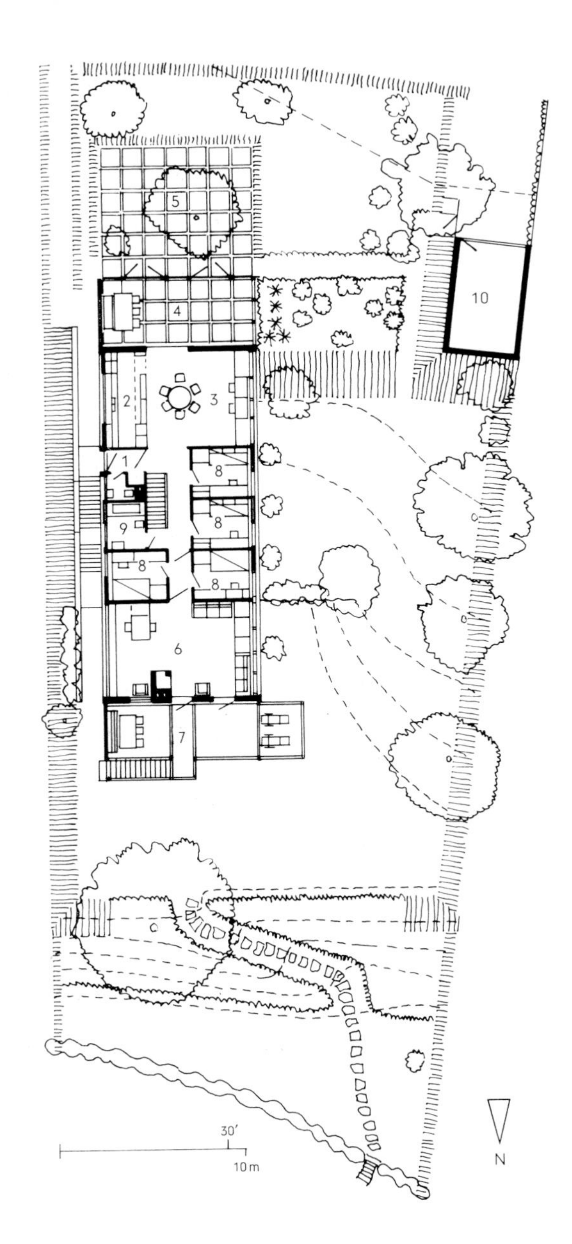

3. Plan. Key: 1 entrance, 2 kitchen, 3 dining room and childrens lounge, 4 garden room, 5 terrace, 6 living room, 7 balcony, 8 bedroom, 9 bathroom, 10 garage.
4. North side lounge with exit to the balcony. Walls and fireplace of water-scrubbed brick, ceiling of untreated spruce.
5. Sitting room with Børge Mogensen's own furniture.
6. Open-plan room with dining area, built-in furniture and light-weight partitions screening the kitchen. On the right, the garden room facing south.

3. Grundriß. Legende: 1 Eingang, 2 Küche, 3 Eßplatz und Spielzimmer, 4 Gartenzimmer, 5 Terrasse, 6 Wohnraum, 7 Balkon, 8 Schlafzimmer, 9 Badezimmer, 10 Garage.
4. Wohnraum am Nordende mit Ausgang zum Balkon. Wände und Kamin bestehen aus Naturziegeln, die Decke aus unbehandeltem Fichtenholz.
5. Wohnraum mit Børge Mogensens eigenen Sitzmöbeln.
6. Gemeinschaftsraum mit Eßplatz, eingebauten Möbeln und den Trennwänden des Küchenbereiches. Rechts das nach Süden liegende Gartenzimmer.

1. West side of the annex, with the window shutters fixed in the horizontal position and the door shutters turned outwards.
2. Cross-section and plan. Key: 1 terrace, 2 bedroom with two beds, 3 bedroom with one bed, 4 built-in cupboard and washbasin, 5 nurse's room, 6 shower bath, 7 W.C.
3. During the spring and autumn, the house can be used for shorter periods by merely opening the side-hung glass door shutters.
4. The annex during the summer, with all shutters and windows completely open.
5. The annex during the winter, with all the shutters closed.

1. Westansicht des Gästehauses mit den waagerecht ausgeklappten Fensterläden und den als seitlichem Sichtschutz geöffneten Türläden.
2. Querschnitt und Grundriß. Legende: 1 Terrasse, 2 Zweibettzimmer, 3 Einbettzimmer, 4 Einbauschrank und Waschbecken, 5 Mädchenzimmer, 6 Dusche, 7 WC.
3. Im Frühjahr und Herbst kann das Haus bei kürzerem Aufenthalt dadurch benutzt werden, daß man nur die seitlich eingehängten Läden der Glastüren öffnet.
4. Das Haus im Hochsommer, wenn alle Läden und Fenster ausgeklappt sind.
5. Das Haus im Winter, mit völlig geschlossenen Läden.

Vilhelm Wohlert

Annex to the summer residence of Niels Bohr, Tisvilde, North Zealand, 1957

The small summer house annex, containing five guest rooms, stands at the edge of Tisvilde Woods and is built as a timber house with external cladding of dark-stained boards. During the winter, the house is completely closed and shuttered; during the summer, it opens up like a fine piece of furniture. When the side-hung shutters of the glass doors are opened, they form partitions between the parts of the terrace belonging to the different guest rooms. The large top-hung window shutters are, during the summer, fixed in the horizontal position so as to form a continuous sun roof. Similarly, the windows and doors proper can be turned inwards against the party walls so that the connection between bedrooms and sun terrace is completely open. Like all joinery, the insides of the shutters are painted with white oil paint.

Gästehaus des Sommersitzes von Niels Bohr in Tisvilde im Norden der Insel Seeland, 1957

Das kleine Gästehaus mit fünf Zimmern, das etwas entfernt vom Hauptgebäude in einem dichten Gehölz errichtet wurde, besteht aus einer Holzkonstruktion, die außen mit dunkel gebeizten Brettern verschalt ist. Im Winter bleibt das Haus unbenutzt und wird mit Fensterläden verschlossen, während es sich im Sommer wie ein schönes Möbelstück öffnet. Die seitlich eingehängten Läden der Glastüren bilden in offener Stellung Trennwände zwischen den Freisitzplätzen vor den einzelnen Gastzimmern. Die großen, in Oberscharnieren beweglichen Klappläden werden im Sommer waagerecht ausgeschwenkt, so daß sie ein durchgehendes Vordach bilden und als Sonnenschutz dienen. Ebenso können die eigentlichen Fenster und Türen seitwärts so weit zurückgeklappt werden, daß sich die Schlafräume in voller Breite auf die Sonnenterrasse öffnen. Die Innenseiten der Läden sind wie alle übrigen Tischlerarbeiten mit weißer Farbe gestrichen.

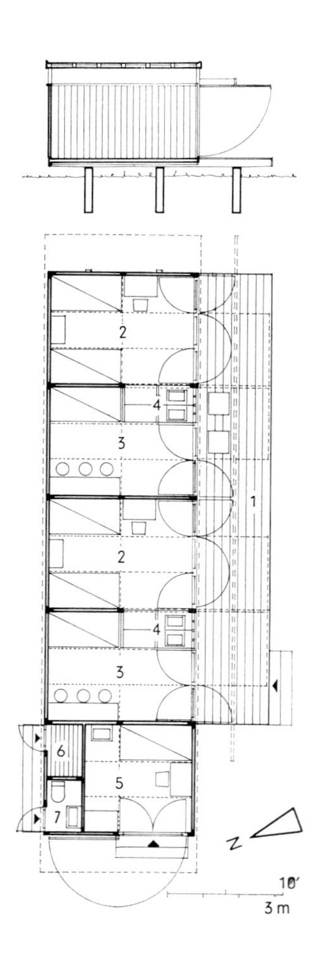

1. View of the house from the eastern slope.
2. Cross-section.

1. Ansicht des Hauses vom Ostabhang her.
2. Schnitt.

Erik Korshagen

Architect's own summer house at Rørvig, North-West Zealand, 1961
The summer house is situated close to the sea on an almost overgrown slope of a heath studded with pine and birch trees. The large thatched roof is supported by a strong timber structure and its large eaves protect the open gallery which surrounds the dwelling proper. This gallery serves as access to the different rooms of the house. For the time being, the large attic is not used. All the woodwork consists of dark-stained deal. Further down the slope is a car port protected by a large thatched roof of its own.

Sommerhaus des Architekten in Rørvig im Nordwesten der Insel Seeland, 1961
Das Sommerhaus steht in der Nähe des Meeres auf einem fast völlig überwachsenen Abhang in einer Heidelandschaft mit lockerem Kiefern- und Birkenbestand. Das große Strohdach wird von einer kräftigen Holzkonstruktion getragen und beschützt mit seinem großen Überhang den offenen Umgang, der den Hauskern auf allen vier Seiten umgibt und die einzelnen Räume des Hauses verbindet. Der große Dachboden wird zur Zeit noch nicht ausgenutzt. Die Holzkonstruktion besteht aus dunkelgebeiztem Kiefernholz. Weiter unten auf dem Grundstück ist ein Wageneinstellplatz eingerichtet, der ebenfalls von einem großen Strohdach beschützt wird.

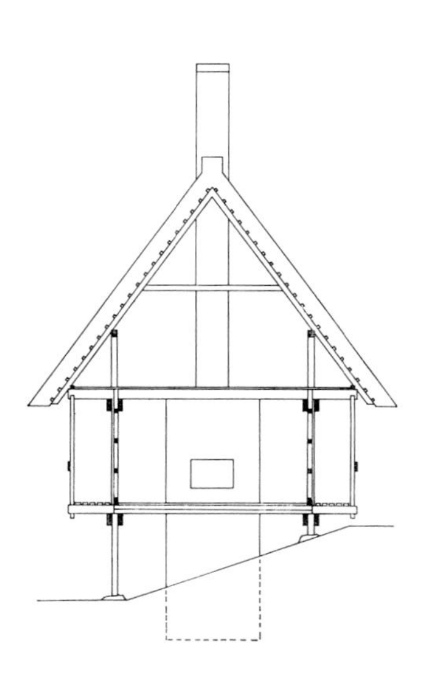

3. The area protected by the large thatched roof of the car port is also used for hobby activities, fuel stores, etc.
4. Close-up of the west side. Each column has its own stone foundation.
5. Plan. Key: 1 sitting room, 2 dining area and kitchen, 3 small bedroom, 4 bathroom and W.C., 5 cloakroom, 6 bedroom.
6. The sitting room is placed at the south corner. The gallery is reached from the outside via the large stepping stone on the west side of the house.
7. The sitting room offers a view through the branches of the pine trees onto a meadow which forms part of a permanent open space.

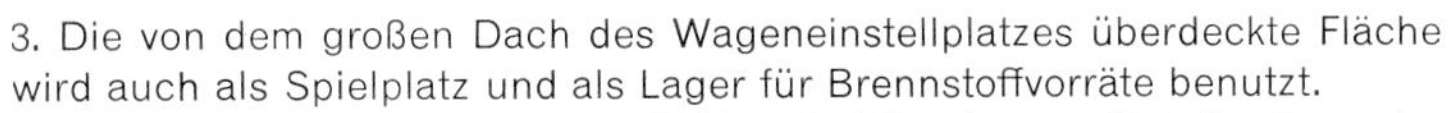

3. Die von dem großen Dach des Wageneinstellplatzes überdeckte Fläche wird auch als Spielplatz und als Lager für Brennstoffvorräte benutzt.
4. Detail der Westseite. Jede der Stützen hat ihr eigenes Steinfundament.
5. Grundriß. Legende: 1 Wohnraum, 2 Eßplatz und Küche, 3 Schlafraum, 4 Bad und WC, 5 Begehbarer Schrankraum, 6 Schlafzimmer.
6. Die Südecke des Hauses mit dem Wohnraum. Der Umgang ist von außen her über den großen Schrittstein an der Westseite zugänglich.
7. Vom Wohnraum aus sieht man durch die Zweige der Kiefern auf eine Wiese, die zu einem Naturschutzgebiet gehört.

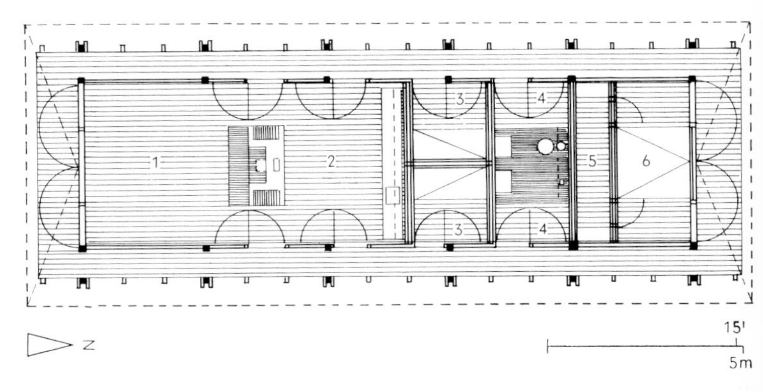

Nils Fagerholt

Summer house at Blåmunkene, North Zealand, 1960
This very simply designed, small summer house is situated on a slope which offers a westward view on a low meadow forming part of a permanent open space but the house also opens up towards east where the site itself is studded with pines. On the west side, the large living room windows are fitted with special shutters which serve partly as sun protection and partly for ventilation purposes. The furniture designed by Poul Kjærholm contributes to the high quality of the house.

Sommerhaus in Blåmunkene im Norden der Insel Seeland, 1960
Dieses sehr einfach gehaltene, kleine Sommerhaus steht auf einem Abhang, der nach Westen einen Ausblick über ein niedriger gelegenes Naturschutzgebiet bietet; doch öffnet sich das Haus auch nach Osten, wo das Grundstück von Kiefern bewachsen ist. Auf der Westseite sind die großen Fenster des Wohnbereiches mit besonderen Läden versehen, die teils zum Sonnenschutz, teils zur Belüftung dienen. Die von Poul Kjærholm entworfenen Serienmöbel tragen zu der hohen Qualität des Hauses bei.

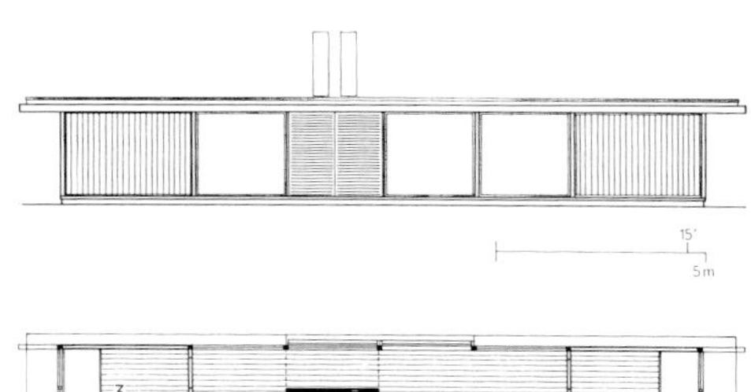

1. West side, with the large sliding windows and shutters.
2. Section and plan. Key: 1 dining kitchen, 2 living room, 3 bedroom, 4 bathroom.

1. Die Westseite mit den großen Schiebefenstern und Fensterläden.
2. Schnitt und Grundriß. Legende: 1 Eßplatz und Küche, 2 Wohnraum, 3 Schlafzimmer, 4 Badezimmer.

3. View from the sitting room, with furniture designed by Poul Kjærholm.
4. Attached to the brick core with kitchen, bath and W.C. is a sheet iron fireplace which was originally designed for this house but was later serially produced.
5. Dining area, with view towards West.

3. Blick aus dem Wohnraum mit den von Poul Kjærholm entworfenen Möbeln.
4. In den aufgemauerten Kern mit Küche, Badezimmer und WC ist ein aus Eisenblech verfertigter Kamin eingebaut, der, ursprünglich für dieses Haus entworfen, später auch serienmäßig hergestellt wurde.
5. Der Eßplatz mit der Aussicht nach Westen.

Søholm housing estate, Klampenborg near Copenhagen, 1950–55
The estate lies at the coastal road close to the Sound on a site studded with beautiful old trees, the remnants of the park of a villa now demolished. The layout plan with three different types of chain and terrace houses is governed by the desire to give all the dwelling units a view eastwards across the Sound and, as far as possible, access to the afternoon sun. Due to a number of restrictive regulations, in force at the time of erection, the first terrace houses on the south side have a floor area of approx. 1180 sq. ft. only whilst the later types have an area of about 1400 sq. ft. Even so, the architect succeeded in creating finely differentiated dwellings, which are particularly attractive in the case of the southern houses where the first floor lounge has a view across the Sound and where the rooms in the lower floor have intimate contact with the well-protected outdoor areas of the private garden. A noteworthy feature, too, is the open connection between lounge and dining area in the lower floor. All the houses are erected in yellow brick. Roofing of asbestos cement.

Siedlung Søholm in Klampenborg bei Kopenhagen, 1950–55
Die Siedlung Søholm liegt an der Küstenstraße (Strandvej) des Øresunds auf einem mit schönen, alten Bäumen bestandenen Gelände, das ursprünglich den Park einer inzwischen abgerissenen Patriziervilla bildete. Der Bebauungsplan mit seinen drei verschiedenen Arten von Ketten- und Reihenhäusern wurde durch den Wunsch bedingt, allen Wohnungen sowohl Aussicht nach Osten auf den Øresund als auch möglichst viel Nachmittagssonne zu geben. Aus Gründen, die mit verschiedenen Beschränkungen zur Zeit der Bauausführung zusammenhängen, haben die zuerst erstellten Reihenhäuser am Südrand eine Wohnfläche von nur 110 m², während die Wohnfläche der übrigen Typen 130 m² beträgt. Dennoch ist es geglückt, reich differenzierte Wohnungen zu schaffen. Besonders gelungen sind die am Südrand des Baugebiets errichteten Haustypen, deren Wohnraum im Obergeschoß Aussicht über den Øresund bietet, während im Erdgeschoß zwischen den Wohnräumen und den geschützten Freisitzplätzen der Privatgärten eine gute Verbindung besteht. Bemerkenswert ist auch der fließende Übergang zwischen Wohnraum und Eßplatz im Erdgeschoß. Alle Häuser wurden aus gelben Backsteinen errichtet. Die Dächer bestehen aus Eternit.

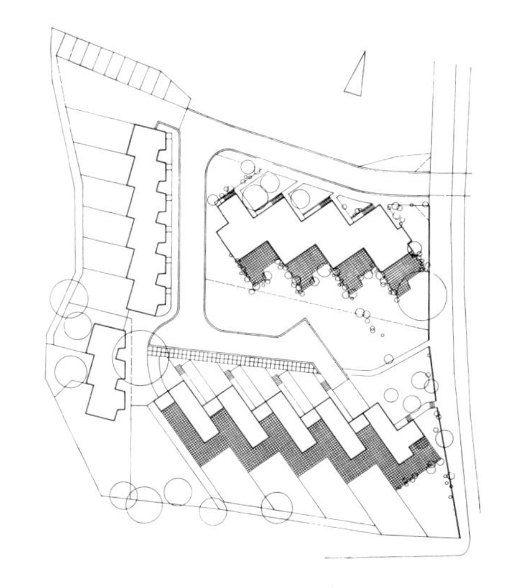

1. Site plan, 1 in 2000.
2. The southernmost group of terrace houses, seen from North-East.

1. Lageplan 1 : 2000.
2. Blick von Nordosten auf die südlichste Gruppe von Reihenhäusern.

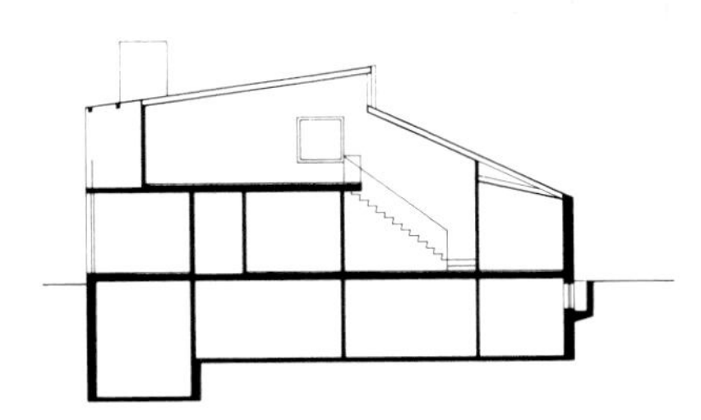

3. Section, 1 in 400.
4. South east side of one of the southern terrace houses, with its private garden in the foreground.
5. Chain houses; plans of upper floor, ground floor and lower floor, 1 in 400. Key: 1 entrance, 2 dining area, with stairs leading to upper floor, 3 kitchen, 4 bedrooms, 5 bathroom, 6 living room, 7 balcony, 8 garage, 9 utility rooms, 10 boiler room.

3. Schnitt 1 : 400.
4. Südostfassade eines der südlichen Reihenhäuser mit dem eigenen Garten im Vordergrund.
5. Kettenhäuser; Grundrisse von Obergeschoß, Erdgeschoß und Untergeschoß. Legende: 1 Eingang, 2 Eßplatz mit Treppe zum Obergeschoß, 3 Küche, 4 Schlafzimmer, 5 Bad, 6 Wohnraum, 7 Balkon, 8 Garage, 9 Wirtschaftsräume, 10 Heizung.

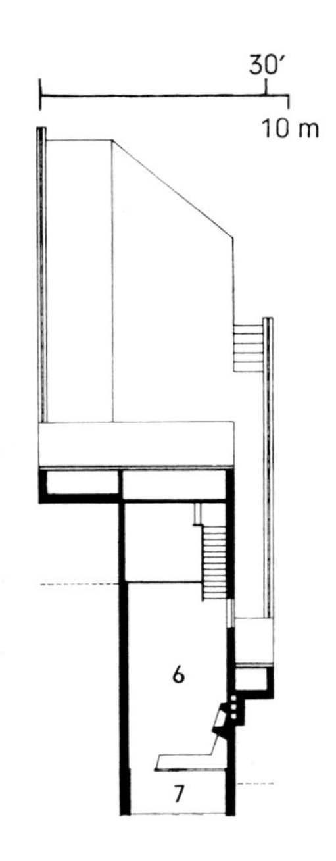

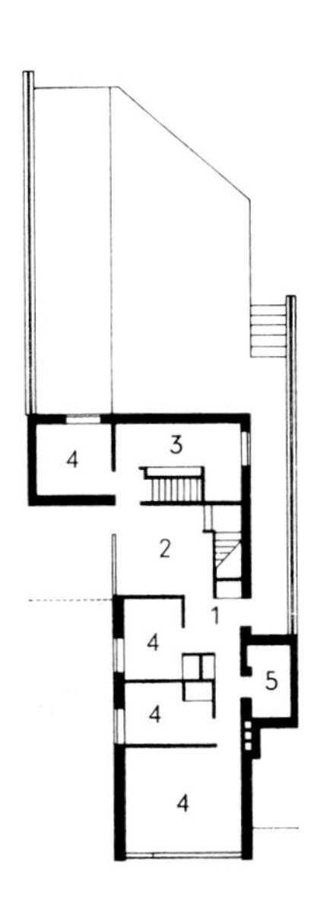

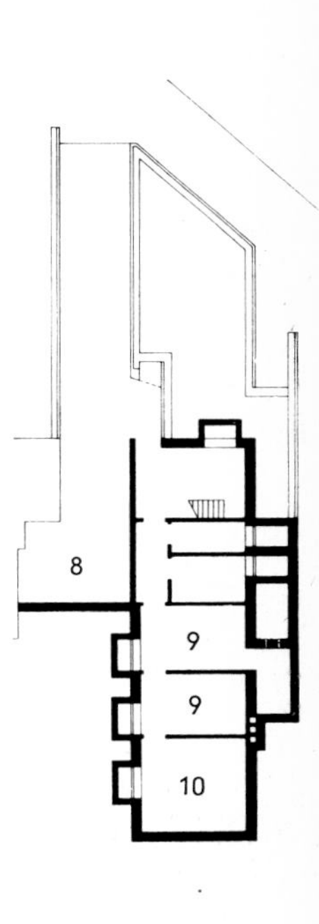

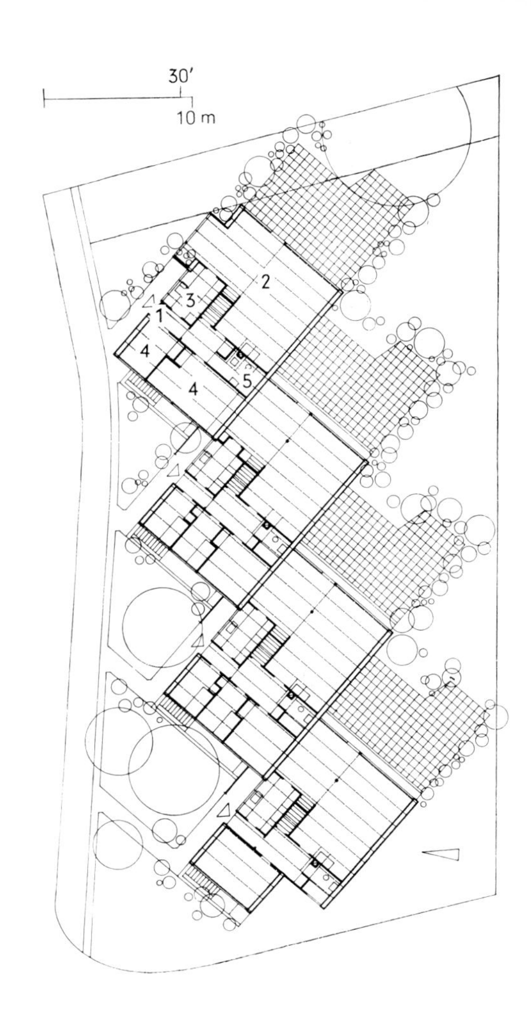
30'
10 m
1
2
3
4
4
5

1. The concatenated court-houses are closely adapted to the contour lines of the undulating ground.

1. Die zu Ketten verbundenen Hofhäuser sind den Höhenverhältnissen des hügeligen Geländes genau angepaßt.

Jørn Utzon

◁ 6. View from the first floor lounge down to the dining area, with its exit to an outdoor terrace.
7. Terrace houses, plan. Key: 1 entrance, 2 living and dining room, 3 kitchen, 4 bedrooms, 5 bathroom and W.C.
8. The easternmost house in the south row is Arne Jacobsen's own. View from the first floor lounge towards the stairs leading down to the dining area. The lounge has evening sun through the high-level window.

◁ 6. Blick vom Wohnraum im Obergeschoß hinunter auf den Eßplatz und den Ausgang zur Gartenterrasse.
7. Reihenhäuser, Grundriß. Legende: 1 Eingang, 2 Wohn- und Eßraum, 3 Küche, 4 Schlafzimmer, 5 Bad und WC.
8. Das östlichste Haus der südlichen Reihe wird von Arne Jacobsen selbst bewohnt. Vom Wohnraum im Obergeschoß sieht man die Treppe, die zum Eßplatz hinunterführt. Durch das hochliegende Fenster erhält der Raum Abendsonne.

Kingohusene Court Houses at Elsinore, 1958–60

Sixty court houses conforming to a module of 15 × 15 metres are placed on undulating ground, so combined in rows that all the houses benefit from the specific possibilities of the site to catch the sun and a view across the common open space. The height of the walls surrounding the court-house units is varied so that they permit a view yet, at the same time, a privacy protection against the neighbours. The garden court represents a valuable addition to the dwelling which has a relatively modest floor area ranging from 1180 to 1400 sq. ft. All the houses are erected in yellow brick, all the woodwork is dark-stained. At the time of erection, the estate represented one of the least expensive housing schemes in Denmark.

Hofhaussiedlung Kingohusene in Helsingør, 1958–60

Auf einem hügeligen Gelände wurden 60 Hofhäuser von je 15 × 15 m Grundfläche so verkettet, daß alle Häuser von den besonderen Gegebenheiten dieses Areals profitieren, Aussicht über eine gemeinschaftliche Grünanlage haben und gut besonnt sind. Die Begrenzungsmauern der Hofhauseinheiten haben verschiedene Höhe; auf diese Weise behindern sie die Aussicht nicht, bieten jedoch hinreichenden Schutz gegen Einblick von den Nachbargrundstücken. Die verhältnismäßig bescheidene Wohnfläche von 110 bis 130 m² wird durch den Gartenhof in gelungener Weise ergänzt. Alle Häuser sind aus gelbem Backstein errichtet, alle Holzkonstruktionen dunkel gebeizt. Als diese Häuser gebaut wurden, stellte die Siedlung Kingohusene eines der preiswertesten Wohnprojekte in Dänemark dar.

2. Towards the road, the facades are almost wholly enclosed, and the few small windows are covered with blinds.
3. Site plan, 1 in 3000.

2. Nach den Zufahrtswegen hin sind die Hausfronten der Hofhäuser bis auf wenige kleine Öffnungen völlig geschlossen.
3. Lageplan 1:3000.

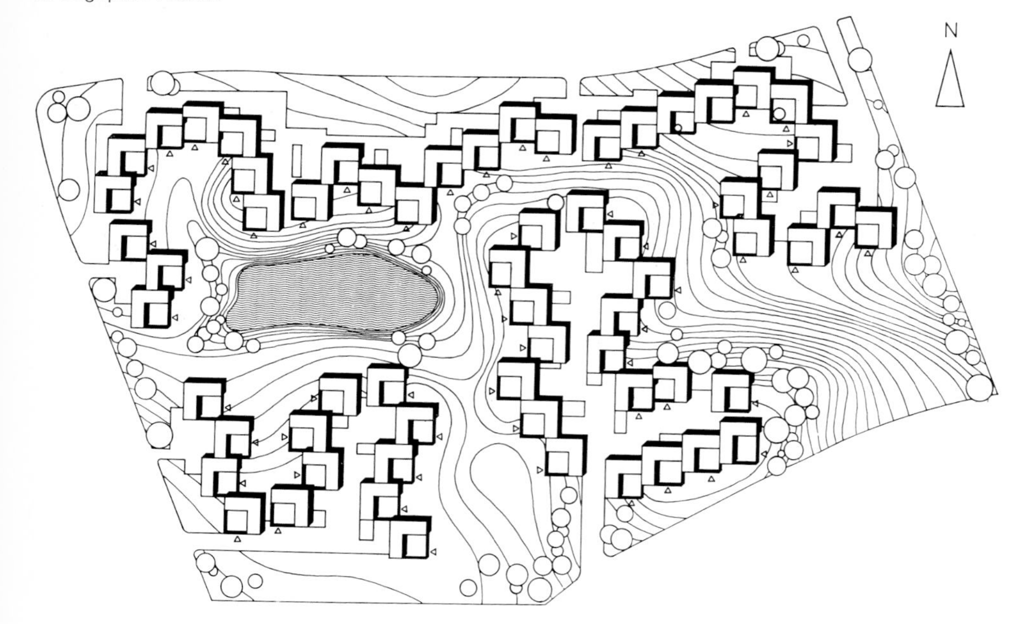

4. Section and plans of the two house types. Key: ▷ 1 entrance, 2 living room, 3 study, 4 terrace, 5 kitchen, 6 bedroom, 7 bathroom, 8 heating plant, 9 garden court, 10 garage.
5. Where ground and orientation are suitable, the garden courts are opened up at the outer corners.
6. By adhering to the same leitmotif and the same building materials, the variegated shapes are impressively integrated.
7. On the garden court side, the dwellings are opened up with large windows. Each family uses its garden court in its own way.

4. Schnitt und Grundrisse der beiden Haustypen. ▷ Legende: 1 Eingang, 2 Wohnraum, 3 Arbeitszimmer, 4 Terrasse, 5 Küche, 6 Schlafzimmer, 7 Badezimmer, 8 Heizraum, 9 Gartenhof, 10 Garage.
5. Wo die Gelände- und Orientierungsverhältnisse es zulassen, öffnen sich die Gartenhöfe an den Außenecken.
6. Durch Beibehalten der leitmotivartig verwendeten Mauerzinnen und der gleichen Baustoffe werden die durchweg verschiedenen Formen zu einer eindrucksvollen Einheit zusammengefaßt.
7. Nach den Gartenhöfen zu öffnen sich die Wohnungen mit großen Fensterflächen. Jede Familie nutzt ihren Gartenhof auf ihre eigene Weise.

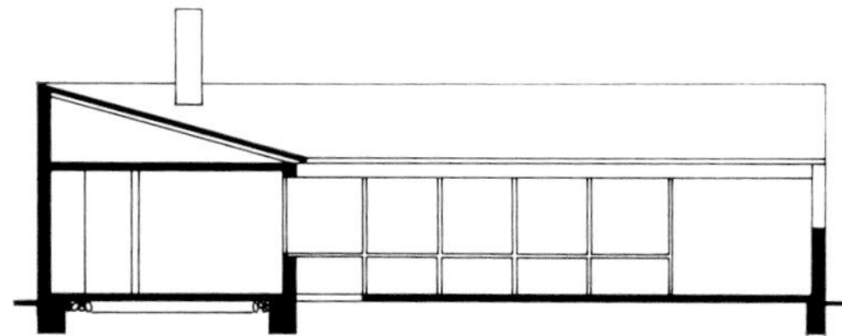

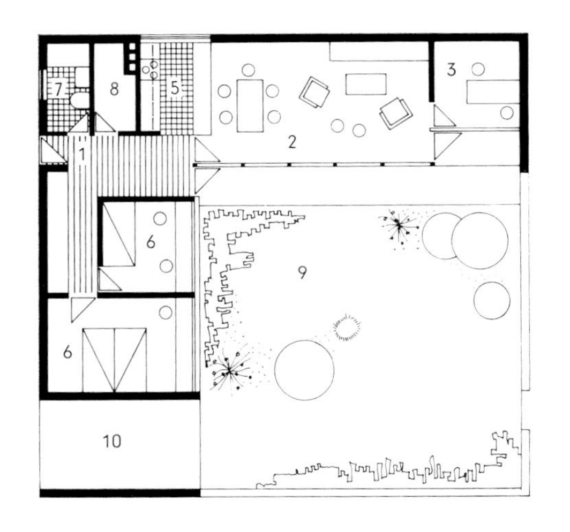
7
8
5
3
2
1
6
9
6
10

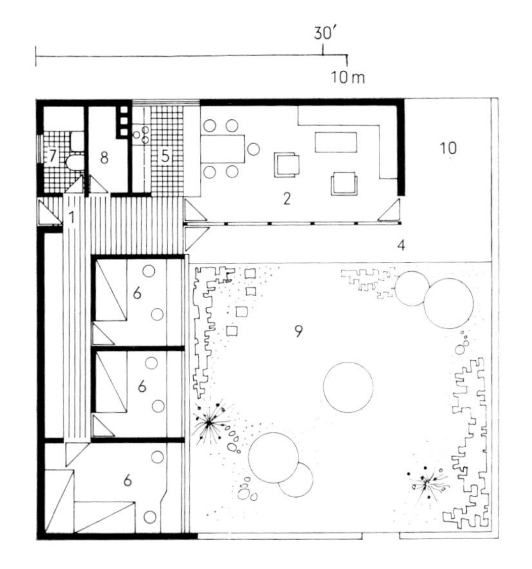
30′
10 m
7
8
5
2
10
1
4
6
9
6
6

Jørn Utzon

Terrace houses at Fredensborg, North Zealand, 1962–63

This estate has been erected by a Danish association ("Foreningen Dansk Samvirke") for Danes who have returned to their home country from residence abroad. The estate comprises court-houses and terrace houses, flats for single persons, and a community centre with club premises and restaurant. The site at the outskirts of the town of Fredensborg slopes down westwards onto a beautiful open landscape with fields and woods. Utzon has here impressively varied the court-house motif with freely arranged court-houses, already applied at Elsinore. By skilfully placing the rows of houses, he has given the little township at the outskirts of Fredensborg a markedly urban character, with access roads to each individual house; at the same time, the community centre as well as the terraces of the individual court-houses have a view across the open landscape. As with the Kingohusene estate, these houses are integrated by using but a small number of materials: yellow brick and deal which is either left untreated or is dark-stained with the single variation of a red glazing colour.

Terrassenhaussiedlung in Fredensborg im Norden der Insel Seeland, 1962–63

Eine dänische Genossenschaft namens »Foreningen Dansk Samvirke« ist der Bauherr einer Wohnsiedlung, die für zurückgekehrte Auslandsdänen bestimmt ist. Zu dieser Siedlung gehören Familienwohnungen in Hof- und Reihenhäusern, Wohnungen für einzelstehende Personen sowie ein Gemeinschaftszentrum mit Klublokalen und Restaurant. Der Baugrund liegt in unmittelbarer Nähe der kleinen Stadt Fredensborg und geht, nach Westen abfallend, in eine schöne, offene Landschaft mit Feldern und Wäldern über. Hier hat Utzon das bereits in Helsingør entwickelte Motiv der frei stehenden Reihen von Hofhäusern auf eindrucksvolle Weise variiert. Durch die buchtenförmige Anordnung der Hausreihen verlieh er der kleinen Siedlung einen ausgesprochenen städtischen Charakter. Jedes einzelne Haus ist an eine Zufahrtsstraße angeschlossen, während das Zentrum und die einzelnen Hofhaus-Terrassen zugleich einen Ausblick in die offene Landschaft bieten. Wie bei den Kingohusene wurde der Eindruck der Einheitlichkeit durch die Verwendung ganz weniger Baustoffe erreicht: gelber Backstein und Kiefernholz, das entweder unbehandelt belassen oder dunkel gebeizt ist. Einzige Abweichung sind die Fensterrahmen, teils mit roter Glasurfarbe gestrichen.

1. Park land, with a view towards the open landscape in the West.
2. Site plan.

1. Einer der zungenförmigen Parkstreifen mit Aussicht über die offene Landschaft im Westen
2. Lageplan.

3. All the houses are erected in yellow brick. Roofs, walls and chimney flues are covered by yellow pantiles.
4. Towards the access roads, the court-houses have the appearance of seclusion.
5. Plan of "type B" house. Key: 1 dining and living room, 2 bedroom, 3 bathroom, 4 kitchen 5 box room, 6 garage.

3. Alle Häuser wurden aus gelbem Backstein errichtet. Dächer, Mauern und Schornsteine sind mit gelben Dachpfannen abgedeckt.
4. Von den Zufahrtsstraßen her gesehen machen die Hofhäuser einen streng geschlossenen Eindruck.
5. Grundriß eines Hofhauses (Typ B). Legende: 1 Eß- und Wohnraum, 2 Schlafzimmer, 3 Badezimmer, 4 Küche, 5 Wirtschaftsraum, 6 Garage.

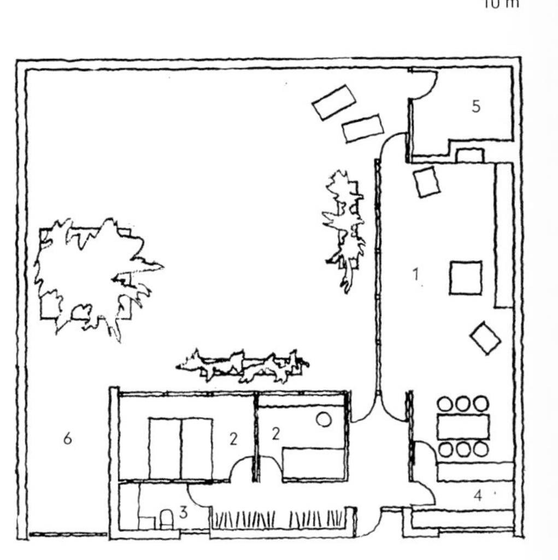

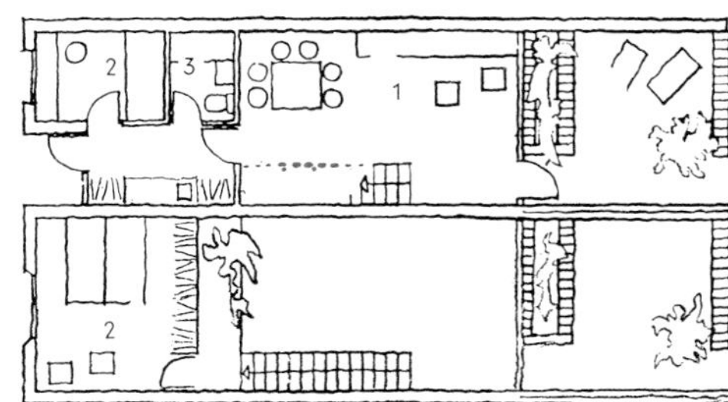
2
3
1
2

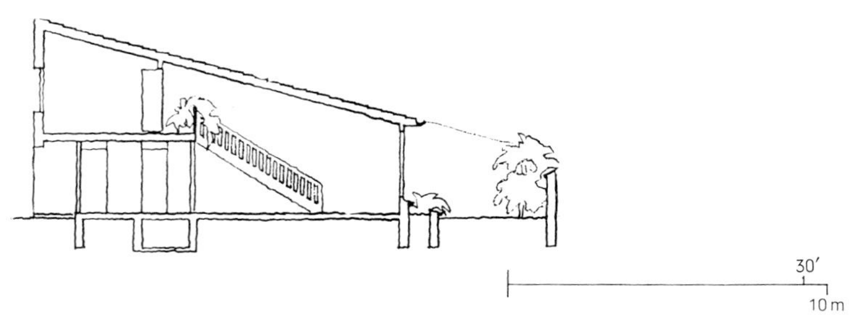
30'
10 m

◁ 6. The enclosed road spaces are connected with the common open space by narrow alley-ways and stairs.
7. Each house has its own protected garden court, with access to the common open space.
8. Plan and section of terrace house. Key: 1 dining an living room, 2 bedroom, 3 bathroom.
9. The large terrace of the community centre is paved with yellow clinkers. Latticework and frames of the clubhouse windows are painted with red glazing colour. The remaining woodwork is of untreated deal.

◁ 6. Schmale Wohnwege und Treppen verbinden die abgeschlossenen Straßenräume mit den offenen Grünflächen.
7. Jedes Haus hat seinen eigenen geschützten Hofraum mit Zugang zur gemeinschaftlichen Grünfläche.
8. Grundriß und Schnitt eines Reihenhauses. Legende: 1 Eß- und Wohnraum, 2 Schlafzimmer, 3 Badezimmer.
9. Die große Terrasse des Zentrums wurde mit gelben Klinkern ausgelegt. Die Fenstergitter und -rahmen des Klublokals sind mit roter Glasurfarbe gestrichen. Im übrigen ist das Kiefernholz der Holzkonstruktionen unbehandelt belassen.

10. All the woodwork in the club premises has been left untreated; the walls are painted white, the floors covered with Höganäs tiles. The club premises are decorated by donations from Danes abroad; Utzon himself was responsible for the furniture design.
11. The large clubroom has access to smaller premises on the first floor.
12. Plan of club centre. Key: 1 entrance, 2 cloakroom, 3 club centre, 4 club premises, 5 dining room, 6 kitchen, 7 guest room, 8 terrace.

10. Die Holzkonstruktion des Klubhauses ist unbehandelt belassen, die Wände sind weiß gestrichen, die Fußböden mit Höganäsfliesen belegt. Die Möbel für die Klubzimmer, die mit Geschenken von Auslandsdänen ausgeschmückt sind, wurden vom Architekten selbst entworfen.
11. Vom Hauptraum des Klubzentrums erreicht man eine Anzahl von kleineren Klubzimmern im Obergeschoß.
12. Klubzentrum, Grundriß des Erdgeschosses. Legende: 1 Eingang, 2 Garderobe, 3 Klubzentrum, 4 Klublokale, 5 Restaurant, 6 Küche, 7 Gastzimmer, 8 Terrasse.

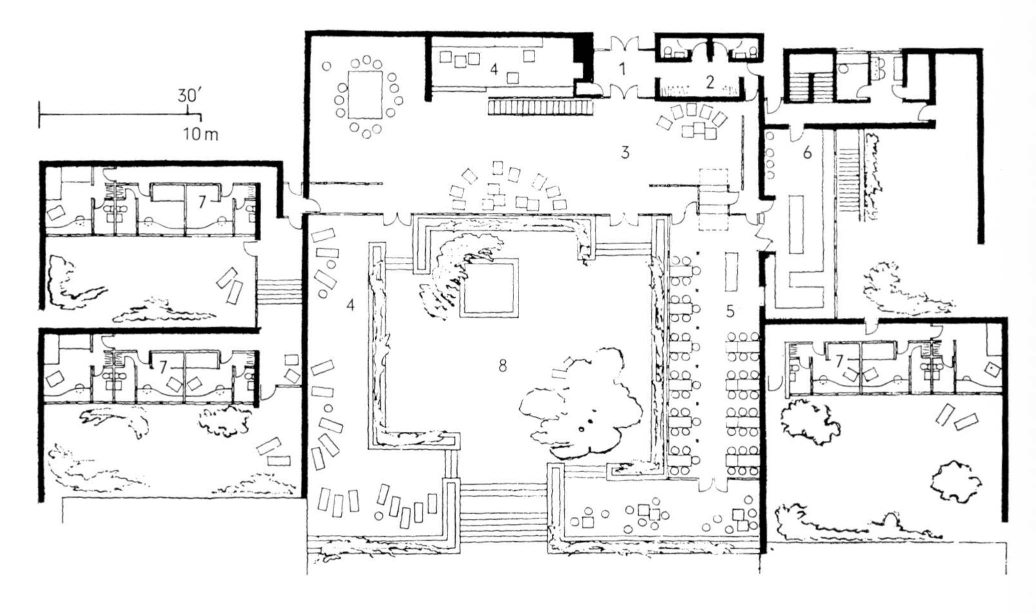

1. Walkway in the court-house area. The white, rough-cast outer walls consist of prefabricated units. The walkway is paved with concrete tiles.
2. Site Plan, 1 in 13700. Key: A court-house area, B multistorey housing, C terrace housing, D shopping centre.

1. Fußgängerstraße im Gebiet der Hofhäuser. Die weißverputzten Außenwände bestehen aus vorgefertigten Elementen. Der Wohnweg ist mit Betonplatten belegt.
2. Lageplan 1:13700. Legende: A Hofhauszone, B Mehrgeschossige Bebauung, C Reihenhausbebauung, D Einkaufszentrum.

Architects: Viggo Møller-Jensen, Tyge Arnfred, Mogens J. Pedersen, Jørn Ole Sørensen
Town Planning consultants: Knud Svensson, Peter Bredsdorff
Landscaping: Ole Nørgård

Albertslund South housing estate, Tåstrup near Copenhagen, 1963–68
The estate is situated on relatively flat ground half-way between Copenhagen and Roskilde. The local authorities acquired and pooled a number of agricultural properties and commissioned the preparation of a joint development plan. Subsequently, a number of housing associations joined forces to prepare a common development plan for the housing estate as a whole which is not yet fully completed. Altogether, the estate will contain some 2200 dwelling units consisting of approx. 625 flats of six different types with floor areas ranging from about 430 to about 1000 sq. ft. in three-storey blocks, some 1000 bungalow-type court-houses of four types with floor areas ranging from 1000 to 1300 sq. ft., and some 550 two-storey terrace houses with a gross floor area of approx. 1080 sq. ft. each. There is complete segregation between vehicular and pedestrian traffic. Via footbridges and subways, there is access from all the houses to playground, shopping centre and recreation areas without having to cross any carriageways. The "centre piece" of the area is a little brook which has been canalised and serves as the geographical centre for a number of common service buildings. The houses are erected by an assembly system using prefabricated concrete and timber elements.

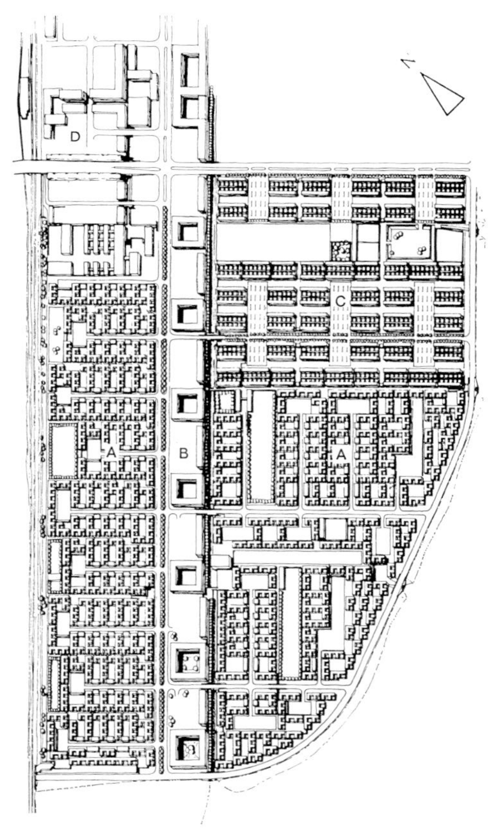

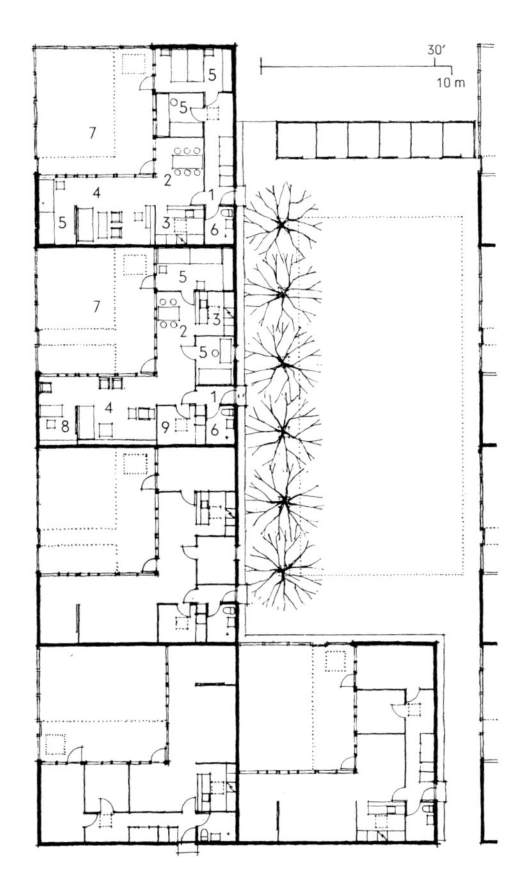

3. Plans of different types of court-houses. Key: 1 entrance, 2 dining area, 3 kitchen, 4 living room, 5 bedroom, 6 bathroom, 7 garden court, 8 study, 9 closet room.
4. The court-houses form angular units which are, towards the walkways, enclosed by black-stained fences.
5. All the windows of the dwellings face the garden court.

3. Grundrisse von Hofhaustypen. Legende: 1 Eingang, 2 Eßplatz, 3 Küche, 4 Wohnraum, 5 Schlafzimmer, 6 Badezimmer, 7 Innenhof, 8 Arbeitszimmer, 9 Arbeitsraum.
4. Die Hofhäuser bilden zusammenhängende Winkelreihen, die nach den Fußgängerstraßen hin mit schwarz imprägnierten Zäunen abgeschlossen sind.
5. Alle Räume eines Winkelhauses wenden sich dem Innenhof zu.

Architekten: Viggo Møller-Jensen, Tyge Arnfred, Mogens J. Pedersen, Jørn Ole Sørensen
Städtebauliche Planung: Knud Svensson, Peter Bredsdorff
Gartenarchitekt: Ole Nørgård

Siedlung Albertslund Süd in Tåstrup bei Kopenhagen, 1963–68
Die Siedlung steht auf verhältnismäßig flachem Gelände auf halbem Wege zwischen Kopenhagen und Roskilde. Von den örtlichen Gemeindebehörden wurde eine Reihe landwirtschaftlicher Grundstücke erworben und zusammengelegt und ein Bebauungsplan in Auftrag gegeben. Daraufhin schlossen sich verschiedene Wohnbaugesellschaften zwecks gemeinschaftlicher Gesamtplanung und Errichtung der ganzen Siedlung zusammen, die auch jetzt noch nicht fertiggestellt ist. Insgesamt wird die Siedlung etwa 2200 Wohnungen umfassen, und zwar etwa 625 Wohnungen von sechs verschiedenen Typen mit Wohnflächen von 40 bis 93 m² in dreigeschossigen Häusern, etwa 1000 eingeschossige Hofhäuser von vier Typen mit 93 bis 127 m², sowie etwa 550 zweigeschossige Reihenhäuser mit einer Gesamtwohnfläche von je 100 m². Fahrverkehr und Fußgängerverkehr sind völlig getrennt. Über Fußgängerbrücken und -unterführungen kann man von allen Häusern her die Spielplätze, Einkaufszentren und Erholungsflächen erreichen, ohne durch den Fahrverkehr behindert zu werden. Das Rückgrat des Gebietes bildet ein kleiner kanalisierter Bach, an dessen Ufern eine Reihe gemeinschaftlicher Anlagen liegen. Die Bauten sind in industrieller Bauweise aus vorgefertigten Beton- und Holzelementen errichtet.

6. The dwelling units in the terrace house area are of the two-storey type and each has its own private back garden. To prevent a view from the upper floor of the neighbouring house, all the windows in this area face the street. The upper floor has a cladding of black asbestos cement.
7. View from one of the terrace houses on to the private back-garden.
8. Between the rows of houses are paved access zones which are suitable as children's playgrounds.

6. Jedes der zweigeschossigen Reihenhäuser hat auf der Rückseite seinen eigenen Gartenhof. Bei diesen Häusern sind alle Obergeschoßfenster nach dem Wohnweg hin orientiert, um einen Einblick vom oberen Stockwerk der Nachbarhäuser zu vermeiden. Das Obergeschoß ist mit schwarzem Eternit verkleidet.
7. Ausblick aus den Wohnräumen im Erdgeschoß eines Reihenhauses auf den dazugehörigen Garten.
8. Zwischen den Reihenhäusern liegen gepflasterte Zugangszonen, die den Kindern gute Spielmöglichkeiten bieten.

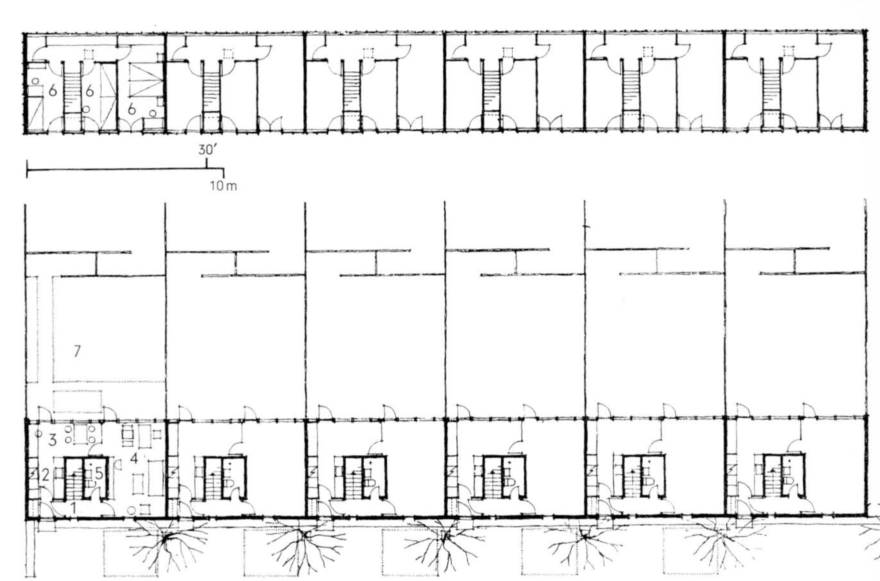

9. The court-houses are interspersed with jointly used playgrounds and sitting areas.
10. Types of terrace houses. Plans of upper floor and ground floor. Key: 1 entrance, 2 kitchen, 3 dining area, 4 living room, 5 bathroom, 6 bedroom, 7 private back-garden.

9. Zwischen den Hofhäusern sind gemeinsame Spiel- und Sitzplätze für die Bewohner ausgespart.
10. Reihenhaustyp. Grundrisse Obergeschoß und Erdgeschoß. Legende: 1 Eingang, 2 Küche, 3 Eßplatz, 4 Wohnraum, 5 Badezimmer, 6 Schlafzimmer, 7 Gartenhof.

F.C. Lund (City Architect / Stadtarchitekt)
Overall planning / Generalplanung: Mogens Irming + Tage Nielsen

Bellahøj housing estate, Copenhagen, 1950–56

A public architectural competition for the development plan for Copenhagen's highest ground, offering a view over large parts of the city, was won in 1945 by architects Mogens Irming and Tage Nielsen. The layout plan and the types of houses recommended in the prize-winning project were largely retained, and the prize-winning architects were appointed as co-ordinators whilst the different groups of tower blocks were assigned to a number of housing associations who brought in their own architects for detailed planning. These architects were Ole Buhl, Dan Fink, Edvard Heiberg, Sven Eske Kristensen, the architectural staff of the Dominia Company as well as the City Architect who was responsible for the buildings here shown. Each of the closely spaced tower blocks consist of two staggered blocks connected by a joint staircase tower. The houses have reinforced concrete walls, cast in sliding forms. The facades are otherwise assembled from relatively small prefabricated concrete units. All the houses are kept in grey and white colour shades.

Hochhaussiedlung Bellahøj in Kopenhagen, 1950–56

Den 1945 öffentlich ausgeschriebenen Architektenwettbewerb für einen Bebauungsplan des höchstgelegenen Baugeländes in Kopenhagen, von dem sich eine Aussicht über große Teile der Stadt bietet, gewannen die Architekten Mogens Irming und Tage Nielsen. Der im preisgekrönten Entwurf vorgesehene Lageplan und die dort vorgeschlagenen Hochhaustypen wurden bei der Ausführung im wesentlichen beibehalten. Die Gewinner des Wettbewerbs bekamen die Oberaufsicht übertragen,da die einzelnen Gruppen von Hochhäusern verschiedenen Wohnungsbaugesellschaften zugeteilt wurden, die die eigentliche Projektierung und Errichtung ihrer Häuser jeweils ihren eigenen Architekten überließen. Dies waren Ole Buhl, Dan Fink, Edvard Heiberg, Sven Eske Kristensen, das Architektenbüro der Dominia-Gesellschaft sowie der Stadtarchitekt, der für die hier gezeigten Häuser verantwortlich war. Jedes der dicht aneinander gestellten Hochhäuser besteht aus zwei gegeneinander versetzten Blöcken, die durch einen gemeinsamen Treppenturm miteinander verbunden sind. Die Häuser wurden als Betonkonstruktion im Gleitschalungsverfahren errichtet. Die Fassaden sind mit verhältnismäßig kleinen vorgefertigten Betonelementen verkleidet. Alle Bauten sind in grauen und weißen Farben gehalten.

1. Site plan, 1 in 9000 / Lageplan 1:9000.

2. The estate seen from Degnemosen Park in the North-West.
3. The staircase towers of the twin blocks are erected in concrete and glass.

2. Die Bebauung vom Degnemosen-Park von Nordwesten her gesehen.
3. Die Treppentürme der Zwillingshäuser bestehen aus Beton und Glas.

4. Typical floor plan. Key: 1 living room, 2 bedroom, 3 kitchen, 4 bathroom, 5 entrance hall, 6 lift, 7 airlock.
5. The estate seen from the North.

4. Normalgeschoßgrundriß. Legende: 1 Wohnraum, 2 Schlafzimmer, 3 Küche, 4 Badezimmer, 5 Diele, 6 Fahrstuhl, 7 Luftschleuse.
5. Ansicht der Siedlung von Norden.

Eva + Nils Koppel

Søllerød Park housing estate at Søllerød near Copenhagen, 1953–55
The estate occupies the tree-studded park of a now demolished old manor house which has inspired the layout plan with its informal arrangement of 19 blocks with two storeys and mansard floor. All the 350 dwelling units share the benefits of the beautiful park. The ground floors of the blocks contain flats with private terraces facing south or west whilst the upper dwellings form one-and-a-half storey maisonettes accessible from galleries at first floor level. The houses are erected in brick, with bearing cross-walls. All the walls are white-washed. Roofs covered with red pantiles, the facades with black cement tiles.

Siedlung Søllerød Park in Søllerød bei Kopenhagen, 1953–55
Um den schönen alten Baumbestand des ehemaligen, parkartigen Landsitzes zu erhalten, wurden die 19 zweigeschossigen Wohnblöcke mit ausgebautem Dachgeschoß unregelmäßig über das Baugelände verteilt. Alle 350 Wohnungen der Siedlung kommen so in den Genuß der gepflegten Parklandschaft. Die Wohnungen im Erdgeschoß der abgetreppten Wohnblöcke haben eigene, nach Süden oder Westen orientierte Terrassen, während die übrigen Wohnungen sich als Maisonette-Typen durch 1½ Geschosse erstrecken und über Laubengänge in Höhe des ersten Stockes erschlossen werden. Die Häuser sind aus Backstein mit tragenden Querwänden errichtet. Alle tragenden Mauern sind weiß gekalkt und die Fassaden mit schwarzen Zementfliesen verkleidet. Die Dächer sind mit roten Pfannenziegeln gedeckt.

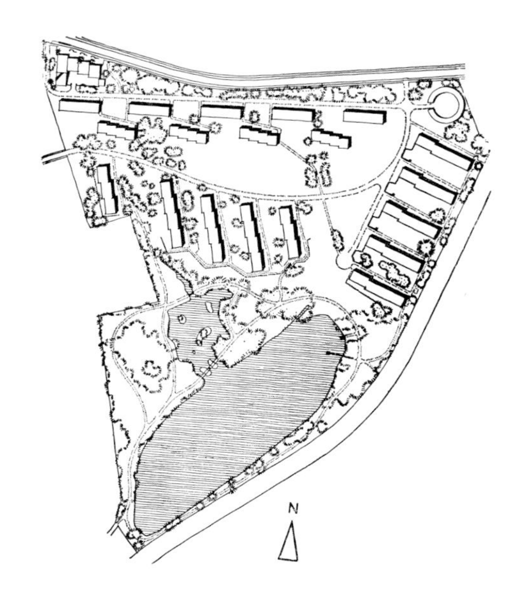

1. Site plan, 1 in 8200.
2. The south and west side of the blocks, with protected outdoor sitting areas in front of the ground floor flats.

1. Lageplan 1:8200.
2. Süd- und Westseite der Wohnblöcke mit geschützten Freisitzplätzen vor den Wohnungen des Erdgeschosses.

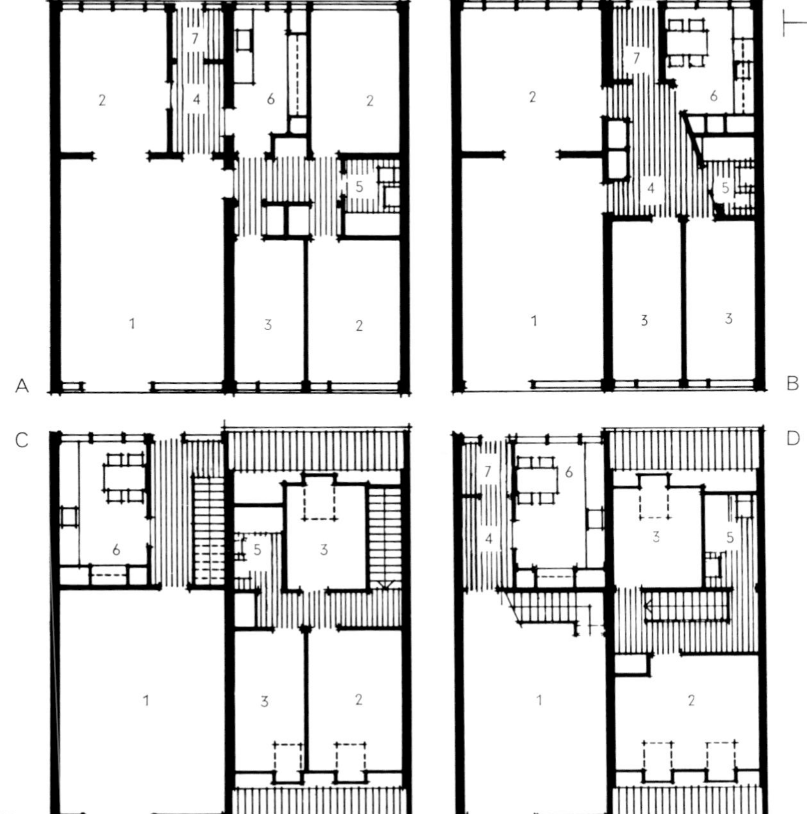

3. In order to ensure their adaptation to the undulating ground, many of the blocks are divided into several staggered sections.
4. The bedrooms of the upper maisonettes are placed in the mansard floor.
5. Plans. Key: A house of type I, B house of type IIA, C house of type IIB, D house of type III; 1 lounge, 2 room, 3 small room, 4 hall, 5 bathroom, 6 dining kitchen, 7 lumber room.

3. Um sich dem hügeligen Gelände anzupassen, bestehen viele der Wohnblöcke aus verschiedenen, gegeneinander verschobenen Abschnitten.
4. Die Schlafräume der oberen Wohnungen sind in das Dachgeschoß verlegt.
5. Grundrisse. Legende: A Wohnungstyp I, B Typ IIA, C Typ IIB, D Typ III; 1 Wohnraum, 2 Zimmer, 3 Kammer, 4 Diele, 5 Bad, 6 Eßküche, 7 Abstellraum.

Arne Jacobsen

Bellevue Bay housing estate, Klampenborg near Copenhagen, 1961

The Bellevue Bay housing estate is adjacent to Arne Jacobsen's earlier Bellavista housing estate (1933). It comprises a four-storey block of flats placed on a low basement. All the flats have a view across the Sound. The block has a relatively great depth which is utilised for a fireside lounge in the centre. In the foreground are five atrium houses where all the lounges are placed on the east side, offering a view over the Sound. Otherwise, the dwellings receive daylight through two inner courtyards.

Wohnhausgruppe an der Bellevue-Bucht in Klampenborg bei Kopenhagen, 1961

Die Anlage an der Bellevue-Bucht schließt sich an Arne Jacobsens frühere Wohnsiedlung Bellavista aus dem Jahr 1933 an und besteht aus einem Block mit Wohnungen in vier Obergeschossen über einem niedrigen Sockelgeschoß. Alle Wohnungen bieten Aussicht über den Øresund. Die verhältnismäßig große Tiefe der Häuser ist in der Mitte für ein Kaminzimmer ausgenutzt. Im vorderen Teil des Grundstückes stehen fünf Atriumhäuser, deren Wohnräume auf der Ostseite liegen, damit auch sie Aussicht über den Sund haben. Die übrigen Räume sind auf zwei innere Lichthöfe orientiert.

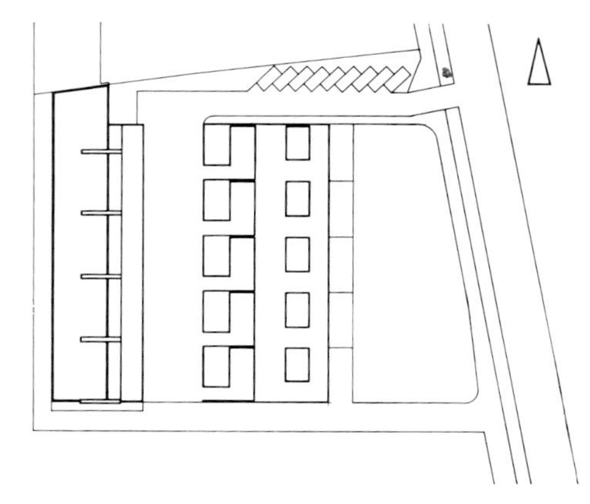

1. Site plan, 1:2000/Lageplan 1:2000.

2. Typical floor plan. Key: 1 entrance, 2 living room and balcony, 3 fireside lounge, 4 bedroom, 5 bathroom and W.C., 6 kitchen, 7 dining area.

2. Normalgeschoßgrundriß. Legende: 1 Eingang, 2 Wohnraum mit Balkon, 3 Kaminzimmer, 4 Schlafraum, 5 Bad und WC, 6 Küche, 7 Eßplatz.

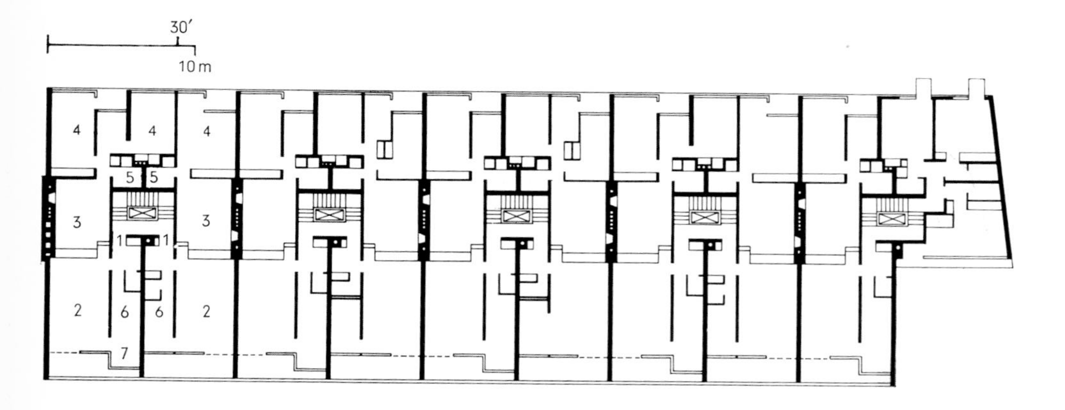

3. The housing estate seen from the coastal road. In the foreground, the single-storey atrium houses, erected in yellow brick.
4. Below the four-storey block are garages, and entrances to the internal stairs.
5. The markedly horizontal character of the building is emphasised by the white balcony parapets. In the background, the Bellavista estate dating back to 1933 is just visible.

3. Ansicht vom Øresund und der Küstenstraße her. Im Vordergrund die eingeschossigen Atriumhäuser, die aus gelbem Backstein errichtet sind.
4. Unter dem viergeschossigen Block befinden sich Garagen und die Zugänge zu den Innentreppen.
5. Die weißen Balkonbrüstungen unterstreichen den stark horizontalen Charakter des Gebäudes. Im Hintergrund ist ein Teil der im Jahre 1933 errichteten Bellavista-Siedlung zu sehen.

Jean Fehmerling

Skodsborgparken block of flats, Skodsborg near Copenhagen, 1962
This block of flats, consisting of five main storeys and a low basement, is placed on the ridge of a north-south orientated slope between the coastal road and the large woods on the west side. The site formerly used for a few summer houses now offers accommodation for nearly 300 families, with a view over woods and beach. The blocks are placed parallel to the coastal road and attractively emphasise the contour lines of the ground. The buildings are erected with bearing cross-walls of brick and prefabricated concrete units for the facade.

Wohnblöcke Skodsborgparken in Skodsborg bei Kopenhagen, 1962
Mit ihren fünf Obergeschossen über einem niedrigen Untergeschoß stehen diese Blöcke auf der Kante eines nord-südlich verlaufenden Abhangs zwischen der Küstenstraße (Strandvej) am Øresund und den großen Waldungen auf der Westseite. Wo früher nur ganz wenige Familien ihre Sommervillen hatten, erhalten jetzt fast 300 Familien die Möglichkeit, die Aussicht über Wald und Strand zu genießen. Die Bebauung liegt parallel zur Küstenstraße und folgt in gelungener Weise den großen Linien des Geländes. Die Häuser haben tragende Querwände, die Fassaden bestehen aus vorgefertigten Betonelementen.

1. The finest of the tall trees on the eastern slope have been preserved from the days of the old summer house gardens.
2. Site plan, 1 in 4000.

1. Auf den Osthängen sind die schönsten der großen Bäume aus den alten Villengärten stehengelassen.
2. Lageplan 1:4000.

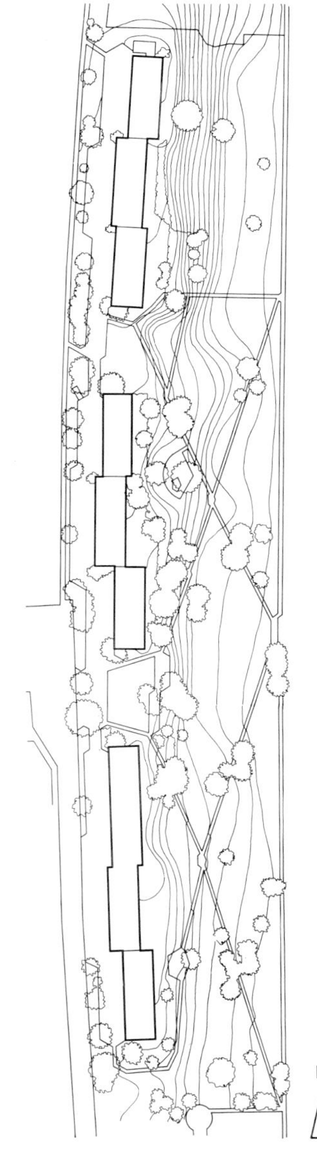

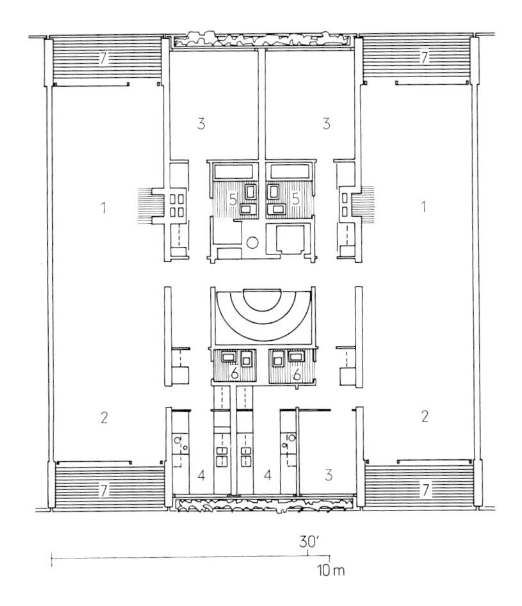

3. Typical floor plan. Key: 1 living room, 2 dining area, 3 bedroom, 4 kitchen, 5 bathroom and W.C., 6 W.C., 7 loggia.
4. The estate seen from the West.
5. View on the Sound from one of the top-storey flats.

3. Normalgeschoßgrundriß. Legende: 1 Wohnraum, 2 Eßplatz, 3 Schlafzimmer, 4 Küche, 5 Bad und WC, 6 WC, 7 Loggia.
4. Ansicht der Bebauung von Westen.
5. Blick aus einer Dachwohnung auf den Øresund.

Henning Jensen + Torben Valeur

Eskemosegård housing estate at Birkerød near Copenhagen, 1958–59
In 1952, Henning Jensen was awarded the First Prize in a public architectural competition for a development plan for a particularly attractive undulating site between Birkerød and Sjælsø. The scheme comprised both blocks of flats and small houses. It is only the multi-storey blocks which have been erected in co-operation with Torben Valeur, but essential features of the competition projects have been preserved in the long, slightly curved residential street on the east side of an attractive, low stretch of ground which can be overlooked from most of the flats. A shopping centre and a multi-storey garage are placed close to the entrance on the valley side. The different types of flats have continuous stairs which also provide accommodation for store rooms. The estate continues a functional Danish tradition with simple construction and materials. There are bearing cross-walls, facade cladding of brick, red tiled roofs, and black tarred window frames.

Wohnblockgruppe Eskemosegård in Birkerød bei Kopenhagen, 1958–59
Im Jahr 1953 wurde Henning Jensen in einem offenen Wettbewerb der erste Preis für den Bebauungsplan eines landschaftlich schönen, hügeligen Geländes zwischen Birkerød und Sjælsø zuerkannt. Der Wettbewerb sah sowohl mehrgeschossige Wohnblöcke als auch Einfamilienhäuser vor. Sechs Jahre später wurde nur der aus mehrgeschossigen Häusern bestehende Abschnitt ausgeführt, den Jensen zusammen mit Torben Valeur entwarf. Dabei wurden jedoch wesentliche Züge des Wettbewerbsentwurfs beibehalten, so die lange, schwach gebogene Wohnstraße auf der Ostseite einer breiten Talmulde, auf die sich von den meisten Wohnungen ein freier Ausblick bietet. Ein Einkaufszentrum und eine Sammelgarage liegen in unmittelbarer Nähe der Zufahrt auf der Talseite. Die Treppenhausbereiche mit wohnungsnahen Abstell- und Nebenräumen ziehen sich quer durch die Hausblöcke; Waschküche und Trockenraum liegen unmittelbar vor jeder Wohnungstür. Die Bebauung setzt die funktionelle dänische Tradition mit einfachen Bauweisen und Baustoffen fort. Die tragenden Mauern sind quergestellt, die Fassaden sind mit Backsteinen verkleidet, die Dächer mit roten Ziegeln gedeckt und die Holzteile der Fensterzonen schwarz geteert.

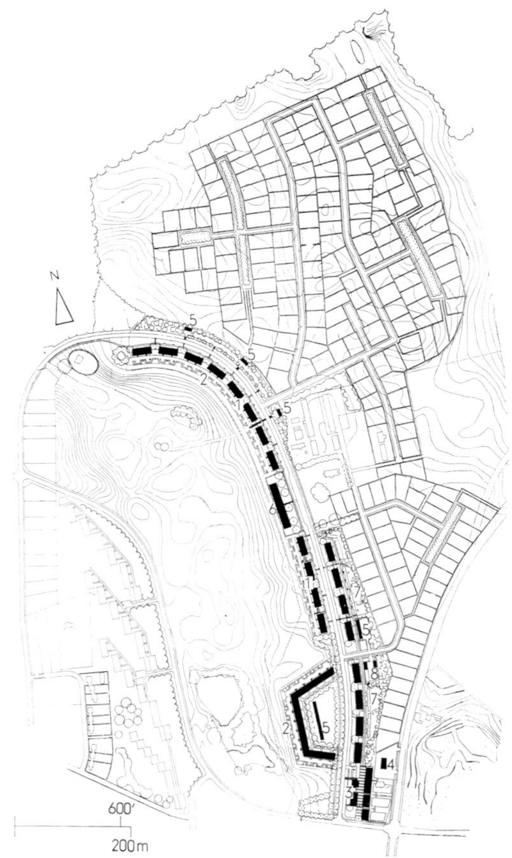

1. The estate faces West with a view across a broad valley.
2. Site plan. Key: 1 two storey buildings, 2 outdoor arbours, 3 shopping centre, 4 service station, 5 garages, 6 kindergarten, 7 playground, 8 heating plant.
3. Cross-section and plan. Key: 1 hall, 2 lounge, 3 bedroom, 4 small room, 5 room, 6 dining kitchen, 7 bathroom, 8 balcony, 9 stores, 10 cupboard room, 11 drying room, 12 utility room and laundry.
4. The entrance zone shows the harmony of the materials.
5. Residential street with short blocks which leave views across the valley even from the street.

1. Die Bebauung zieht sich in einem großen Bogen um eine westwärts abfallende Talmulde herum.
2. Lageplan. Legende: 1 Zweigeschossige Wohnhäuser, 2 Sitz- und Spielbereiche im Freien, 3 Einkaufszentrum, 4 Tankstelle, 5 Garagen, 6 Kindergarten, 7 Spielplatz, 8 Heizungszentrale.
3. Querschnitt und Grundriß. Legende: 1 Diele, 2 Wohnraum, 3 Schlafraum, 4 Kleines Zimmer, 5 Zimmer, 6 Eßküche, 7 Bad und WC, 8 Balkon, 9 Abstellraum, 10 Schrankraum, 11 Trockenraum, 12 Waschküche.
4. Die Eingangspartie zeigt den Zusammenklang der Materialien.
5. Kurze Blocks auf der Westseite der Zufahrtsstraße lassen den gegenüberliegenden Häusern noch ausreichende Durchblicke auf die Talmulde.

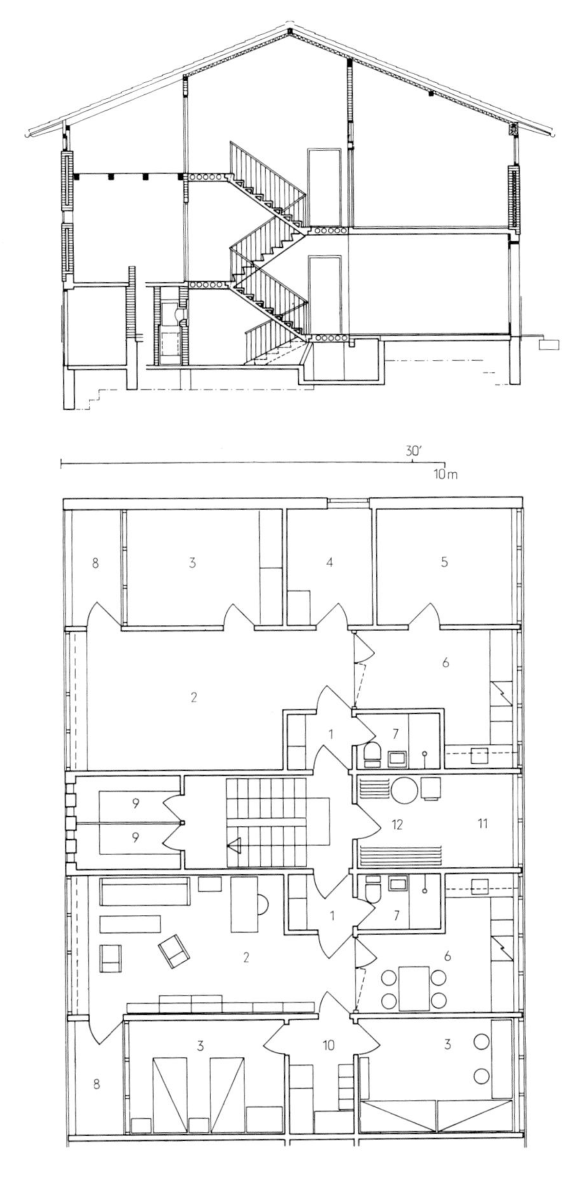

Halldor Gunnløgsson + Jørn Nielsen

Præstevænget multi-storey block of flats, Ballerup, Copenhagen, 1964
Due to difficult soil conditions, a development plan originally envisaging low-rise houses in an area to the North-West of Copenhagen had to be abandoned in favour of a 15-storey block. This block is placed on a strong concrete foundation with garages in the basement, and with playgrounds on the east side at the entrance doors to the tower block itself. Since lifts are provided for any two of the flats on each floor, the gallery on the east side is used as an emergency exit only. The bearing cross walls and structural floors are cast in situ whilst all the other structural components are assembled from prefabricated units.

Wohnhochhaus Præstevænget in Ballerup bei Kopenhagen, 1964
Schwierige Bodenverhältnisse führten dazu, daß die ursprünglichen Pläne für eine niedrige Bebauung im Nordwesten von Kopenhagen abgeändert und die geplanten Wohnungen in einem einzigen Hochhaus mit 15 Wohngeschossen über kräftigem Betonfundament zusammengefaßt werden mußten. Im Untergeschoß befinden sich Garagen, während unmittelbar vor den Eingängen auf der Ostseite Kinderspielplätze vorgesehen sind. Je zwei Wohnungen des gleichen Stockwerks haben einen Aufzug für sich, so daß der Laubengang auf der Ostseite nur als Fluchtweg bei Brandgefahr dient. Die tragenden Querwände und Geschoßdecken bestehen aus Ortbeton, während alle übrigen Elemente vorgefertigt wurden.

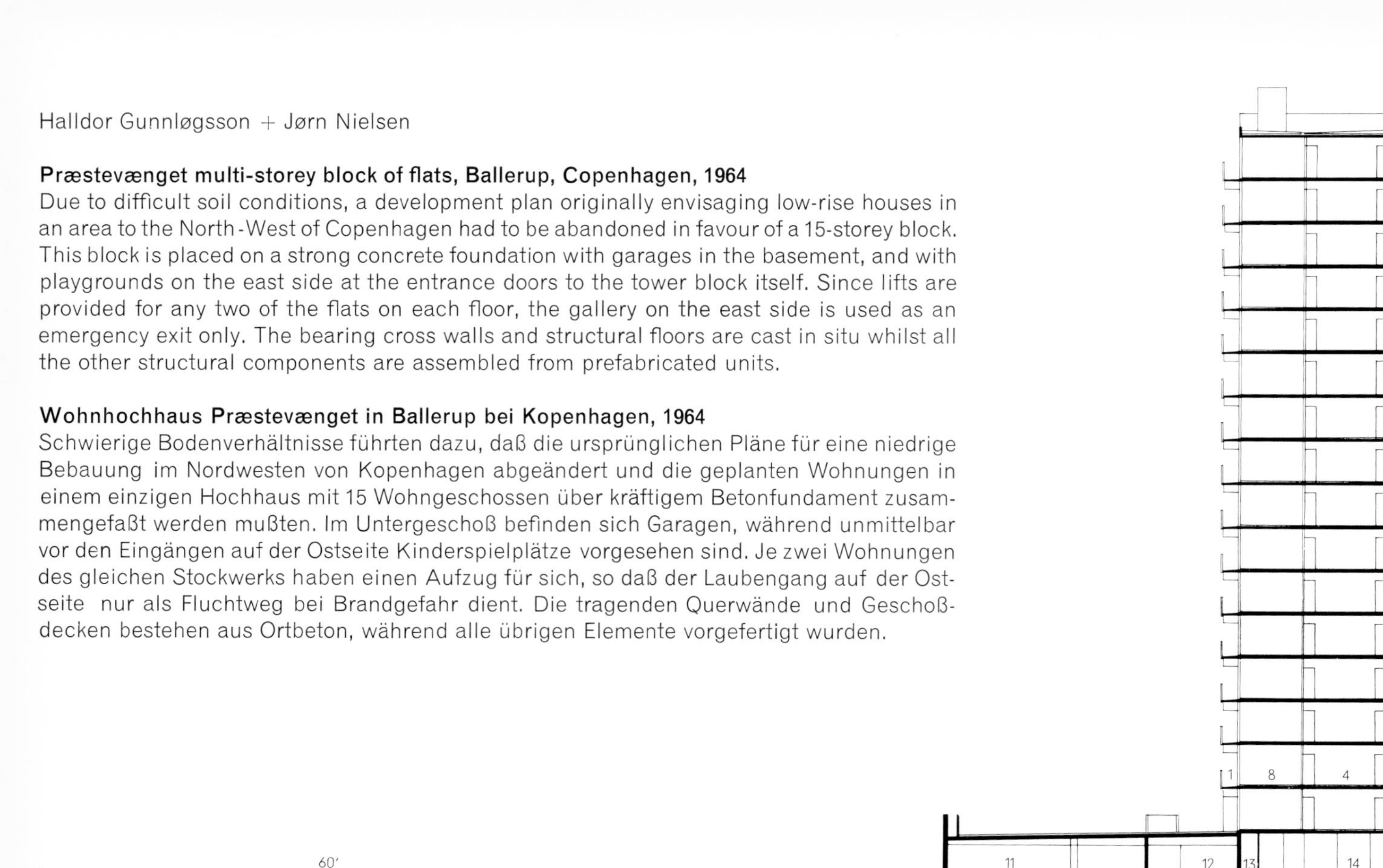

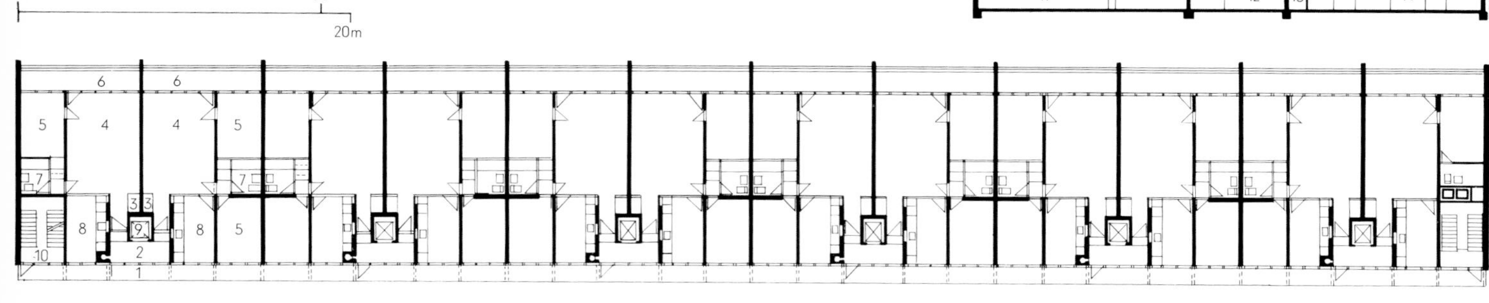

1. Cross-section and plan of typical floor. Key: 1 gallery, 2 hall, 3 cloakroom, 4 lounge, 5 bedroom, 6 balcony, 7 bathroom and W.C., 8 kitchen, 9 lift, 10 emergency stairs, 11 garage, 12 bicycle cellar, 13 silo, 14 stores room.
2. The tower block, seen from the west. Visible cross walls, balcony floors and parapets are left in untreated concrete.

1. Querschnitt und Grundriß eines Normalgeschosses. Legende: 1 Lauben, 2 Aufzugvorraum, 3 Garderobe, 4 Wohnraum, 5 Schlafraum, 6 Loggia, 7 Badezimmer und WC, 8 Küche, 9 Aufzug, 10 Nottreppe, 11 Garage, 12 Fahrradkeller, 13 Silo, 14 Abstellraum.
2. Ansicht des Hochhauses von Westen. Die sichtbaren Querwände, die Kragplatten der Loggien und die Brüstungen bestehen aus schalungsrauh belassenem Beton.

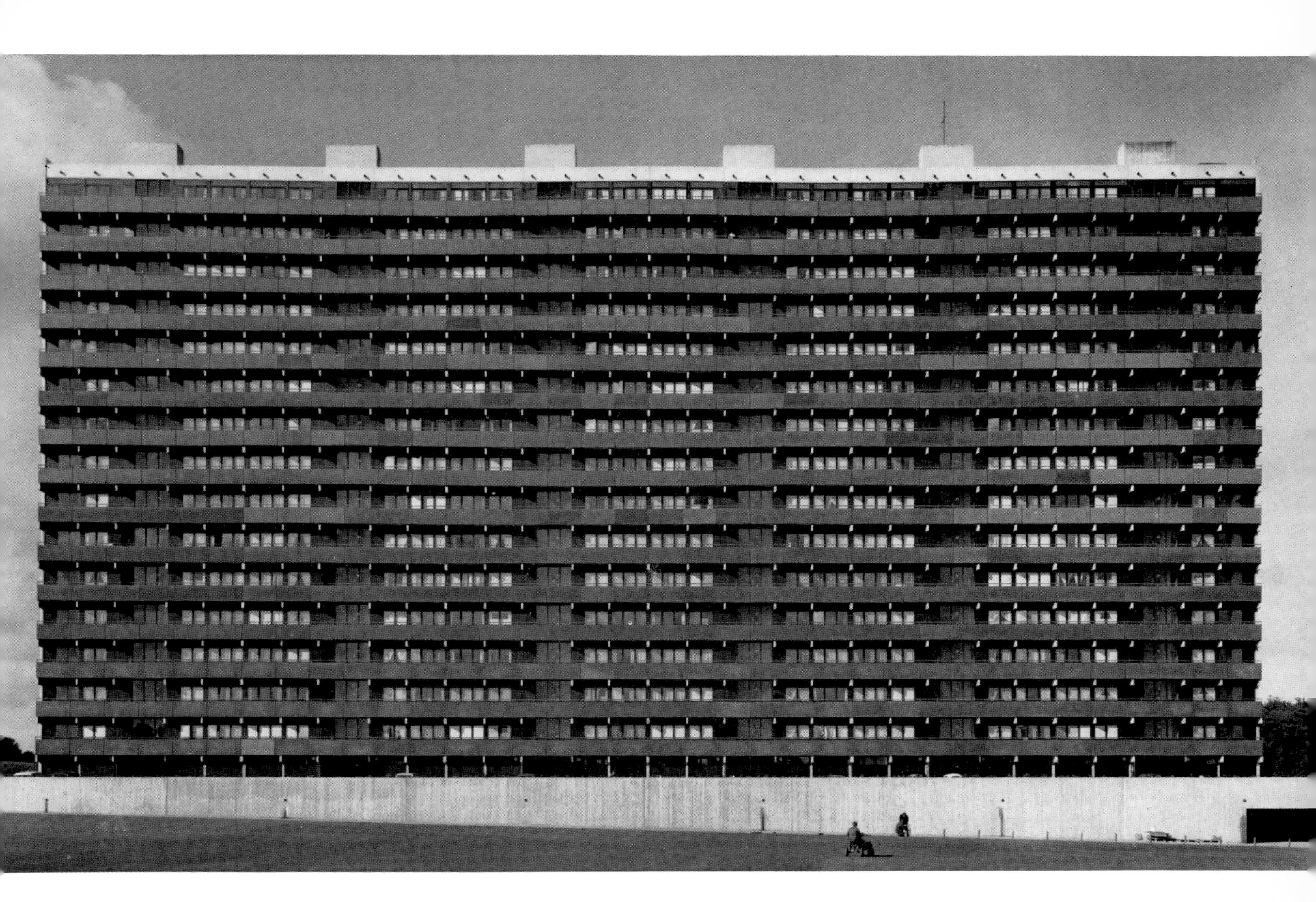

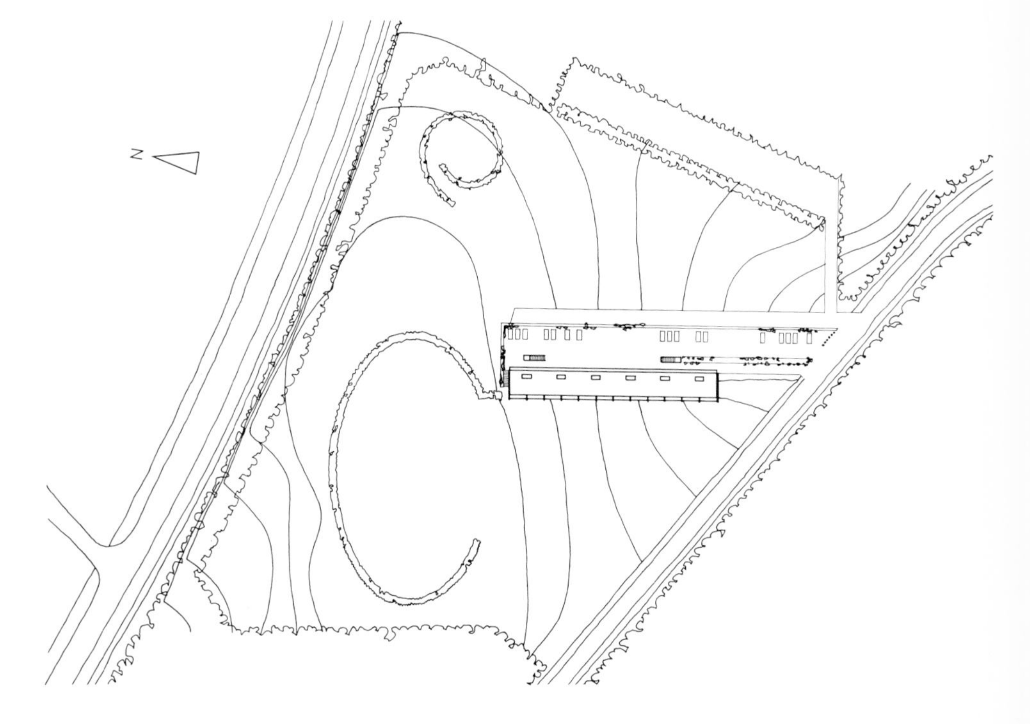

3. The balcony parapets on the east side are covered with grey-black asbestos cement.
4. Site plan, 1 in 3450.

3. Die Brüstungen der Laubengänge auf der Ostseite sind mit grauschwarzen Eternitplatten verkleidet.
4. Lageplan 1:3450.

Poul Ernst Hoff, Bennet Windinge, Jorgen Juul Møller, Kai Agertoft, Alex Poulsen

Høje Gladsaxe housing estate, Gladsaxe near Copenhagen, 1964–68
A housing scheme with a total of 1880 dwelling units, designed and erected as an entity through collaboration of several major firms of architects. The estate is situated in the North-West of Copenhagen on high ground to the North of a large park with bird sanctuaries (Utterslev Mose). The houses are retracted as far as possible from the park, leaving large open spaces in front of them. The dwellings are concentrated in five 16-storey blocks and about ten lower blocks with four and nine storeys. The housing estate also comprises extensive joint facilities, shopping centre, crèche and kindergarten, schools, sportsground and church. There is a consistent segregation of vehicular and pedestrian traffic. The houses are constructed entirely by assembly methods, using prefabricated units.

Siedlung Høje Gladsaxe in Gladsaxe bei Kopenhagen, 1964–68
Bei dieser Siedlung handelt es sich um ein Gemeinschaftsprojekt verschiedener großer Architekturbüros für die Erstellung von insgesamt 1880 Wohnungen. Das Wohngebiet liegt auf einem hochgelegenen Gelände nordwestlich von Kopenhagen an der Nordseite eines großen Naturschutzparkes mit Vogelschutzgebieten (Utterslev Mose). Die Wohnungen verteilen sich auf fünf 16geschossige Hochhäuser und ungefähr zehn niedrigere, vier- und neungeschossige Blöcke, die soweit wie möglich vom Park abgerückt und von diesem durch große Freiflächen getrennt sind. In das Bauprogramm mit eingeschlossen sind umfangreiche Gemeinschaftsanlagen, Einkaufszentrum, Kindergärten, Schulen, Sportplätze und Kirche. Die Trennung des Fahrverkehrs vom Fußgängerverkehr ist konsequent durchgeführt. Die Bauten wurden ausschließlich aus vorgefertigten Elementen errichtet.

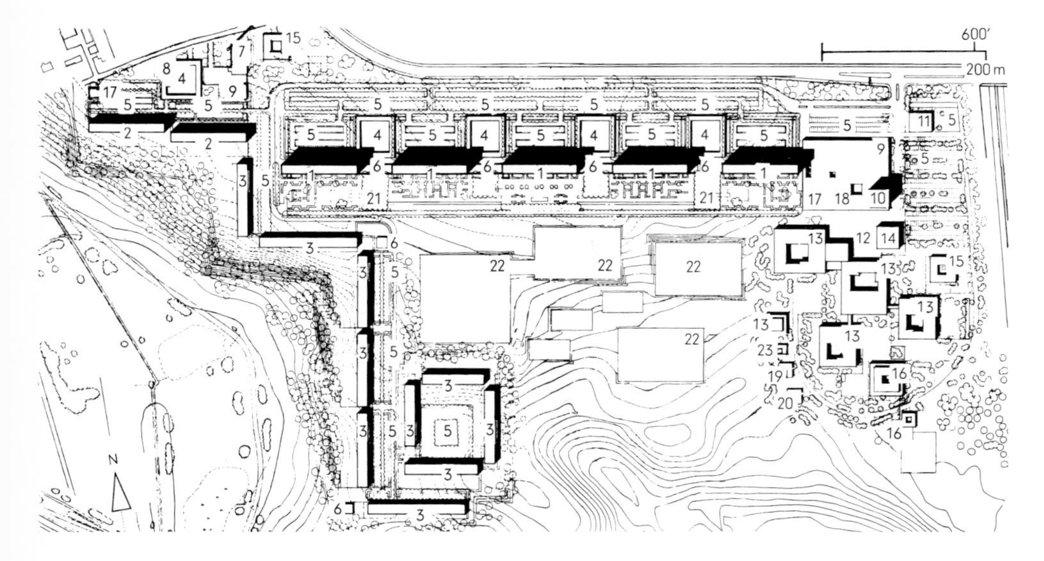

1. Site plan. Key: 1 16-storey blocks, 2 9-storey blocks, 3 4-storey blocks, 4 garages, 5 car park, 6 washhouses, 7 heating plant, 8 motorcar repair shop, 9 shops, 10 nine-storey tower block, 11 service station, 12 shopping centre, 13 schools, 14 church, 15 crèche and kindergarten, 16 spare time centre with junk playground, 17 youth clubs, 18 banqueting premises, 19 headmaster's dwelling, 20 vicarage, 21 terraces, 22 sportsground, 23 school caretaker.
2. The housing estate seen from the park (Utterslev Mose) in the South.

1. Lageplan. Legende: 1 16geschossige Wohnblöcke, 2 9geschossige Wohnblöcke 3 4geschossige Wohnblöcke, 4 Garagen, 5 Parkplätze, 6 Wäscherei, 7 Heizzentrale, 8 Autoreparaturwerkstatt, 9 Läden, 10 9geschossiges Turmhaus, 11 Tankstelle, 12 Piazza, 13 Schulen, 14 Kirche, 15 Kleinkinderheim und Kindergarten, 16 Freizeitzentrum mit Bauspielplatz, 17 Jugendklubs, 18 Gesellschaftslokale, 19 Wohnung des Schuldirektors, 20 Pfarrhaus, 21 Terrassen, 22 Fußballplätze, 23 Wohnung des Schulwarts.
2. Die Südseite der Siedlung vom Naturschutzpark Utterslev Mose her gesehen.

3. Floor plan, nine and sixteen-storey blocks. Key: A three-room flats, B one-room flats, C four-room flats; 1 gallery, 2 vestibule, 3 hall, 4 dining kitchen, 5 lounge, 6 bedroom, 7 small room, 8 bathroom and W.C., 9 box room, 10 stores room, 11 balcony.
4. On the south sides of the sixteen-storey tower blocks are children's playgrounds.
5. The sixteen-storey blocks, seen from South-East. The balcony parapets are of concrete and are, like all the other structural components of the block, assembled from prefabricated units.

3. Normalgeschoßgrundriß (Ausschnitt) der 9- und 16geschossigen Wohnblöcke. Legende: A Dreizimmerwohnung, B Einzimmerwohnung, C Vierzimmerwohnung; 1 Laubengang, 2 Aufzugvorhalle, 3 Diele, 4 Eßküche, 5 Wohnraum, 6 Schlafraum, 7 Kleineres Zimmer, 8 Badezimmer und WC, 9 Schrankraum, 10 Abstellraum, 11 Balkon.
4. Die Kinderspielplätze liegen vor den Südfassaden der 16geschossigen Hochhäuser.
5. Ansicht der 16geschossigen Hochhausscheiben von Südosten her. Die Balkonbrüstungen aus Beton bestehen ebenso wie alle anderen Bauteile aus vorgefertigten Elementen.

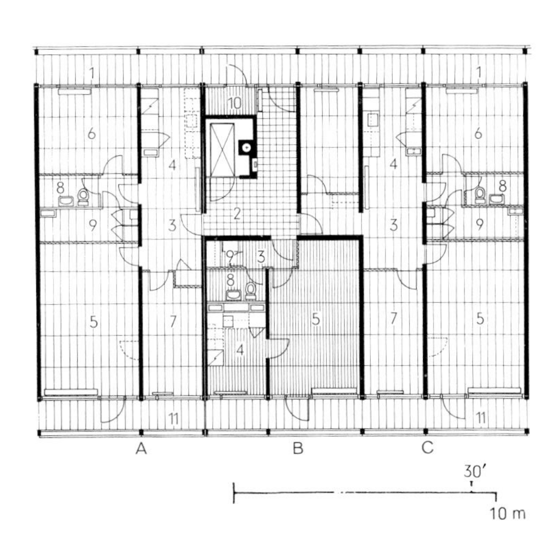

C. F. Møller

4th of May College, students hostel, Århus, Jutland, 1949

To support the victims of the resistance movement, a "Freedom Fund" was established just after the last war. The Fund was used for the erection of a number of colleges throughout the country, designed for students who seek advanced education in courses of at least two years' duration. In Århus, the "4. Mai-kollegiet" was erected on a site formerly occupied by allotment gardens. The finest trees were preserved in the large garden court which now forms the centre of the 55 dormitories and common rooms, placed in single-storey buildings which are staggered in adaptation to the contour lines. The buildings are erected of red-brown brick and covered by pantile roofs.

1. The college seen from North-East, with the assembly room and dwellings of the north wing in the foreground.
2. Site plan. Key: 1 main entrance, 2 caretaker, 3 vestibule, 4 cloak room, 5 assembly hall, 6 stage, 7 common room, 8 toilets, 9 office, 10 lounge, 11 dining room, 12 bedroom, 13 kitchen, 14 bathroom, W.C., 15 painter's studio, 16 music room, 17 sales kiosk, 18 school warden.

Kollegium des 4. Mai, Studentenwohnheim in Århus, Jütland, 1949

Zur Unterstützung der Opfer des Freiheitskampfes wurde gleich nach dem letzten Weltkrieg der sogenannte Freiheits-Fonds errichtet, mit dessen Hilfe in verschiedenen Orten Dänemarks eine Reihe von Fortbildungsschulen für eine mindestens zweijährige Weiterbildung von Studenten errichtet wurde. In Århus wurde das »4. Maj-Kollegiet« in einem früheren Schrebergartengelände errichtet, dessen schönste Bäume in einer großen zentralen Grünanlage erhalten blieben. Um diese Grünanlage herum wurden eingeschossige, abschnittsweise dem Gelände angepaßte Flügelbauten mit insgesamt 55 Zimmern und Versammlungsräumen errichtet. Die Gebäude sind aus rotbraunem Backstein errichtet und mit Pfannenziegeln gedeckt.

1. Ansicht von Nordosten mit den Versammlungsräumen und Wohnungen des Nordflügels im Vordergrund.
2. Lageplan. Legende: 1 Haupteingang, 2 Zugang zur Hausmeisterwohnung, 3 Vorhalle, 4 Garderobe, 5 Aula, 6 Bühne, 7 Aufenthaltsraum bei der Aula, 8 Toiletten, 9 Büro, 10 Wohnraum, 11 Eßzimmer, 12 Schlafzimmer, 13 Küche, 14 Bad und WC, 15 Maleratelier, 16 Musikraum, 17 Verkaufskiosk, 18 Zugang zur Wohnung des Heimleiters.

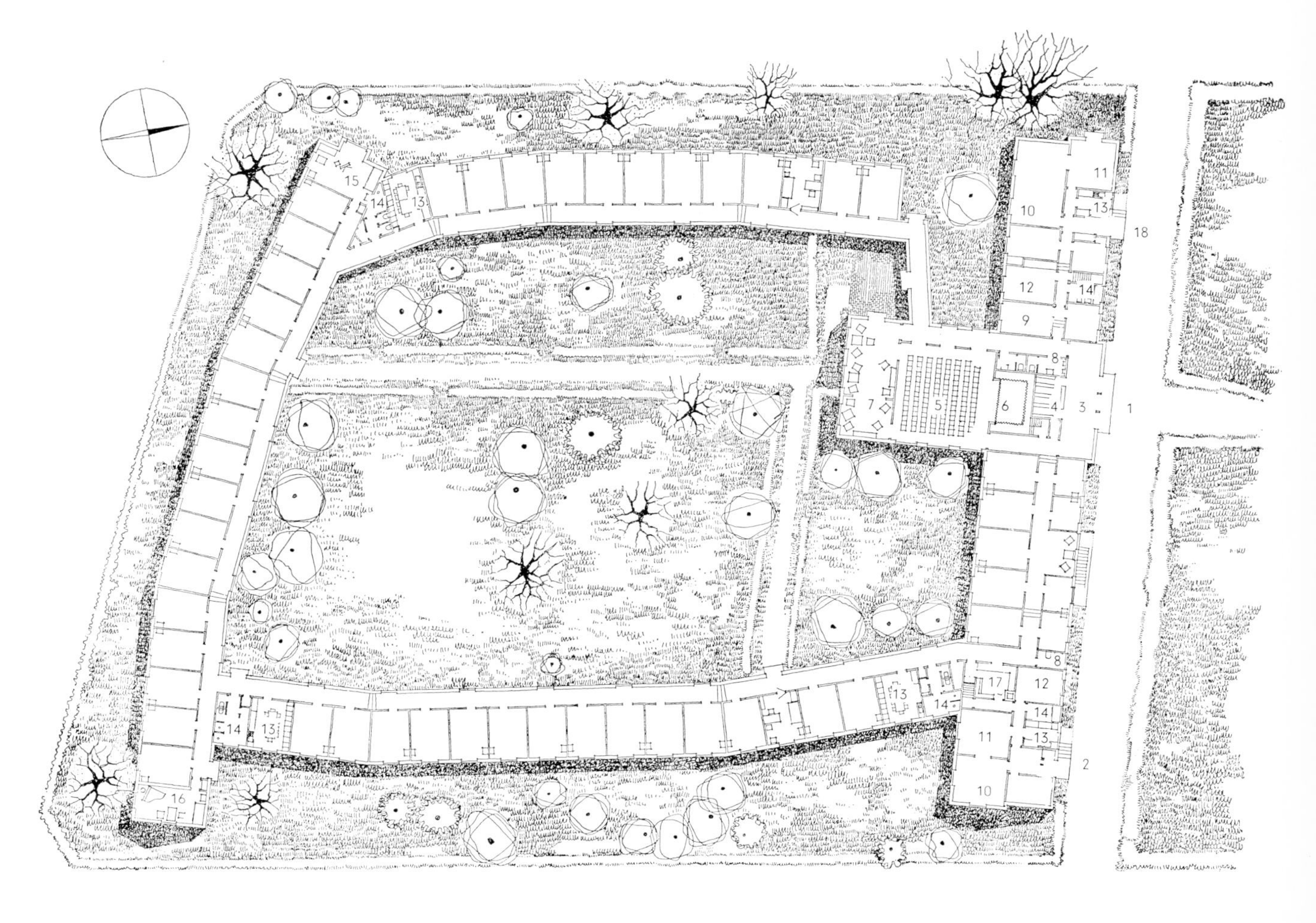

3. The college rooms give on to narrow gardens. Access to the central garden court is from the surrounding college corridors.
4. The college corridors have white-washed walls and floors of hard-burned clinkers.

3. Die einzelnen Studentenzimmer gehen nach außen auf schmale Grünstreifen. Die zentrale Grünanlage ist von den Korridoren aus zugänglich.
4. Die Wände der Korridore sind verputzt, ihre Fußböden bestehen aus hartgebrannten Klinkern.

Kay Fisker

Mothers' Help Organisation, Administrative Building and Block of Flats, Copenhagen, 1955
The Mothers' Help Organisation is an institution which, being financed by public funds, provides guidance and assistance to pregnant women, married as well as unmarried, as well as mothers with small children. The Copenhagen headquarters of the institution are situated in the town centre amidst a residential area with five storey tenement houses at Strandboulevarden. In two blocks staggered in relation to each other, the building accommodates the offices for administration and consultants as well as 61 self-contained service flats for single mothers with a child. The building also contains a lecture room and a number of joint service facilities. The building is erected in yellow brick. The central corridor system applied to both wings is externally apparent from their end walls. An annex on the south side with a number of joint service facilities has been added recently.

Verwaltungsgebäude und Kollektivhaus der Mütterhilfe in Kopenhagen, 1955
Die Mütterhilfe ist eine aus öffentlichen Mitteln finanzierte Einrichtung, die schwangeren Frauen – verheiratet oder ledig – sowie Müttern mit Kleinkindern mit Rat und Tat zur Seite steht. Der Hauptsitz des Instituts steht in Kopenhagen zentral am Strandboulevard mitten zwischen fünfgeschossigen Wohnbauten. In dem einen der beiden gegeneinander versetzten Blöcke sind die Verwaltungs- und Beratungsräume des Institutes untergebracht, im anderen 61 abgeschlossene Kleinwohnungen für alleinstehende Mütter mit Kind. Zum Raumprogramm gehören außerdem ein Vortragssaal und eine Anzahl von Gemeinschaftseinrichtungen. Das Gebäude ist aus gelbem Backstein errichtet. Das Zentral-Korridorsystem der beiden Gebäudeteile läßt sich am Außenbau an den doppelten Stirnmauern der beiden Flügel klar ablesen. Vor kurzem wurde die Anlage durch weitere Kleinwohnungen erweitert.

1. Under the pergola in the courtyard are outdoor benches for residents and staff.
2. The building seen from North-East (Strandboulevarden) with the administration building in the foreground and the block of service flats with the main entrance from Svendborggade.
3. Typical floor plan. Key: 1 block of service flats, 2 administration building, 3 room, 4 child, 5 kitchen, 6 W.C., 7 lift, 8 lecture room, 9 office, 10 director's office, 11 secretariat.
4. North-west side of the building, facing Strandboulevarden.

1. Freisitzplätze für Bewohner und Personal unter der Pergola im Innenhof.
2. Die Nordostseite vom Strandboulevard aus gesehen, mit dem Verwaltungsgebäude im Vordergrund und dem anschließenden Wohnbau, dessen Haupteingang sich in einer Seitenstraße befindet.
3. Grundriß eines Normalgeschosses. Legende: 1 Kollektivbau, 2 Bürohaus, 3 Wohnraum einer Kleinwohnung, 4 Kinderzimmer, 5 Küche, 6 Toilette, 7 Fahrstuhl, 8 Sitzungszimmer, 9 Büro, 10 Büro des Direktors, 11 Sekretariat.
4. Die Fassade zum Strandboulevard, von Nordwesten gesehen.

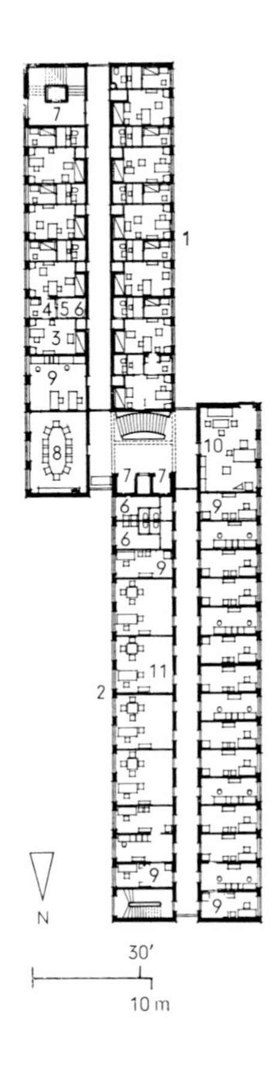

1. The central garden has the character of a large park with informally placed groups of trees.
2. Site plan. Key: 1 main entrance, 2 administration, 3 assembly room, 4 canteen, 5 patients, 6 clock tower, 7 resident mechanic, 8 duct.
3. Between lounge and covered outdoor space, the corridor is widened into a high-roofed room with top lighting.

1. Die zentrale Grünanlage macht den Eindruck eines großen Parks mit einzelnen Baumgruppen.
2. Lageplan. Legende: 1 Haupteingang, 2 Verwaltung, 3 Versammlungshalle, 4 Kantine, 5 Patienten, 6 Uhrenturm, 7 Wohnung des Maschinenmeisters, 8 Kanal.
3. Zwischen dem Aufenthaltsraum und dem überdeckten Freisitzplatz erweitert sich der Korridor zu einem Wohnraum mit Oberlicht.

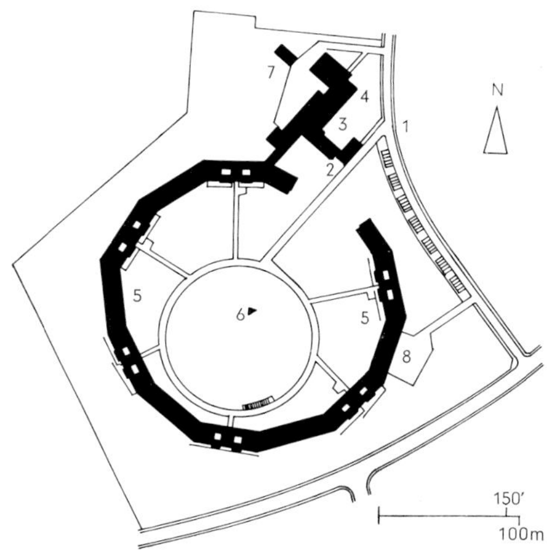

F.C. Lund + Hans Chr. Hansen

Ringbo hostel for elderly psychiatric patients at Bagsværd, near Copenhagen, 1964
The hostel has 280 beds for older psychiatric patients, spread over 12 wards arranged in the form of a ring which surrounds a large open space. Each ward has its own dining and sitting room as well as its own garden. An extension of the corridor area near the sitting room of each ward has a raised roof with top lighting which has the dual purpose of interrupting the monotony of the corridors and of improving the daylight conditions for the lounge. A continuous corridor system in the basement provides a venue for the transport of meals and laundry from a central plant near the main entrance. The outer walls are of light-weight concrete. All the other walls are clad with asbestos cement and black or red stained wood. The roofing consists of corrugated asbestos cement slabs.

Ringbo, Psychiatrisches Pflegeheim für ältere Patienten, Bagsværd bei Kopenhagen, 1964
Das Pflegeheim bietet Unterkunft für 280 Patienten. Ihre Betten sind auf zwölf ringförmig verkettete Abteilungen verteilt, die sich um eine große Grünanlage gruppieren. Jede Abteilung hat ihren eigenen Speise- und Aufenthaltsraum sowie Freisitzplätze in Verbindung mit einem Garten. Die Aufenthaltsräume, die durch eine Erweiterung des Korridors entstehen, haben einen besonderen Dachaufbau mit Oberlicht, teils um die Einförmigkeit der Ränge zu unterbrechen, teils um die Tageslichtverhältnisse der Aufenthaltsräume zu verbessern. Im Keller dient ein System von durchgehenden Korridoren zur Verteilung von Speisen und Wäsche, die von einer Zentralanlage in der Nähe des Haupteinganges geliefert werden. Die Außenwände sind aus Leichtbeton, die übrigen Wandverschalungen bestehen aus Eternit oder schwarz und rot imprägniertem Holz, die Dächer aus Welleternit.

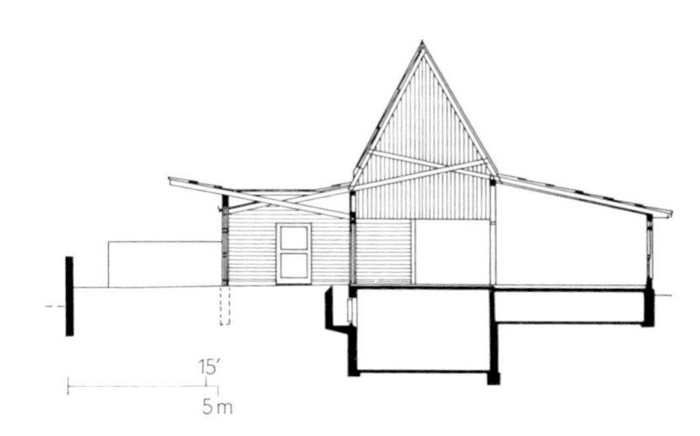

4. Cross-section through terrace and lounge.
5. The outer and inner gardens are connected by a subway.
6. For reasons of orientation, two of the twelve wards turn their back to the central garden. The privacy of the outdoor sitting areas is protected by concrete walls.

4. Querschnitt durch Terrasse und Aufenthaltsraum.
5. Die inneren und äußeren Gartenanlagen sind durch eine Unterführung verbunden.
6. Aus Orientierungsgründen wenden zwei der zwölf Abteilungen der zentralen Grünanlage den Rücken zu. Die Freisitzplätze sind durch Betonmauern gegen Einblick von außen geschützt.

Kay Fisker

Voldparken elementary school at Husum, near Copenhagen, 1951–57

The design of the school is closely adapted to that part of the near-by Voldparken housing estate which Kay Fisker completed a few years before the school was built. The school comprises a single-storey section for infants with 10 classrooms, each associated with an outdoor area, and a main building consisting of two three-storey wings around a joint staircase. The East wing contains 19 standard classrooms, the West wing a number of special classrooms. The school also comprises two gymnastic halls and a large sports hall. All the buildings are linked by half-covered walkways in connection with the centrally placed playground. The buildings are erected in yellow brick. The large roofs and parapets of the three-storey wings are clad with asbestos cement. On the park side, the school is bordered by fort-like semicircular walls which surround some of the outdoor areas reserved for infants.

Voldparken-Grundschule in Husum bei Kopenhagen, 1951–57

Der Entwurf für diese Schule ist dem Teil der benachbarten Voldparken-Siedlung angepaßt, der nach den Plänen von Kay Fisker einige Jahre vor Beginn des Schulbaus fertiggestellt wurde. Die Schulanlage besteht aus einer eingeschossigen Abteilung für die Unterstufe mit zehn Klassenzimmern, denen jeweils eine entsprechende Freifläche zugeordnet ist, und aus einem dreigeschossigen Hauptschultrakt, dessen beide Flügel sich um einen gemeinsamen Treppenturm gruppieren. Im östlichen Flügel befinden sich 19 Normalklassenräume, im westlichen Flügel eine Anzahl von Fachklassenzimmern. Der ganze Komplex wird durch zwei Turnhallen und eine große Sporthalle vervollständigt. Alle Gebäude sind miteinander durch überdeckte Gänge verbunden, die ihrerseits mit dem zentral gelegenen Pausenhof in Verbindung stehen. Die Gebäude sind aus gelbem Backstein errichtet. Die großen Dachflächen sowie die Brüstungen der dreigeschossigen Gebäude wurden mit Eternit verkleidet. Nach dem Park zu wird die Schule durch bastionsartige, halbrunde Mauern abgeschlossen, die einen Teil der Freiluftklassen für die Unterstufe umgeben.

1. The main building, with the corridor side of the special classroom wing on the left and the end of the standard classroom wing on the right of the common staircase. The end wall of the sports hall can just be glimpsed on the extreme right.
2. One of the infants' classrooms with its own outdoor area. The window sides are protected against the sun by the large overhang of the roof and by awnings at door height.
3. Ground floor plan. Key: 1 entrance, 2 staircase, 3 standard classroom wing, 4 special classroom wing, 5 infants, 6 open air classroom, 7 toilets, 8 bathroom, 9 gymnastics hall, 10 sports hall, 11 changing rooms, 12 sportsground, 13 playground for older children, 14 playground for infants, 15 woodcraft, 16 standard classroom, 17 school dentist, 18 nurse and medical officer, 19 caretaker's flat, 20 bicycle parking, 21 school gardens.

1. Ansicht des Hauptschultrakts mit der Korridorseite des Fachklassenflügels (links) und der Stirnseite des Normalklassenflügels (Mitte), die das Pultdach der Treppenhaus-Vorhalle durchschneidet. Ganz rechts ist gerade noch die Sporthalle sichtbar.
2. Ein Klassenzimmer der Unterstufe mit dem dazugehörigen Außenraum. Die Fensterflächen sind gegen die Sonne durch das auskragende Dach und durch eine horizontale Blende in Türhöhe abgeschirmt.
3. Grundriß des Erdgeschosses. Legende: 1 Eingang, 2 Treppenhaus, 3 Normalklassenflügel, 4 Fachklassenflügel, 5 Unterstufe, 6 Freiluftklasse, 7 Toiletten, 8 Bäder, 9 Turnhalle, 10 Sporthalle, 11 Umkleideräume, 12 Sportplätze, 13 Pausenhof für größere Kinder, 14 Pausenhof für kleinere Kinder, 15 Werkraum für Holzarbeiten, 16 Normalklasse, 17 Schul-Zahnarzt, 18 Krankenschwester und Arzt, 19 Wohnung des Hausmeisters, 20 Abstellraum für Fahrräder, 21 Schulgärten.

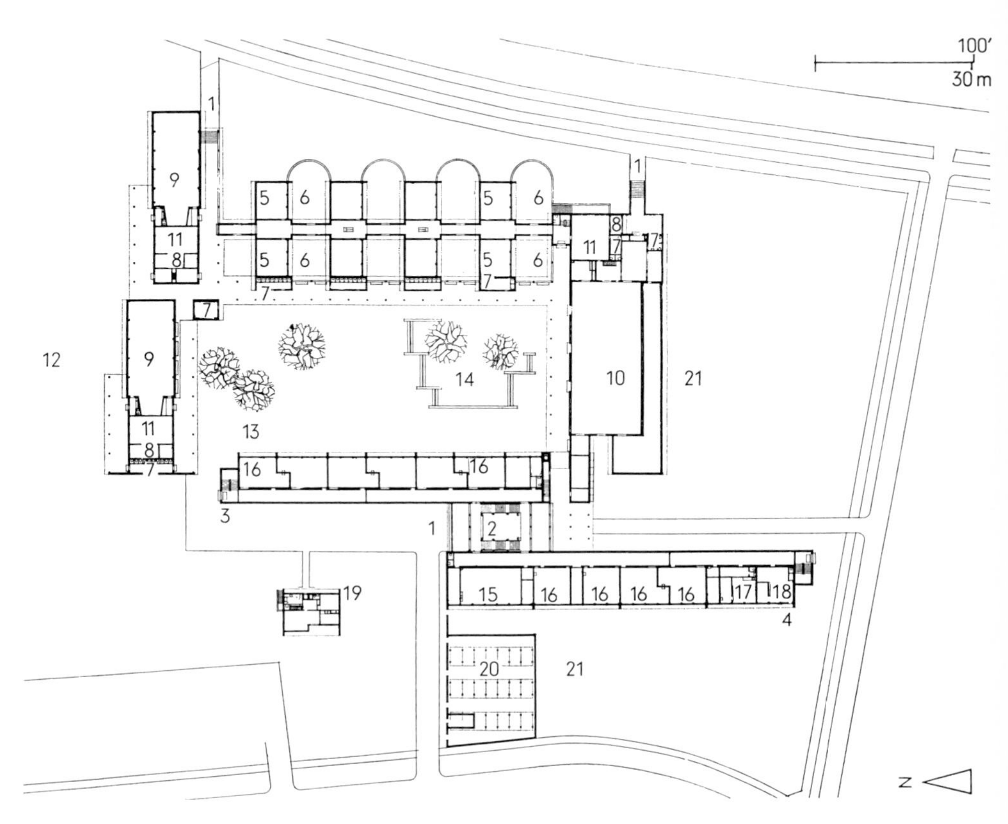

Arne Jacobsen

Munkegårds elementary school at Gentofte near Copenhagen, 1952–56
Munkegårds School is situated in a rather unattractive mixed residential area in one of Copenhagen's northern suburbs. With great success, Arne Jacobsen has tried to endow the school with special environmental values by placing the 24 standard classrooms in pairs in single-storey pavilions, each with its own specially designed garden court. A simple system of cross corridors connects the classrooms with assembly hall, masters' room and a two-storey wing with special classrooms. Gymnastics halls and bicycle sheds are placed as self-contained buildings within the playground. The walls are of yellow brick both outside and inside. All woodwork is painted white, the roofs are covered with aluminium. Arne Jacobsen was also responsible for designing the furniture and the flora of the different garden courts.

Munkegårds-Grundschule in Gentofte bei Kopenhagen, 1952–56
Die Munkegårdsschule steht in einem wenig ansprechenden, gemischten Wohnviertel in einem nördlichen Vorort von Kopenhagen. Arne Jacobsen ist es gelungen, der Anlage dadurch eine überdurchschnittliche Qualität zu verleihen, daß er die 24 Normalklassen paarweise in einstöckigen Pavillons unterbrachte und jeder Doppelklasse einen eigenen Gartenhof zuteilte. Ein einfaches System von querlaufenden Korridoren verbindet die Klassenzimmer mit der Aula, dem Lehrerzimmer und einem zweigeschossigen Fachklassentrakt. Turnhallen und Fahrradaufbewahrung begrenzen als selbständige Gebäude den großen Pausen- und Spielhof. Sowohl die Außenmauern als auch die Trennwände bestehen aus gelbem Backstein. Alle Holzteile sind weiß gestrichen, die Dächer sind aus Aluminium. Arne Jacobsen war auch für den Entwurf des Mobiliars und für die Bepflanzung der einzelnen Gartenhöfe verantwortlich.

1. Part of the group of school buildings, seen from the South. In the background the two-storey wing with special classrooms.
2. All the garden courts are different in respect of paving, flora and decoration which consists of castings of classic or modern sculptures.

1. Ein Teil der Schulanlage von Süden. Im Hintergrund der zweigeschossige Fachklassentrakt.
2. Die einzelnen Gartenhöfe unterscheiden sich durch verschiedene Pflasterung, Bepflanzung und Ausschmückung mit Abgüssen klassischer oder moderner Skulpturen.

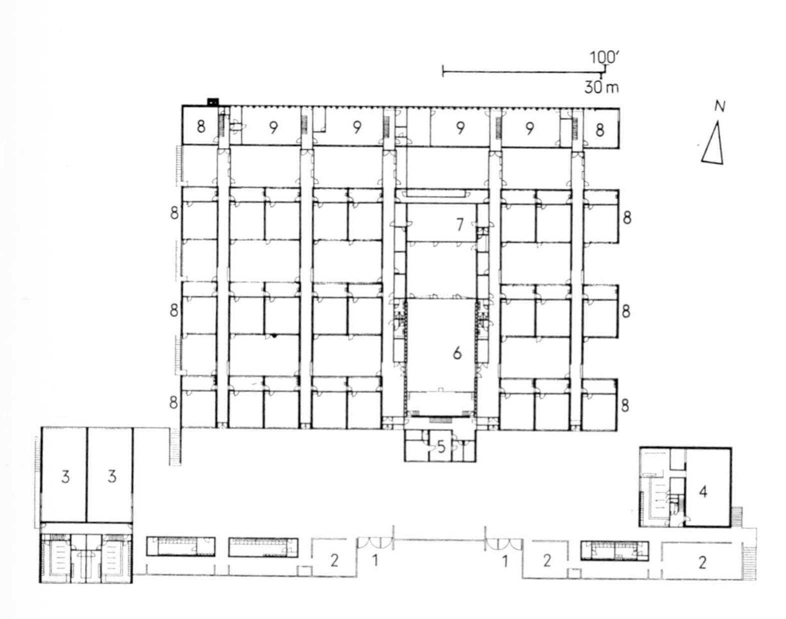

3. Pool of water in the garden court in front of the two-storey wing with the special classrooms.
4. Garden court with the assembly hall in the background. From the corridors, there is access and view to all the garden courts.
5. Plan. Key: 1 main entrance, 2 bicycle sheds, 3 gymnastics hall for older children, 4 gymnastics hall for younger children, 5 offices, 6 assembly hall, 7 teacher's room, 8 standard classrooms, 9 special classroom.

3. Wasserbecken in einem der Gartenhöfe vor dem zweigeschossigen Fachklassengebäude.
4. Gartenhof mit der Aula im Hintergrund. Auch von den Korridoren sind alle Gartenhöfe zugänglich und übersehbar.
5. Grundriß. Legende: 1 Haupteingang, 2 Fahrradständer, 3 Turnhalle für größere Schüler, 4 Turnhalle für Schüler der Unterstufe, 5 Verwaltungsräume, 6 Aula, 7 Lehrerzimmer, 8 Normalklassen, 9 Fachklassen.

6. The roof profile of the classroom provides good daylight conditions for all the desks in the room.
7. Each classroom is associated with an ante-room which can be used for group work.
8. The drinking water fountains on the playground are made of Swedish marble.

6. In den Klassenzimmern sorgen hochliegende Fensterbänder für gleichmäßig gute Belichtung und Belüftung.
7. Zu jedem Klassenzimmer gehört ein Vorraum, der für Gruppenarbeit benutzt werden kann.
8. Die Trinkbrunnen des Pausen- und Spielhofs bestehen aus schwedischem Marmor.

9. The assembly hall, seen from the garden court in front of it. The light fittings of the assembly hall are placed in recesses of the brick side walls; these recesses also serve an acoustic purpose.
10. East side of caretaker's and headmaster's houses.

9. Die Aula vom davorliegenden Gartenhof aus. Die Beleuchtungskörper sind in Vertiefungen der Seitenwände untergebracht, die auch zur akustischen Dämpfung beitragen.
10. Die Ostseite der Hausmeister- und Direktorwohnungen.

1. Standard classroom wing seen from the East, with the low section for infants and the steep hoods of the staircases, each of which provides access to four classrooms.

1. Ansicht des Normalklassenflügels von Osten, mit dem eingeschossigen Trakt der Unterstufe links und den steilen Hauben über den Treppenhäusern, die je vier Klassenzimmer erschließen.

F.C. Lund + Hans Chr. Hansen

Hanssted elementary school at Vigerslev near Copenhagen, 1954–58
The school is situated on a site embellished with fine old trees. In the vicinity of the southern boundary are a low wing with five classrooms for infants and a two-storey wing with 16 standard classrooms forming groups of four around a joint staircase and cloakroom group. Special classrooms and gymnastics hall are placed in a two-storey wing parallel to the main road. Staircase and bearing cross-walls are of yellow brick. Otherwise, the outer walls are clad with asbestos cement fixed by wooden battens. Roofing of asbestos cement.

Hanssted-Grundschule in Vigerslev bei Kopenhagen, 1954–58
Die Schule wurde auf einem Gelände mit schönen alten Bäumen errichtet. An seinem Südrand steht ein eingeschossiges Gebäude mit fünf Klassenzimmern für die Unterstufe sowie ein zweigeschossiger Trakt mit 16 Normalklassenzimmern, die in Gruppen von je vier an eine gemeinsame Treppen- und Garderobenanlage angeschlossen sind. Fachklassen und Turnhalle liegen in einem zweigeschossigen Flügel, der mit der Hauptstraße parallel läuft. Treppenhäuser und tragende Querwände wurden aus gelbem Backstein gemauert. Im übrigen sind die Außenwände mit Eternittafeln verschalt, die von Holzleisten gehalten werden. Die Dächer bestehen ebenfalls aus Eternit.

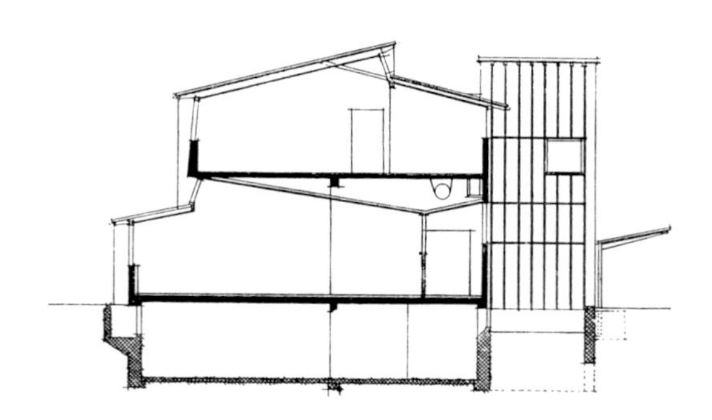

2. The playground is situated in a parklike area to the North of the standard classroom wing.
3. The roof profile of the standard classroom provides good daylight conditions for desks both near the window and away from it.
4. Cross-section of South wing, 1:300.
5. Ground floor plan. Key: 1 standard classrooms, 2 special classrooms.
6. A view along the special classroom wing from the outside stairs leading to the gymnastic hall.
7. Special classroom wing seen from South-East, with the external access to the gymnastics hall on the first floor. The first floor wall has a cladding of asbestos cement.

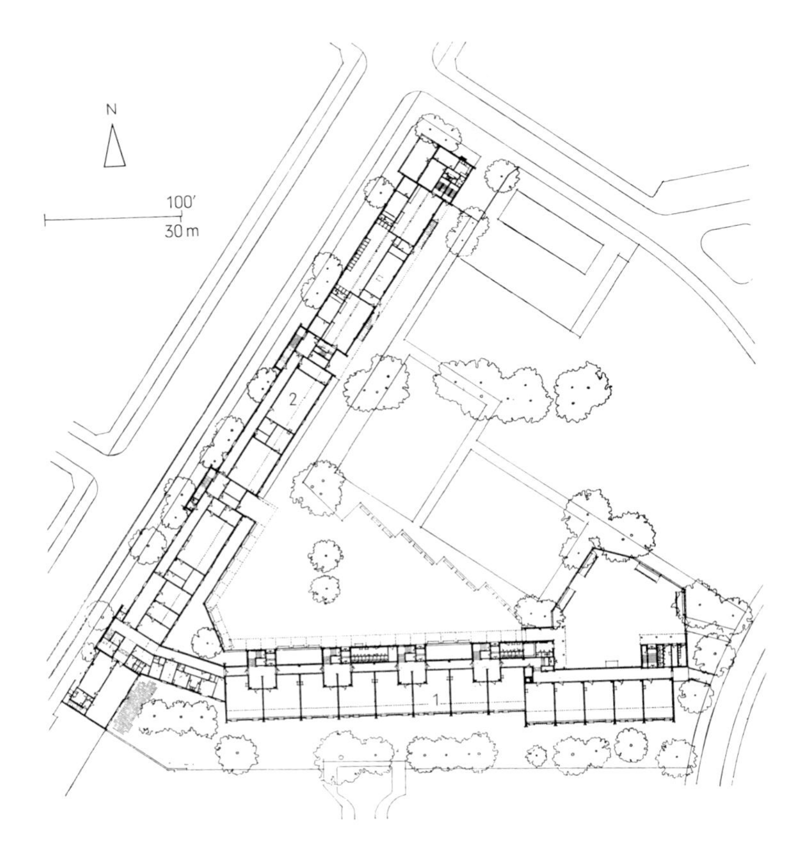

2. Der Pausenhof liegt in einem parkartigen Gelände auf der Nordseite des Normalklassenflügels.
3. Das Dach der Normalklassen ist so ausgestaltet, daß nicht nur die Plätze in der Nähe des Fensters, sondern auch die entfernteren Arbeitsplätze gut belichtet sind.
4. Querschnitt durch den Südflügel, 1:300.
5. Grundriß des Erdgeschosses. Legende: 1 Normalklassen, 2 Fachklassen.
6. Ein Längsblick am Fachklassengebäude entlang, von der außenliegenden Galerie der Turnhalle aus.
7. Der Fachklassenflügel von Südosten gesehen, mit dem außenliegenden Zugang zur Turnhalle im Obergeschoß, dessen Außenwand mit Eternittafeln verschalt ist.

Gehrdt Bornebusch, Max Brüel, Henning Larsen, Jørgen Selchau

Vangebo elementary school at Søllerød near Copenhagen, 1957–60
Vangebo School is situated to the North of Copenhagen in an area rich in woods and lakes, and the school itself borders on the South side of a wood protected by the nature preservation acts. The basic idea of the scheme was to assign, to each of the 24 standard classrooms, a protected garden and to give the entire school environment a robust yet at the same time congenial character. Gymnastics halls and dwellings are placed along the access road whilst the special classrooms on the North side are placed in short buildings with central corridors, separated from each other by enclosed courtyards. All the outer walls are of yellow brick. The woodwork is dark stained or painted with a deep red glazed colour.

Vangebo-Grundschule in Søllerød bei Kopenhagen, 1957–60
Die Vangeboschule liegt in einer wald- und seereichen Landgemeinde im Norden von Kopenhagen und grenzt im Süden an einen unter Naturschutz stehenden Wald an. Der Entwurf der Anlage war von dem Gedanken bestimmt, jedes der 24 Normalklassenzimmer mit einem geschützten Gartenhof zu verbinden, außerdem wurde versucht, der Schule einen zugleich robusten und freundlichen Charakter zu geben. Die Turnhallen und Wohnungen liegen an der Zufahrtsstraße, während die Fachklassen auf der Nordseite in kurzen Gebäuden mit Mittelkorridoren untergebracht sind, die durch ringsum eingeschlossene Höfe voneinander getrennt werden. Alle Außenwände bestehen aus gelbem Backstein. Das Holz ist dunkel imprägniert oder mit tiefroter Glasurfarbe gestrichen.

1. Facing the access road are gymnastics halls with their high-level windows.
2. Pergola at the playground, with a glimpse, on the left, into one of the garden courts of the standard classroom building.

1. An der Zufahrtsstraße die Turnhallen mit ihren hochliegenden Fenstern.
2. Pergola am Pausen- und Spielplatz. Links ein Einblick in einen der Gartenhöfe, die zu den Normalklassen gehören.

3. Metalled roads between the pavilions of the standard classrooms where the high windows provide good sun and daylight conditions despite the comparatively close spacing of the buildings.
4. The garden courts between the standard classrooms have a luxuriant character.

3. Verbindungsweg zwischen den Pavillons mit den Normalklassenzimmern. Durch die hohen Fenster erhalten die Klassenräume trotz der verhältnismäßig dichten Bebauung genügend Sonne und Tageslicht.
4. Die Gartenhöfe zwischen den Normalklassenpavillons machen einen intimen Eindruck.

5. Floor plan. Key: 1 administrative offices, 2 school clinic, 3 special classrooms, 4 master's room, 5 vestibule, 6 main corridor, 7 classroom, 8 auxiliary classroom, 9 group room, 10 toilets, 11 gymnastics hall, 12 changing rooms, 13 playground, 14 caretaker's dwelling, 15 headmaster's dwelling, 16 sports ground, 17 entrance, 18 bicycle ramp.

5. Grundriß. Legende: 1 Verwaltung, 2 Schulklinik, 3 Fachklassen, 4 Lehrerzimmer, 5 Vorhalle, 6 Hauptkorridor, 7 Klassenzimmer, 8 Zusätzlicher Unterrichtsraum, 9 Gruppenraum, 10 Toiletten, 11 Turnhalle, 12 Umkleideräume, 13 Pausen- und Spielfläche, 14 Wohnung des Hausmeisters, 15 Wohnung des Direktors, 16 Sportplatz, 17 Eingang, 18 Rampe für Radfahrer.

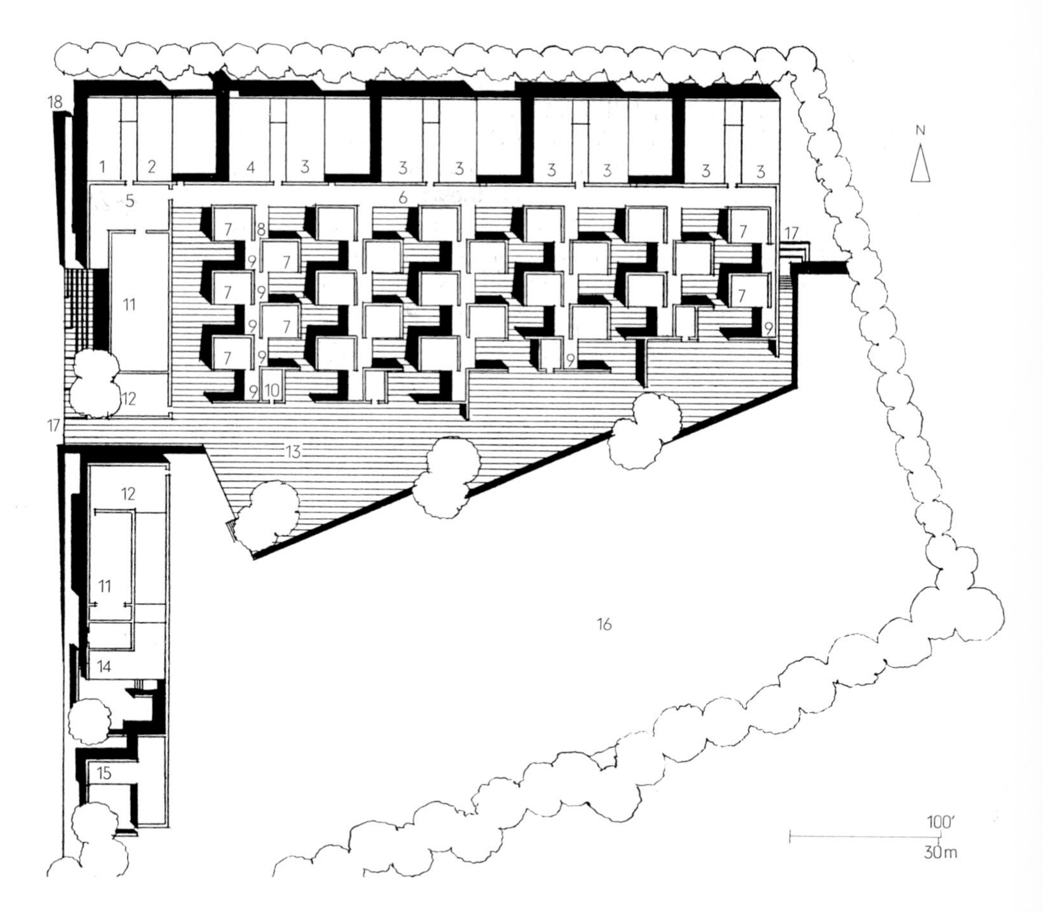

6. The wide corridor between the standard and special classrooms sections.
7. The garden courts provide good facilities for outdoor group work.
8. The classroom walls are of yellow brick whilst the wooden covering of the ceiling is painted in a dark red glazed colour.

6. Der breite Korridor zwischen den Normalklassen- und Fachklassenabteilungen.
7. Die Gartenhöfe bieten gute Möglichkeiten für die Gruppenarbeit im Freien.
8. Die Wände der Klassenzimmer bestehen aus gelbem Backstein, die Holzverschalung der Decke ist mit dunkelroter Naturfarbe angestrichen.

Arne Gravers + Johan Richter

Grenå Grammar School at Grenå, Jutland, 1964

This school, designed for pupils ranging from 12 to 19 years of age, is based on a special classroom principle pure and simple. They are no standard classrooms, but each special classroom is designed and equipped in relation to the special requirements dictated by each subject. That is why a large joint cloakroom has been provided in the centre of the building where the pupils can leave their books, satchels, and luncheon packets and where there is easy access both to the assembly hall and to all the classrooms. The classrooms face outwards towards broad terraces which provide facilities for outdoor teaching and where the pupils can stay during the breaks. School and terraces are placed on a bastion-like platform protected by walls and raised about 3 ft. above ground. The buildings are erected in red brick.

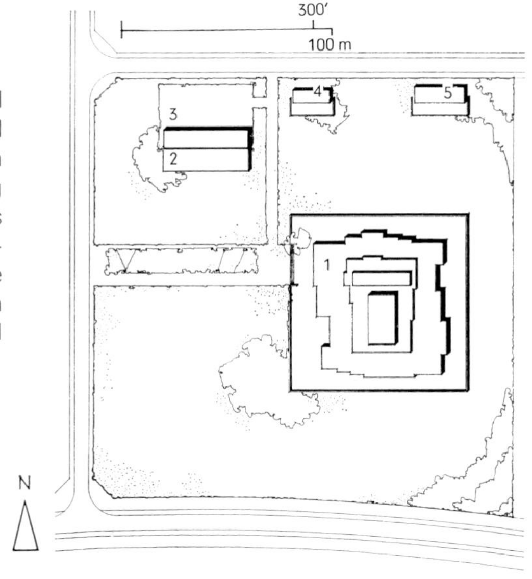

4. In front of the classrooms are broad terraces with outdoor benches. The widely overhung roof is covered with dark painted boards.

4. Vor den Klassenzimmern liegen breite Terrassen mit Freisitzplätzen. Das auskragende Dach ist mit dunkel gestrichenen Brettern verschalt.

◁ 1. Site plan. Key: 1 school building, 2 gymnastics hall, 3 car park, 4 caretaker, 5 headmaster.
2. Grenå Grammar School, seen from the West.
3. The school, here seen from South-West, is situated on a low bastion surrounded by open flat ground overgrown with heather and studded with low fir trees.

◁ 1. Lageplan. Legende: 1 Schulgebäude, 2 Turnhalle, 3 Parkplatz, 4 Wohnung des Hausmeisters, 5 Wohnung des Direktors.
2. Ansicht von Westen.
3. Die hier von Südwesten gezeigte Schule steht auf einer niedrigen Plattform mitten in einem offenen, flachen, mit Heidekraut und Zwergkiefern bewachsenen Gelände.

Arne Gravers + Johan Richter

Gymnasium in Grenå in Jütland, 1964

Dieses Gymnasium für Schüler von 12 bis 19 Jahren ist durchweg nach dem Fachklassenprinzip angeordnet. Es gibt keine Normalklassenzimmer; dafür ist jeder Fachklassenraum so gestaltet und ausgestattet, wie es das betreffende Sonderfach erfordert. Aus diesem Grunde wurde im Zentrum des Gebäudes eine große Gemeinschaftsgarderobe für die Mäntel und Taschen der Schüler vorgesehen, von wo aus sowohl die Aula als auch alle Unterrichtsräume leicht erreichbar sind. Den Klassenzimmern sind nach außen breite Terrassen vorgelagert, die die Möglichkeit für den Unterricht im Freien bieten und als Pausenplatz dienen. Schule und Terrassen liegen auf einer von niedrigen Mauern umgebenen, bastionartigen Plattform, die ungefähr 1 m über das Gelände angehoben ist. Die ganze Anlage wurde in rotem Backstein errichtet.

5. The special classrooms are echeloned towards the surrounding terraces, providing good facilities for protected outdoor spaces for group teaching.
6. The assembly hall, here seen from the vestibule, with its stage and its high-level side lighting is placed in the centre of the building. The walls of the assembly hall are in stark blue, the ceiling in ochre yellow.
7. Section and ground floor plan. Key: 1 entrance, 2 assistant headmaster, 3 headmaster, 4 medical officer, 5 toilets, 6 senior common room, 7 kitchen, 8 main cloakroom, 9 vestibule, 10 sculpture, 11 pool of water, 12 main hall (also serving as dining hall), 13 stage. Rooms without numbers are special classrooms for specific subjects.
8. The pool of water separates the vestibule from the assembly hall.

5. Die Klassenräume springen untereinander gestaffelt auf die umlaufenden Terrassen vor, so daß sich geschützte Freisitzplätze für den Gruppenunterricht ergeben.
6. Die hier von der Vorhalle aus gezeigte Aula mit Bühne liegt in der Mitte der Anlage und ist mit hoch gelegenen Seitenfenstern versehen. Die Wände der Aula sind in einem kräftigen Blau gehalten, die Decke in Ocker.
7. Schnitt und Grundriß des Erdgeschosses. Legende: 1 Eingang, 2 Stellvertretender Direktor, 3 Direktor, 4 Schularzt, 5 Toiletten, 6 Gemeinschaftsraum, 7 Küche, 8 Hauptgarderobe, 9 Vorhalle, 10 Skulptur, 11 Wasserbecken, 12 Aula (auch als Speisesaal benutzt), 13 Bühne. Die nicht numerierten Räume sind Fachklassenzimmer.
8. Das Wasserbecken trennt die Vorhalle von der Aula.

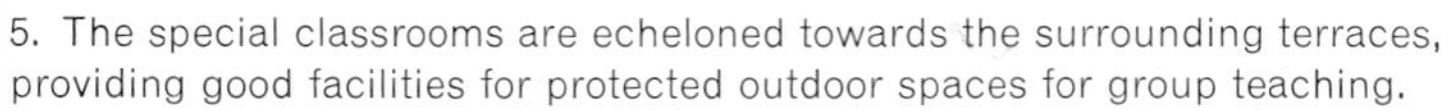

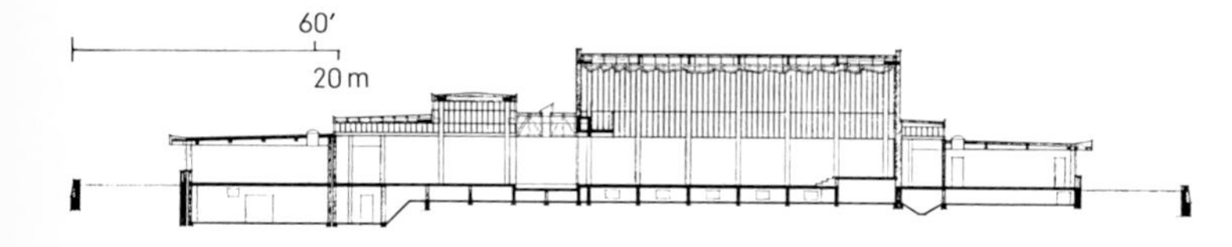

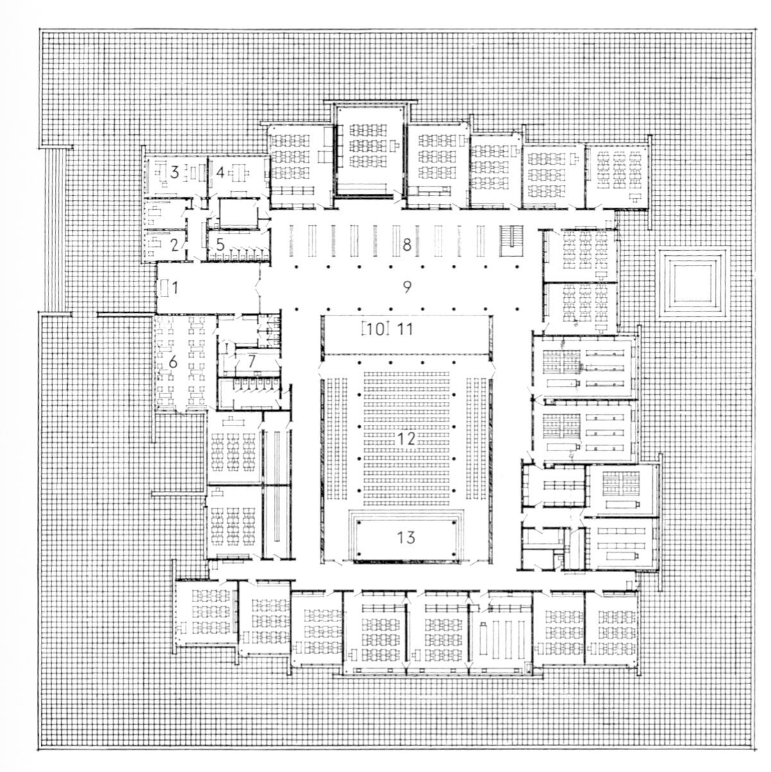

1. The school seen from the sports ground, with the special classroom wing (left), the gymnastics halls and the indoor swimming pool. All the walls are erected in yellow brick, the roofing is of white asbestos cement.
2. Cross-section and longitudinal section of standard classroom building.

1. Die Schule von den Sportplätzen im Süden aus gesehen, mit dem Fachklassengebäude (links), den beiden Turnhallen und der Schwimmhalle. Alle Mauern sind aus gelbem Backstein, die Dächer mit weißem Eternit abgedeckt.
2. Querschnitt und Längsschnitt durch ein Normalklassengebäude.

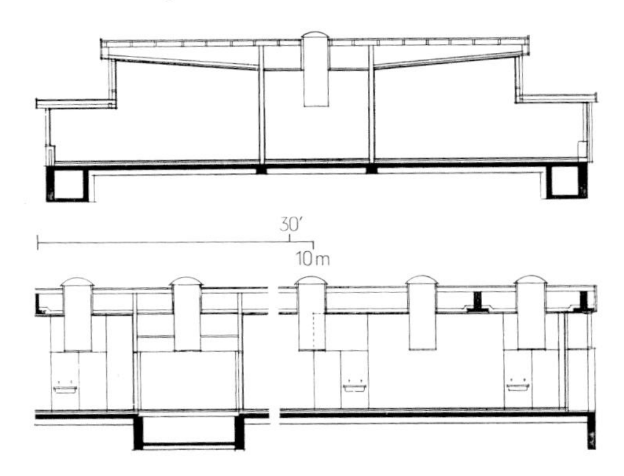

Arne Jacobsen

Nyager elementary school at Rødovre, Copenhagen, 1965
In a limited competition Arne Jacobsen was awarded the First Prize for a functional, clearly arranged plan. On each side of a central corridor axis are the east and west orientated standard classrooms with short corridors, facing the garden courts which are used jointly by six or seven classrooms. In a building near the western edge of the site are all the special classrooms, surrounding a wide central corridor which serves as a foyer. The gymnastics halls as well as an indoor swimming pool are associated with the sports ground on the south side. A dominating architectural feature is provided by the overhung concrete roofs of the classroom buildings which permitted the adoption of an angular cross-section for the window walls, resulting in differentiated lighting conditions for the classrooms themselves.

Nyager-Grundschule in Rødovre, Kopenhagen, 1965
In einem begrenzten Wettbewerb wurde Arne Jacobsen der erste Preis für einen funktionell klar disponierten Entwurf zugeteilt. Auf jeder Seite einer zentralen Korridoranlage liegen die nach Osten und Westen orientierten Normalklassenzimmer. Sie werden durch kurze Mittelkorridore erschlossen und öffnen sich auf Gartenhöfe, die von jeweils sechs oder sieben Klassen gemeinsam benutzt werden. In einem langgestreckten Baukörper am Westrand des Grundstücks sind alle Fachklassenzimmer an einem breiten Mittelkorridor aufgereiht, der mit seinen Schaukästen eine Art Foyer bildet. Die Turnhallen und eine Schwimmhalle wurden auf die Südseite gelegt, wo sie unmittelbar mit den anschließenden Sportplätzen verbunden sind. Charakteristisches architektonisches Merkmal der ganzen Anlage sind die auskragenden Dächer und die abgewinkelten Fensterfronten, die für eine differenzierte Belichtung der Klassenräume sorgen.

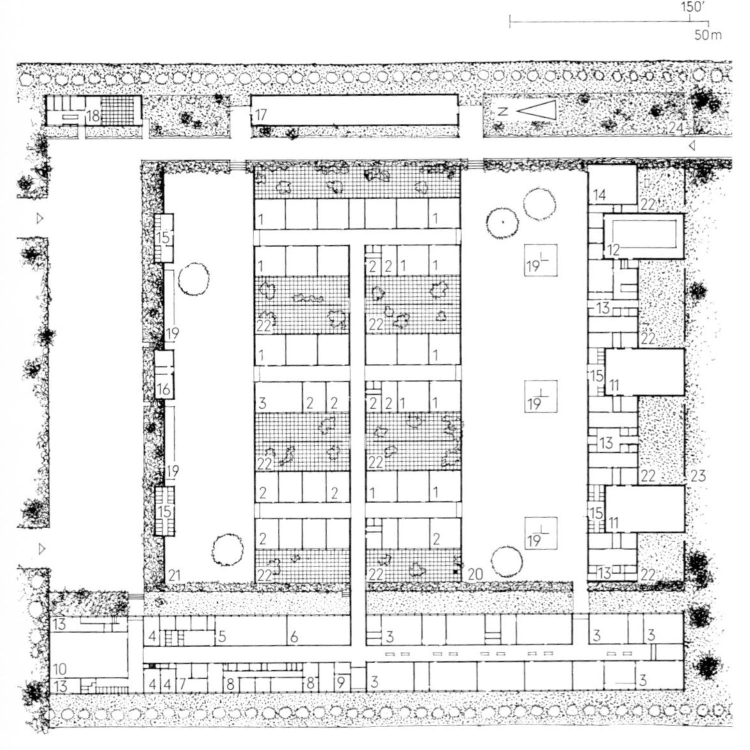

3. The playground for older children has a covered shelter of steel and glass. The wind protection walls are of concrete, painted yellow.
4. Ground floor plan. Key: 1 standard classroom, 2 special classroom, 3 subject classroom, 4 administration, 5 masters' room, 6 library, 7 medical officer, 8 dental officer, 9 psychologist, 10 playhall for infants, 11 gymnastics hall, 12 indoor swimming pool, 13 changing rooms, 14 heating plant, 15 toilets, 16 implements, 17 bicycle sheds, 18 caretaker's dwelling, 19 shelter, 20 playground for older children, 21 playground for infants, 22 garden court, 23 sports ground, 24 botanical garden.

3. Auf dem Pausen- und Spielhof für größere Kinder stehen Schutzdächer aus Stahl und Glas, mit halbhohen Schirmwänden aus gelb gestrichenem Beton.
4. Grundriß des Erdgeschosses. Legende: 1 Normalklasse, 2 Spezialklasse, 3 Fachklasse, 4 Verwaltung, 5 Lehrerzimmer, 6 Bibliothek, 7 Schularzt, 8 Schulzahnarzt, 9 Schulpsychologe, 10 Unterstufen-Spielsaal, 11 Turnhalle, 12 Schwimmhalle, 13 Umkleideräume, 14 Heizungsanlage, 15 Toiletten, 16 Geräte, 17 Fahrräder, 18 Wohnung des Hausmeisters, 19 Schutzdach, 20 Pausenhof und Spielplatz für größere Kinder, 21 Pausenhof und Spielplatz Unterstufe, 22 Gartenhof, 23 Sportplätze, 24 Schulgarten.

5. The different flora of the garden courts was chosen by Arne Jacobsen himself. The screen walls which prevent a direct view from one classroom into the one opposite, are decorated with reliefs.
6. The angular cross-section of the window walls ensures good lighting conditions even in the rear of the classroom.
7. Central corridor in the special classroom wing, with showcases where some of the school's collections are permanently displayed.

5. Die Bepflanzung der Gartenhöfe wurde von Arne Jacobsen selbst entworfen. Die Schirmwände, die einen Einblick von den gegenüberliegenden Klassenzimmern aus verhindern, sind zum Teil mit Reliefs geschmückt.
6. Die abgewinkelten Fensterwände mit dem hochliegenden Fensterband schaffen auch im hinteren Teil der Klassenräume gute Lichtverhältnisse.
7. Der Mittelkorridor des Fachklassengebäudes mit den Schaukästen, in denen ein Teil der Schulsammlungen dauernd ausgestellt ist.

Nils Andersen + Salli Besiakov

Køge Grammar School, Køge, Zealand, 1965
The design of the school, obtained as the result of a public architectural competition, follows the special classroom principle; there are therefore no standard classrooms. Much attention has been paid to the congenial environment of the premises used during the breaks: a large, centrally placed vestibule is provided which also comprises the dining areas in close contact with the outdoor terraces. Assembly hall and music room form the core, obtaining daylight through high-level windows above the surrounding roofs. Radiating from the foyer are the four classroom wings. Any monotony of the corridors has been avoided by repeated changes in their width as well as in daylight access conditions.With its yellow brick walls and different roof heights, the group of buildings rises above the flat ground like a well-composed sculpture.

Gymnasium in Køge auf der Insel Seeland, 1965
Die Schule, deren Entwurf aus einem offenen Wettbewerb stammt, ist nach dem Fachklassenprinzip gebaut, unter Verzicht auf Normalklassenzimmer. Mit Erfolg wurde großer Wert darauf gelegt, für die Pausen in einer großen zentralen Halle eine freundliche Atmosphäre zu schaffen; aus diesem Grund ist auch der Eßbereich in unmittelbarer Nähe der Außenterrassen untergebracht. Aula und Musiksaal bilden das Zentrum und sind durch hoch über den anschließenden Dächern gelegene Fenster belichtet. Von der Halle gehen windmühlenförmig vier Seitenflügel mit Klassenzimmern aus. Bei den Korridoren wurde jede Einförmigkeit durch mehrfachen Wechsel der Gangbreite und der Belichtungsverhältnisse vermieden. Mit ihren gelben Backsteinmauern und den verschiedenen Dachhöhen erhebt sich die Anlage über dem flachen Gelände wie eine gut komponierte Skulptur.

1. School yard and school buildings seen from the South, with the dining area and the large windows of the vestibule.

1. Schulhof und Schulgebäude von Süden, mit den großen Fensterflächen des Eßbereichs und der Vorhalle.

2. Ground floor plan. Key: 1 terrace, 2 lily pond, 3 vestibule, 4 dining area, 5 assembly hall, 6 music room, 7 stage, 8 changing room, 9 special classroom, 10 library, 11 collection and stores, 12 lecture rooms, 13 laboratories, 14 medical officer, 15 master's room, 16 inspector, 17 headmaster, 18 milkroom, 19 gymnastics hall, 20 bathrooms, 21 drying room, 22 bicycle stores, 23 heating plant, 24 caretaker.
3. The school buildings seen from South-East. Assembly hall and music room rise above the other buildings.

2. Grundriß des Erdgeschosses. Legende: 1 Terrasse, 2 Wasserbecken, 3 Vorhalle, 4 Eßbereich, 5 Aula, 6 Musiksaal, 7 Bühne, 8 Umkleideräume, 9 Fachklassenräume, 10 Bibliothek, 11 Sammlungen, 12 Lehrsäle, 13 Laboratorien, 14 Schularzt, 15 Lehrerzimmer, 16 Verwaltung, 17 Direktor, 18 Milchausgabe, 19 Turnhallen, 20 Duschräume, 21 Trockenraum, 22 Abstellraum für Fahrräder, 23 Heizzentrale, 24 Hausmeister.
3. Ansicht von Südosten. Aula und Musiksaal überragen die übrigen Gebäude.

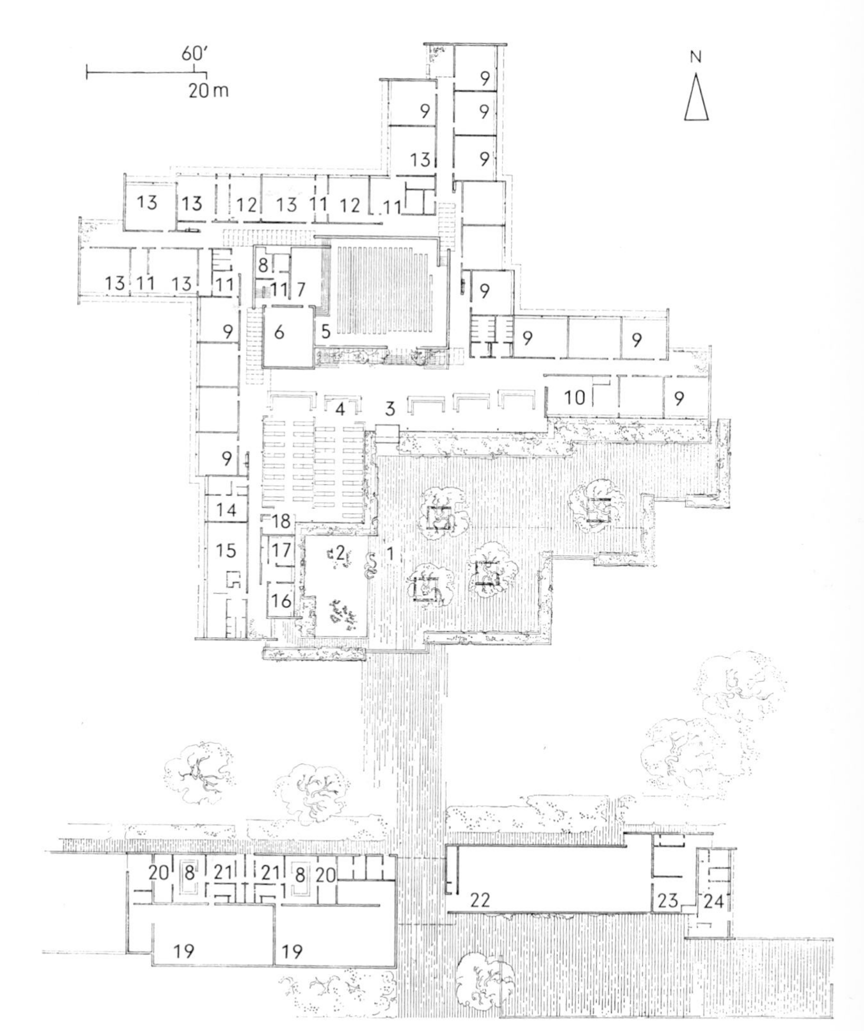

4. A pool of water on the forecourt terrace is immediately adjacent to the dining area windows. The main entrance of the school is on the right.
5. Benches, protected by low screen walls, are provided in the vestibule.
6. The access rooms to the different classrooms have varying width and daylight conditions.

4. Ein Wasserbecken auf der Terrasse schließt unmittelbar an die Fensterwand des Eßbereichs an. Rechts dahinter der Haupteingang.
5. Von niedrigen Mauern umgebene Sitznischen in der Vorhalle.
6. Die Korridore der einzelnen Klassenzimmerflügel haben wechselnde Breiten und Belichtungsverhältnisse.

7. The rear part of the vestibule receives additional daylight through a skylight at the stairs leading to the assembly hall. Floors and stairs are covered with ceramic tiles.

7. Der rückwärtige Teil der Vorhalle erhält durch ein Oberlicht am Treppeneingang der Aula zusätzliches Tageslicht. Fußböden und Treppen sind mit keramischen Fliesen belegt.

Henning Larsen

Klostermarken elementary school at Roskilde, Zealand, 1965
The design for this school is the result of a public architectural competition which took place in 1960. The school is erected on high ground offering a view over Roskilde Fjord and large parts of the town, and falling towards north-west. The layout plan has been so arranged that the buildings are adapted to the sloping ground by a continuous, terraced concourse which is, at its northern end, extended into a dining area facing an outdoor terrace. The concourse separates the standard classrooms, which are placed in parallel single-storey wings on the South side, from the special classrooms which are separated from each other by internal courtyards. Close to the main entrance is an assembly hall and, at the northern end near the sports ground, an indoor swimming pool. The building is erected in reinforced concrete and has been, to a large extent, assembled from precast concrete units.

Klostermarken-Grundschule in Roskilde auf der Insel Seeland, 1965
Der Entwurf für diese Schule ist das Ergebnis eines offenen Wettbewerbs, der 1960 stattfand. Das hochliegende Grundstück bietet einen Ausblick über den Roskilde-Fjord sowie über große Teile der Stadt und der Hügellandschaft im Nordwesten. Baulich folgt die Anlage dem ansteigenden Gelände mit einer in Nord-Südrichtung durchgehenden, terrassenförmig abgetreppten Wandelhalle, die sich nach Norden zu einem Eßbereich mit davorliegender Freiluftterrasse erweitert. Die Wandelhalle trennt die Normalklassenzimmer, die in parallelen, nach Süden orientierten, eingeschossigen Flügeln untergebracht sind, von den Fachklassenräumen in den ostwärts liegenden Anbauten, die untereinander ebenfalls durch Innenhöfe getrennt sind. Am Haupteingang liegt eine Aula und am Nordende in der Nähe der Sportplätze eine Schwimmhalle. Die ganze Anlage ist eine reine Stahlbetonkonstruktion und wurde zu einem großen Teil aus vorgefertigten Betonelementen montiert.

1. On the north side, the school ends in a broad terrace. A concrete wall separates the terrace from the sports ground.

1. Auf der Nordseite ist die Schule durch eine breite Terrasse abgeschlossen. Terrasse und Sportplätze werden durch eine Betonmauer voneinander getrennt.

2. Section and plan. Key: 1 standard classroom, 2 auxiliary classroom, 3 needlework, 4 handicraft, 5 school kitchen, 6 special classrooms, 7 reading room, 8 lending room, 9 medical officer, clinic, 10 administration, inspector, 11 master's room, 12 vestibule, 13 assembly hall, 14 music room.
3. The ground between the buildings is terraced with concrete platforms and stairs.
4. The terrace in front of the dining area serves as playground.

2. Schnitt und Grundriß. Legende: 1 Normalklassen, 2 Zusätzlicher Unterrichtsraum, 3 Handarbeiten, 4 Werkunterricht, 5 Schulküche, 6 Fachklassen, 7 Lesezimmer, 8 Leihbibliothek, 9 Schularzt und Klinik, 10 Verwaltung und Schuldirektor, 11 Lehrerzimmer, 12 Vorhalle, 13 Aula, 14 Musiksaal.
3. Zwischen den Gebäuden ist das Gelände durch Betonterrassen und Treppen dem Gefälle angepaßt.
4. Die Terrasse auf der Nordseite dient als Pausenhof und Spielplatz.

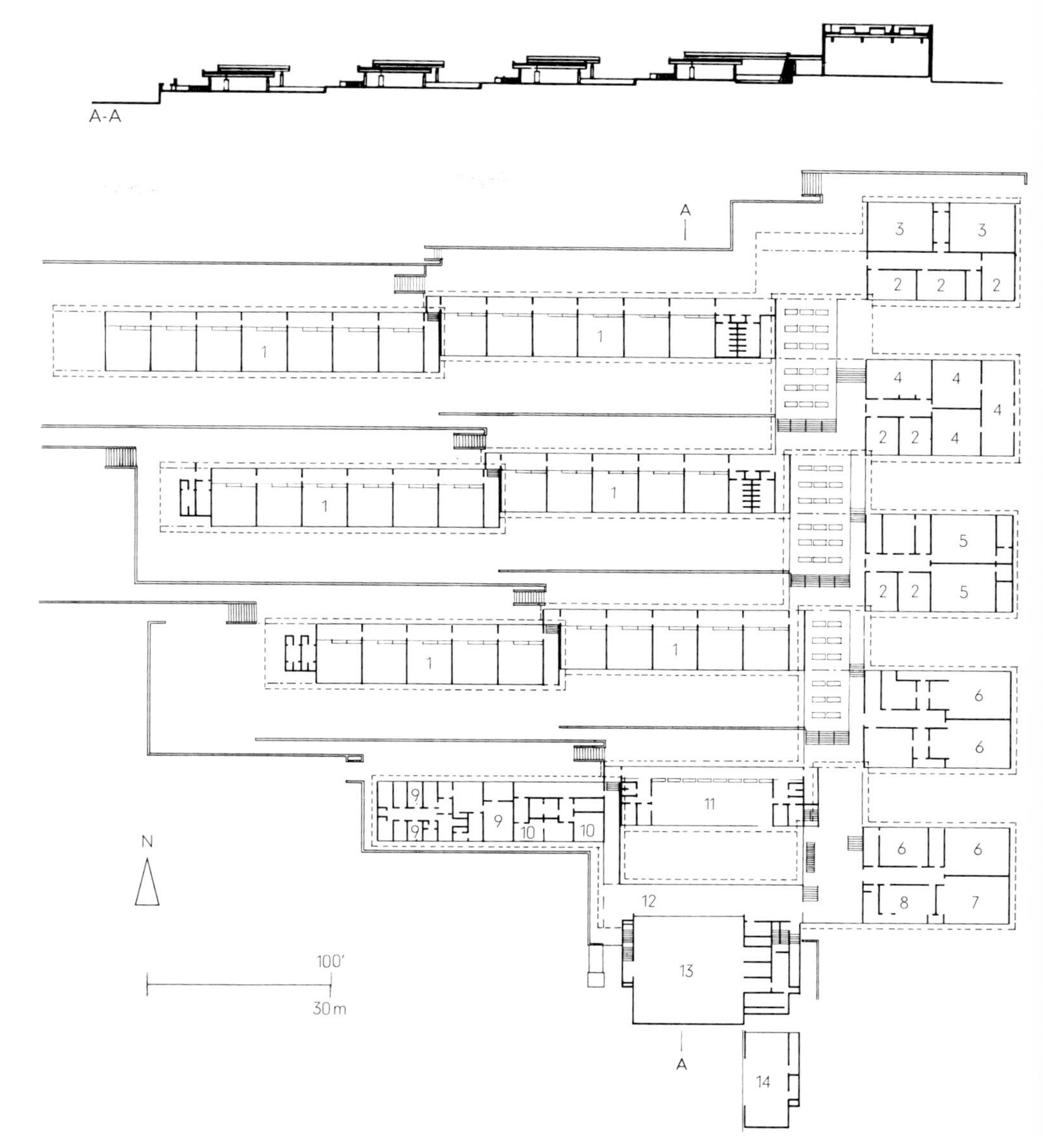

5. Extension at the north end of the concourse, with the dining area. The reinforced concrete beams and girders are left untreated, both inside and outside.
6. The indoor swimming pool opens up towards a solarium which was not yet ready when the photograph was taken.
7. All the classrooms face south. The party walls between the classrooms are of brick, and painted.

5. Nach Norden zu erweitert sich der Hauptkorridor zu einer Halle mit Eßbereich. Die Stahlbetonbalken und -stützen sind in den Innenräumen und am Außenbau unbehandelt gelassen.
6. Die Schwimmhalle öffnet sich auf ein Sonnenbad, das zum Zeitpunkt der Aufnahme noch nicht fertiggestellt war.
7. Alle Klassenzimmer sind nach Süden orientiert. Die Trennwände zwischen den Klassenräumen bestehen aus Backstein und sind gestrichen.

1. Longitudinal section, 1 in 800.
2. Cross-section.
3. Top view.
4. Ground floor plan. Key: 1 dormitories, 2 lecture rooms, 3 dining room, 4 kitchen, 5 assembly hall, 6 common rooms, 7 garden court.

1. Längsschnitt 1:800.
2. Querschnitt.
3. Dachaufsicht.
4. Grundriß des Erdgeschosses. Legende: 1 Schlafräume, 2 Unterrichtsräume, 3 Speisesaal, 4 Küche, 5 Auditorium, 6 Aufenthaltsräume, 7 Gartenhof.

Jørn Utzon

Højstrup College at Elsinore, Zealand, Project, 1958

In a public architectural competition for an educational centre of the Trade Union Congress, Jørn Utzon was awarded the First Prizes for a project which is based on a platform raised above the ground. Vehicular traffic is relegated to the level below the platform whilst the school proper is placed above it. In the revised project all the teaching premises are placed on a single floor with a view over the beautiful park whilst the lounges and club rooms are facing an internal courtyard. All the dormitories are concentrated in a tower block on the North side of the ground. The school was planned to be constructed in reinforced concrete with a saddle roof covering the teaching room and lounges. The assembly room in the south-eastern corner is to be covered by a free dome structure. The project was abandoned in 1962.

Lehranstalt Højstrup in Helsingør auf der Insel Seeland, Entwurf 1958

In einem offenen Architektenwettbewerb für ein Ausbildungszentrum der Gewerkschaften wurde Jørn Utzon der erste Preis für ein Projekt zuerkannt, das eine kräftig vom Gelände abgehobene Plattform vorsah. Der gesamte Fahrverkehr sollte unter diese Plattform verlegt werden, auf der sich die Gebäude erheben. Bei der Umarbeitung des ersten Preises sind sämtliche Unterrichtsräume in einem einzigen Geschoß konzentriert und haben einen freien Ausblick über die parkartige Umgebung, während die Aufenthalts- und Klubräume einem Innenhof zugewandt sind. Alle Schlafräume sind in einem am Nordrande vorgesehenen Hochhaus untergebracht. Es war geplant, die Schule aus Stahlbeton mit einem Faltdach über den Unterrichts- und Aufenthaltsräumen zu errichten. Für das Auditorium in der Südostecke war eine frei geformte Schalenkonstruktion vorgesehen. Das Projekt wurde 1962 aufgegeben.

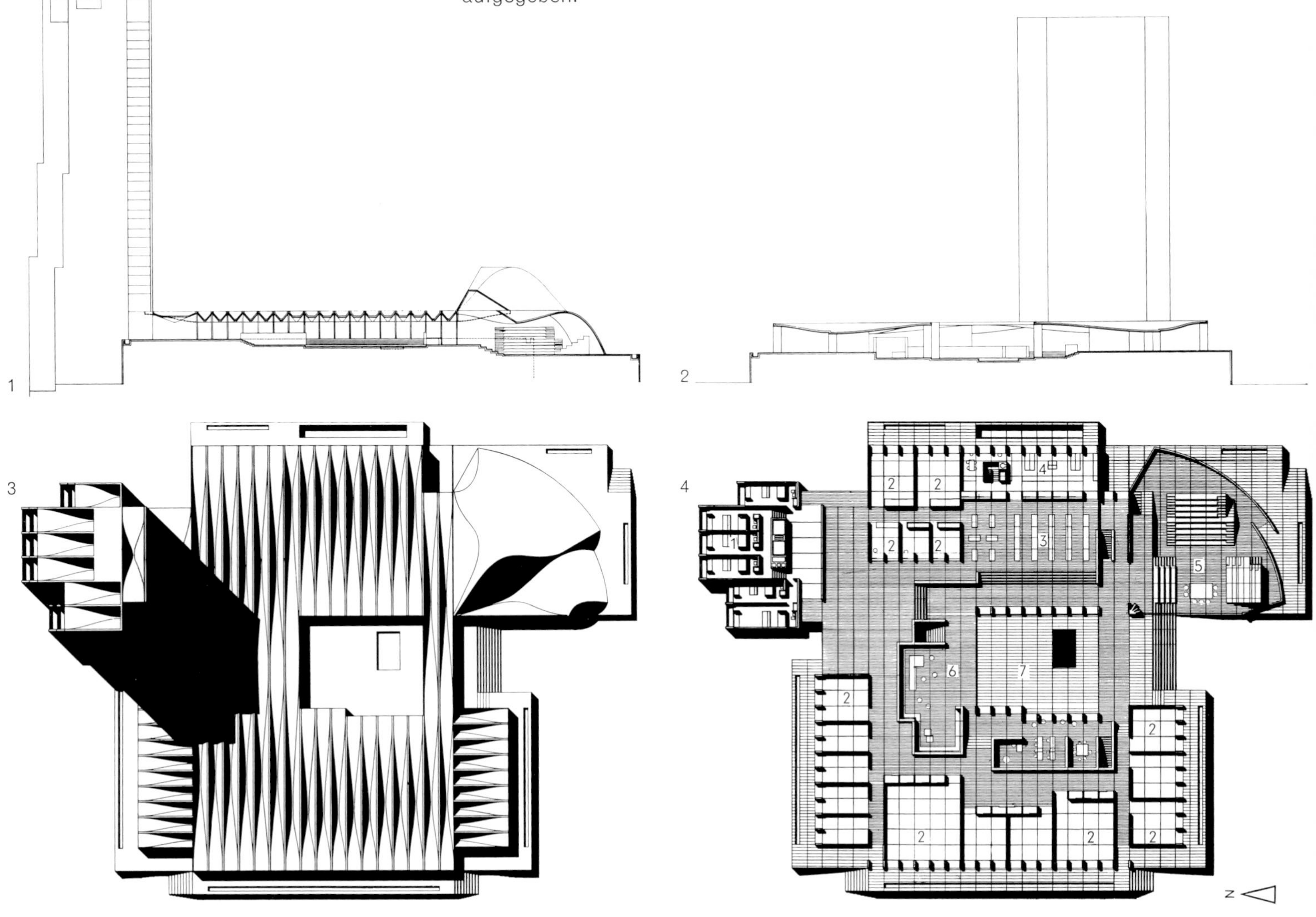

1. With its light aluminium cladding, the tower block with the dormitories forms a contrast to the seemingly heavy buildings of red brick.

1. Mit seiner leichten Aluminiumverkleidung bildet das Hochhaus für die Studenten einen Gegensatz zu den schweren roten Backsteinbauten.

Viggo Møller-Jensen + Tyge Arnfred

Herning College, Herning, Jutland, 1962
The area around the town of Herning is flat, and the tower block at the outskirts of the town, housing the College dormitories, forms a striking feature in the flat landscape. The tower block is in reinforced concrete with aluminium cladding. All the other buildings are single-storey houses grouped around internal courtyards which provide outdoor seats well protected against the blusterous climate. The low buildings are of red brick with dark-stained woodwork. The roof is covered with black asphalt roofing.

Hochschule in Herning, Jütland, 1962
Die Umgebung der Stadt Herning ist völlig eben, so daß ein Hochhaus am Stadtrand – wie der Neubau des Studentenhauses der Hochschule – auf das Stadtbild einen beherrschenden Einfluß hat. Das Hochhaus wurde aus Stahlbeton errichtet und mit Fassadenelementen aus Aluminium verkleidet. Die übrigen Gebäude sind eingeschossig um Innenhöfe herum gebaut, die bei dem stürmischen Klima geschützte Sitzplätze im Freien bieten. Die niedrigen Flügel bestehen aus rotem Backstein mit dunkel imprägniertem Holz, die Dächer sind mit schwarzer Dachpappe gedeckt.

2. Section and ground floor plan. Key: 1 courtyard, 2 garage and kitchen courtyard, 3 common room, 4 lecture rooms, 5 auditorium, 6 classroom wing, 7 inspector's dwelling, 8 dining room, 9 kitchen, 10 garages, 11 bicycle sheds, 12 female staff, 13 bathrooms, 14 teachers' lodgings, 15 gymnastics hall (not yet built).
3. The school building seen from the West, with the long classroom wing in front of the tower block and the auditorium on the extreme right.

2. Schnitt und Grundriß des Erdgeschosses. Legende: 1 Hof, 2 Garagen und Küchenhof, 3 Aufenthaltsraum, 4 Unterrichtsräume, 5 Hörsaal, 6 Lehrsaalgebäude, 7 Wohnung des Direktors, 8 Mensa, 9 Küche, 10 Garagen, 11 Fahrräder, 12 Wohnungen für weibliches Personal, 13 Baderäume, 14 Lehrerwohnungen, 15 Turnhalle (noch nicht gebaut).
3. Die Anlage von Westen gesehen, mit dem langen Flügel der Unterrichtsräume vor dem Hochhaus und dem Hörsaalgebäude ganz rechts.

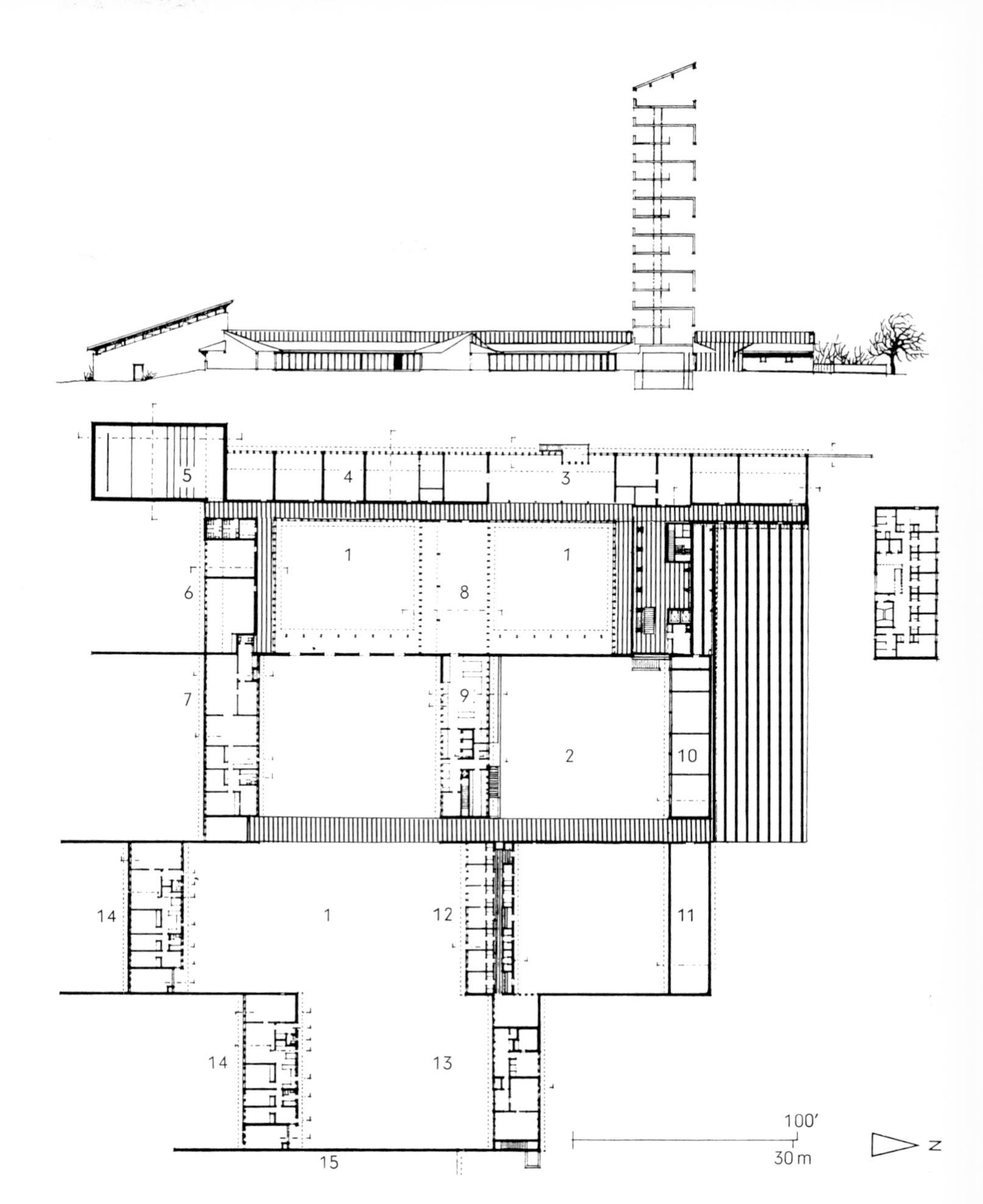

4. Both sides of the dining room face internal courtyards. The inclined roof provides additional sunlight from the South.
5. The auditorium is amphi-theatrically designed. The recesses in the brick walls are provided for acoustic reasons.
6. Students' common room, with lowered ceiling of redstained boards above the fireplace zone.
7. Students gathering around the fireplace in the common room.
8. The windows on the South side of the tower block are staggered in relation to each other in order to preserve the surface effect.

4. Die Mensa öffnet sich beiderseits auf Innenhöfe. Durch das schräge Dachprofil bringt ein hochliegendes Fensterband auf der Südseite zusätzlich Sonne in den Raum.
5. Im Hörsaal folgen die ansteigenden Bankreihen der Neigung des Pultdachs. Die Löcher in den Backsteinwänden sind aus akustischen Gründen vorgesehen.
6. Der Aufenthaltsraum der Studenten mit der abgehängten Rasterdecke aus rot imprägnierten Brettern über der Kaminzone.
7. Um den Kamin im Aufenthaltsraum versammelte Studenten.
8. Die Fenster auf der Südseite des Hochhauses sind gegeneinander verschoben, um den flächigen Charakter beizubehalten.

1. The college seen from North-East, with the shell-shaped valley in the foreground.

1. Ansicht von Nordosten, mit der muschelförmigen Talmulde im Vordergrund.

Karen + Ebbe Clemmensen

Skive Training College, Skive, Jutland, 1957–59
The architects were entrusted with the design of this College as a result of a public competition in 1955. The undulating high ground is attractively utilised by adapting the long, staggered classroom wing to the shell-shaped valley below. The large halls of the training college – gymnastics halls and assembly hall – are grouped around a paved garden court together with the administrative offices and the vestibule. The classroom wing is a reinforced concrete framework structure with prefabricated infilling panels. The roofs are covered with corrugated asbestos cement.

Lehrerseminar in Skive, Jütland, 1957–59
Den Architekten wurde der Bau dieses mit einer Schule kombinierten Seminars als Ergebnis eines offenen Wettbewerbs im Jahre 1955 übertragen. Das wellige Gelände ist auf geschickte Weise durch den weiten Bogen der südlichen Flügelbauten und den Anschluß des langen, abgetreppten Klassenzimmergebäudes an die muschelförmige Talmulde ausgenutzt. Die Großräume des Seminars – Turnhallen und Aula – sind gemeinsam mit den Verwaltungsräumen und der Vorhalle um einen gepflasterten Hof gruppiert. Das Klassenzimmergebäude besteht aus einer Stahlbetonkonstruktion mit vorgefertigten Brüstungselementen. Die Dächer sind mit Welleternit gedeckt.

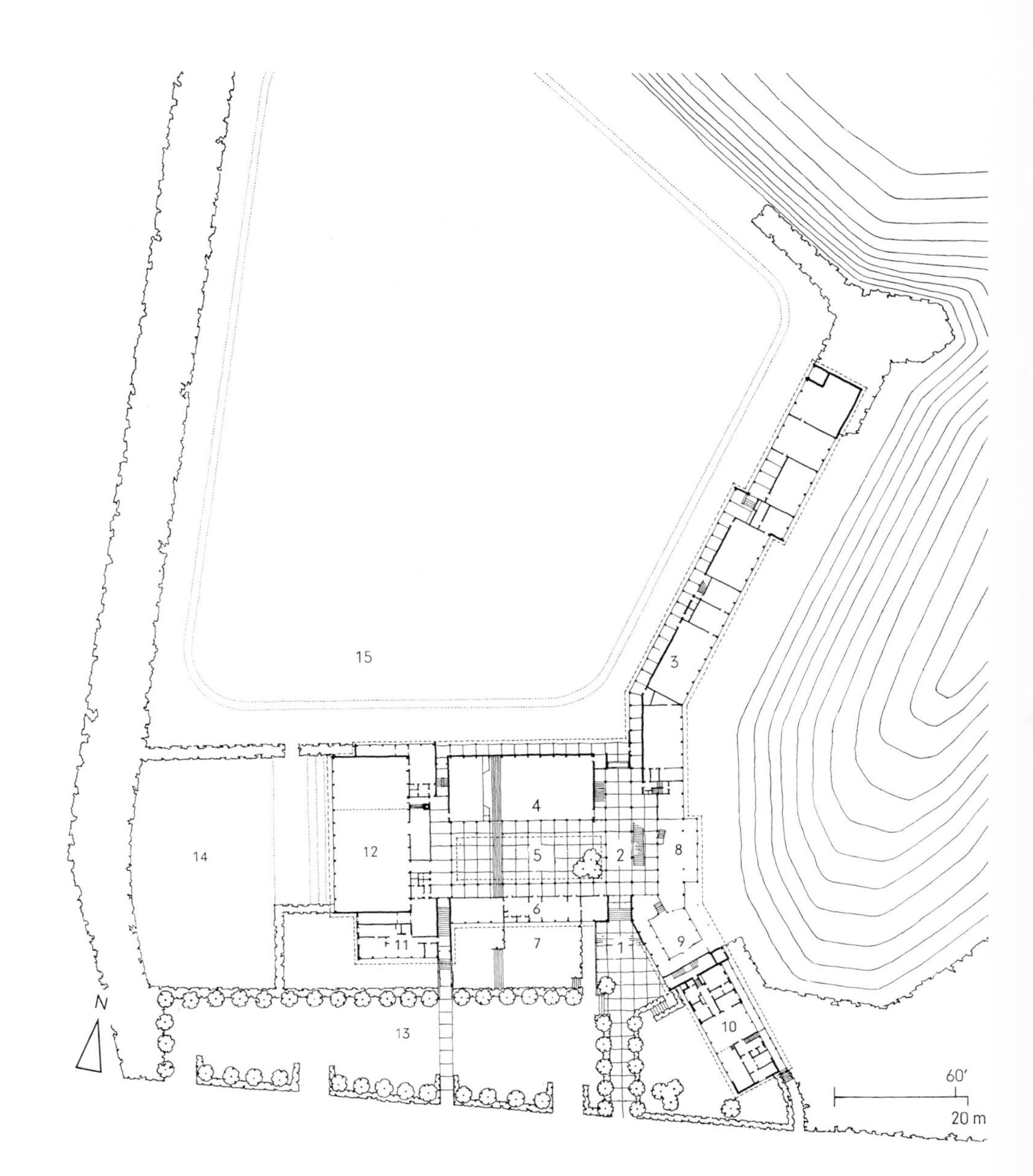

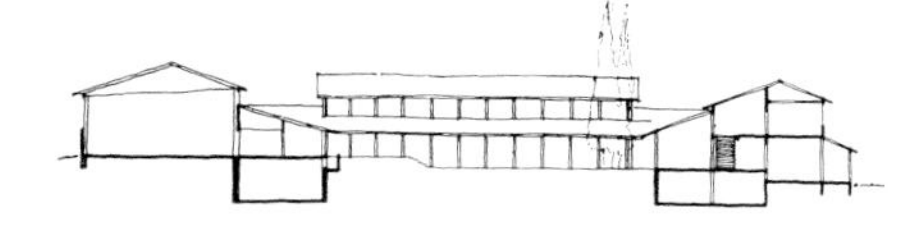

2. Section and ground floor plan. Key: 1 entrance, 2 vestibule, 3 special classrooms, 4 assembly hall, 5 garden court, 6 administration, 7 garden reserved for teachers, 8 canteen, 9 students' common room, 10 principal's dwelling, 11 caretaker's dwellings, 12 gymnastics halls, 13 car park, 14 sports court, 15 sports ground.
3. In front of the canteen on the East side are outdoor tables and benches.

2. Schnitt und Grundriß des Erdgeschosses. Legende: 1 Eingang, 2 Vorhalle, 3 Fachklassen, 4 Aula, 5 Hof, 6 Verwaltung, 7 Lehrergarten, 8 Kantine, 9 Aufenthaltsraum der Studenten, 10 Wohnung des Direktors, 11 Wohnung des Hausmeisters, 12 Turnhallen, 13 Parkplatz, 14 Wettkampfbahn, 15 Sportplatz.
3. Sitzplätze im Freien vor der Ostseite in Verbindung mit der dahinter liegenden Kantine.

4. The garden court, seen from the vestibule. All external woodwork is treated with clear varnish. The courtyard is laid out with paving stones.
5. The garden court with the gymnastics hall in the background and the windows of the assembly hall on the right.
6. The staircase windows face the garden court. Flooring of ceramic clinkers, ceiling covered with untreated deal.

4. Der gepflasterte Innenhof, von der Vorhalle her gesehen. Alle außenliegenden Holzkonstruktionen sind farblos imprägniert.
5. Der Innenhof mit der Turnhalle im Hintergrund und den Aulafenstern rechts.
6. Die Fenster des Treppenhauses sind dem Innenhof zugewandt. Der Fußboden ist mit Klinkern belegt, die Decke mit unbehandelten Kiefernbrettern verschalt.

Kay Fisker, C.F. Møller, Povl Stegmann

1. In the central valley of the University park, a little brook has been converted into a lake. On the left the book tower of the State Library, in the centre the main building with assembly hall, and on the extreme right the Chemico-Physical Institute.

1. In der Talmulde im Zentrum des Universitätsparks wurde ein kleiner Wasserlauf zu einem See aufgestaut. Links der Bücherturm der Staatsbibliothek, in der Mitte das Hauptgebäude mit der Aula, ganz rechts das Chemisch-physikalische Institut.

University at Århus, Jutland, 1933–68

The park-like character of the University was suggested in the prize-winning project of 1931, prepared by Kay Fisker, C.F. Møller and Povl Stegmann. The project envisaged that all the different institutions of the University should be housed in buildings informally placed around an attractive, undulating valley. The first building, the Chemico-Physical Institute, has a strictly prismatic appearance, with yellow brick and non-cantilevered roof of yellow tiles. This basic principle and the same materials have been adopted for all the later buildings so that the whole group has preserved a rare character of integrity at all stages of the building programme. The main building was erected in 1942–46. The State Library with its prominent book tower and the buildings for offices and students' hostels were added later, being completed in 1964. Stegmann left the work in 1937 and Kay Fisker in 1942 so that C.F. Møller was solely responsible for all the subsequent buildings. C.Th. Sørensen acted as landscape gardener. New buildings are still under construction in the area.

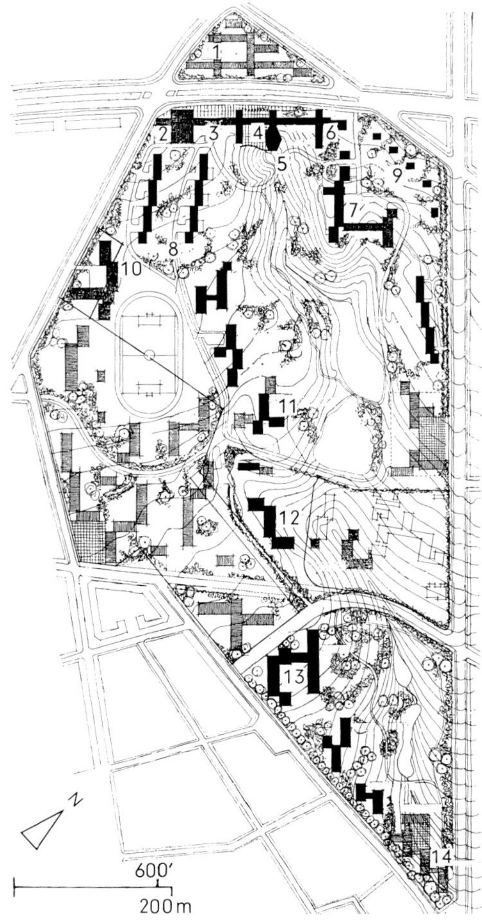

Kay Fisker, C.F. Møller, Povl Stegmann

Universität in Århus, Jütland, 1933–68

Der parkartige Charakter der Universitätsanlage geht auf den Wettbewerbsentwurf zurück, für den Kay Fisker, C.F. Møller und Povl Stegmann im Jahr 1931 den ersten Preis erhielten. Das Projekt sah vor, alle Institutionen der Universität in frei stehenden Baukörpern unterzubringen, die auf dem schönen, hügeligen Gelände um eine Talmulde herum gruppiert werden sollten. Das erste Gebäude, das Chemisch-physikalische Institut, hat eine streng-prismatische Form und ist aus gelbem Backstein errichtet, wobei das nicht überstehende Dach ebenfalls mit gelben Ziegeln gedeckt ist. Diese Grundform und die gleichen Baustoffe wurden auch bei allen späteren Bauten verwendet, so daß die Gesamtanlage zu jedem Zeitpunkt eine sonst selten zu beobachtende Einheitlichkeit bewahrte. Das Hauptgebäude wurde in den Jahren 1942–46 errichtet. Die Staatsbibliothek mit dem charakteristischen Bücherturm, das Verwaltungsgebäude und das Studentenhaus entstanden als letzte; sie wurden 1964 fertiggestellt. Im Jahr 1937 schied Stegmann und fünf Jahre später Kay Fisker aus dem Vorhaben aus, so daß C.F. Møller für alle seither errichteten Bauten allein verantwortlich war. Die Gartenanlagen gestaltete C.Th. Sørensen. Weitere Gebäude werden zur Zeit noch auf dem Gelände errichtet.

2. The Institute for Chemistry, Physics and Anatomy, which was the first University building to be erected, became the prototype for all subsequent buildings.
3. Site plan. Key: 1 students' hostel and administration, 2 library, 3 humanistics, 4 jurisprudence, 5 assembly hall, 6 theology, 7 physics and mathematics, 8 students' colleges, 9 lecturers' dwellings, 10 chemistry, 11 museum of natural history, 12 anatomy, 13 dentistry, 14 art museum.

2. Das als erstes errichtete Institut für Chemie, Physik und Anatomie wurde zum Vorbild für alle weiteren Gebäude.
3. Lageplan. Legende: 1 Studentenhaus und Verwaltung, 2 Bibliothek, 3 Geisteswissenschaften, 4 Jura, 5 Aula, 6 Theologie, 7 Physik und Mathematik, 8 Studentenkollegs, 9 Professorenwohnungen, 10 Chemie, 11 Naturkundemuseum, 12 Anatomie, 13 Zahnheilkunde, 14 Kunstmuseum.

4. The main building with the large hexagonal assembly hall, erected in 1942–46. In front of the terrace, which is bordered by an arcade, an amphitheatrically arranged outdoor auditorium faces the park.
5. Ground floor plan. Key: 1 assembly hall, 2 outdoor auditorium, 3 festival site, 4 concourse, 5 forecourt, 6 vestibule, 7 training hall, 8 theology, 9 institute, 10 lunch canteen, 11 studies, 12 professor, 13 auditorium, 14 cloak room, 15 W.C., 16 lecturer's room, 17 teachers' conference room, 18 administration, 19 ramp.

4. Das in den Jahren 1942–46 errichtete Hauptgebäude mit der großen sechskantigen Aula. Unter der von Arkadenbögen begrenzten Terrasse liegt zum Park hin ein Freiluftauditorium, das wie ein Amphitheater angelegt ist.
5. Grundriß des Erdgeschosses. Legende: 1 Aula, 2 Freiluftauditorium, 3 Festplatz, 4 Wandelhalle, 5 Vorplatz, 6 Vorhalle, 7 Übungssaal, 8 Theologische Fakultät, 9 Institut, 10 Kantine, 11 Studiensaal, 12 Professorenzimmer, 13 Hörsaal, 14 Garderobe, 15 WC, 16 Dozentenzimmer, 17 Sitzungssaal der Fakultät, 18 Verwaltung, 19 Rampe.

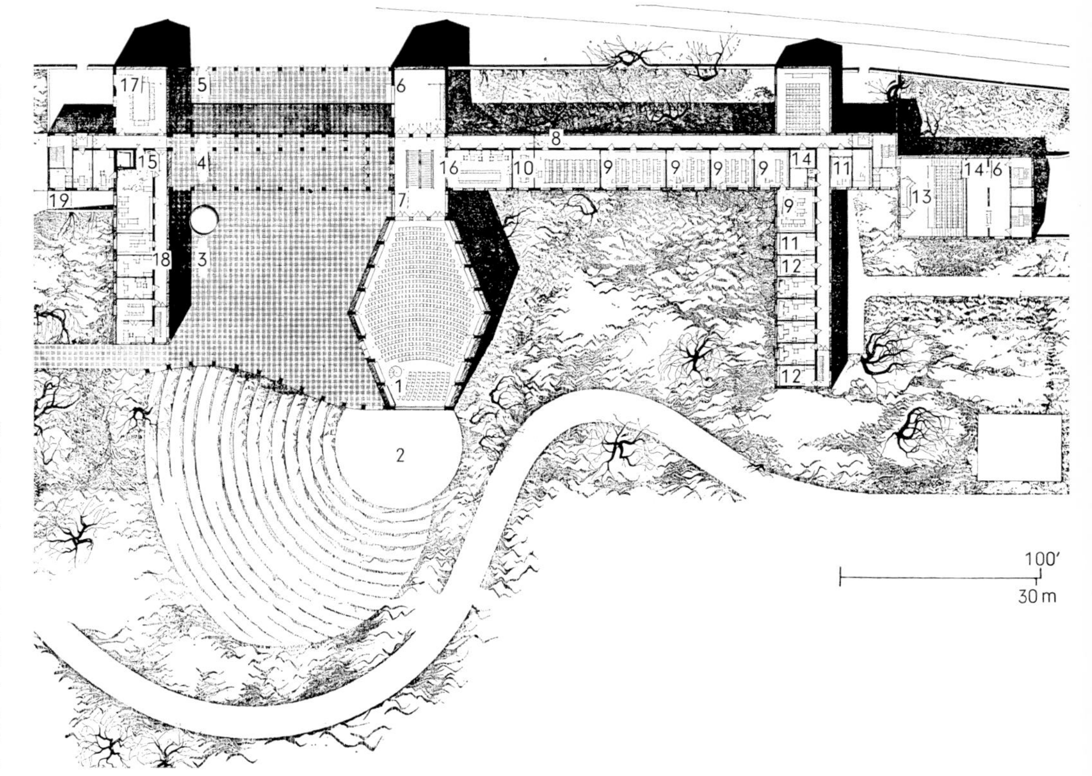

9. The North wall of the main building has been given an ornamental treatment. The main entrance is behind a forecourt, bordered by an arcade. ▷
10. Museum of Natural History, built during the years 1937–39.
11. State Library. First floor plan and section. Key: A lower basement, B upper basement, C ground floor, D first floor, E second floor; 1 staircase, 2 information, 3 book orders, outgoing and incoming books, 4 catalogue room, 5 periodicals reading room, 6 students' reading room, 7 main reading room, 8 passage to University, 9 book tower magazine, 10 lifts, 11 preparation of catalogues, 12 librarian, 13 despatch, 14 packing room.

9. Die Stirnmauer des Hauptgebäudes auf der Nordseite trägt ein dekoratives Backsteinmuster. Der Haupteingang liegt an einem Vorhof, der von einem Bogen begrenzt wird. ▷
10. Das Naturkundemuseum, in den Jahren 1937 bis 1939 erbaut.
11. Staatsbibliothek. Grundriß des ersten Obergeschosses und Querschnitt. Legende: A Unterer Keller, B Oberer Keller, C Erdgeschoß, D Erstes Obergeschoß, E Zweites Obergeschoß; 1 Treppenraum, 2 Auskunft, 3 Bestellungen, Ausgabe und Rückgabe, 4 Katalogsaal, 5 Zeitschriftenlesesaal, 6 Studentenlesesaal, 7 Hauptlesesaal, 8 Durchgang zur Universität, 9 Bücherturm, 10 Aufzüge, 11 Katalogisierung, 12 Bibliothekar, 13 Versand, 14 Packraum.

6. Like the other buildings, the assembly hall is constructed in brick. The roof is supported by visible reinforced concrete columns. The wall decorations have acoustic purposes. The chairs are covered with pigskin, the sofas with calves' hide.
7. The brick walls are left untreated in corridors and staircases. The floors are covered with clinkers.
8. The windowless book tower of the State Library, seen from North-West.

6. Die Aula ist wie die übrigen Gebäude der Universität aus Backstein errichtet. Das Dach wird von sichtbar belassenen Stahlbetonbindern getragen. Das dekorative Muster der Wände ist akustisch bedingt. Die Stühle sind mit Schweinsleder und die Sofas mit Kalbsleder bezogen.
7. Im Innern sind die Backsteinwände in den Korridoren und Treppenräumen unbehandelt belassen. Die Fußböden sind mit Klinkern belegt.
8. Der völlig fensterlose Bücherturm der Staatsbibliothek, von Nordwesten gesehen.

NATUR

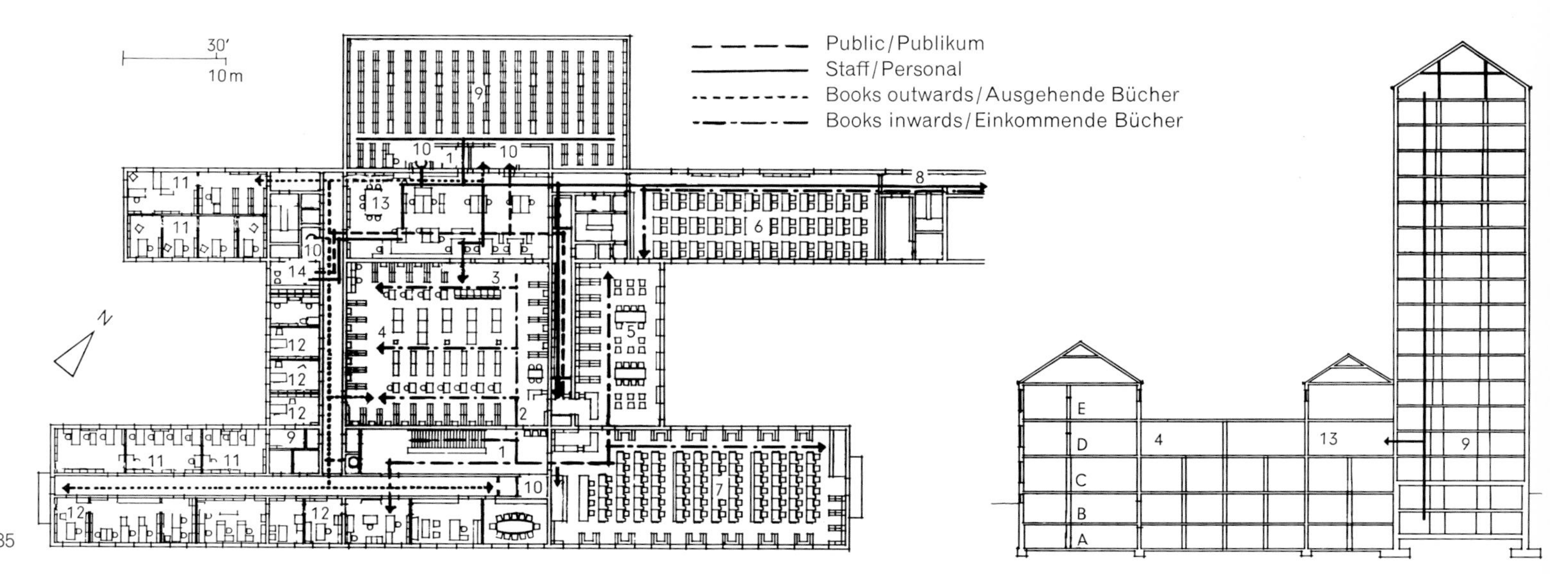
30'
10 m
N
Public/Publikum
Staff/Personal
Books outwards/Ausgehende Bücher
Books inwards/Einkommende Bücher
1
2
3
4
5
6
7
8
9
10
11
12
13
14
A
B
C
D
E

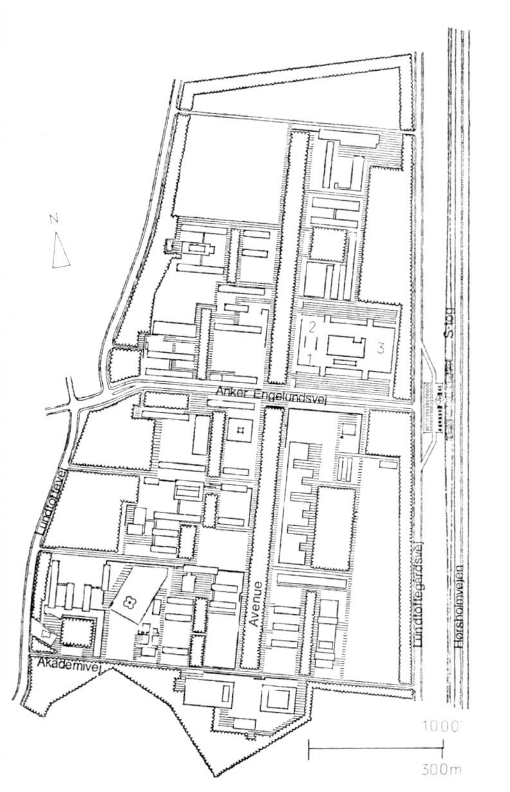

Nils Koppel

Technical University at Lundtofte near Copenhagen, 1959–68

In 1958, it was decided to move the Technical University together with the newly founded Engineering Academy from central Copenhagen to a slightly undulating site to the north of the city where the new University is designed for 5000 students. The different institutions are housed in informally arranged buildings in units of reasonable size so that the possibility of future extensions is preserved to the greatest possible extent. For economic reasons, all the laboratories are accommodated in two- or three-storey "standard buildings" of 50 to 100 metres length, with certain possibilities of variations. The buildings containing halls, lecture rooms, libraries, canteens, etc. are unobtrusively designed as cubic blocks with the same yellow brick cladding as the standard houses. A broad, landscaped boulevard serves to hold all the many buildings together and to support the impression of unity. Ole Nørgård is acting as landscape gardener. The campus is still under construction.

Technische Hochschule in Lundtofte bei Kopenhagen, 1959–68

Im Jahre 1958 wurde beschlossen, die Technische Hochschule und die 1957 gegründete Dänische Ingenieurakademie aus der Innenstadt von Kopenhagen herauszunehmen. Auf einem leicht hügeligen Gelände nördlich von Kopenhagen wurde eine neue Anlage projektiert, die für insgesamt 5000 Studenten berechnet ist. Die einzelnen Institute sind in frei stehenden Gebäuden mittlerer Größe untergebracht, wobei die Voraussetzungen für eine spätere Erweiterung weitgehend offengehalten sind. Aus wirtschaftlichen Gründen wurde für die Laborgebäude ein Standardtyp mit zwei oder drei Stockwerken von 50 bis 100 m Länge mit gewissen Variationsmöglichkeiten entwickelt. Hallen, Hörsäle, Bibliothek, Mensa und so weiter sind unaufdringlich in kubischen Blöcken untergebracht, die aus dem gleichen Backstein wie die Standardtypen errichtet wurden. Ein breiter, bepflanzter Boulevard dient als Sammelader, die durch die gesamte Anlage führt und dazu beiträgt, den großen Baukomplex zu einem einheitlichen Ganzen zu verbinden. Die Gartengestaltung liegt in den Händen von Ole Nørgård. Die Anlage ist noch im Bau.

1. All the buildings are given a strict, cubic shape and a facade cladding of yellow bricks. All woodwork is dark-stained.
2. Site plan. Key: 1 administration, 2 auditorium, 3 library.
3. Cross-section of three-storey standard house and floor plan of the electrical engineers' house.
4. A two-storey standard house with continuous window parapets of yellow brick.
5. A group of standard houses in the electrical engineering section. The difference in ground level is taken up by retaining walls clad with grey Opdal stone.

1. Alle Gebäude haben eine klare kubische Form und Fassaden aus gelbem Backstein. Sämtliche Holzteile sind dunkel imprägniert.
2. Lageplan. Legende: 1 Verwaltung, 2 Auditorium, 3 Bibliothek.
3. Querschnitt durch ein dreigeschossiges Gebäude des Standardtyps sowie Grundriß des Institutsgebäudes der Elektroingenieure.
4. Ein zweigeschossiges Gebäude des Standardtyps mit durchgehenden Fensterbrüstungen aus gelbem Backstein.
5. Eine Gruppe von Standardtypen in der Abteilung für Elektroingenieure. Die Höhenunterschiede des Geländes werden von Stützmauern aufgefangen, die mit grauem Opdalstein verkleidet sind.

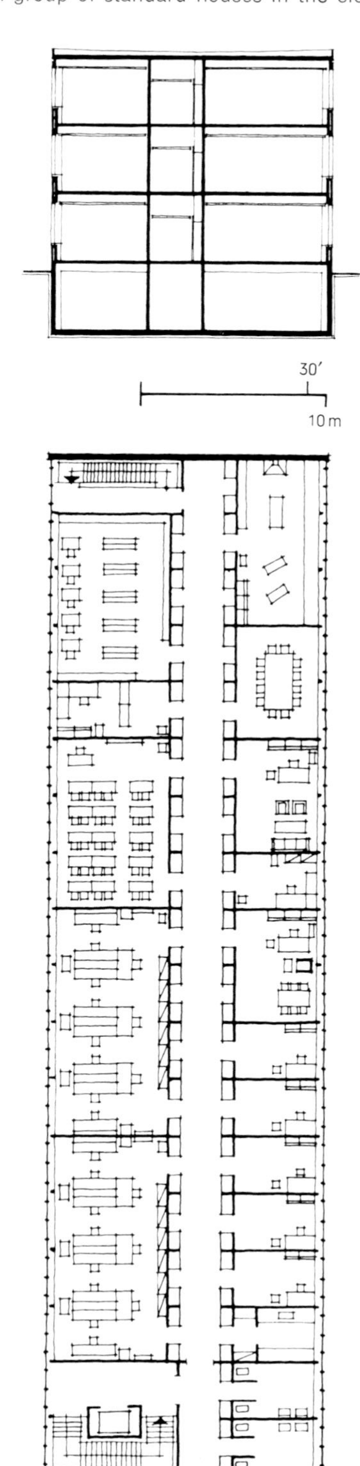

6. The larger institutes are accommodated in several standard houses, linked by passages of steel and glass.
7. Detail of standard house facade. Between the brick parapets the window zones can be varied and replaced by standard open or closed sections.
8. Chemical laboratory.
9. Vestibule in the auditorium building.

6. Die großen Institute bestehen aus mehreren Gebäuden des Standardtyps, die durch leichte, aus Stahl und Glas errichtete Korridore miteinander verbunden sind.
7. Ausschnitt aus der Fassade eines Standardgebäudes. Zwischen den Backstein-Brüstungen können die Fensterzonen abgewandelt und gegen genormte offene oder geschlossene Einheiten ausgetauscht werden.
8. Ein Übungslabor im Chemischen Institut.
9. Die Vorhalle im Hörsaalgebäude.

Jørgen Bo + Vilhelm Wohlert

Louisiana gallery of modern art, Humlebæk, North Zealand, 1958
One of the old villas by the coastal road along the Sound has an exceptionally beautiful position in a park studded with tall trees. Steep slopes lead down to the Sound in the East and to Lake Humlebæk in the North-West. Here, a modern art gallery has been erected through private initiative in conjunction with the old villa, destined for changing exhibitions of significant works of modern international art and of the museum's own collection of contemporary Danish art. In arranging the new houses, the architects tried to keep the greater part of the large park free from buildings. Three large exhibition halls are placed in the northern most corner of the site where they face the park with large windows and are connected with the old villa by corridors of varying width. Also included in the scheme are a library and a cafeteria. A fourth exhibition hall was completed in 1966. All the walls are whitewashed. The robust roof beams consist of laminated deal. The beam ends are protected by gilded aluminium sheets. Bargeboards are of teak wood. Inside, the walls are kept white whilst the floors are covered with brown-red tiles.

Louisiana-Kunstgalerie in Humlebæk im Norden der Insel Seeland, 1958
Eine der alten Villen an der Küstenstraße am Øresund liegt besonders schön in einem aus großen Bäumen bestehenden Park. Gegen Osten fällt das Gelände steil zum Sund und gegen Nordwesten zum Humlebæker See ab. Aus privater Initiative wurde hier in Zusammenhang mit der alten Villa ein modernes Museum geschaffen, das für Wechselausstellungen moderner internationaler Kunst und eigener Sammlungen dänischer Gegenwartskunst bestimmt ist. Bei der Anordnung der Neubauten haben die Architekten versucht, den größten Teil des großen Parkes von der Bebauung freizuhalten. Drei große Ausstellungsgebäude stehen an der nördlichsten Ecke des Grundstücks, wo sie sich zum Park hin mit großen Fensterflächen öffnen und mit der alten Villa durch einen Gang von wechselnder Breite verbunden sind. Zur Anlage gehören auch ein Bibliotheksgebäude und ein Selbstbedienungscafé. Ein vierter Ausstellungssaal wurde 1966 gebaut. Alle Außenwände sind weiß gekalkt. Die kräftigen Dachbalken bestehen aus verleimtem Schichtholz. Die Balkenenden sind durch goldeloxierte Aluminiumplatten geschützt. Die Randbalken bestehen aus Teakholz. Auch die Innenwände sind weiß gehalten, während die Fußböden aus braunroten Keramikfliesen bestehen.

1. The large exhibition halls have high-level windows.

1. Die großen Ausstellungsbauten haben hochliegende Fensterbänder.

2. Pool of water between two of the exhibition buildings.
3. Site plan. Key: 1 main entrance, 2 old villa, 3 connecting passages, 4 galleries, 5 library, 6 cafeteria terrace, 7 Lake Humlebæk, 8 the Sound.

2. Wasserbecken zwischen zwei Ausstellungsbauten.
3. Lageplan. Legende: 1 Haupteingang, 2 Alte Villa, 3 Verbindungsgang, 4 Ausstellungsbauten, 5 Bibliothek, 6 Terrasse des Selbstbedienungscafés, 7 Humlebæker See, 8 Øresund.

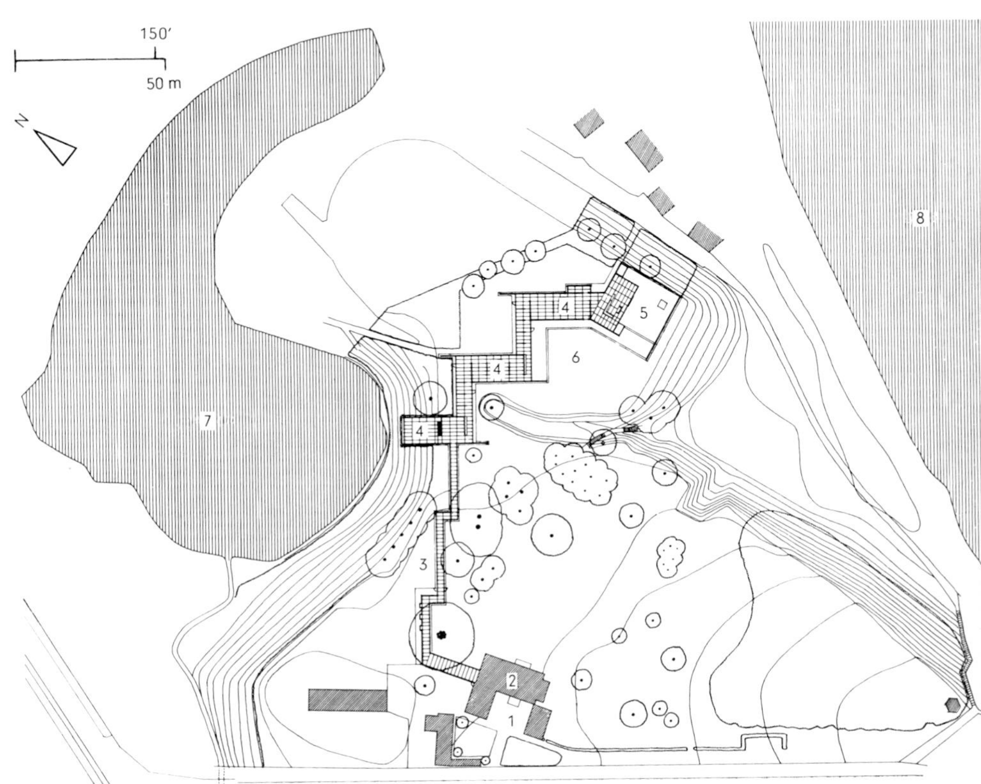

4. The long passageways face the park and the trunks of the old trees with large windows.
5. One of the exhibition halls offers a view over the lake below.
6. The new exhibition hall, completed in 1966.
7. Fireplace lounge in the exhibition hall closest to the Sound, next door to the cafeteria.
8. Some of the passageways are extended so as to provide facilities for the display of paintings on light screen walls.

4. Zum Park mit den alten Bäumen hin öffnen sich die langen Verbindungsgänge mit großen Fensterflächen.
5. Eines der Ausstellungsgebäude bietet einen Ausblick über den Humlebæker See.
6. Der 1966 fertiggestellte neue Ausstellungsbau.
7. Der am weitesten im Osten gelegene Bau hat ein Kaminzimmer, an das sich das Selbstbedienungscafé anschließt.
8. Einige der Verbindungsgänge sind verbreitert, um dadurch eine Möglichkeit für die Ausstellung von Gemälden auf leichten Scherwänden zu bieten.

Jørn Utzon

Silkeborg art gallery, Project, 1963

On the initiative of the painter Asger Jorn, who donated a collection of contemporary European art to the museum of the town of Silkeborg in central Jutland, Utzon prepared a project for a new museum building. Having regard to the surrounding low-rise buildings, the architect has placed the greater part of the new building in a three-storey deep pit below ground whilst the only part projecting above ground is a clerestory of about one storey's height. The several sections of the pit have different ceiling heights and lighting effects and are viewed by the visitors from a ramp which enables them to see the premises as well as the displays from any direction. As with the opera house in Sydney, the curved structures are based on strictly geometrical designs. The interior of the building is to be painted white whilst the sculptured clerestory is to be covered with multicoloured ceramic teils.

3. Plans at roof level (a), ground level (b), gallery level (c), and bottom level (d). Key: 1 main entrance, 2 information, 3 kitchen, 4 kitchen entrance, 5 cafeteria, 6 existing building, 7 cloakroom, 8 toilets, 9 store room. ▷

3. Grundrisse in der Ebene des Daches (a), in Straßenebene (b), in der Ebene der Galerie (c) und in der niedrigsten Ebene (d). Legende: 1 Haupteingang, 2 Auskunft, 3 Küche, 4 Kücheneingang, 5 Cafeteria, 6 Bestehendes Gebäude, 7 Garderobe, 8 Toiletten, 9 Lagerraum. ▷

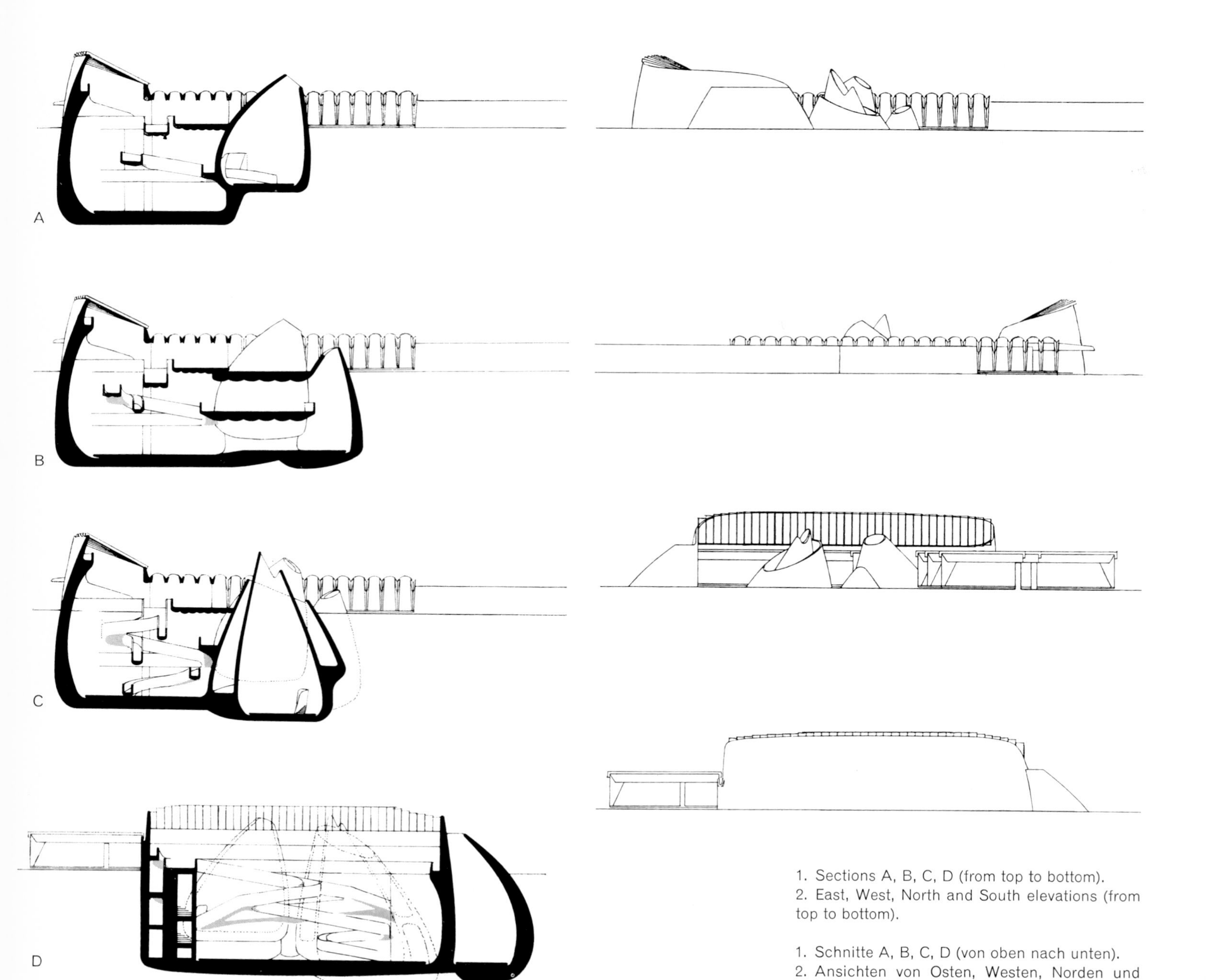

1. Sections A, B, C, D (from top to bottom).
2. East, West, North and South elevations (from top to bottom).

1. Schnitte A, B, C, D (von oben nach unten).
2. Ansichten von Osten, Westen, Norden und Süden (von oben nach unten).

Jørn Utzon

Kunstmuseum in Silkeborg, Projekt 1963

Zur Unterbringung einer Sammlung moderner europäischer Kunst, die der Maler Asger Jorn dem Museum der Stadt Silkeborg in Mittel-Jütland schenkte, arbeitete Utzon auf Veranlassung von Asger Jorn ein Projekt für einen neuen Museumsbau aus. Mit Rücksicht auf die umliegende, niedrige Bebauung soll der größte Teil des Neubaus in einer etwa drei Geschosse tiefen Grube in den Boden eingelassen werden, während nur ein einziges Geschoß mit hohen Oberlichtern über das Gelände herausragen wird. Die verschiedenen Abschnitte der Grube haben unterschiedliche Deckenhöhen und Beleuchtungsverhältnisse und werden auf einer Rampenanlage durchwandert, die es ermöglicht, sowohl die Räume als auch die Kunstwerke von allen Seiten zu betrachten. Wie beim Opernhaus in Sydney war der Architekt darauf bedacht, die Konstruktion aus gekrümmten Betonflächen auf streng geometrischer Grundlage zu entwickeln. Innen soll das Gebäude weiß gestrichen werden, während das plastisch gestaltete Obergeschoß mit keramischen Fliesen in kräftigen Farben verkleidet werden soll.

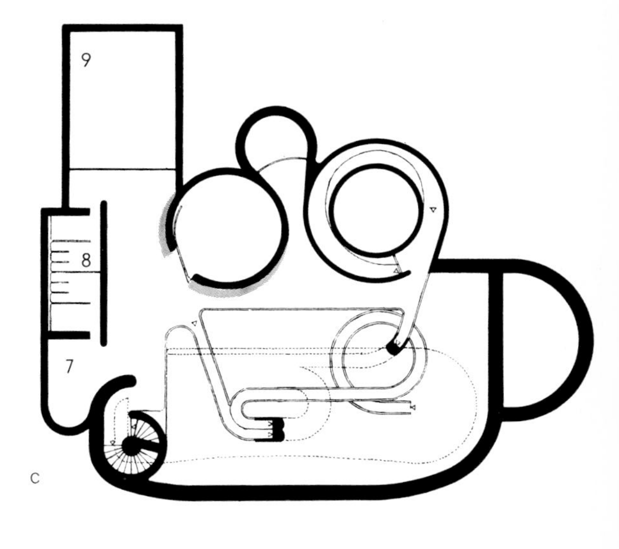

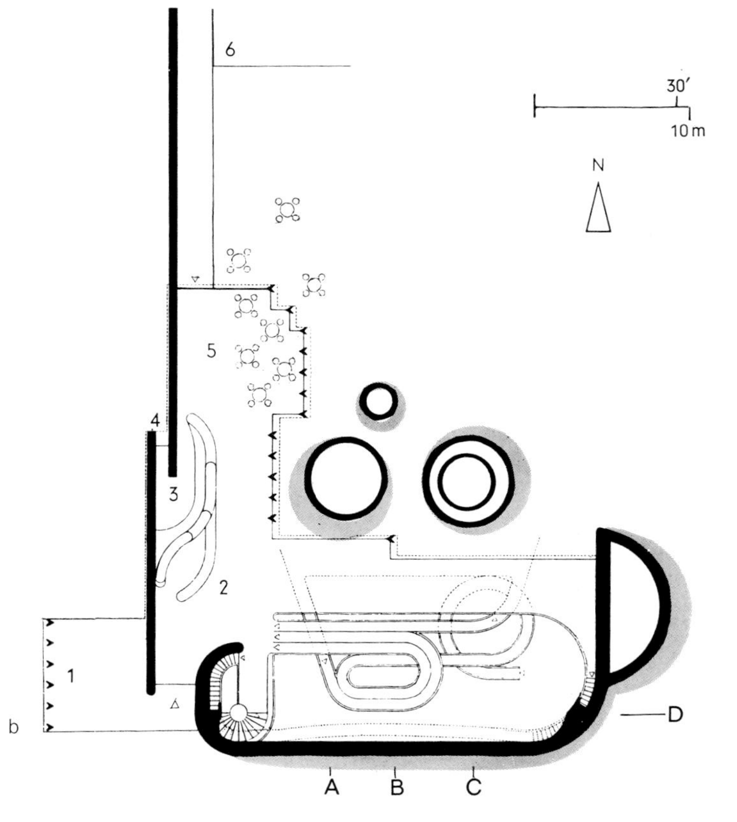

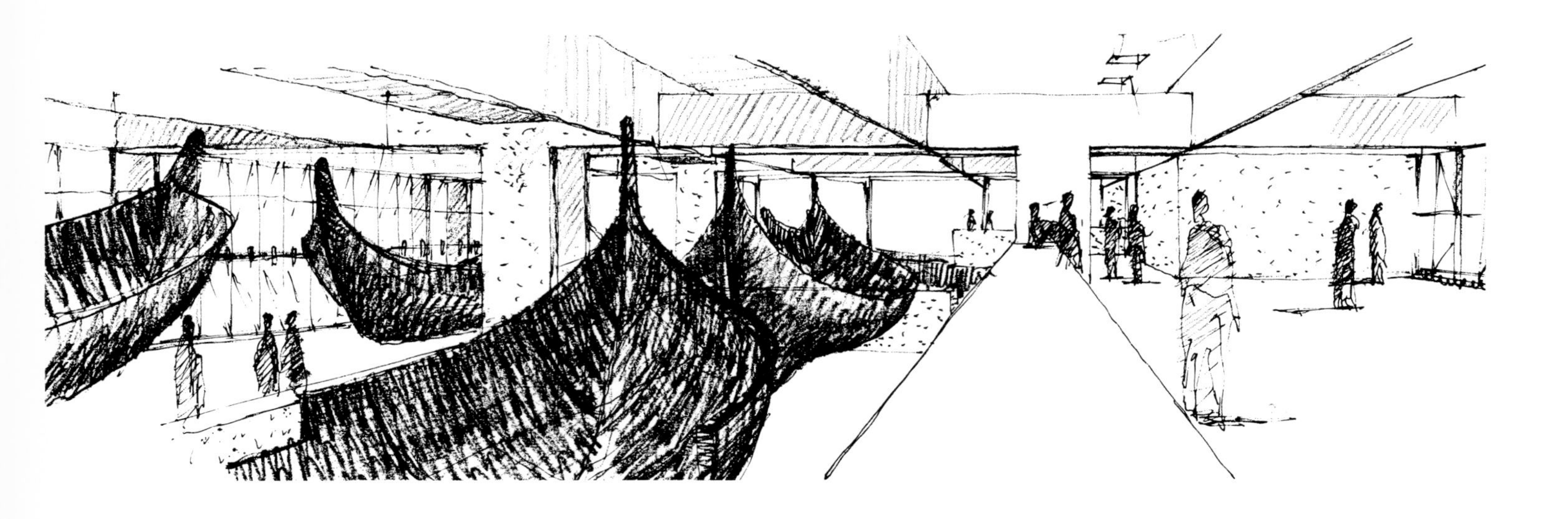

Erik Chr. Sørensen

Museum for Viking boats at Roskilde, Zealand, Project, 1963 (Under construction)
A few years ago, a small fleet of Viking boats was discovered in Roskilde Fjord. In 1963, a number of architects were invited to participate in a competition for a museum building for the five boats. The First Prize was awarded to Erik Christian Sørensen whose project is about to be realised at Roskilde. The building, half projecting into the Fjord itself, has a terraced floor so that the visitors will be able to walk on three different levels, viewing the boats both from above and from below. The museum will have large windows on the North side and screened toplighting so that the boats are not exposed to direct sunlight. The building is erected in reinforced concrete with strong bearing columns and continuous girders.

1. Interior of the museum.
2, 3. Model photographs of the museum, seen from North-West and North-East respectively, with the large windows facing the fjord.

1. Ansicht des Innenraums.
2, 3. Modellansichten des Museums von Nordwesten und Nordosten, mit den großen Fensterflächen zum Fjord.

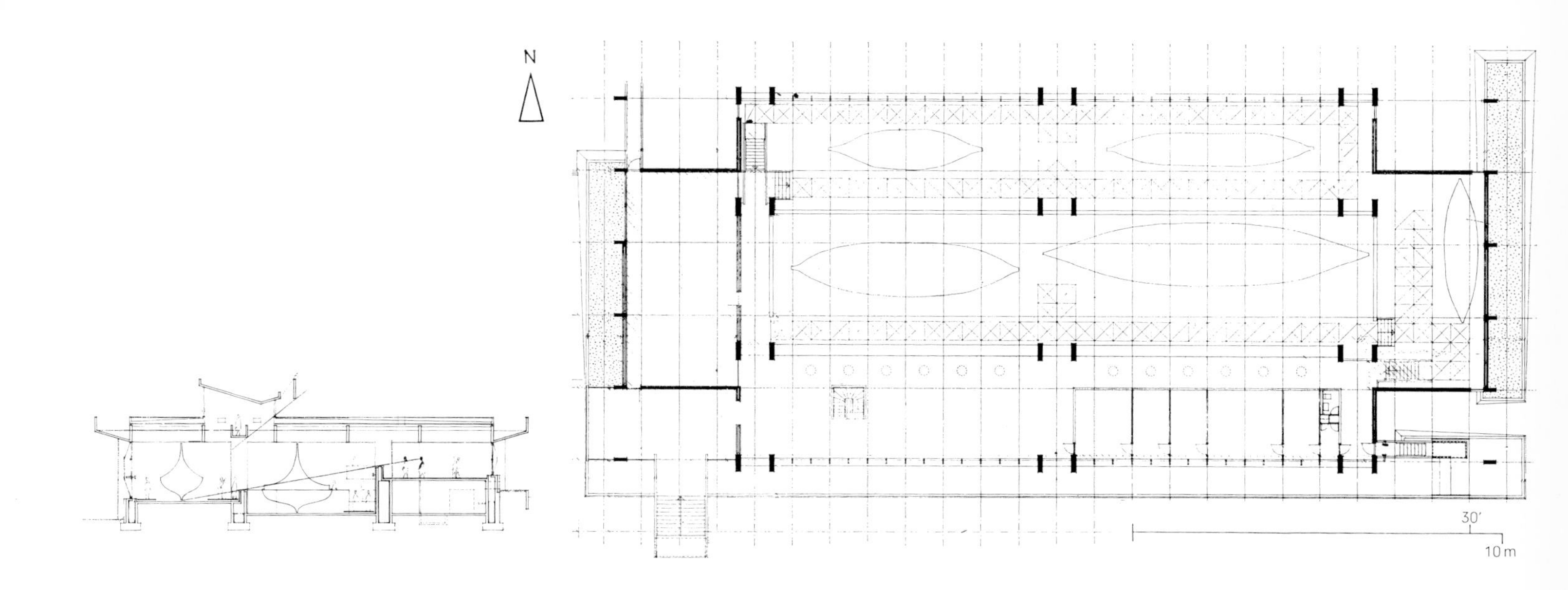

Erik Chr. Sørensen

Museum für Wikingerschiffe in Roskilde, Insel Seeland, Projekt 1963 (zur Zeit im Bau)
Für die kleine Flotte von Wikingerschiffen, die vor einigen Jahren im Roskilde-Fjord entdeckt worden war, wurde 1963 ein begrenzter Architektenwettbewerb für ein Museumsgebäude ausgeschrieben, das die fünf Schiffe aufnehmen soll. Das von Erik Christian Sørensen ausgearbeitete, mit dem ersten Preis bedachte Projekt wird zur Zeit in Roskilde ausgeführt. Das Gebäude ragt zur Hälfte in den Fjord hinaus. Der Fußboden ist terrassenförmig abgestuft, so daß die Besucher sich auf drei Ebenen bewegen und die Schiffe sowohl von oben als auch von unten besichtigen können. Das Museum hat große Glasfenster auf der Nordseite und abgeschirmte Oberlichter, damit die Schiffe nicht unmittelbar dem Sonnenlicht ausgesetzt sind. Das Gebäude wird aus Stahlbeton mit kräftigen Stützen und durchgehenden Trägern errichtet.

4. Cross-section.
5. Plan.
6. Isometric view of the building without roof; isometric view of the roof structure.

4. Querschnitt.
5. Grundriß.
6. Isometrie ohne Dach und Isometrie der Dachkonstruktion.

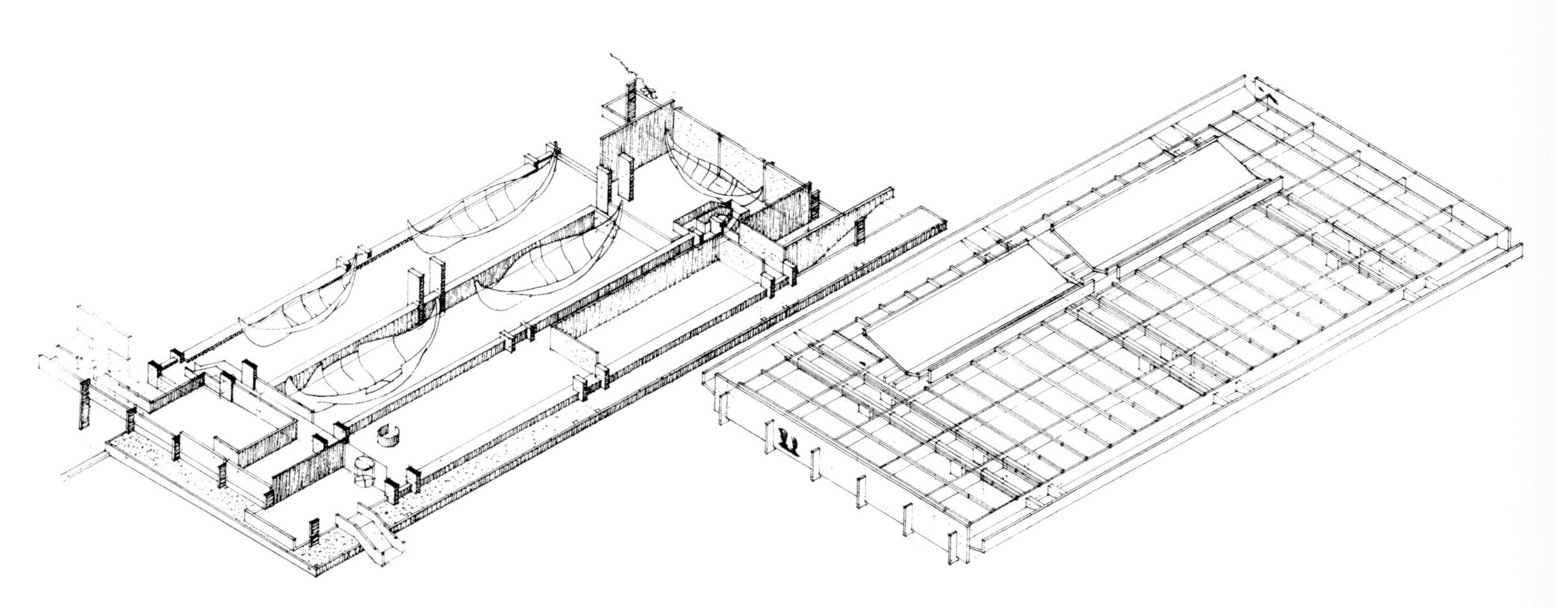

Gunnar Jensen + Finn Monies

Seaside resort at Sandvig, Bornholm, Baltic, 1960

The seaside resort is situated at the northern tip of the island of Bornholm in a rocky area. A stringent budget called for simplified design of the buildings for cashier, sales kiosk and changing rooms. The changing room building has a butterfly roof covered with asbestos cement slabs, supported by a continuous wall below the roof valley and by the steam pipes at the eaves. The light screen walls forming the outer curtain of the building can be dismantled during the winter so that the cores around the cloakrooms and toilets are the only enclosed units to remain.

Ostseebad Sandvig auf der Insel Bornholm, 1960

Das Bad liegt an der Nordspitze Bornholms an einem steinigen Strand. Finanzielle Gesichtspunkte bedingten eine möglichst einfache Gestaltung der Bauten für Kartenverkauf, Kiosk und Garderobe. Das Umkleidegebäude besteht im wesentlichen aus einem V-förmigen Eternitdach, das auf einer durchgehenden Mauer unter dem Mittelknick und an den Außenseiten auf Stützen aus Heizungsrohren ruht. Die leichten Schirmwände, die das Gebäude außen begrenzen, können im Winter entfernt werden, so daß dann nur noch die gemauerten Kerne um die Garderobe und die Duschräume als geschlossene Einheiten verbleiben.

1. The butterfly roof of the changing room building seen from the sales kiosk.

1. Das Schmetterlingsdach des Umkleidegebäudes, vom Kiosk her gesehen.

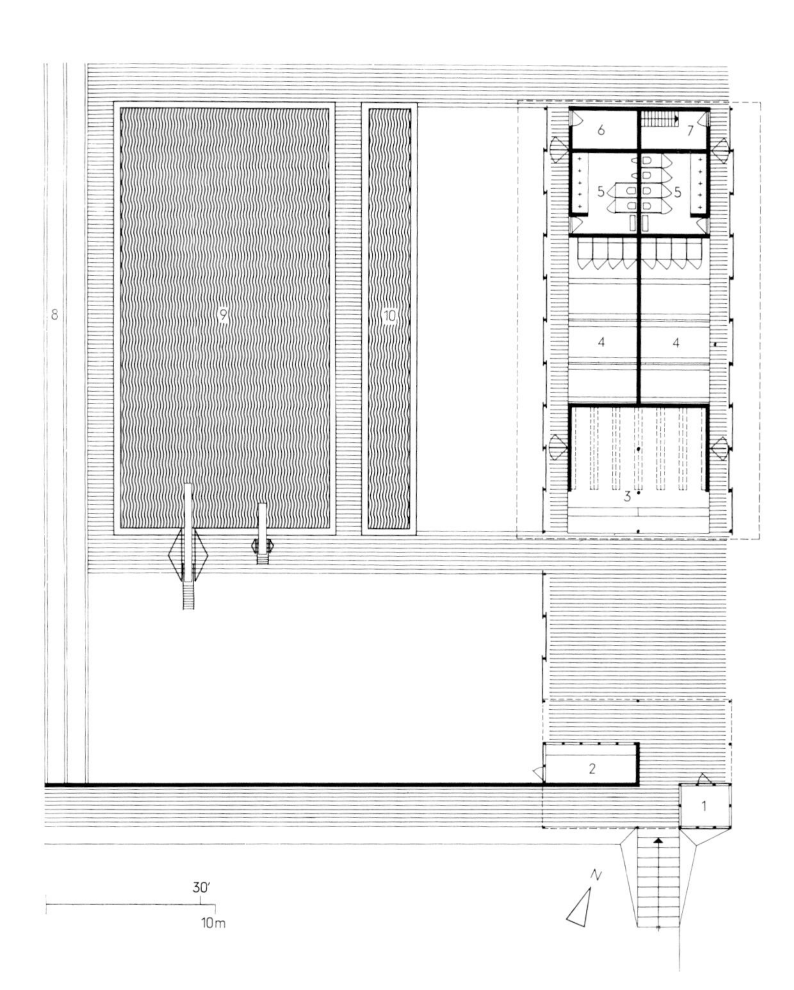

2. Plan. Key: 1 cashier, 2 sales kiosk, 3 cloakroom, 4 changing rooms, 5 toilets and shower bath, 6 chlorination plant, 7 stores room and stairs leading to pump room basement, 8 spectators, 9 swimming pool with 3 m and 1 m diving boards, 10 paddling pool for children.
3. Changing room building, seen from the beach.
4. Model photograph of the group of buildings.
5. The swimming pool is of concrete, the diving boards are of tubular steel.

2. Grundriß. Legende: 1 Kasse, 2 Verkaufskiosk, 3 Garderobe, 4 Umkleideräume, 5 Toiletten und Duschen, 6 Chloranlage, 7 Abstellraum und Treppen, die zum Keller mit der Pumpenanlage führen, 8 Zuschauer, 9 Schwimmbecken mit 3-m- und 1-m-Sprungbrettern, 10 Planschbecken für Kinder.
3. Das Umkleidegebäude vom Strand aus.
4. Modellbild der Anlage.
5. Die Sprungtürme bestehen aus Stahlrohren.

Torben Stokholm + Christian Pedersen

Stadium at Ålborg, Jutland, 1963
The stadium is situated in a residential district in the outskirts of Ålborg. It consists of a stadium and an indoor sports hall, both of which are mainly assembled from prefabricated reinforced concrete units. The canopies of the grandstand are built as steel structures.

Stadion der Stadt Ålborg in Jütland, 1963
Die Anlage liegt in einem Villenviertel am Stadtrand von Ålborg. Sie besteht aus einem Stadion und einer geschlossenen Sporthalle, die beide zu einem großen Teil aus vorgefertigten Stahlbetonelementen errichtet wurden. Die baldachinartigen Schutzdächer der Tribünen sind reine Stahlkonstruktionen.

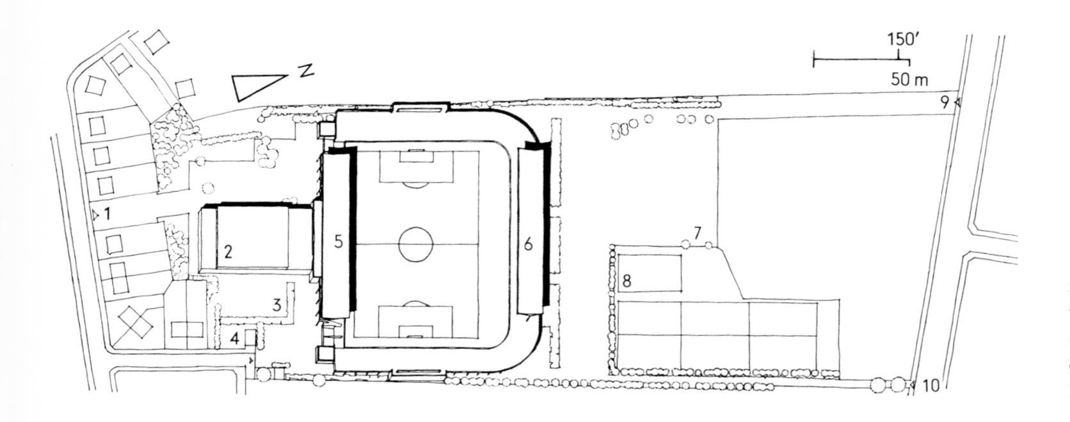

1. Site plan. Key: 1 main entrance, 2 sports hall, 3 car park for players and press, 4 caretaker's flat, 5 spectators' seats, 6 covered stand for standing spectators, 7 car park for 390 cars, 8 tennis courts, 9 to car park, 10 pedestrians.
2. The stadium, seen from the car park.

1. Lageplan. Legende: 1 Haupteingang, 2 Sporthalle, 3 Parkplatz für Spieler und Presse, 4 Wohnung des Platzwarts, 5 Zuschauer (Sitzplätze), 6 Überdeckte Tribüne (Stehplätze), 7 Parkplatz für 390 Wagen, 8 Tennisplätze, 9 Einfahrt zum Parkplatz, 10 Fußgänger.
2. Das Stadion vom Parkplatz aus.

3. The grandstand of the stadium. The underside of the steel structure of the canopies is covered in aluminium.
4. Plan of grandstands. Key: 1 exits, 2 spectators' stand, 3 covered stand for spectators, 4 covered seats, 5 radio and press enclosure, 6 bar, 7 cafeteria.

3. Die baldachinartigen Schutzdächer der Tribünen sind auf der Unterseite mit Aluminium verkleidet.
4. Grundriß der Tribünenanlagen. Legende: 1 Ausgänge, 2 Zuschauerränge, 3 Überdeckte Stehplätze, 4 Überdeckte Sitzplätze, 5 Reservierte Sitze für Rundfunk- und Pressevertreter, 6 Bar, 7 Selbstbedienungsrestaurant.

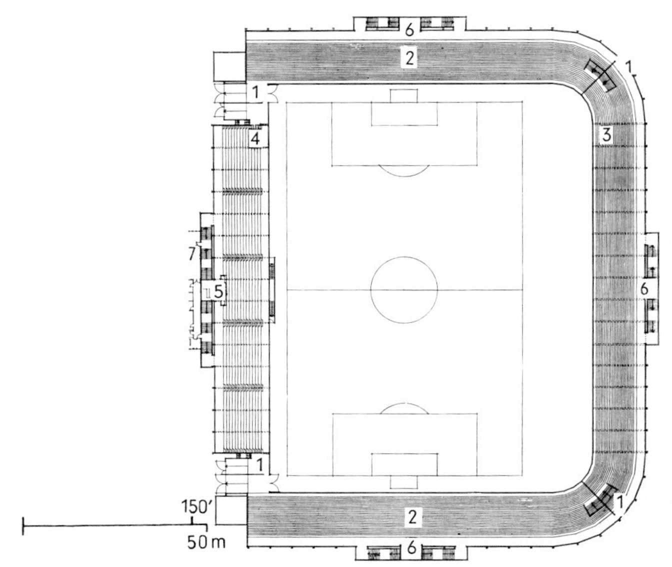

5. The terraced steps of the grandstand and the screen walls are, like the bearing concrete trestlework below them, assembled from prefabricated units.
6. The grandstands of the stadium are supported by prefabricated concrete trestleworks.

5. Die Terrassenstufen der Tribünen und die Brüstungen sind ebenso wie die eigentliche Tragkonstruktion aus vorgefertigten Betonelementen errichtet.
6. Vorgefertigte Betonbinder und -stützen tragen die Tribünen der Stadionanlage.

7. The sports hall has a direct link with the stadium. The hall, too, is assembled from prefabricated concrete units.

7. Die Sporthalle steht in unmittelbarer Verbindung mit dem Stadion. Sie ist ebenfalls aus vorgefertigten Betonelementen errichtet.

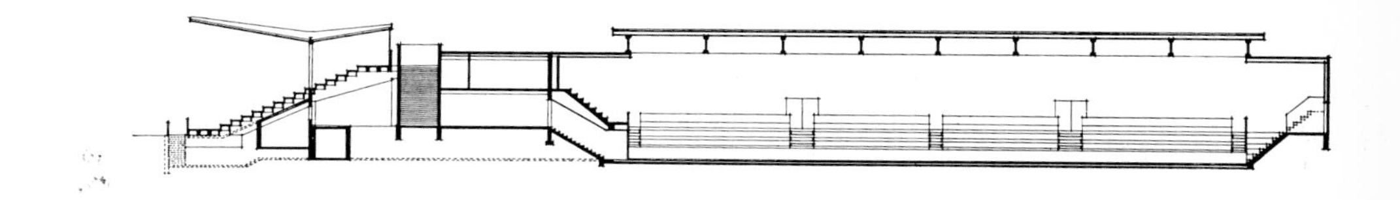

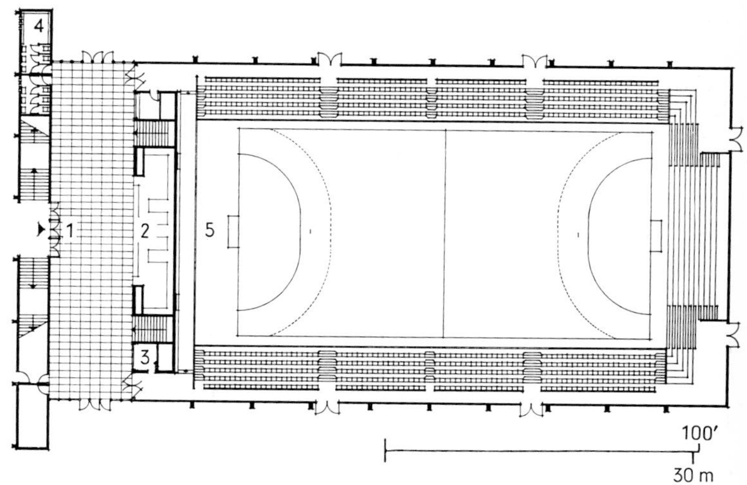

8. The separate seats in the grandstand are made of glass fibre-reinforced polyester.
9. Longitudinal section of grandstand and hall, and ground floor plan. Key: 1 vestibule, 2 cloakroom, 3 kiosk, 4 toilets, 5 hall.

8. Die einzelnen Sitze der Tribünen bestehen aus glasfaserverstärktem Polyester.
9. Längsschnitt durch Tribüne und Sporthalle und Hallengrundriß. Legende: 1 Vorhalle, 2 Garderobe, 3 Kiosk, 4 Toiletten, 5 Halle.

Arne Jacobsen

Swimming pool at Lyngby, Copenhagen, Project, 1964

The swimming pool is to be built in direct connection with Lyngby Stadium on the South side. On a terrace-shaped bastion, bordered on the South side by a paddling pool, extending over the whole length, stands a single-storey building with changing rooms. The inclined roof reaches its greatest height above the diving boards. Each of the six large roof girders consists of seven prefabricated concrete units, assembled with pre-tensioning cables. Crossbeams of approx. 6 metres width, likewise to be assembled from prefabricated concrete units, form open sunbathing terraces protected by screen walls, which provide a view partly over the stadium on the South side and partly, through large windows, onto the swimming pool below. One of the roof terraces is planned to be enclosed and equipped as a restaurant.

Schwimmstadion in Lyngby bei Kopenhagen, Projekt 1964

Das Schwimmstadion soll in direkter Verbindung mit dem südlich von Lyngby gelegenen Stadion gebaut werden. Auf einer terrassenförmigen Plattform, die auf der Südseite von einem über die ganze Länge reichenden Planschbecken begrenzt wird, steht ein eingeschossiges Gebäude mit Umkleideräumen und Schwimmbecken. Das pultförmige Dach der Schwimmhalle erreicht über dem Sprungturm seine größte Höhe. Jeder der sechs großen Dachträger besteht aus sieben vorgefertigten Betonelementen, die durch Vorspannkabel zusammengehalten werden. Querliegende, ungefähr sechs Meter breite, V-förmige Plattenbalken, die ebenfalls aus vorgefertigten Betonelementen zusammengesetzt werden sollen, bilden offene Sonnenterrassen, die von Schirmwänden beschützt sind und eine Aussicht teils über das Stadion im Süden, teils durch Glasfenster auf die darunterliegende Schwimmhalle bieten. Eine der Dachterrassen soll umschlossen und als Restaurant eingerichtet werden.

1. Model photograph of the building, seen from above.

1. Modellansicht der Anlage von oben.

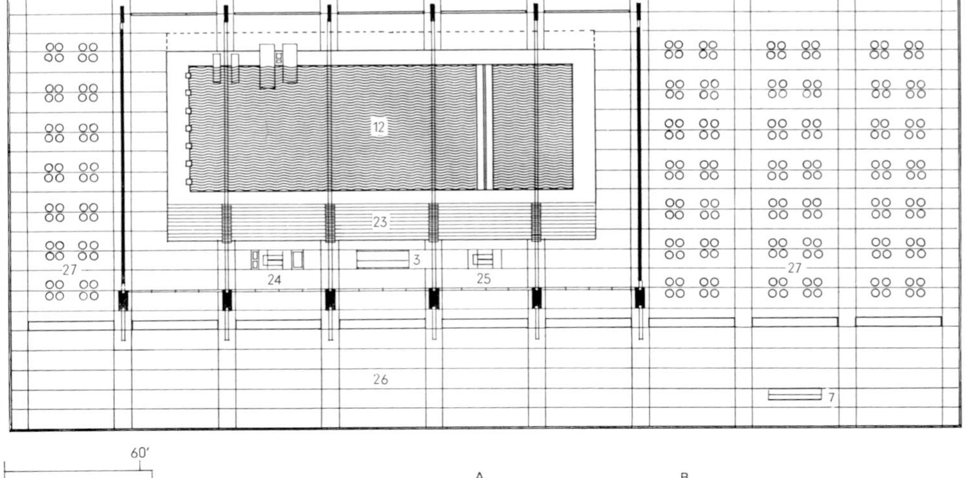

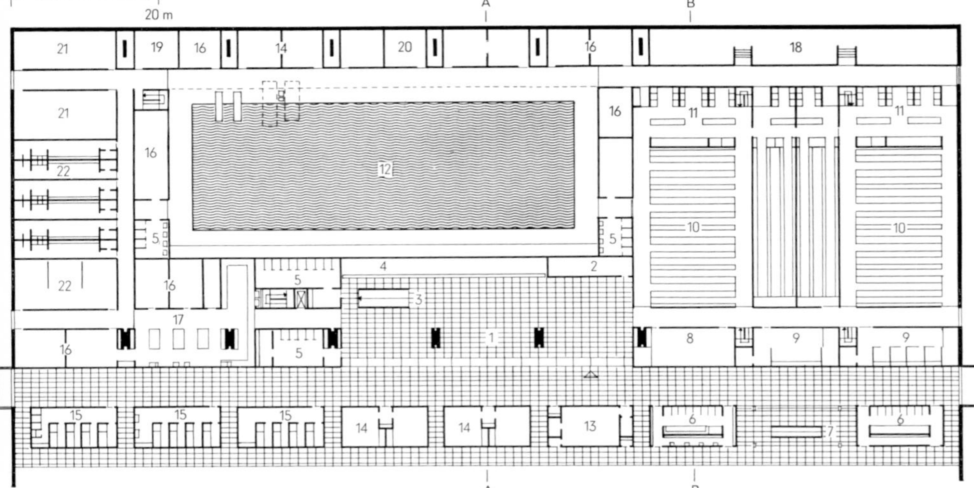

2. Roof and ground floor plans. Key: 1 vestibule, 2 box office, 3 spectators, 4 cloakroom, 5 toilets, 6 changing rooms and baths, 7 up to terrace, 8 administration, 9 hairdresser, 10 changing rooms, 11 bathrooms, 12 pool, 13 kiosk, 14 club premises, 15 sports hotel, 16 stores, 17 kitchen, 18 physical training, 19 sick room ward, 20 radio and television, 21 craftsmen, 22 staff, 23 seats, 24 to restaurants, 25 to solarium, 26 sunbathing terraces, 27 top lighting.

2. Grundrisse von Plattformgeschoß und Untergeschoß. Legende: 1 Vorhalle, 2 Kasse, 3 Aufgang zu den Zuschauerplätzen, 4 Garderobe, 5 Toiletten, 6 Umkleideräume und Wannenbad, 7 Aufgang zur Terrasse, 8 Verwaltung, 9 Friseur, 10 Umkleideräume, 11 Baderäume, 12 Schwimmbecken, 13 Kiosk, 14 Klublokale, 15 Hotel für Sportler, 16 Abstellraum, 17 Küche, 18 Gymnastik, 19 Krankenzimmer, 20 Radio und Fernsehen, 21 Handwerker, 22 Personal, 23 Tribüne mit Sitzplätzen, 24 Aufgang zum Restaurant, 25 Aufgang zum Sonnenbad, 26 Sonnenterrassen, 27 Oberlichtkuppeln.

3. Model photograph of the swimming pool seen from South.
4. Cross-sections A-A (swimming pool) and B-B (changing rooms). Key: 1 paddling pool, 2 terrace, 3 club premises, 4 passage, 5 vestibule, 6 installations, 7 pool, 8 restaurant, 9 changing rooms, 10 hairdresser 11 tub baths, 12 women's baths, 13 shower baths, 14 sauna, 15 physical training, 16 solarium.
5. Model photograph of the swimming pool seen from East.
6. Model photograph of the swimming pool seen from North.

3. Modellansicht der Schwimmhalle von Süden.
4. Schnitte A-A (Schwimmhalle) und B-B (Umkleideräume). Legende: 1 Planschbecken, 2 Terrasse, 3 Klublokale, 4 Durchgang, 5 Vorhalle, 6 Installationen, 7 Schwimmbecken, 8 Restaurant, 9 Umkleideräume, 10 Friseur, 11 Wannenbad, 12 Römisches Bad, 13 Duschraum, 14 Sauna, 15 Gymnastik, 16 Sonnenbad.
5. Modellansicht der Schwimmhalle von Osten.
6. Modellansicht der Schwimmhalle von Norden.

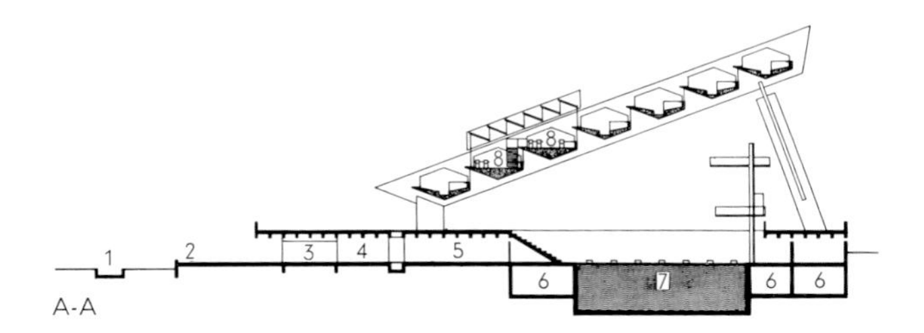

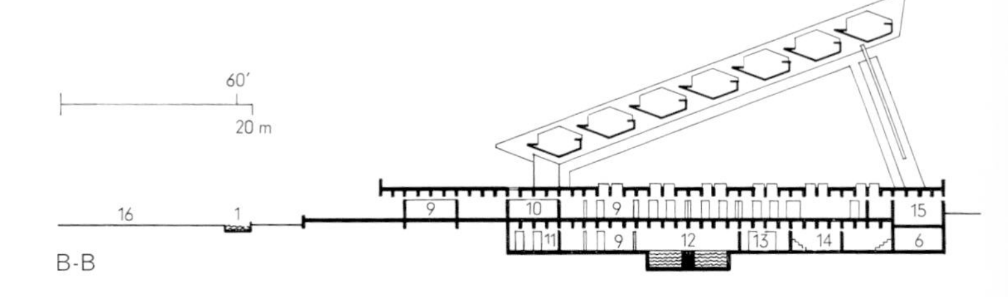

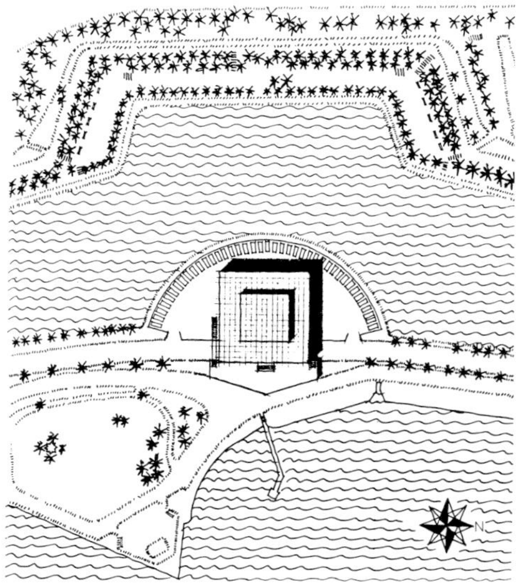

Eva + Nils Koppel

Restaurant Langelinie Pavilion in Copenhagen, 1957
The well-known Langelinie Walk in Copenhagen is situated between the harbour and the old fortifications, Kastellet. In a public architectural competition for the design of a pavilion to replace a restaurant building destroyed during the war, Nils and Eva Koppel were awarded the First Prize for a project which was subsequently carried out. A low-level carriageway which used to follow the contour lines of the old moat is now taken right through the basement of the building where the main entrance and vestibule are placed. At the level of the Langelinie Walk, and with a view in all directions, is the main floor with the restaurant and the banqueting rooms around the kitchen. In a retracted upper floor, the Royal Danish Yacht Club has its premises. The steel profiles of the structure are painted black, the wall panels grey-blue.

Restaurant im Langelinie-Pavillon, Kopenhagen, 1957
Die Langelinie-Promenade in Kopenhagen liegt zwischen dem Hafen und der alten Festung Kastellet. In einem offenen Wettbewerb für den Entwurf eines Pavillons als Ersatz für ein Restaurantgebäude, das während des Krieges zerstört worden war, gewannen Nils und Eva Koppel den ersten Preis mit einem Projekt, das anschließend ausgeführt wurde. Eine Fahrstraße, die früher den Höhenlinien des alten Festungsgrabens folgte, ist jetzt direkt durch das Untergeschoß geführt, in dem sich der Haupteingang und das Foyer befinden. Auf Höhe der Promenade mit Aussicht nach allen vier Himmelsrichtungen liegt das Hauptgeschoß mit Restaurant und Gesellschaftsräumen um die Küche herum. In einem zurückgesetzten Obergeschoß sind die Räume des Königlich Dänischen Yachtklubs untergebracht. Die Stahlprofile der Konstruktion wurden schwarz gestrichen, die Wandfelder graublau.

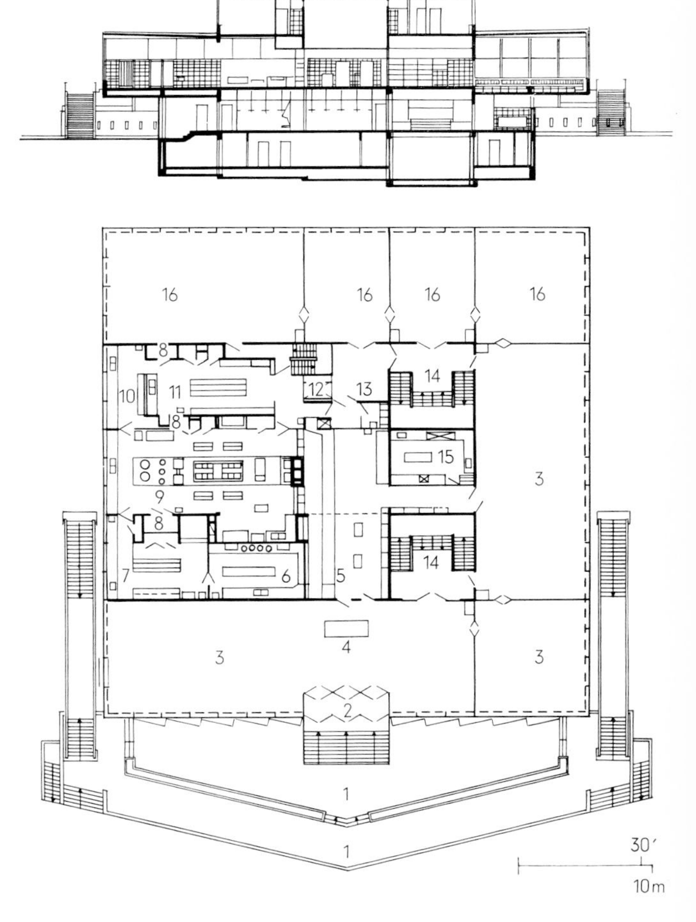

1. The pavilion with the open-air restaurant terrace facing the Langelinie Walk and harbour.
2. Site plan.
3. The pavilion, seen between the old trees of the fortifications, with the moat in the foreground.
4. View from the restaurant towards north, showing the moat on the left-hand side and the harbour on the right-hand side of the carriageway which is taken directly through the basement of the house.
5. The banqueting rooms face the moat. Furniture designed by Jørgen Høj, lamp fitting by Poul Henningsen.
6. Section and plan of restaurant floor. Key: 1 terrace, 2 porch, 3 restaurant, 4 pastry buffet, 5 buffet, 6 coffee kitchen, 7 pastry cook, 8 refrigerator room, 9 warm kitchen, 10 cold kitchen, 11 Smørrebrød kitchen, 12 lift, 13 ante-room, 14 stairs, 15 scullery, 16 banqueting rooms.

1. Der Pavillon mit seinem der Promenade und dem Hafen zugewandten Terrassenrestaurant.
2. Lageplan.
3. Der Pavillon mit dem alten Festungsgraben im Vordergrund.
4. Blick aus dem Restaurant nach Norden mit dem Festungsgraben auf der linken Seite und dem Hafen auf der rechten Seite der Fahrstraße, die direkt durch das Untergeschoß des Hauses geführt ist.
5. Die Gesellschaftsräume liegen nach Osten zum Festungsgraben hin. Die Möbel wurden von Jørgen Høj, die Kugellampe von Poul Henningsen entworfen.
6. Schnitt und Grundriß des Restaurantgeschosses. Legende: 1 Terrasse, 2 Windfang, 3 Restaurant, 4 Küchenbuffet, 5 Buffet, 6 Kaffeeküche, 7 Konditorei, 8 Kühlraum, 9 Warme Küche, 10 Kalte Küche, 11 Smørrebrød-Küche, 12 Fahrstuhl, 13 Vorraum, 14 Treppe, 15 Spülküche, 16 Gesellschaftsräume.

Arne Jacobsen

SAS Royal Hotel, with restaurant and air terminal, Copenhagen, 1958–60

The SAS Hotel, occupying a central position in Copenhagen, consists of a long two-storey wing whose horizontality is emphasized by a continuous ribbon of windows, and of an 18-storey hotel tower. At the southern end of the low building are hotel foyer, restaurant and shops, at the northern end the air terminal. The entire group is raised on a reinforced concrete framework structure. The hotel tower is covered by a curtain wall of thin, grey aluminium profiles with breast panels of grey-green glass. The low wing has a covering of grey-green enamelled steel plates.

SAS-Hotel Royal mit Restaurant und SAS-Empfangsgebäude, Kopenhagen, 1958–60

Das im Zentrum der Stadt errichtete Gebäude besteht aus einem langen zweigeschossigen Flügelbau, dessen durchgehendes Fensterband die Horizontale betont, und aus einem 18-geschossigen Hotelturm. Der Südteil des flachen Traktes nimmt Hotelfoyer, Restaurant und Läden auf, der Nordteil die Abfertigungsräume der skandinavischen Luftfahrtgesellschaft. Die ganze Anlage ist als Stahlbeton-Skelettkonstruktion ausgeführt. Der Hotelturm wurde mit einem Curtain-wall aus dünnen, grau eloxierten Aluminiumprofilen und Brüstungselementen aus graugrünem Glas verkleidet. Der niedrige Anbau hat eine Verkleidung aus graugrün emaillierten Stahltafeln.

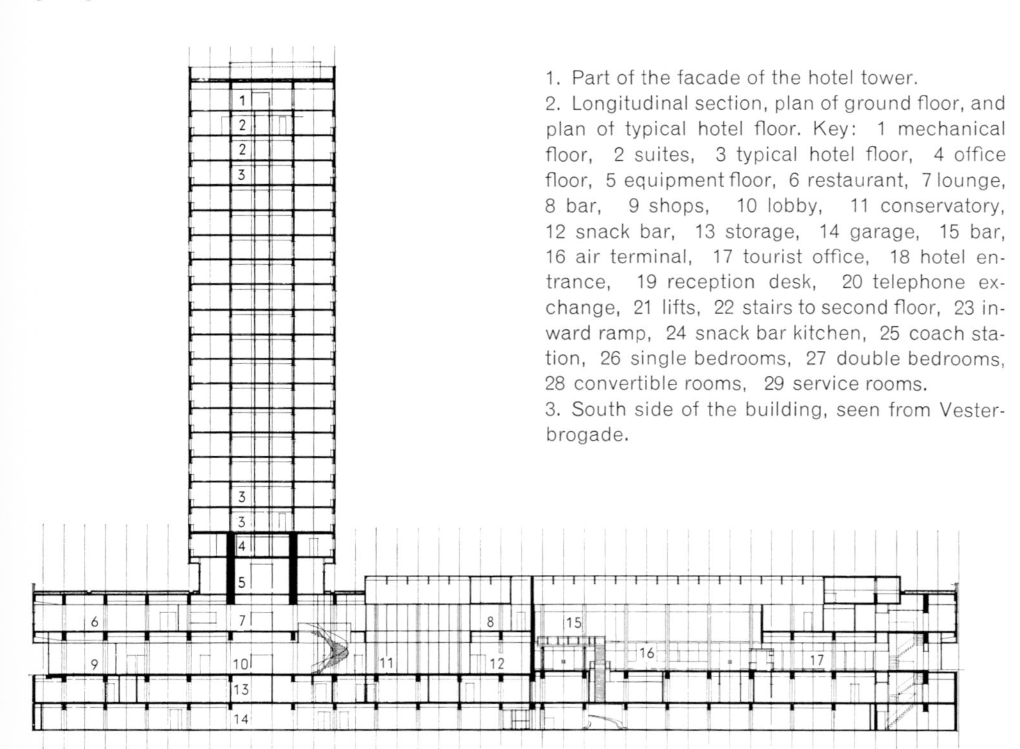

1. Part of the facade of the hotel tower.
2. Longitudinal section, plan of ground floor, and plan of typical hotel floor. Key: 1 mechanical floor, 2 suites, 3 typical hotel floor, 4 office floor, 5 equipment floor, 6 restaurant, 7 lounge, 8 bar, 9 shops, 10 lobby, 11 conservatory, 12 snack bar, 13 storage, 14 garage, 15 bar, 16 air terminal, 17 tourist office, 18 hotel entrance, 19 reception desk, 20 telephone exchange, 21 lifts, 22 stairs to second floor, 23 inward ramp, 24 snack bar kitchen, 25 coach station, 26 single bedrooms, 27 double bedrooms, 28 convertible rooms, 29 service rooms.
3. South side of the building, seen from Vesterbrogade.

1. Ausschnitt aus der Fassade des Hotelturms.
2. Längsschnitt, Grundriß des Erdgeschosses und Grundriß eines Normalgeschosses im Hotelturm. Legende: 1 Technische Installationen, 2 Hotelsuiten, 3 Hotel-Normalgeschoß, 4 Bürogeschoß, 5 Installationsgeschoß, 6 Restaurant, 7 Lounge, 8 Bar, 9 Läden, 10 Lobby, 11 Wintergarten, 12 Snackbar, 13 Vorräte, 14 Garage, 15 Bar, 16 SAS-Abfertigung, 17 Reisebüro, 18 Hoteleingang, 19 Empfang, 20 Telefonvermittlung, 21 Aufzüge, 22 Treppe zum ersten Obergeschoß, 23 Einfahrtrampe, 24 Küche der Snackbar, 25 Autobus-Haltestelle, 26 Einbettzimmer, 27 Zweibettzimmer, 28 Wandelbare Zimmer, 29 Service.
3. Die Südseite des Gebäudes, von der Vesterbrogade aus gesehen.

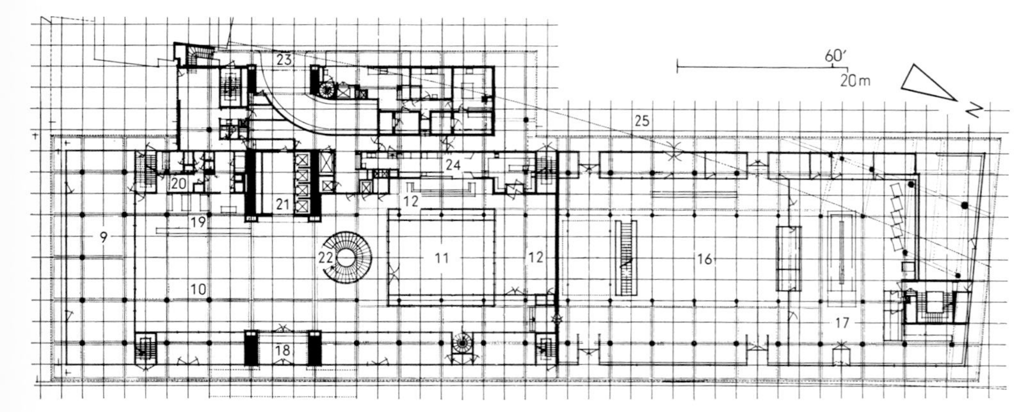

SAS
BOSCH
A3

◁ 4. The spiral stairs between foyer and restaurant are suspended from steel cables. The doubled-up steel plates of the steps are covered with green carpeting. The balustrade panels are of smoked coloured plexiglass.
5. The hotel foyer in the low wing, surrounded by shops which have access both from the foyer and from the street. A conservatory, with top lighting, provides daylight for the rear part of the foyer. Flooring of light grey marble, ceiling painted dark green. All furniture is designed by Arne Jacobsen.
6. Lift landing. Walls of polished black marble.
7. The conservatory is surrounded by double glass walls; in the space between these walls, different types of orchids are suspended. In the background, the hotel snack bar.
8. The circular top lights of the restaurant also accommodate the smoke-coloured glass globes of the light fittings. Furniture, curtains, carpets and cutlery are designed by Arne Jacobsen.
9. Restaurant vestibule with furniture and fittings designed by Arne Jacobsen.

◁ 4. Die Wendeltreppe zwischen Foyer und Restaurant ist an Stahlkabeln aufgehängt. Die aus gefalzten Stahlplatten bestehenden Stufen sind mit einem grünen Teppich belegt. Die Füllungen des Treppengeländers bestehen aus rauchfarbenem Plexiglas.
5. Das Hotelfoyer im niedrigen Anbau ist von Läden umgeben, die sowohl von der Halle als auch von der Straße her zugänglich sind. Ein mit Oberlicht versehener Wintergarten bringt auch dem rückwärtigen Teil des Foyers Tageslicht. Der Fußboden besteht aus hellgrauem Marmor, die Decke ist dunkelgrün gestrichen. Alle Möbel wurden von Arne Jacobsen entworfen.
6. Vorraum der Hotelaufzüge. Wände aus poliertem schwarzen Marmor.
7. Der Wintergarten ist von doppelten Glaswänden umgeben, zwischen denen Orchideenpflanzen aufgehängt sind. Im Hintergrund die Snackbar des Hotels.
8. Innerhalb der kreisrunden Oberlichter im Restaurant ist für die rauchfarbenen Glasglocken der künstlichen Beleuchtung Platz gelassen. Möbel, Vorhänge, Teppiche und Tischbestecke sind von Arne Jacobsen entworfen.
9. Foyer des Restaurants mit von Arne Jacobsen entworfenen Möbeln und Lampen.

1. The hotel, seen from the West.

1. Die Westseite des Hotels.

Knud Friis + Elmar Moltke Nielsen

Hvide Hus hotel and restaurant at Ebeltoft, Jutland, 1962–63
The hotel is situated on a slope North of Ebeltoft, affording an attractive view across Ebeltoft Fjord and the Mols peninsula. The hotel rooms are placed on terraces down the slope and each room has a wide balcony of its own. Access road and foyer are on the East side. The restaurant is on the top floor and is linked with a large terrace where meals are served in the open. The hotel is erected in reinforced concrete, painted white. The terraces between the different rooms are divided by screens.

Hotel und Restaurant Hvide Hus in Ebeltoft, Jütland, 1962–63
Das Hotel liegt an einem Abhang nördlich von Ebeltoft mit schöner Aussicht über den Fjord und die Halbinsel Mols. Die Hotelzimmer sind terrassenförmig angelegt, und jedes Zimmer hat einen breiten Balkon. Zufahrt und Foyer befinden sich auf der Ostseite. An das im Dachgeschoß gelegene Restaurant schließt sich eine große Terrasse an, auf der ebenfalls serviert wird. Das Haus ist aus weißgestrichenem Stahlbeton errichtet. Zwischen den einzelnen Zimmern sind die Terrassen durch Schirmwände abgeteilt.

2. Part of the terraces on the West side.
3. Cross-section, plans of top floor and ground floor. Key: 1 entrance, 2 hall, 3 bar, 4 reception, 5 office, 6 cloakroom, 7 lift, 8 staff entrance, 9 staff dining room, 10 banqueting room, 11 lounge, 12 restaurant, 13 scullery, 14 kitchen, 15 dressing room, 16 terrace.
4. The hotel and its view across Ebeltoft Fjord and the Mols peninsula, seen from the East.

2. Teil der Terrassenanlage auf der Westseite.
3. Querschnitt und Grundrisse von Dachgeschoß und Erdgeschoß. Legende: 1 Eingang, 2 Halle, 3 Bar, 4 Empfang, 5 Büro, 6 Garderobe, 7 Fahrstuhl, 8 Personaleingang, 9 Personalspeisesaal, 10 Gesellschaftsraum, 11 Aufenthaltsraum, 12 Restaurant, 13 Spülküche, 14 Küche, 15 Anrichte, 16 Terrasse.
4. Ostansicht mit der Zufahrt und dem Blick über den Ebeltoft-Fjord und die Halbinsel Mols.

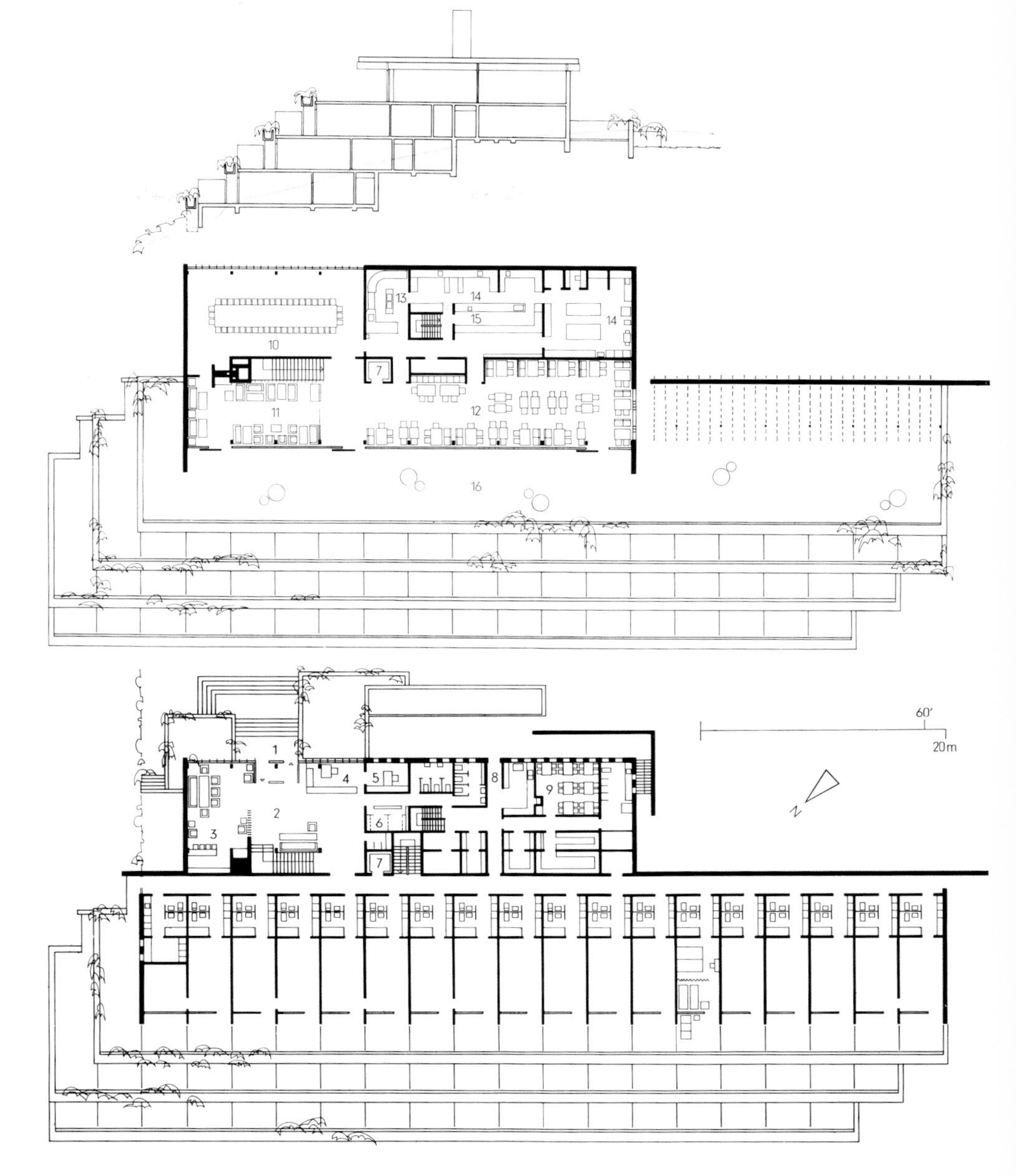

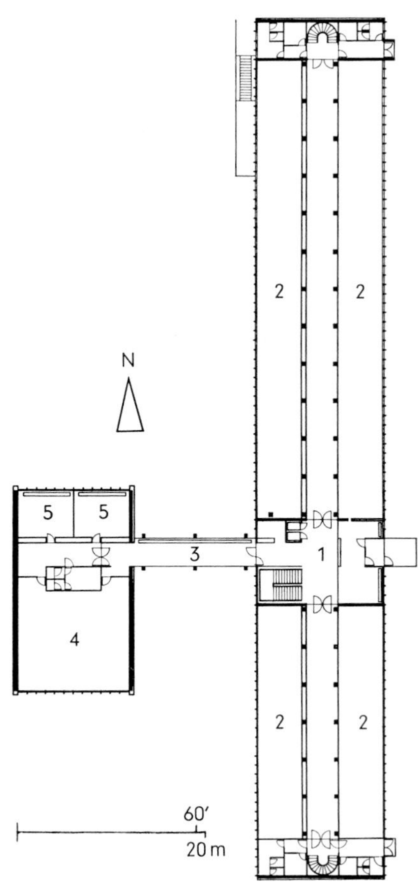

Arne Jacobsen

Town Hall at Rødovre near Copenhagen, 1955
The town hall is situated in a residential area in the vicinity of Rødovre's local shopping centre on a flat common which now also accommodates a library designed by Arne Jacobsen. The town hall consists of a three-storey office wing, linked with a single-storey pavilion in which the council chamber and the committee rooms are placed. The bearing structure of the office block consists of reinforced concrete columns placed along the central corridor from which the structural floors are cantilevered. The facades of the long sides are composed of curtain walls with lightgreen glass panels, and windows framed by steel profiles. The end walls are covered with black marble.

Rathaus der Gemeinde Rødovre bei Kopenhagen, 1955
Das Rathaus steht zwischen Wohnbauten in der Nähe des örtlichen Einkaufszentrums inmitten einer Grünfläche, auf der inzwischen eine ebenfalls von Arne Jacobsen entworfene Bibliothek errichtet worden ist. Der Komplex besteht aus einem dreigeschossigen Verwaltungsgebäude und einem frei stehenden, eingeschossigen Pavillon, in dem der Ratssaal und zwei Ausschußzimmer untergebracht sind. Die Geschoßdecken des Bürogebäudes kragen von einer Doppelreihe tragender Stahlbetonstützen zu beiden Seiten des Mittelflurs frei aus. Die Fassaden der Längsseiten sind als Curtain-walls mit Stahlprofilen und hellgrünen Glasbrüstungen ausgebildet. Die Stirnwände sind mit schwarzen Marmorplatten verkleidet.

1 Main entrance with a canopy supported by steel columns. The two undersides, staggered in relation to each other, are painted light-green and orange-red respectively.
2. Ground floor plan. Key: 1 entrance hall, 2 offices, 3 passage connecting the main building with the council chamber, 4 council chamber, 5 committee rooms.
3. South side with the low council chamber building and the marble-covered end wall of the office block.
4. West side, with the low council chamber pavilion in the foreground.

1. Der Haupteingang mit dem auf Stahlstützen ruhenden Vordach und dem niedrigen Kragdach über der Tür. Die beiden Unterseiten sind hellgrün beziehungsweise orangerot gestrichen.
2. Grundriß des Erdgeschosses. Legende: 1 Eingangshalle, 2 Büros, 3 Verbindungsgang zwischen Hauptgebäude und Ratssaal, 4 Ratssaal, 5 Sitzungszimmer.
3. Ansicht von Süden mit dem niedrigen Ratssaalpavillon (links) und der marmorverkleideten Stirnmauer des Büroflügels.
4. Die Westfassade mit dem Sitzungsgebäude im Vordergrund.

5. Corridor connecting the office block with the council chamber pavilion.
6. The flooring of the council chamber is of marble, the walls are painted yellow-green. The white ceiling reflects the light of 121 small lamps which are fitted to suspended steel tubes.
7. The stringers and steps of the main stairs are made of steel plates and suspended from steel tubes. The banister panels are of pre-stressed glass. The stringers are painted olive-green, the steel tubes red; the steps are covered with grey plastics.

5. Verbindungsgang zwischen Verwaltungsgebäude und Ratssaalpavillon.
6. Der Ratssaal mit Marmorboden und gelbgrün gestrichenen Wänden. Die weißgestrichene Decke reflektiert das Licht von 121 Lampen, die an aufgehängten Stahlrohren befestigt sind.
7. Wangen und Stufen der Haupttreppe bestehen aus Stahlblech, die Geländerfüllungen aus vorgespanntem Glas. Die Treppe ist an Rundstahlstäben aufgehängt. Ihre Seitenwangen sind olivgrün, die Rundstäbe rot gestrichen. Die Stufen sind mit grauem Kunststoff belegt.

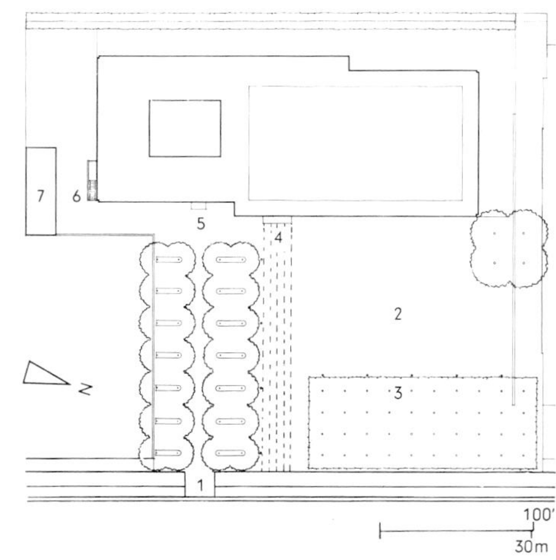

Halldor Gunnløgsson + Jørn Nielsen

Town Hall at Tårnby near Kastrup, Copenhagen, 1958–59
The design is the result of a public architectural competition. The town hall is situated in a mixed residential and commercial district in the island of Amager South of Copenhagen. Two staggered two-storey blocks each contain offices on three sides; one of the blocks surrounds a large hall with top lighting, the other an open courtyard with a pool of water. At ground floor level, a vestibule provides a transition between courtyard and hall. Above the vestibule, on the first floor, is the council chamber, facing the courtyard. The building is in reinforced concrete; all the inside columns and beams remain visible. On the outside, the building has a cladding of Norwegian marble.

Rathaus von Tårnby bei Kastrup, Kopenhagen, 1958–59
Das Rathaus, dessen Entwurf das Ergebnis eines offenen Architektenwettbewerbs ist, steht in einem gemischten Wohn- und Geschäftsviertel auf der Insel Amager südlich von Kopenhagen. Jeder der beiden seitlich gegeneinander versetzten zweigeschossigen Bauteile enthält auf drei Seiten Büros; der eine Flügelbau umschließt eine mit Oberlicht versehene Ratshalle, der andere einen offenen Hof mit Wasserbecken. Im Erdgeschoß bildet eine Vorhalle den Übergang zwischen Hof und Ratshalle. Über der Vorhalle liegt im Obergeschoß der Ratssaal, mit Blick auf den Hof. Die Konstruktion besteht aus sichtbar belassenen Stahlbetonstützen und -trägern. Außen ist das Gebäude mit norwegischem Marmor verkleidet.

1. Tårnby town hall, seen from the paved forecourt on the east side. The large hall is recognisable from the outside by its flat roof with the large cantilever above the high-level top lighting.
2. Site plan. Key: 1 entrance and exit, 2 paved forecourt, 3 car park, 4 main entrance, 5 entrance to welfare office, 6 stairs to bicycle basement, 7 garages.

1. Das Rathaus von dem im Osten anschließenden gepflasterten Vorplatz aus gesehen. Die große Ratshalle ist von außen an ihrem flachen Dach zu erkennen, das über den hochliegenden Fensterbändern weit auskragt.
2. Lageplan. Legende: 1 Ein- und Ausfahrt, 2 Gepflasterter Vorplatz, 3 Parkplatz, 4 Haupteingang, 5 Eingang zum Wohlfahrtsamt, 6 Treppe zum Fahrradkeller, 7 Garagen.

3. Longitudinal section, and ground floor plan. Key: 1 large hall, 2 pool of water, 3 vestibule, 4 welfare office, 5 archives, 6 canteen, 7 bicycle basement, 8 council chamber, 9 balcony, 10 shelter room, 11 waiting room, 12 educational officer, 13 valuer, 14 registrar, 15 treasurer, 16 cashier, 17 accountant.
4. The large hall, seen from the low vestibule, furnished by Poul Kjærholm. The hall is kept in shades of grey, whilst the stringers of the stairs and the edges of the balconies are painted lake-red.

3. Längsschnitt und Grundriß des Erdgeschosses. Legende: 1 Große Halle, 2 Wasserbecken, 3 Vorhalle, 4 Wohlfahrtsamt, 5 Archive, 6 Speisesaal, 7 Fahrradkeller, 8 Ratssaal, 9 Erschließungsgalerie, 10 Luftschutzraum, 11 Warteraum, 12 Schulbehörde, 13 Katasteramt, 14 Einwohnermeldeamt, 15 Steueramt, 16 Kasse, 17 Buchhaltung.
4. Ansicht der Ratshalle von der niedrigen Vorhalle aus, die mit Serienmöbeln (Entwurf Poul Kjærholm) ausgestattet ist. Die Halle ist in grauen Farbtönen gehalten, während die Treppenwangen und die Vorderkanten der Galerie lackrot gestrichen sind.

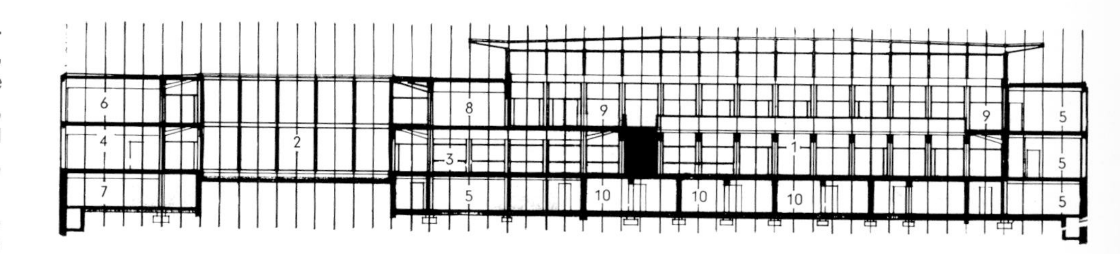

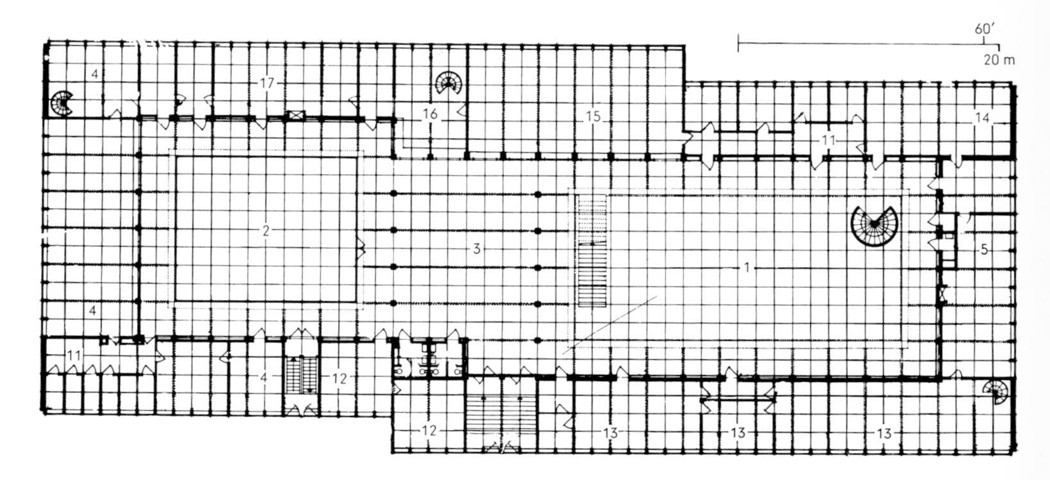

5. From the large hall, there is a view past the stairs and through the vestibule on to the courtyard with the pool of water.
6. Main entrance on the east side. The stairs are covered with Norwegian marble.
7. The sculpture placed in the pool of water in the courtyard is by Torsten Johansson.

5. Von der Ratshalle her hat man durch Treppe und Vorhalle einen Ausblick auf Hof und Wasserbecken.
6. Der Haupteingang auf der Ostseite mit Treppenstufen aus norwegischem Marmor.
7. Im Wasserbecken des Hofes ist eine Skulptur des Bildhauers Torsten Johansson aufgestellt.

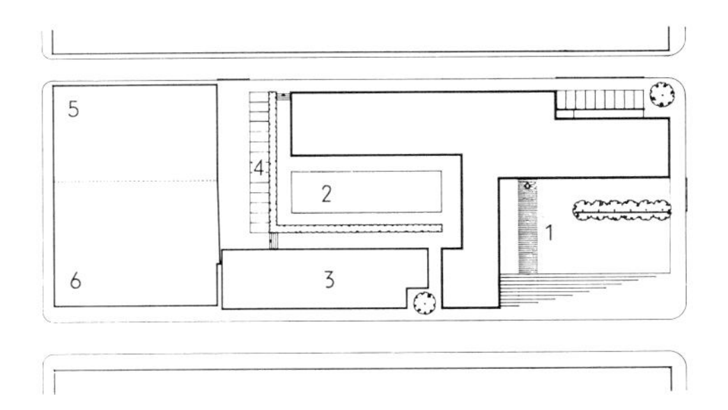

1. Administration building of the town hall, seen at night from the forecourt, with the council chamber annex on the left.
2. Site plan. Key: 1 forecourt, 2 planned town hall garden, 3 planned office block, 4 car park, 5 subsequently added car park, 6 private houses.

1. Nachtansicht des Verwaltungsgebäudes, vom Platz vor dem Haupteingang aus gesehen; links der Ratssaalanbau.
2. Lageplan. Legende: 1 Terrassierter Platz am Eingang, 2 Geplanter Rathausgarten, 3 Geplantes Geschäftshaus, 4 Parkplatz, 5 Spätere Parkplatzerweiterung, 6 Privathäuser.

Halldor Gunnløgsson + Jørn Nielsen

Town Hall at Fredericia, Jutland, 1963–64

In 1956, Gunnløgsson and Jørn Nielsen were awarded the First Prize in a public architectural competition for a tidy and attractive project, comprising both a new municipal administration building and an office block. So far, it is only the municipal building which has been erected. Its original layout plan with two staggered office wings and a low transverse annex with the council chamber has been preserved though the reasoning behind it is not fully apparent as long as the office block has not been built. The administration building has a reinforced concrete framework and is clad with bronze. The council chamber building has in-situ-cast concrete walls which have been left untreated. The lightweight roof above the skylight of the council chamber is supported by steel trestlework.

Rathaus der Stadt Fredericia in Jütland, 1963–64

Im Jahre 1956 wurde den Architekten Gunnløgsson und Jørn Nielsen in einem offenen Architektenwettbewerb der erste Preis für ein übersichtliches und interessantes Projekt zuerkannt, das sowohl ein neues städtisches Verwaltungsgebäude als auch ein Geschäftshaus umfaßte. Bisher konnte nur das Verwaltungsgebäude ausgeführt werden, bei dessen Grundriß jedoch die ursprünglich vorgesehene Form mit zwei gegeneinander versetzten Büroflügeln und einem niedrigen, quergestellten Ratssaalanbau beibehalten wurde – eine Anordnung, die nicht ganz motiviert erscheint, solange das Geschäftshaus noch nicht errichtet ist. Das eigentliche Verwaltungsgebäude hat eine Stahlbeton-Skelettkonstruktion und ist mit Bronze verkleidet. Die Ortbetonwände des Ratssaalanbaus sind unbehandelt belassen. Das leichte Dach über dem hochliegenden Fensterband des Ratssaals wird von Stahlbindern getragen.

3. The town hall seen from the North, with the concrete wall of the council chamber annex in the background. The three-storey office wing has a cladding of bronze.
4. Administrative building of the town hall, seen from the East, with the main entrance at the corner of the paved forecourt.

3. Das Rathaus von Norden, mit den Betonwänden des Ratssaalanbaus im Hintergrund. Das dreigeschossige Verwaltungsgebäude hat eine Bronzeverkleidung.
4. Das Verwaltungsgebäude von Osten gesehen, mit dem Haupteingang an der Ecke des gepflasterten Terrassenplatzes.

5. Section and ground floor plan. Key: 1 administration building, 2 council chamber, 3 committee rooms, 4 register, 5 vestibule, 6 treasurer, 7 rates collector.
6. The walls of the vestibule are of light-grey limestone brick. The reinforced concrete structures are left untreated. The balcony balustrades are of oak, the floor is paved with brown clinkers.
7. The council chamber walls are covered with oak panels. Floors of grey marble. The steel structures of the roof are painted red.

5. Schnitt und Grundriß des Erdgeschosses. Legende: 1 Verwaltungsgebäude, 2 Ratssaal, 3 Sitzungszimmer, 4 Standesamt, 5 Vorhalle, 6 Stadtkämmerer, 7 Steueramt.
6. Die Wände der Vorhalle bestehen aus hellgrauem Kalksandstein. Die Stahlbetonkonstruktion ist unbehandelt belassen. Galeriebrüstung aus Eichenholz, Fußboden mit braunen Klinkern belegt.
7. Die Wände des Ratssaals sind mit Eichenholzpaneelen verkleidet. Der Fußboden besteht aus grauem Marmor. Die Stahlbinder des Daches sind rot gestrichen.

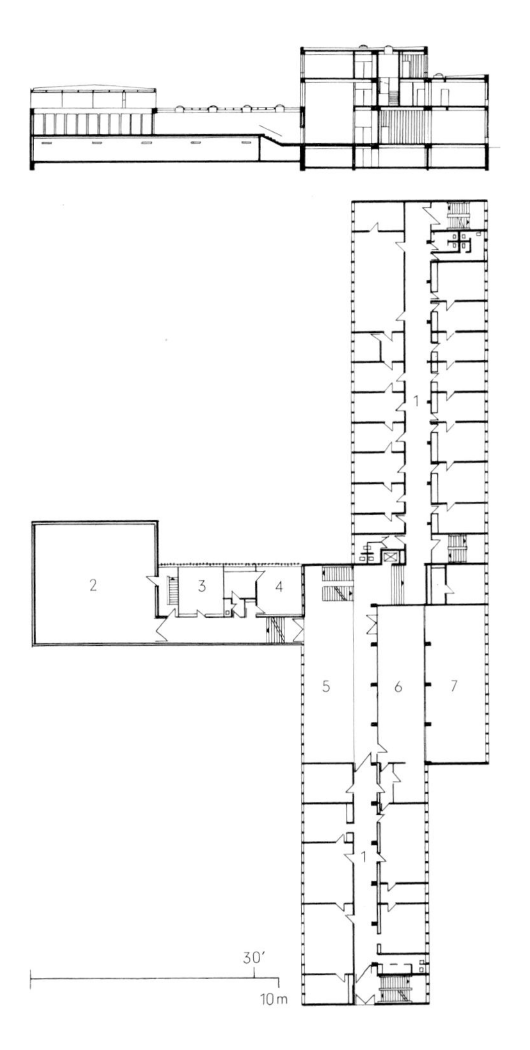

1. East side, facing the street (Nyropsgade).
2. Section; plans of 7th floor, typical floor, and ground floor (from top to bottom).

1. Die Ostseite des Gebäudes nach der Straße zu (Nyropsgade).
2. Querschnitt; Grundrisse vom 7. Obergeschoß, Normalgeschoß und Erdgeschoß (von oben nach unten).

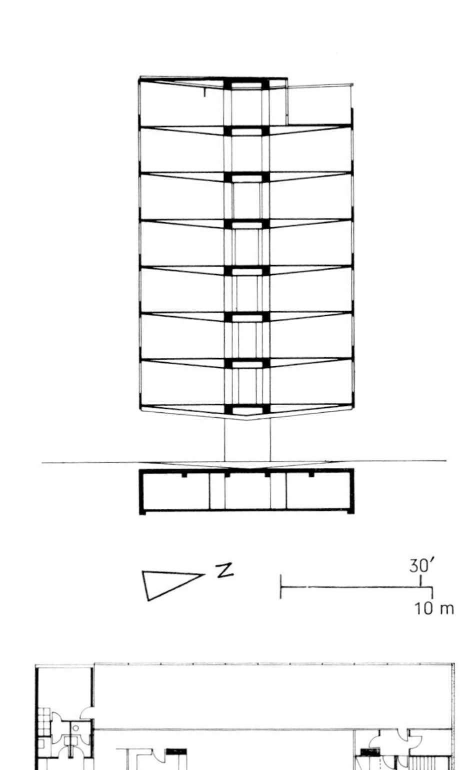

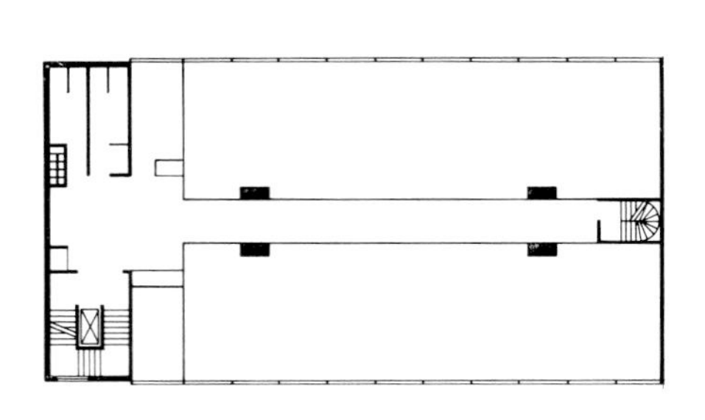

Arne Jacobsen

Headquarters of Messrs. Jespersen & Søn, Copenhagen, 1955

The building is supported by the in-situ-cast end walls and two massive columns in the ground floor which, on the upper floors, are split into two slender columns on either side of the central corridor. From here, the structural floors are cantilevered. The curtain wall facades are of wood with aluminium clad bars and with window breast walls of green glass. The windows towards the street (Nyropsgade) cannot be opened, those facing the courtyard are horizontally hinged thermopane windows. The entire ground floor is left open as the authorities insisted on free passage.

Bürogebäude der Firma Jespersen & Søn in Kopenhagen, 1955

Die vertikalen Tragelemente des Gebäudes bestehen aus Ortbeton-Wandscheiben an den Stirnseiten und aus zwei massiven Stahlbetonpfeilern, die sich in den oberen Stockwerken in je ein schlankes Stützenpaar spalten, zwischen dem der Mittelkorridor der zweibündigen Anlage verläuft. Von hier aus kragen die Geschoßdecken nach beiden Seiten weit aus. Die Fassade, ein reiner Curtain-wall, besteht aus aluminiumverkleideten Holzrahmen mit Fensterbrüstungen aus grünem Glas. Die Fenster auf der Straßenseite sind fest verglast, während sie auf der Hofseite aus Wendeflügeln mit Thermopanescheiben bestehen. Einer Auflage der Behörden folgend, ist das gesamte Untergeschoß als Durchfahrt offen gelassen.

3. The glass-encased emergency stairs in the open passage below the building.
4. Street front, seen from North-East.

3. Die voll verglaste Nottreppe nimmt einen Teil der offenen Durchfahrt unter dem Haus ein.
4. Die Straßenfront von Nordosten.

1. Street view of shop window.
2. The shop as seen from the gallery towards the street. The walls are covered with framed oak panels.

1. Straßenansicht der Schaufensterfront.
2. Blick vom Zwischengeschoß durch den Laden zur Straße. Die Wände bestehen aus Eichenholzpaneelen.

Vilhelm Wohlert + Kaare Klint

Optician's shop of Messrs. F.A. Thiele A/S, Copenhagen, 1956
In 1944, Kaare Klint was entrusted with the reconstruction of the shop of the old optician's firm, F.A. Thiele, in Købmagergade. The project was deferred, and was only resumed in 1951 in collaboration with Vilhelm Wohlert. Kaare Klint died in 1954 so that Wohlert alone became responsible for the detailed design and execution of the work. Interior joinery is of smoked oak treated with wax; tables and barriers are of teak, the ceiling is painted white.

Optikergeschäft der Firma F.A. Thiele A/S in Kopenhagen, 1956
Im Jahr 1944 wurde Kaare Klint die Aufgabe erteilt, den Laden der alten Optikerfirma F.A. Thiele in der Købmagergade umzubauen. Das Projekt wurde aufgeschoben und erst 1951 in Zusammenarbeit mit Vilhelm Wohlert wiederaufgenommen. Kaare Klint starb 1954, so daß Wohlert die Detailplanung und Ausführung des Umbaus allein durchführte. Die Inneneinrichtung besteht aus geräuchertem, mit Wachs behandeltem Eichenholz. Tische und Handläufe sind aus Teakholz, die Decke ist weiß gestrichen.

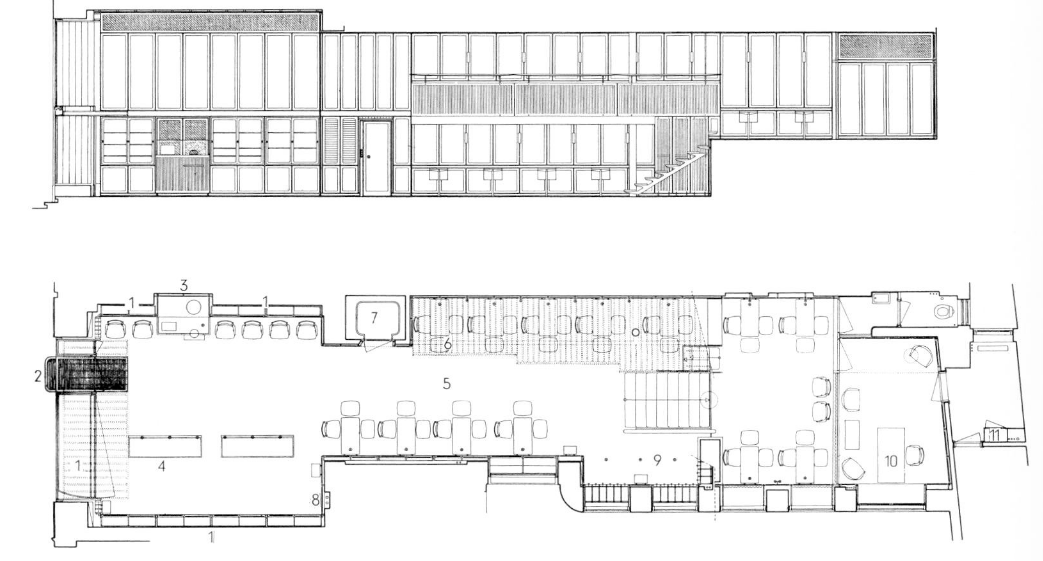

3. Stairs leading to the gallery.
4. The shop, seen towards the display window.
5. Longitudinal section and plan. Key: 1 showcase, 2 entrance, 3 cashier, 4 sales counter, 5 space for 18 optician's tables, 6 gallery, 7 lift, 8 pneumatic conveyor, 9 drawers for spectacles, 10 manager's office, 11 cloakroom.

3. Treppe zum Zwischengeschoß.
4. Blick durch den vorderen Teil des Ladens.
5. Längsschnitt und Grundriß. Legende: 1 Schaufensterauslage, 2 Eingang, 3 Kasse, 4 Ladentisch, 5 Stellfläche für 18 Optikertische, 6 Zwischengeschoß, 7 Fahrstuhl, 8 Rohrpost, 9 Einbauregale für Brillen, 10 Büro des Prokuristen, 11 Garderobe.

1. Part of the facade towards Lille Kongensgade. The retracted ground floor provides sufficient space for an arcade along the shop windows.
2. Ground floor plan. Key: A Lille Kongensgade, B Kongens Nytorv; 1 arcade, 2 entrance, 3 escalators, 4 exit ramp from parking garage, 5 entrance ramp to parking garage, 6 courtyard, 7 covered courtyard, 8 restaurant à'Porta, 9 self-service shop.
3. On the side facing Bremerholm, the authorities insisted on the provision of balconies on each floor to serve as emergency exits. By means of a close network of bars, the impression of a full-face frontage is maintained at least in fore-shortened perspective.
4. Facade towards Bremerholm at the corner of Lille Kongensgade.
5. Through the small piazza at Bremerholm, the department store is in direct contact with Copenhagen's main shopping street, Strøget.

1. Ausschnitt aus der Fassade zur Lille Kongensgade. Das zurückgenommene Erdgeschoß läßt für eine Passage vor den Schaufenstern Platz.
2. Grundriß des Erdgeschosses. Legende: A Lille Kongensgade, B Kongens Nytorv; 1 Passage, 2 Eingang, 3 Rolltreppen, 4 Ausfahrtrampe des Parkhauses, 5 Einfahrtrampe des Parkhauses, 6 Hof, 7 Lichthof, 8 Restaurant à'Porta, 9 Selbstbedienungsabteilung.
3. Am Bremerholm verlangten die Behörden zur Straße hin offene Notausgangsgalerien in den Obergeschossen. Durch ein dichtes Netz von Sprossen ist jedoch die Flächenhaftigkeit der Hausreihe jedenfalls in der perspektivischen Verkürzung bewahrt.
4. Fassade an der Ecke von Bremerholm und Lille Kongensgade mit den als Fluchtweg dienenden offenen Außengalerien.
5. Durch die kleine Piazza am Bremerholm steht das Warenhaus mit Kopenhagens wichtigster Geschäftsstraße (Strøget) in Verbindung.

Erik Møller

Magasin du Nord department stores, Copenhagen, 1959

The oldest part of the Magasin du Nord department stores, situated at Kongens Nytorv, was built in 1893 by architect Albert Jensen. Erik Møller's task was to integrate a number of subsequent additions and yet another annex into a single unit while preserving the original building and its adjacent property with the popular Copenhagen restaurant à'Porta. With its four-storey buildings, the annex is in harmony with the scale of the older districts and the elevation of the old houses in the vicinity. The curtain wall panels between the bars of the new building are of black split slate.

Warenhaus Magasin du Nord in Kopenhagen, 1959

Der älteste, am Kongens Nytorv gelegene Teil des großen Warenhauses Magasin du Nord wurde 1893 vom Architekten Albert Jensen erbaut. Erik Møllers Aufgabe bestand darin, das ursprüngliche Gebäude und das daneben liegende Haus mit dem beliebten Kopenhagener Restaurant à'Porta zu erhalten und mit den späteren Anbauten sowie einem weiteren Neubau zu einer Einheit zusammenzufassen. Mit seinen viergeschossigen Fronten ordnet sich der Neubau maßstäblich sowohl dem umliegenden älteren Stadtteil als auch dem Flächencharakter der alten Hausreihen im Straßenbild ein. Beim Curtain-wall des neuen Gebäudes bestehen die Brüstungsfelder zwischen den Metallsprossen aus schwarzen, bruchrauhen Schieferplatten.

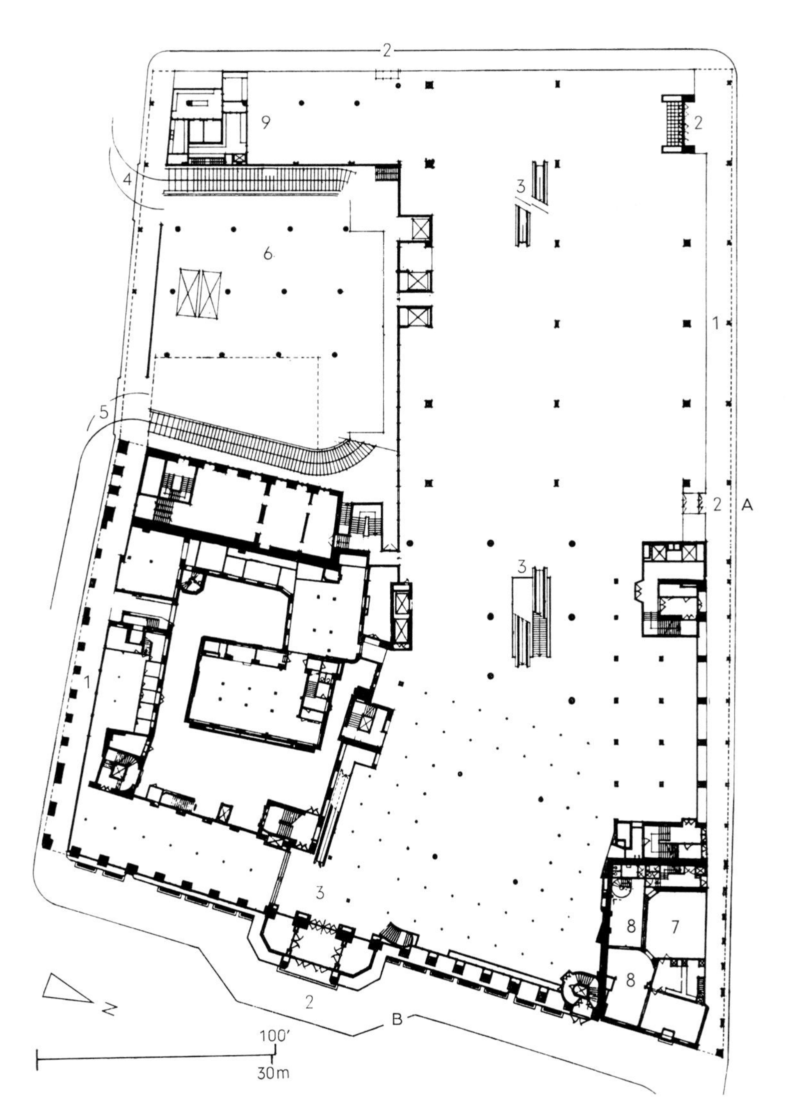
2
9
2
4
3
6
1
5
2
A
3
1
3
8
7
8
2
B
N
100'
30m

NORD MAGASIN DU NORD
Magasin
HAFNIA

Palle Suenson

Headquarters building of Messrs. F.L. Schmidt & Co., Copenhagen, 1954–56

The principal activity of Messrs. F.L. Schmidt & Co. is the erection of cement factories throughout the world. The headquarters building of the firm is situated in an industrial estate in the Copenhagen district of Valby. Two staggered, north-south orientated wings with eight and four storeys, respectively, contain the drawing and commercial offices whilst the vestibule and management offices are placed in a two-storey block with retracted roof storey. The laboratories are housed in a low annex in the rear of the site. The bearing structure of the buildings consists of 30 cm wide and 75 cm deep brick pillars spaced at 120 cm centres. The bronze windows are deeply recessed, and owing to the marked vertical relief effect, the facades are of heavy and robust appearance, in attractive compositional contrast to the light, widely cantilevered roof of the management wing. The buildings are faced with specially manufactured deep-red Flensborg tiles.

Bürogebäude der Firma F.L. Schmidt & Co. in Kopenhagen, 1954–56

Die Firma F.L. Schmidt & Co. befaßt sich vor allem damit, Zementfabriken in der ganzen Welt zu errichten. Ihr Hauptverwaltungsgebäude liegt in einem Industriebezirk im Kopenhagener Stadtteil Valby. Zwei gegeneinander versetzte, nord-südlich orientierte Gebäude mit acht beziehungsweise vier Geschossen nehmen die Zeichen- und Verwaltungsbüros auf, während die Empfangshalle und die Direktionsbüros in einem zweigeschossigen Baukörper mit zurückgesetztem Dachgeschoß untergebracht sind. Die Laboratorien befinden sich in einem niedrigen Anbau im rückwärtigen Teil des Grundstücks. Die Tragkonstruktion der Gebäude besteht aus 30 cm breiten und 75 cm tiefen, gemauerten Pfeilern, die in einem Abstand von 120 cm voneinander stehen. Die Fenster in Bronzerahmen sind weit zurückgezogen, so daß die Fassaden durch die starke vertikale Reliefwirkung einen schweren und robusten Eindruck machen. In spannungsvollem Gegensatz hierzu steht das weit auskragende, leichte Dach des Direktionsgebäudes. Die Bauten sind aus besonders hergestellten, tiefroten Flensburgziegeln errichtet.

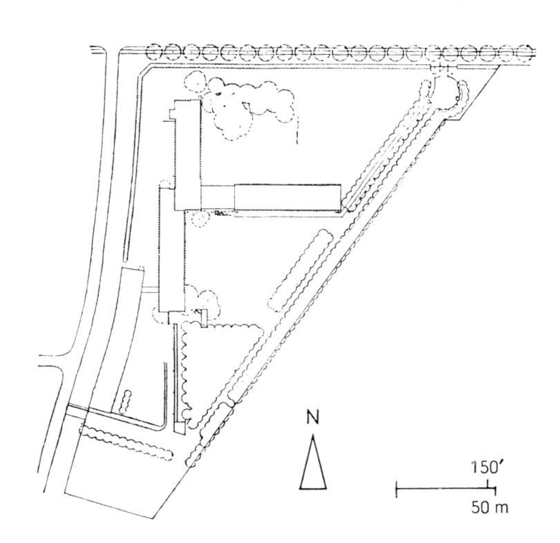

1. The north wing of the administration building seen from the East, with the low wing containing the management offices in the foreground on the left. The eight-storey block contains the drawing offices.
2. Site plan.

1. Der Nordflügel des Verwaltungsgebäudes von Osten, mit dem niedrigen Direktionsgebäude im Vordergrund links. Das achtgeschossige Gebäude enthält die Zeichenbüros.
2. Lageplan.

3. The gallery in the vestibule is supported by 17 metres long beams of prestressed concrete.
4. The south wing of the administration building seen from the East, with the entrance yard. The two-storey building with the management offices is here seen on the right.
5. Vestibule with stairs leading to the gallery and to the management offices on the first floor.

3. Das Zwischengeschoß der Empfangshalle ruht auf 17 m langen Spannbetonträgern.
4. Der viergeschossige Südflügel von Osten, mit dem Eingangshof. Rechts das zweigeschossige Direktionsgebäude.
5. Die Empfangshalle mit der Treppe zum Zwischengeschoß und zu den Direktionsbüros im ersten Stock.

Erik Chr. Sørensen

Office building and data processing centre, Copenhagen, 1962
The building is situated at Lersø Park Allé in an industrial estate where the use of red brick and the landscaping of the open spaces was obligatory. The building has a bearing structure of in-situ-cast concrete. The deck above the ground floor is supported by three longitudinal column-cum-girder systems whilst the roof above the first floor is supported by cross beams stretching between the extreme rows of columns. The brick facades are not load-bearing.

Bürogebäude und Rechenzentrum in Kopenhagen, 1962
Das Gebäude liegt an der Lersø Park Allé in einem Industriebezirk, wo die Anwendung roter Ziegel und eine parkartige Bepflanzung der Freiflächen behördlich vorgeschrieben ist. Das Gebäude hat eine Skelettkonstruktion aus Ortbeton. Die Decke über dem Erdgeschoß ruht auf drei längsorientierten Reihen von Stützen und Unterzügen, während das Dach über dem Obergeschoß auf Querträgern aufliegt, die sich zwischen den äußeren Stützenreihen spannen. Die aus Backsteinen bestehenden Außenwände haben keine tragende Funktion.

1. Entrance side of the building.
2. Cross-section, plans of upper floor and ground floor. Key: 1 screen walls of 1.40 metres height, 2 punching room, 3 sorting, 4 distribution, 5 postal despatch, 6 IBM machines, 7 glass wall, 8 stores, 9 tape archive, 10 technical stores, 11 screen walls of 2 metres height, 12 cloakroom, 13 hall, 14 lavatories, 15 staff entrance, 16 canteen, 17 offices, 18 vestibule, 19 main entrance, 20 supervisor's office.

1. Die Eingangsseite des Gebäudes.
2. Querschnitt und Grundrisse von Obergeschoß und Erdgeschoß. Legende: 1 Sichtschutzwände von 1,40 m Höhe, 2 Kartenlochung, 3 Sortierung, 4 Verteilung, 5 Postversand, 6 IBM-Maschinen, 7 Glaswand, 8 Lager, 9 Magnetbandarchiv, 10 Technisches Zubehör, 11 Sichtschutzwände von 2 m Höhe, 12 Garderobe, 13 Vorraum, 14 Toiletten, 15 Personaleingang, 16 Kantine, 17 Büros, 18 Eingangshalle, 19 Haupteingang, 20 Bürochef.

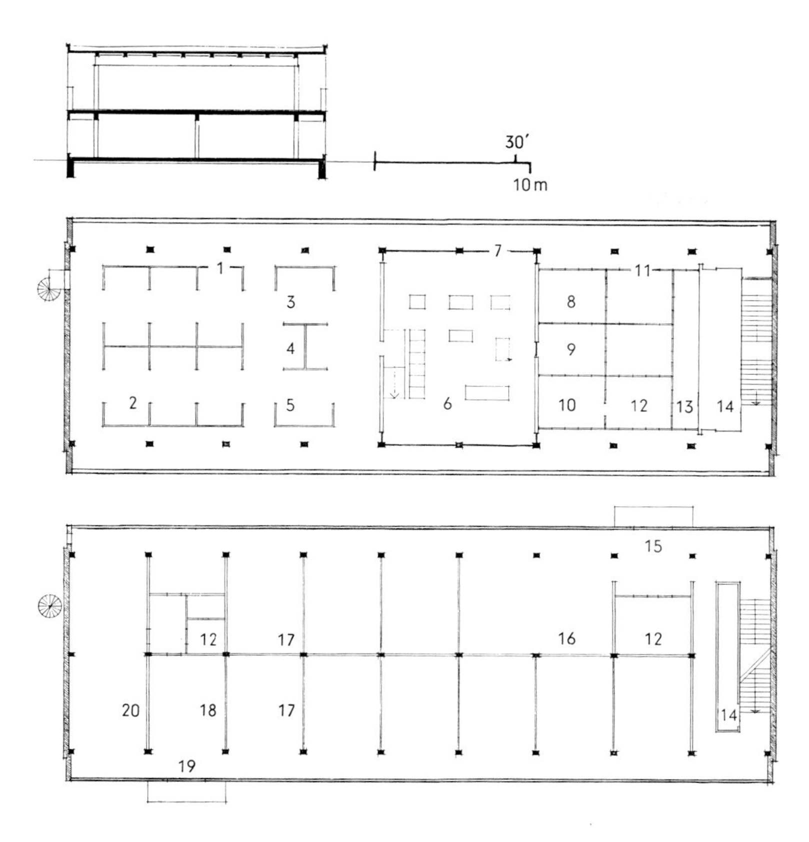

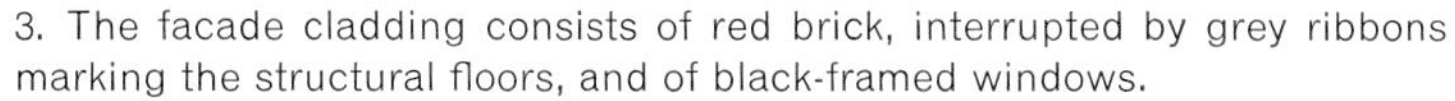

3. The facade cladding consists of red brick, interrupted by grey ribbons marking the structural floors, and of black-framed windows.
4. Hall on the first floor, with the exposed cross beams of reinforced concrete
5. Interior of the ground floor offices, showing the longitudinal column systems.

3. Fassadenausschnitt. Brüstungsverkleidung aus rotem Backstein, in Höhe der Geschoßdecken durch grau gestrichene Streifen unterbrochen; Fenster mit schwarz gestrichenen Rahmen.
4. Die Halle im Obergeschoß mit den sichtbaren, querlaufenden Stahlbetonträgern.
5. Innenansicht der Büroräume im Erdgeschoß mit den längsorientierten Stützenreihen.

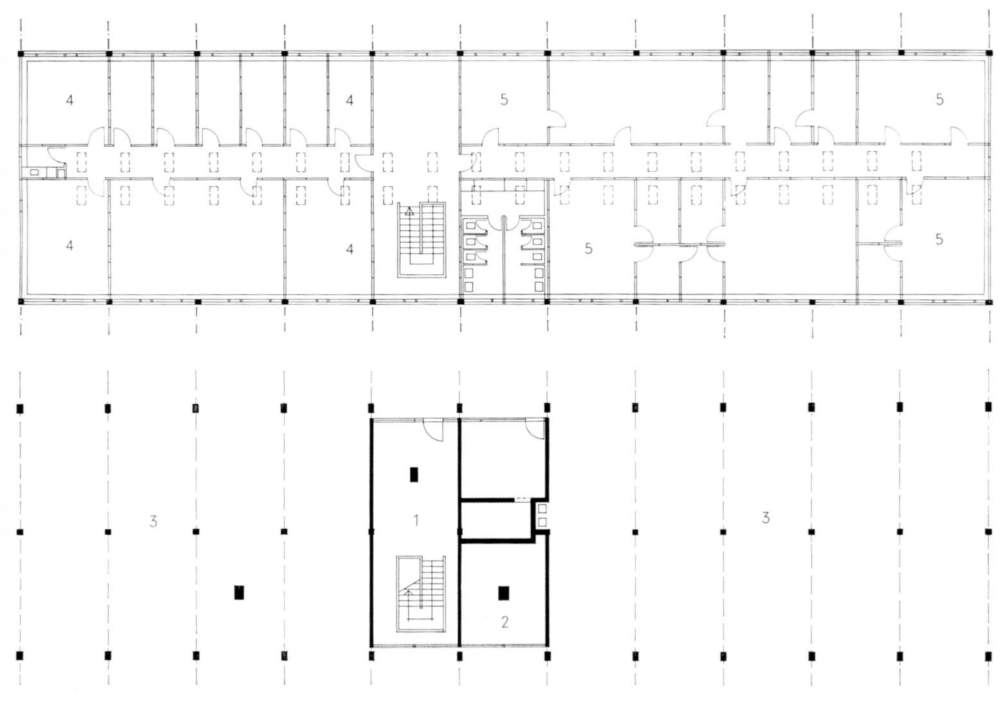

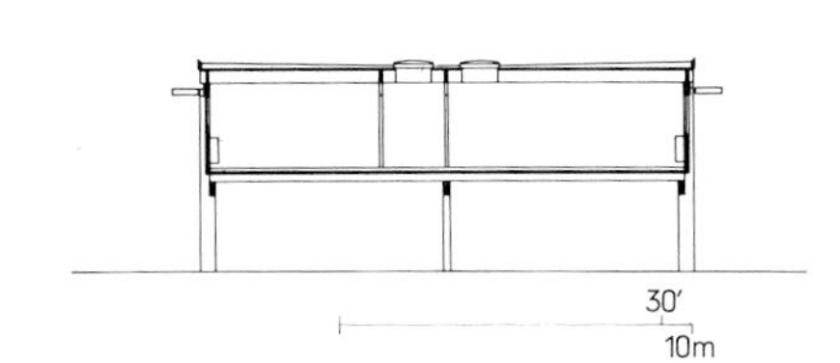

1. Main frontage of the administration building.
2. Plans of first floor and ground floor; cross section. Key: 1 vestibule, 2 garage, 3 car park, 4 offices, 5 laboratories and drawing offices.
3. The in-situ assembled prefabricated concrete units – columns, beams and ribbed plates – are left untreated in the facade. The window breast panels are of white asbestos cement on black frames, the sun screens are of impregnated wood.

1. Die Längsseite des Verwaltungsgebäudes.
2. Grundrisse von Obergeschoß und Erdgeschoß und Querschnitt. Legende: 1 Eingangshalle und Treppenhaus, 2 Garage, 3 Wageneinstellplätze, 4 Büros, 5 Labors und Zeichenbüros.
3. Die an Ort und Stelle montierten, vorgefertigten Betonelemente – Stützen, Träger und Rippenplatten – werden in der Fassade unbehandelt belassen. Die Fensterbrüstungen bestehen aus weiß gestrichenen Eternitplatten in schwarzen Rahmen. Sonnenschutzlamellen aus imprägniertem Holz.

Knud Peter Harboe

Office building of Messrs. N. Foss Electric A/S, Hillerød, North Zealand, 1961
The principal architectural feature of this building lies in the bearing structure itself which can be clearly discerned from the outside. The building is assembled from prefabricated reinforced concrete units, viz. columns, beams and I-shaped ribbed plates. The ground floor is kept open as a car park.

Verwaltungsgebäude der N. Foss Electric A/S, Hillerød im Norden der Insel Seeland, 1961
Das Schwergewicht des architektonischen Eindrucks liegt bei diesem Gebäude auf der Konstruktion, die sich von außen klar ablesen läßt. Es handelt sich um ein aus vorgefertigten Stahlbetonelementen errichtetes Gebäude, das aus Stützen, Trägern und I-förmigen Rippenplatten zusammengesetzt ist. Das Untergeschoß des Hauses wurde als Wageneinstellplatz freigehalten.

1. The street frontage of the new building appears to consist of open balconies in reinforced concrete, stretching between bearing walls of yellow brick.
2. The entrance with its granite stairs is retracted from the street. Window frames and ceiling covers are of bronze.

1. Die Straßenseite des Bankneubaus mit den Stahlbeton-»Balkonen«, die zwischen den tragenden Seitenwänden aus gelbem Backstein eingespannt scheinen.
2. Der Eingang mit der Granittreppe ist von der Straße zurückgesetzt. Fensterrahmen und Dekkenverkleidung sind aus Bronze.

Poul Kjærgaard, Ole Jung, Svend Limkilde, Bent Mortensen, Jørgen Strunge, Pauli Wulff
Assistant/Mitarbeiter: Finn Gaardboe

Building of Hammerum Herreds Savings Bank at Herning, Jutland, 1964
In 1964 an existing bank building dating from the beginning of this century, in the High Street of Herning, was reconstructed and extended by a new building next door. The latter consists of a service hall with a gallery facing the street, and a retracted roof storey. The brick sidewalls of the service hall penetrate the street facade which gives the appearance of wide concrete balconies suspended between the sidewalls. The old building now contains a loans department in direct connection with the new premises. The yellow brick walls as well as the reinforced concrete are left untreated, both externally and internally.

Hammerum Herreds Sparkasse in Herning, Jütland, 1964
Ein zu Anfang des Jahrhunderts errichtetes Bankgebäude an der Hauptstraße von Herning wurde im Jahre 1964 umgebaut und durch einen Neubau erweitert. Der Neubau besteht aus einem Kundenraum mit eingeschobener Galerie auf der Straßenseite und einem zurückgesetzten Dachgeschoß. Die Backstein-Seitenwände des Kundenraumes sind über die Straßenfront hinaus nach vorn gezogen, so daß diese aus breiten, zwischen seitlichen Mauerscheiben eingespannten Betonbalkonen zu bestehen scheint. Im alten Gebäude ist in unmittelbarer Verbindung mit dem Kundenraum ein Kreditbüro eingerichtet. Sowohl die gelben Backsteinwände als auch die Stahlbetonflächen sind innen und außen unbehandelt belassen.

3. Bank premises with top lighting and, on the right, with the reinforced concrete gallery which accommodates a conference room. Furniture and fittings are of light oak. ▷

3. Der Kundenraum mit Oberlichtbändern und der in Sichtbeton ausgeführten Galerie (rechts), auf der sich ein Sitzungszimmer befindet. Einbauten aus hellem Eichenholz. ▷

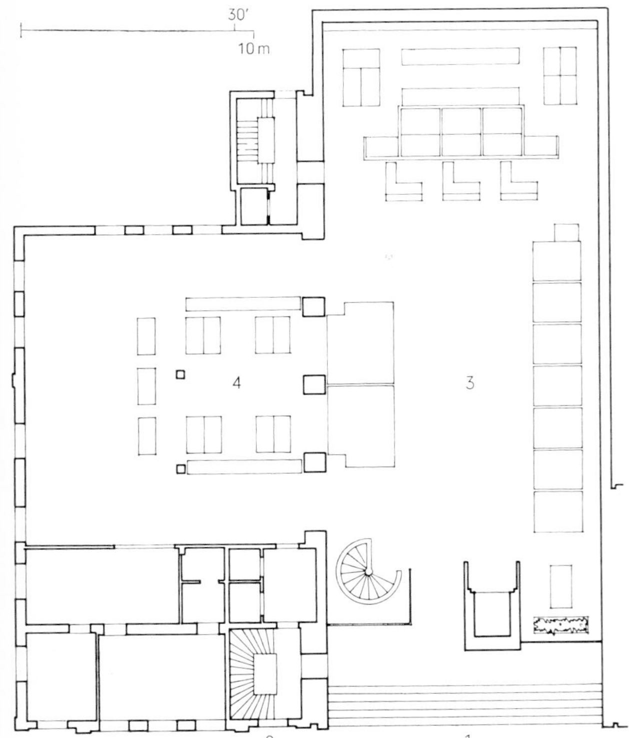

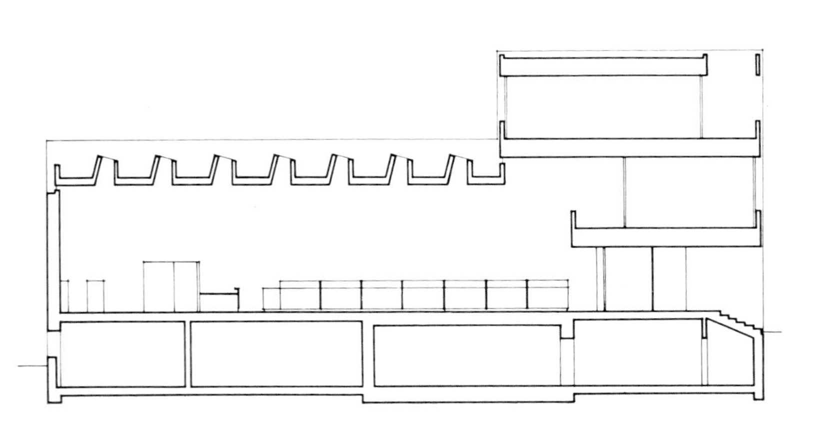

4. The loans department in the old building (on the left) is in open connection with the new premises. Flooring of Øland tiles.
5. Ground floor plan and section. Key: 1 entrance to new building, 2 old building, 3 deposits department, 4 loans department.

4. Das Kreditbüro im Altbau (links) steht mit dem neuen Kundenraum in offener Verbindung. Fußbodenbelag aus Ølandfliesen.
5. Grundriß und Schnitt des Erdgeschosses. Legende: 1 Eingang zum Neubau, 2 Altbau, 3 Depositenkasse, 4 Kreditbüro.

Arne Jacobsen

Toms Fabrikker A/S, factory at Ballerup near Copenhagen, 1961
Toms Fabrikker are manufacturers of chocolate. The group of buildings, erected in 1961, is situated at Ballerup to the North-West of Copenhagen on a flat site which is covered with lawn and attractive vegetation. The group forms a well-composed unit of clearly identifiable buildings – a three-storey administration building, a large rectangular factory hall, and a heating plant – associated with a group of chimneys, oil tanks and silos with strong vertical accent. The buildings are in reinforced concrete and have a cladding of concrete integrally cast with white-grey ceramic tiles. The factory hall has pyramid-shaped top lighting of artificial glass.

Toms Fabrikker A/S in Ballerup bei Kopenhagen, 1961
Toms Fabrikker stellen Schokolade und Süßwaren her. Die 1961 errichtete Werksanlage liegt in Ballerup nordwestlich von Kopenhagen auf einem ebenen Gelände mit ausgedehnten Grünflächen und Anpflanzungen. Sie bietet ein gut komponiertes Gesamtbild klarer Baueinheiten: ein dreigeschossiges Verwaltungsgebäude, eine große, rechtwinklige Fabrikhalle und eine Heizzentrale, an die sich eine stark vertikal gegliederte Gruppe aus Schornstein, Öltanks und Silos anschließt. Die Gebäude wurden als Stahlbetonkonstruktion errichtet und mit Betonfertigteilen verkleidet, auf deren Außenseite weißgraue keramische Fliesen eingegossen sind. Die Fabrikhalle erhält durch pyramidenförmige Oberlichter aus Kunstglas Tageslicht.

1. View from the administration building across the top lighting of the factory hall towards the group of chimneys and silos.
2. Model of the group of buildings, seen from South-East.

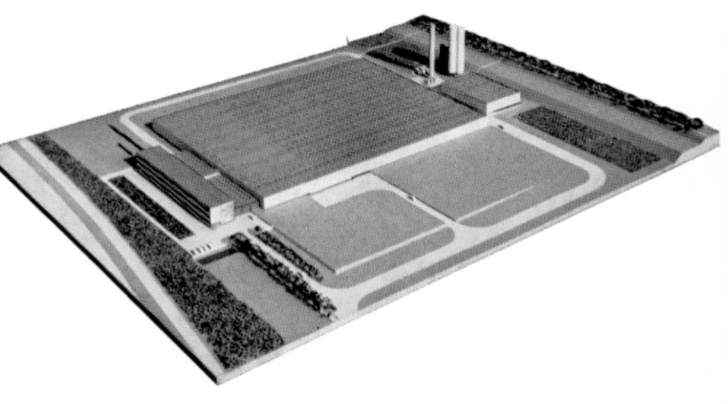

1. Blick vom Verwaltungsgebäude über die Oberlichter der Fabrikhalle hinweg auf Schornstein und Silobauten.
2. Modell der Anlage, von Südosten gesehen.

3, 4. East wall of the administration building with entrance and vestibule with the main stairs, supported by steel profiles.
5. The administration building, seen from South-East. The continuous ribbons of windows are half-covered by adjustable blinds.
6. The cocoa beans silo plant of reinforced concrete and the two oil tanks of steel.

3, 4. Die Ostseite des Verwaltungsgebäudes mit der Eingangszone und dem verglasten Treppenhaus. Die Haupttreppe besteht aus Stahlprofilen.
5. Ansicht des Verwaltungsgebäudes von Südosten. Die durchlaufenden Fensterbänder zur Hälfte durch verstellbare Aluminiumjalousien verdeckt.
6. Siloanlage aus Stahlbeton für Kakaobohnen und die beiden Öltanks aus Stahl.

1. Interior of the despatch hall with the multi-angled reinforced concrete structure of columns and beams.
2. Plans of ground floor and second floor, cross-section and longitudinal section. Key: 1 existing warehouse, 2 manager's office, 3 superintendent's office, 4 store room, 5 unsorted stores, 6 sorted stores, 7 conveyor belt, 8 packing tables, 9 loading bays, 10 despatch, 11 office, 12 dealers' office, 13 stores, 14 bathrooms, 15 cloakroom, 16 lunch canteen, 17 telephone switchboard, 18 head of despatch department, 19 assistants, 20 programming section for electronic data processing, 21 order reception, 22 punched card section for electronic data processing unit, 23 electronic data processing unit, EDB 1401.
3. The main entrance is placed under a protecting cantilever roof in the otherwise enclosed East wall.
4. The office section faces South. The windows are protected against the sun partly by the roof canopy, partly by white wooden slats in copper-clad frames.

1. Innenansicht der Lagerhalle mit den abgeschrägten Stahlbetonstützen und -trägern.
2. Grundrisse des Erdgeschosses und Obergeschosses; Querschnitt und Längsschnitt. Legende: 1 Bestehendes Lagergebäude, 2 Büro des Vertriebsleiters, 3 Büro des Lagerverwalters, 4 Abstellraum, 5 Unsortierte Zugänge, 6 Lager, 7 Zum Versand vorbereitete Sendungen, 8 Packtische, 9 Rampe für Lastwagen, 10 Versand, 11 Büro, 12 Händler-Büro, 13 Nebenraum, 14 Duschraum, 15 Garderobe, 16 Kantine, 17 Telefonzentrale, 18 Leiter der Versandabteilung, 19 Assistenten, 20 Programmabteilung für die elektronische Rechenanlage, 21 Auftragsbearbeitung, 22 Lochkartenabteilung für die elektronische Rechenanlage, 23 Elektronische Rechenanlage, EDB 1401.
3. Der Haupteingang liegt unter einem auskragenden Schutzdach an der sonst geschlossenen Ostseite.
4. Das Verwaltungsgebäude ist nach Süden orientiert. Die Fenster sind gegen die Sonne teils vom auskragenden Dach geschützt, teils von Lamellenblenden aus weiß angestrichenen Holzleisten in kupferverkleideten Rahmen.

Jørgen Bo + Vilhelm Wohlert

Gyldendal's warehouse and despatch hall in Copenhagen, 1963

The new building of the Gyldendal publishing house is an extension of an existing warehouse in the island of Amager to the South of Copenhagen. The extension consists of a hall with skylighting, covering a floor area of approx. 16,000 sq. ft. The light is filtered through suspended canvas and reflected by inclined reinforced concrete beams. The latter rest on reinforced concrete columns and on the surrounding walls. Connected with the hall is a two-storey office section with a single-storey canteen annex. All external walls are of red brick.

Gyldendals Versand- und Lagerhaus in Kopenhagen, 1963

Der Neubau des Buchverlages Gyldendal wurde an ein bestehendes Lagerhaus auf der Insel Amager südlich von Kopenhagen angebaut. Der Erweiterungsbau besteht aus einer 1500 m² großen Halle mit shedähnlichen Oberlichtern. Das einfallende Tageslicht wird durch aufgehängte Leinwände gefiltert und von abgeschrägten Stahlbetonträgern reflektiert. Die Träger ruhen auf sich nach unten verjüngenden Stahlbetonstützen und werden zudem von den umgebenden Mauern abgestützt. An die Halle schließt sich ein zweigeschossiger Verwaltungsbau mit davorliegender eingeschossiger Kantine an. Alle Außenmauern bestehen aus rotem Backstein.

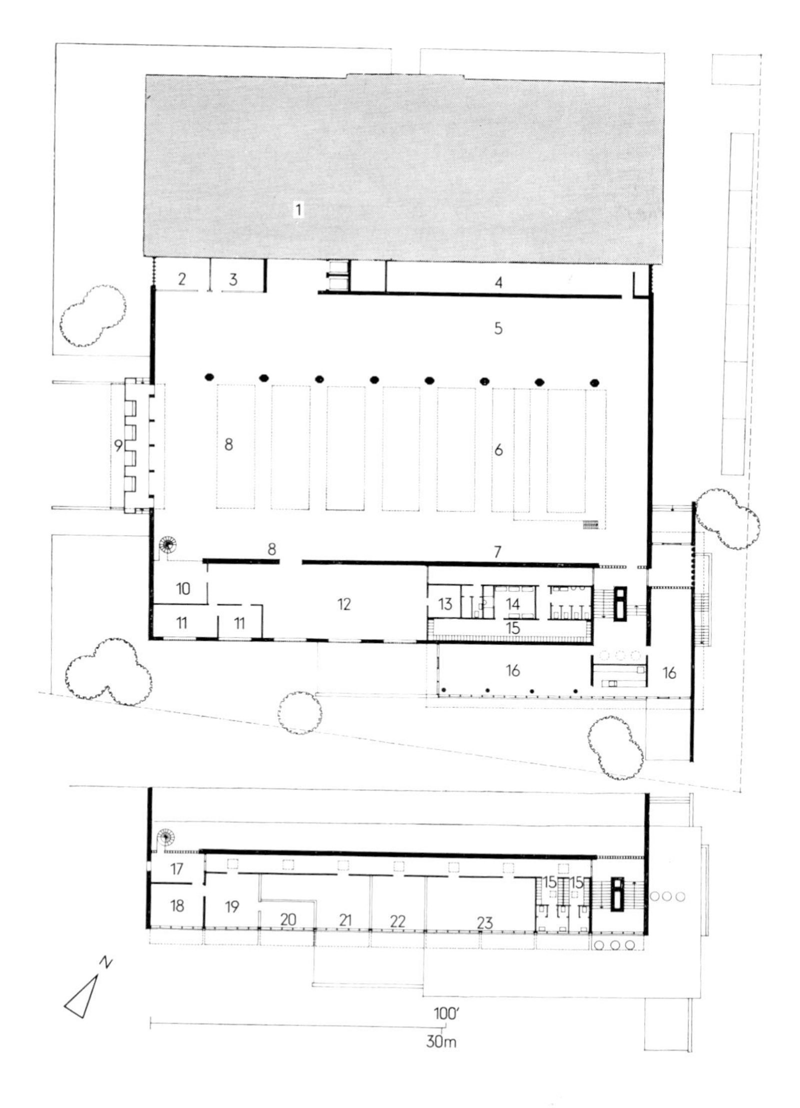
1
2
3
4
5
6
7
8
9
10
11
12
13
14
15
16
17
18
19
20
21
22
23
N
100'
30m

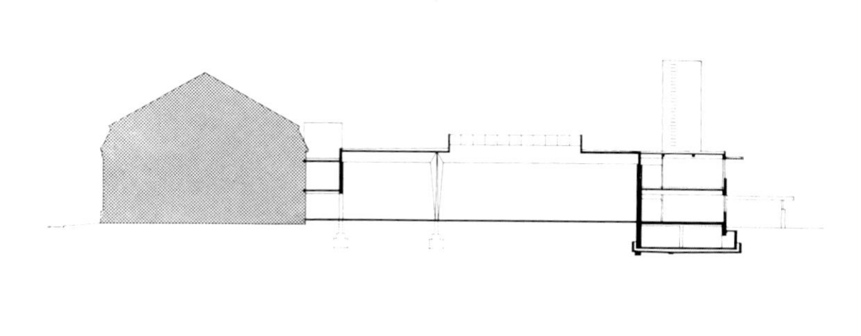

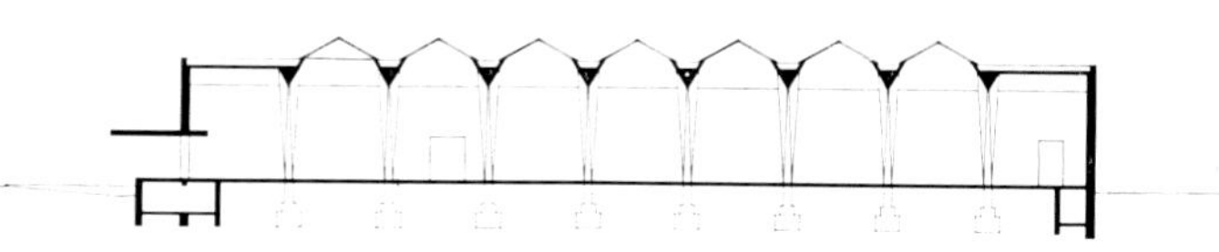

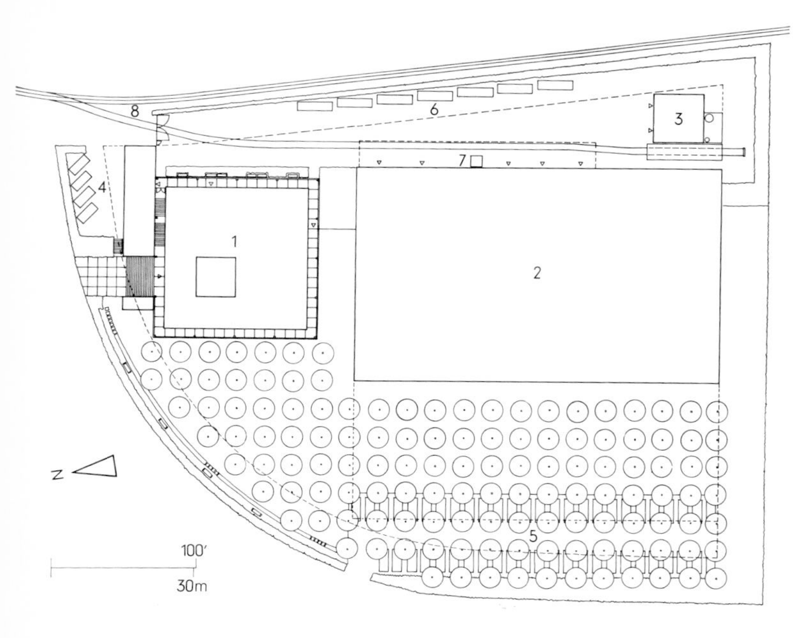

1. Site plan. Key: 1 administration building, 2 warehouse, 3 washing and repairs, 4 car park for visitors, 5 car park, 6 parking area for commercial vehicles, 7 janitor, 8 railway siding.
2. The main entrance is placed in the single-storey administration building. The box roof is overhung to serve as a sun screen.
3. The outer walls of the warehouse are of water-scrubbed lime-sandstone. The rather ornamental tube ends are part of the ventilation plant.
4. Atrium of the administration building.
5. The offices surrounding the atrium are not partitioned. The daylight entering from the atrium is supplemented by top lighting. Artificial light fittings are built into the Oregon pine ceiling.
6. Administration building, north elevation and ground floor plan. Key: 1 main entrance, 2 vestibule, 3 office area, 4 cashier, 5 atrium, 6 manager, 7 office, 8 cloakroom, 9 toilets, 10 conference room, 11 board room, 12 wine tasting, 13 wine stores, 14 archives.

Halldor Gunnløgsson + Jørn Nielsen

Wine stores of Messrs. Georg Bestle A/S at Ballerup near Copenhagen, 1965

The building is situated in a new industrial estate at Ballerup to the North-West of Copenhagen. It consists of a large warehouse containing a 10 metres high hall and a single-storey administration building surrounding an atrium. The roof of the hall is a lattice structure of steel, resting on steel columns. The outer walls are of lime-sandstone. The wine is stored on shelves of 6 to 7 metres height. The office building has a reinforced concrete framework with lime sandstone panels. The roof is of the box type, erected in concrete, with panels of oil-painted wooden lattice work.

Weinhandlung der Firma Georg Bestle A/S in Ballerup bei Kopenhagen, 1965

Der Baukomplex liegt in einem neuen Industrieviertel bei Ballerup nordwestlich von Kopenhagen. Es besteht aus einem großen Lagerhaus mit einer 10 m hohen Halle und einem eingeschossigen Bürogebäude, das einen Innenhof umschließt. Das Dach der Halle besteht aus einer von Stahlstützen getragenen Stahlgitterkonstruktion. Die Außenmauern sind aus Kalksandstein. Der Wein wird auf 6 bis 7 m hohen Regalen gelagert. Das Bürogebäude hat ein Stahlbetonskelett mit Füllwänden aus Kalksandstein und ein Kassettendach aus Betonrippen mit Holzgitterfüllung, die mit Ölfarbe gestrichen ist.

1. Lageplan. Legende: 1 Verwaltungsgebäude, 2 Lagerhalle, 3 Wasch- und Reparaturhalle, 4 Parkplatz für Gäste, 5 Parkplatz, 6 Parkplatz für Lastwagen, 7 Pförtner, 8 Anschlußgleis.
2. Haupteingang im Verwaltungsgebäude. Das Kassettendach kragt als Sonnenschutz aus.
3. Die Außenwände der Lagerhalle bestehen aus geschlämmtem Kalksandstein. Die effektvollen Rohrmündungen gehören zur Ventilationsanlage.
4. Der Innenhof des Verwaltungsgebäudes.
5. Die den Innenhof umgebenden Büros sind nicht unterteilt. Das vom Hofe einfallende Tageslicht wird durch Oberlichtfelder ergänzt. In das Gitterwerk der Decke, das aus Oregon-Pine besteht, sind quadratische Punktstrahler eingebaut.
6. Ansicht der Nordseite und Grundriß des Verwaltungsgebäudes. Legende: 1 Haupteingang, 2 Eingangshalle, 3 Großraumbüro, 4 Kasse, 5 Innenhof, 6 Geschäftsführer, 7 Büro, 8 Garderobe, 9 Toiletten, 10 Sitzungszimmer, 11 Direktion, 12 Weinprobe, 13 Weinlager, 14 Archiv.

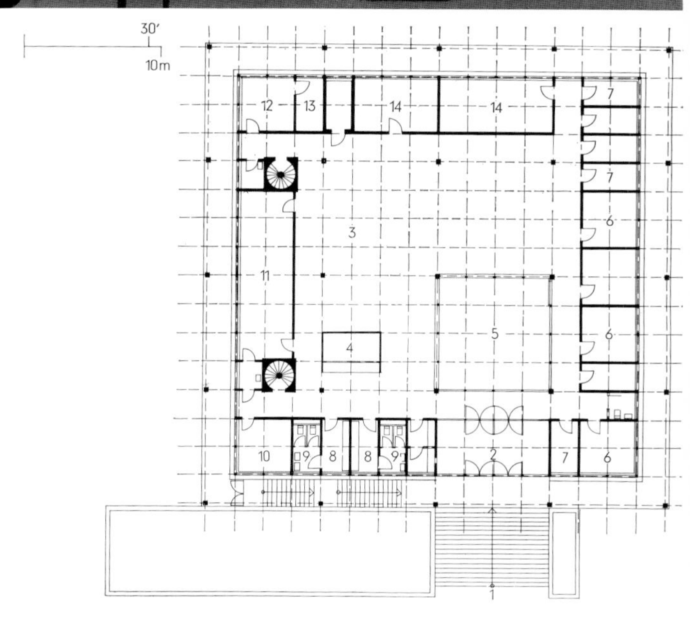
30'
10m
12
13
14
14
7
7
6
3
11
5
6
4
10
9
8
8
9
2
7
6
1

Vilhelm Lauritzen; Mogens Boertmann, Jørgen Anker Heegaard, Helge H. Hoppe

Kastrup Airport, Copenhagen, 1957–60

The airport building is a 70 metres deep block with a three-storey office wing on the North side and a large hall, extending over the full height of the building and provided with gallery floors. Luggage and goods are taken across the building at ground level whilst passengers must go up the stairs to the foyers, restaurants and transit waiting room, all of which are placed on galleries above the goods handling area. Passengers reach the aircraft at upper floor level through approx. 300 metres long "fingers" which, for the time being, can handle up to 35 aircraft. Because of the transverse orientation of the passenger handling system, the building can be extended in the longitudinal direction. The public has access to high-level viewing points both inside the hall on a gallery facing the concourse, and outside on promenade decks, along the roofs of the fingers. The building is erected in reinforced concrete and has a cladding of twin curtain walls of wood and glass.

Flughafengebäude in Kastrup bei Kopenhagen, 1957–60

Das Flughafengebäude besteht aus einem 70 m tiefen Block mit einem dreigeschossigen Bürotrakt an der nördlichen Längsseite und einer großen Halle, die über die volle Höhe des Gebäudes reicht und von seitlichen Galerien begleitet wird. Gepäck und Fracht werden zu ebener Erde quer durch das Gebäude befördert, während die Reisenden sich über Treppen zu den Foyers, Restaurants und Transitwarteräumen begeben müssen, die alle auf den Galerien über der Frachtgutabfertigung untergebracht sind. Zu den Flugzeugen gelangen die Passagiere durch etwa 300 m lange »Finger«, galerieartige Flugsteige in Höhe des ersten Stockes, die zur Zeit Abfertigungsmöglichkeiten für maximal 35 Maschinen bieten. Infolge des querorientierten Abfertigungssystems kann das Gebäude in Längsrichtung erweitert werden. Das Publikum hat Zugang zu hochgelegenen Aussichtspunkten, sowohl im Innern der Halle auf Aussichtsbalkons über der Hauptverkehrsfläche als auch außen auf Promenadendecks über den »Finger«-Bauten. Das Gebäude ist aus Stahlbeton errichtet und mit einem doppelten Curtain-wall aus Holz und Glas verkleidet.

1. One of the long "finger" piers of the airport. Luggage and goods are handled at ground level, passengers on upper floor level. The public have access to promenades on the roof.

1. Einer der langen »Finger«-Flugsteige. Gepäck und Frachtgut laufen durch das Erdgeschoß, während die Fluggäste im Obergeschoß abgefertigt werden. Das Publikum hat Zugang zur Dachpromenade.

2. The terminal building seen from the South, i.e. from the apron, with one of the "finger tips" in the foreground.
3. Site plan. Key: A passenger handling building, B piers, C planned restaurent, D flight briefing building, E canteen, F planned workshop, technical services, G flight kitchen, H maintenance workshop, J traffic and ramp control tower, K emergency power supply, 1 short-time parking, 2 long-time parking, 3 mail, 4 sightseers, 5 apron, 6 access road, 7 plantation, 8 planned railway link.
4. The end wall on the east side with its large windows provides side lighting for the main concourse.
5. The corridor in the fingers is permanently screened against the sun by asbestos cement slats. The traffic control tower is accessible through spiral stairs in the white-painted column.

2. Die Südseite des Abfertigungsgebäudes vom Rollfeld her gesehen, mit einer der »Fingerspitzen« im Vordergrund.
3. Lageplan. Legende: A Abfertigungsgebäude für Fluggäste, B Fingerförmige Flugsteige, C geplantes Restaurant, D Flugpersonal, E Kantine, F Geplantes Werkstattgebäude, technischer Dienst, G Zentralküche für den Bordservice, H Werkstattgebäude, Wartungsdienst, J Kontrollturm für Luftverkehr und Rampenanlage, K Kraftwerk zur Notversorgung; 1 Parkplatz für kurzzeitiges Parken, 2 Parkplatz für längeres Parken, 3 Postverkehr, 4 Besucher, 5 Standplätze für Flugzeuge, 6 Zufahrtsstraße, 7 Anpflanzungen, 8 geplante Eisenbahnverbindung.
4. Durch die große Fensterfläche in der Ostfassade erhält die Abfertigungshalle Seitenlicht.
5. Die Gänge der Flugsteig-»Finger« sind durch horizontale Asbestzementblenden gegen Sonneneinstrahlung abgeschirmt. Der Kontrollturm ist durch eine Wendeltreppe in dem weiß gestrichenen Betonzylinder zugänglich.

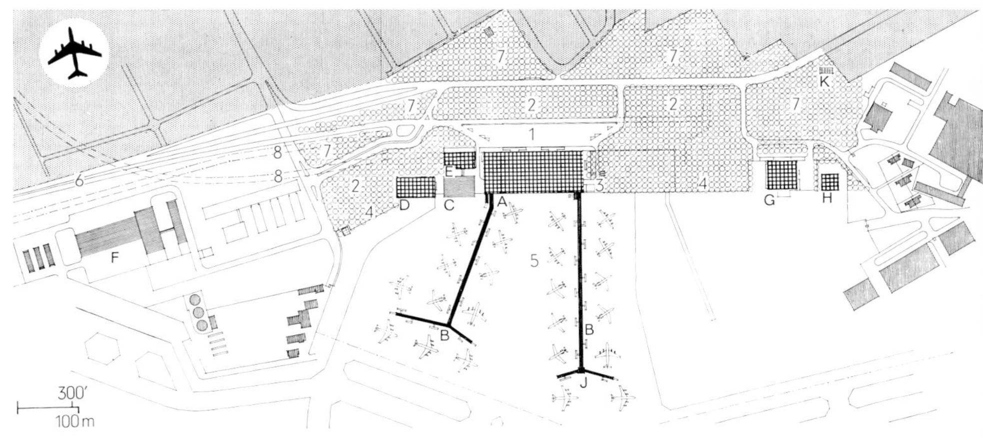
7
7
K
7
2
2
7
1
8
7
6
8
E
2
3
4
4
D
C
A
G
H
F
5
B
B
J
300′
100 m

6. Apron side of the building. For acoustic reasons, the building is insulated with a double layer of glass. The bars of the curtain wall are of wood.
7. The large concourse, seen from the West window.
8. Cross-section of passenger handling building and plan of first floor. Key: 1 departure gallery, 2 airport-tax counter, 3 passport control, 4 cashier, 5 transit lounge, 6 information, 7 shops, 8 bank, 9 post office, 10 transit passengers' entrance, 11 nursery, 12 bar, 13 lifts, 14 stairs to toilets in basement, 15 staff passage, 16 customs, 17 outdoor balcony, 18 stairs to VIP reception and rest lounge, 19 stairs to transit restaurant, 20 toilets, 21 check area, 22 transit passengers' check-in, 23 arrival bridge, luggage delivery, 24 lounge for domestic flights, 25 exit to aircraft, 26 stairs for passengers to aircraft, 27 offices, 28 balcony, 29 upper part of main concourse, 30 transit restaurant, 31 incoming luggage, 32 installations.
9. The concourse extends through the whole length and height of the building. On the right, the stairs and galleries to the three-storey office wing on the North side. The ceiling consists of blue-painted aluminium plates, the flooring of Øland tiles. The walls of the office wing are painted light-green, the columns white, and the stringers and banisters of the stairs vermilion-red.

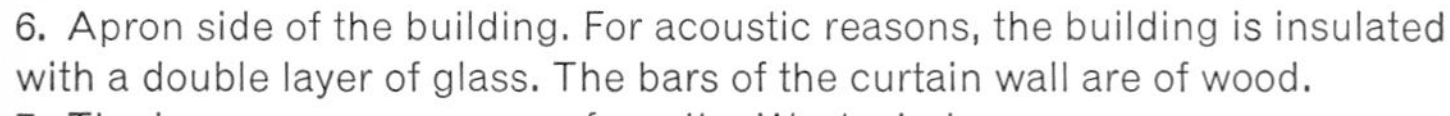

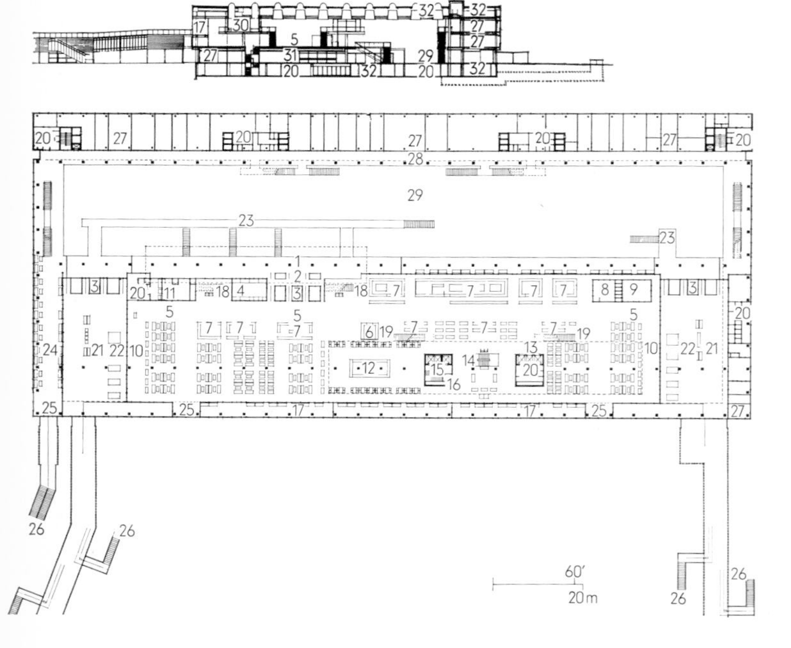

6. Die Fassade des Abfertigungsgebäudes zum Flugplatz ist aus akustischen Gründen mit einer doppelten Glaswand geschlossen. Die Sprossen des Curtain-walls bestehen aus Holz.
7. Die große Abfertigungshalle, durch die westliche Fensterwand gesehen.
8. Querschnitt des Abfertigungsgebäudes und Grundriß des ersten Obergeschosses. Legende: 1 Galerie für abfliegende Fluggäste, 2 Schalter für Fluggastgebühren, 3 Paßkontrolle, 4 Kasse, 5 Transitwarteraum, 6 Auskunft, 7 Läden, 8 Bank, 9 Postamt, 10 Eingang für Transitfluggäste, 11 Spielzimmer für Kinder, 12 Bar, 13 Aufzüge, 14 Treppe zu den Toiletten im Untergeschoß, 15 Durchgang für Personal, 16 Zoll, 17 Offene Terrasse, 18 Treppe zum Empfangs- und Ruheraum für bevorzugte Fluggäste, 19 Treppe zum Restaurant für Transitfluggäste, 20 Toiletten, 21 Eingangskontrolle für Transitfluggäste, 22 Abfertigung für Transitfluggäste, 23 Ankunftsbrücke für Gepäckauslieferung, 24 Warteraum für inländische Flüge, 25 Ausgang zu den Flugzeugen, 26 Treppen für Fluggäste, 27 Büros, 28 Balkon, 29 Luftraum Haupthalle, 30 Restaurant für Transitfluggäste, 31 Ankommendes Gepäck, 32 Installationen.
9. Die Abfertigungshalle erstreckt sich durch die ganze Länge und über die ganze Höhe des Gebäudes. Rechts sind die Treppen und Erschließungsgänge des dreigeschossigen Büroanbaus auf der Nordseite zu sehen. Die Abfertigungsräume für Fluggäste liegen links. Die Decke besteht aus blaugestrichenen Aluminiumplatten, der Fußboden aus Ølandfliesen. Die Wände des Bürogebäudes sind hellgrün gestrichen; die Säulen sind weiß, die Treppenwangen und Geländer zinnoberrot gehalten.

Interior design / Inneneinrichtung: Kay Kørbing

M/S Prinsesse Margrethe liner on the Copenhagen-Oslo route, 1957
The Copenhagen–Oslo liner M/S Prinsesse Margrethe, belonging to the United Steamship Company (D.F.D.S.), can carry some 1200 passengers. The architect participated in the design work for the ship from the outset and contributed to a layout providing good inter-connections between all parts of the ship used by passengers. The integral character is enhanced by adopting similar floor coverings and light fittings. Apart from certain variations in upholstering and colour schemes, all the light furniture designed for the ship is identical in the first and second class saloons.

Passagierschiff M/S Prinsesse Margrethe der Kopenhagen-Oslo-Linie, 1957
Das Schiff Prinsesse Margrethe der Vereinigten Dampfschiffahrtsgesellschaft (D.F.D.S.), das zwischen Kopenhagen und Oslo verkehrt, kann etwa 1200 Passagiere befördern. Der Architekt nahm an der Planung des Schiffes von Anfang an teil und trug dazu bei, gute räumliche Verbindungen zwischen allen Bereichen zu schaffen, die den Passagieren zugänglich sind. Der einheitliche Gesamteindruck wird durch die Wahl gleichartiger Fußbodenbeläge und Beleuchtungskörper unterstrichen. Abgesehen von einigen Abwandlungen der Polsterung und der Farbtöne sind alle für das Schiff entworfenen leichten Möbel in den Salons der ersten und zweiten Klasse vollkommen gleich.

1. M/S Prinsesse Margrethe.
2. Longitudinal section and plans of Boat Deck, A-Deck (A), B-Deck (B), C-Deck (C), D-Deck (D) (from top to bottom). Key: 1 passengers, 2 cargo, 3 deck crew, 4 sun deck, 5 motor engine room casing, 6 pantry, 7 toilets, 8 officers' mess, 9 radio room, 10 deck officer, 11 wheel house, 12 second class hall, 13 second class cafeteria, 14 first class dining room, 15 first class hall, 16 first class writing room, 17 bar, 18 first class smoking saloon, 19 second class dining saloon, 20 saloon, 21 second class smoking saloon, 22 galley, 23 first class cabins, 24 second class cabins.

1. M/S Prinsesse Margrethe.
2. Längsschnitt und Grundrisse vom Bootsdeck, A-Deck (A), B-Deck (B), C-Deck (C), D-Deck (D) (von oben nach unten). Legende: 1 Passagiere, 2 Ladung, 3 Deckmannschaft, 4 Sonnendeck, 5 Maschinenraum-Eindeckung, 6 Anrichte, 7 Toiletten, 8 Offiziersmesse, 9 Funkraum, 10 Deckoffiziere, 11 Radkasten, 12 Foyer 2. Klasse, 13 Selbstbedienungsrestaurant 2. Klasse, 14 Speisesaal 1. Klasse, 15 Foyer 1. Klasse, 16 Schreibzimmer 1. Klasse, 17 Bar, 18 Rauchsalon 1. Klasse, 19 Speisesaal 2. Klasse, 20 Salon, 21 Rauchsalon 2. Klasse, 22 Schiffsküche, 23 Kajüten 1. Klasse, 24 Kajüten 2. Klasse.

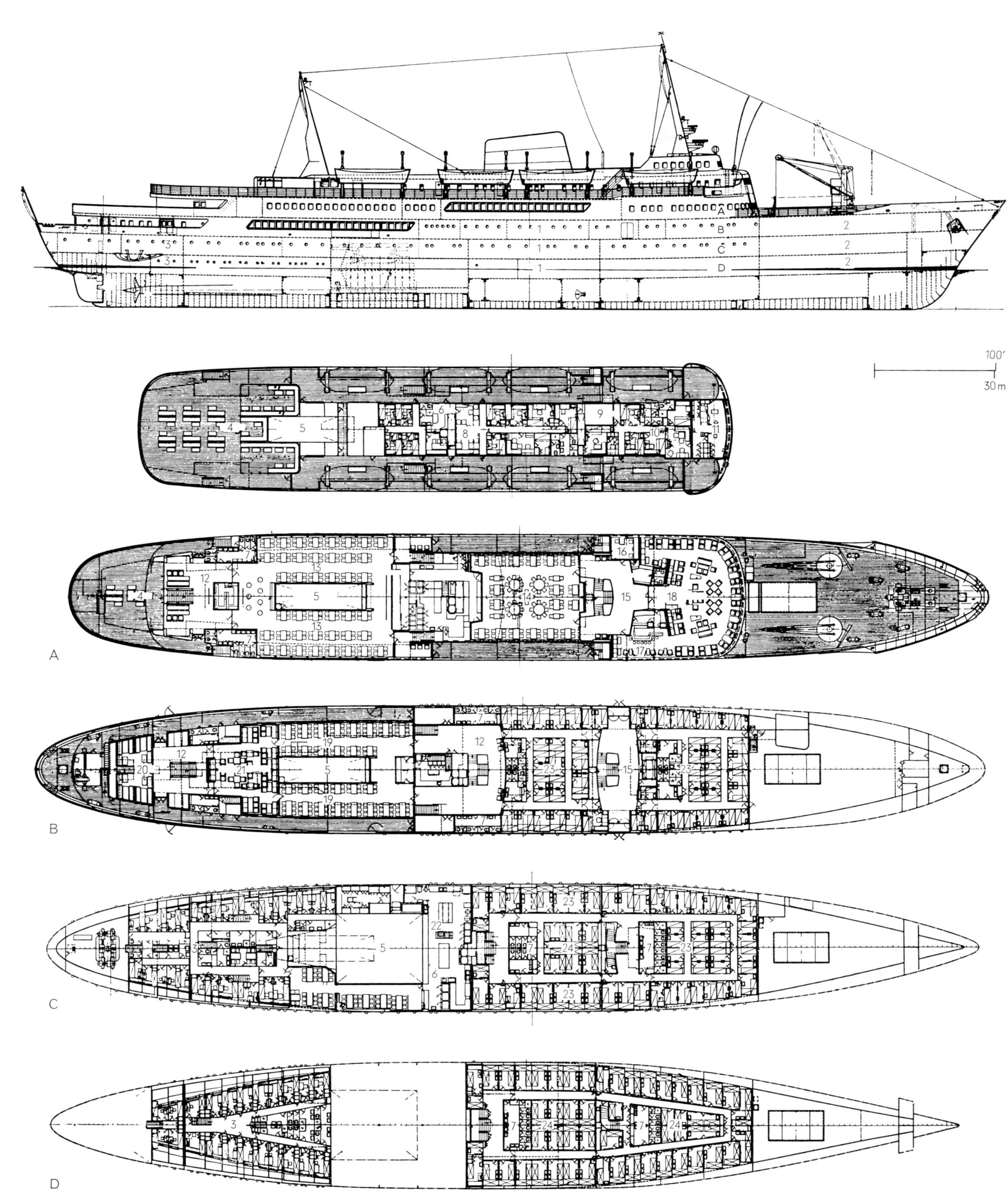

100'
30 m
A
B
C
D

3

4

3. First class hall. Wall panels of Oregon pine.
4. First class writing room. Window frames of anodised aluminium. The glass is extended directly up to the ceiling profile.
5. Second class centre vestibule with wall photographs by Keld Helmer-Petersen.
6. First class smoking saloon.
7. Second class cafeteria.
8. First class dining saloon. Upholstered glass-fibre chairs in blue colour shades along the walls and in orange in the centre of the room.
9. Standing tables at the cafeteria.
10. First class bar. The end wall is decorated by Aagaard Andersen, the bar wall by Svend Dalsgård.

3. Foyer 1. Klasse. Wandverkleidung aus Oregon-Pine.
4. Schreibzimmer 1. Klasse. Rahmen aus eloxiertem Aluminium. Das Glas ist direkt in die Profilierung der Decke eingelassen.
5. Foyer 2. Klasse mit Wandfotografien von Keld Helmer-Petersen.
6. Rauchsalon 1. Klasse.
7. Selbstbedienungsrestaurant 2. Klasse.
8. Speisesaal 1. Klasse. Gepolsterte Glasfaserstühle in Blau längs der Wände und Orange in der Mitte des Saales.
9. Stehtische im Selbstbedienungsrestaurant.
10. Bar 1. Klasse. Die Stirnwand ist von Aagaard Andersen ausgeschmückt, die Wand hinter der Bartheke von Svend Dalsgård.

5

6

7

8

9

10

Carl R. Frederiksen

St. Knud Lavards Church in Lyngby near Copenhagen, 1956–57

The church forms part of a Roman-Catholic community centre at Lyngby, with school, manse, etc. The plan of the church was governed by liturgical requirements. The entrance on the West side and the main altar and St. Mary's altar on the East side are lit by a high window with coloured cathedral glass. The church is constructed in reinforced concrete. Two rows of columns in the nave support the steel lattice work of the roof whilst the columns in the outer walls support the top walls of white-washed sand-lime brick.

St.-Knud-Lavards-Kirche in Lyngby bei Kopenhagen, 1956–57

Die Kirche bildet einen Teil eines katholischen Gemeindezentrums in Lyngby, zu dem auch eine Schule, Priesterwohnung und so weiter gehören. Der Grundriß der Kirche ist von liturgischen Gesichtspunkten bestimmt. Der Eingang auf der Westseite und der Hauptaltar und Marienaltar auf der Ostseite sind von einem hohen Fenster aus farbigem Kathedralglas beleuchtet. Die Kirche ist aus Stahlbeton errichtet. Zwei Säulenreihen im Mittelschiff tragen das Stahlfachwerk des Daches, während die außenliegenden Säulen im Erdgeschoß die geschlossenen Wandflächen des Obergadens aus weiß geschlämmtem Kalksandstein aufnehmen.

1. West side of the church with the main entrance from the terrace-shaped forecourt. The Christ-Monogram and the St. Knud Lavards medallion are designed by the painter Erik Olson.

1. Die Westseite der Kirche mit dem Haupteingang von dem terrassenförmig aufgebauten Vorplatz aus gesehen. Das Christus-Monogramm und das St.-Knud-Lavards-Medaillon sind vom Maler Erik Olson entworfen.

2. The nave seen towards the altar. Ceilings, door-high wall panels and pews are of untreated deal. Electric light fittings of copper. The crucifix above the main altar is of deal; the main altar and St. Mary's altar are of raw concrete.
3. Longitudinal section and ground floor plan. Key: 1 nave, 2 altar, 3 gallery.

2. Der Innenraum zum Altar hin. Decken, türhohe Wandverkleidungen und Gestühl bestehen aus unbehandeltem Kiefernholz. Die Beleuchtungskörper sind aus Kupfer, das Kreuz über dem Hauptaltar aus Kiefernholz, der Hauptaltar und Marienaltar aus unbehandeltem Beton.
3. Längsschnitt und Grundriß des Erdgeschosses. Legende: 1 Kirchenraum, 2 Altar, 3 Empore.

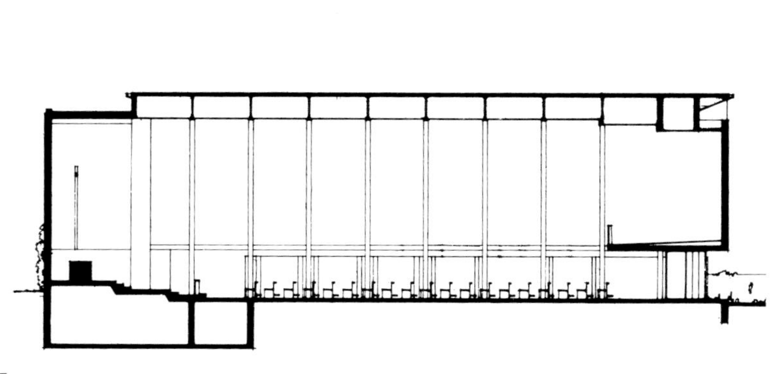

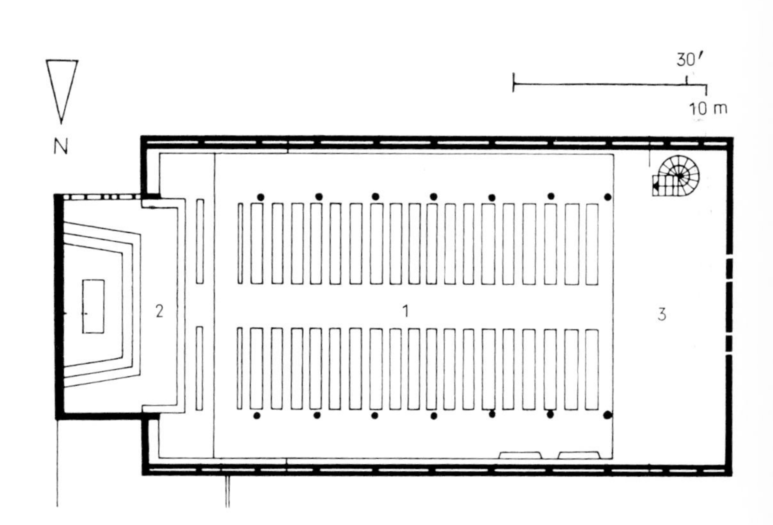

1. The church seen from Hvidovrevej.
2. South elevation and plan. Key: 1 entry, 2 nave, 3 altar, 4 office, 5 sacristy, 6 chapel, 7 store, 8 heating plant, 9 manse I, 10 manse II, 11 garden, 12 courtyard.

1. Die Kirche vom Hvidovrevej aus gesehen.
2. Ansicht von Süden und Grundriß. Legende: 1 Eingang, 2 Kirchenraum, 3 Altar, 4 Büro, 5 Sakristei, 6 Kapelle, 7 Abstellraum, 8 Heizung, 9 Priesterwohnung I, 10 Priesterwohnung II, 11 Garten, 12 Hof.

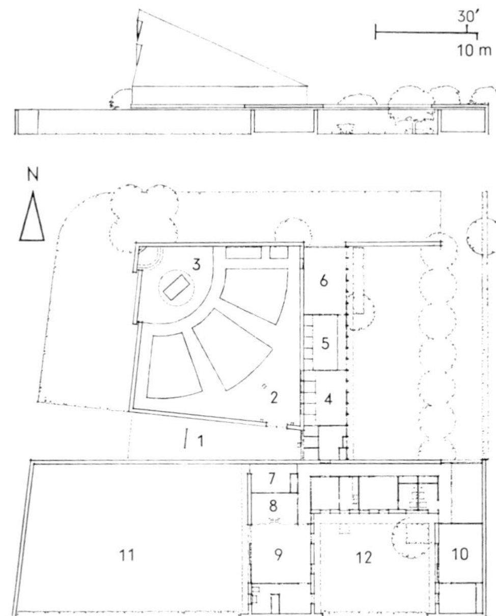

Johan Otto von Spreckelsen

St. Nikolaj Church at Hvidovre, near Copenhagen, 1960
The Roman-Catholic church is situated in a residential area close to the heavily used Hvidovrevej west of Copenhagen. A special feature of the square, but diagonally placed nave is the roof which is a reinforced concrete shell in the form of a hyperbolic paraboloid with its highest point above the altar in one of the corners of the room. Two narrow side windows between the walls throw gleams of light over the black, isolated altar table. A deep and narrow vestibule forms a fine, distance-creating transition between street and nave. Two manses in a one-storey wing are linked with the church. The walls are of untreated brick, inside and outside.

St.-Nikolaj-Kirche in Hvidovre bei Kopenhagen, 1960
Die katholische Kirche steht in einem Wohngebiet an dem stark befahrenen Hvidovrevej westlich von Kopenhagen. Der quadratische, aber diagonal orientierte Kirchenraum erhält seine besondere Note durch die Decke, die aus einer Stahlbetonschale in Form eines hyperbolischen Paraboloids besteht und über dem Altar in einer der Ecken ihren höchsten Punkt erreicht. Zwei schmale Seitenfenster, die in verdeckten Wandschlitzen angeordnet sind, werfen Streiflicht über den schwarzen, frei stehenden Altartisch. Eine tiefe und enge Vorhalle bildet einen wirkungsvollen, distanzschaffenden Übergang zwischen Straße und Kirchenraum. Zwei Priesterwohnungen in einem eingeschossigen Anbau sind der Kirche angeschlossen. Die Wände bestehen innen und außen aus unbehandeltem Backstein.

3. The diagnonally placed altar table of black marble receives side light through high slits between the walls, facing south. The ceiling is covered with untreated deal boards. Furniture and fittings are of oak, and the font of black marble. ▷

3. Der diagonal gestellte Altartisch aus schwarzem Marmor erhält Seitenlicht durch hohe, nach Süden orientierte Wandschlitze. Die Decke ist mit unbehandelten Kiefernholzbrettern verkleidet. Das Mobiliar besteht aus Eichenholz, das Taufbecken aus schwarzem Marmor. ▷

4. Entrance from Hvidovrevej. Walls of yellow brick, timber construction of oak, paving of granite.
5. The narrow vestibule of the church with an attractively illuminated medieval wood sculpture, representing St. Nikolaj.
6. The organ is placed diagonally in relation to the altar. Like the pews, it is made of oak.

4. Eingang vom Hvidovrevej. Mauern aus gelbem Backstein, Holzteile aus Eichenholz, Pflasterung aus Granit.
5. Die enge dunkle Vorhalle der Kirche mit einer eindrucksvoll beleuchteten mittelalterlichen Holzskulptur, die den hl. Nikolaus darstellt.
6. Die mit Eichenholz verkleidete Orgel ist diagonal dem Altar gegenübergestellt.

1. The church seen from the South. The main entrance is below the low roof in front of the belfry.
2. Staircase and belfry.

1. Die Kirche von Süden. Der Haupteingang befindet sich unter dem niedrigen Dach vor dem Glockenturm.
2. Treppen- und Glockenturm.

Rolf Graae + Vilhelm Wohlert

Stengård Church at Gladsaxe, near Copenhagen, 1963–64
The Lutheran church is situated in a residential district to the North of Copenhagen. Porch, aisle, nave, staircase and belfry are composed into an interpenetrating group of buildings forming an entity of highly plastic effect, with the belfry as its climax. The qualities of the red brick are utilised to the full both externally and internally. Thus, walls, altar, pulpit and font are in the same material, forming an integrated unity. Ground floor and gallery of the aisle can either be used as an extension to the nave or as self-contained premises for parish activities.

Stengård-Kirche in Gladsaxe bei Kopenhagen, 1963–64
Die evangelisch-lutherische Kirche liegt in einem Villenviertel nördlich von Kopenhagen. Vorhalle, Seitenschiff, Kirchenraum, Treppenturm und Glockenturm bauen sich wie ineinandergeschachtelte Backsteinkörper zu einer stark plastisch wirkenden Gruppe auf, die im Glockenturm gipfelt. Die Materialreize der roten Backsteinmauern werden sowohl außen als auch innen ausgespielt. So sind Wände, Altar, Kanzel und Taufbecken aus dem gleichen Baustoff zu einer kompositionellen Einheit verbunden. Untergeschoß und Empore des Seitenschiffs können entweder zur Erweiterung des Kirchenraumes oder als selbständige Lokale für das Gemeindeleben verwendet werden.

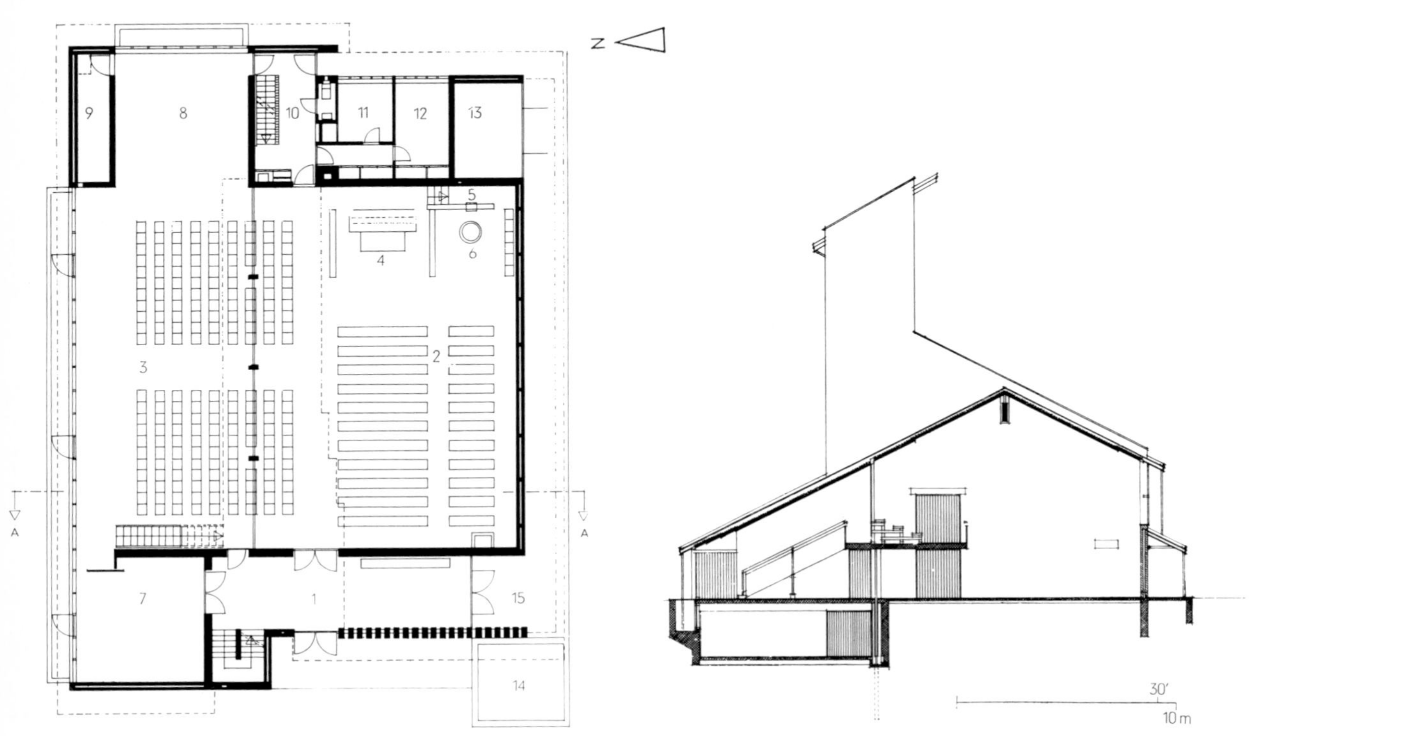

Z
9
8
10
11
12
13
5
4
6
3
2
A
A
7
1
15
14
30'
10 m

3. West side with staircase and belfry.
4. Ground floor plan and section A-A. Key: 1 porch, 2 nave, 3 aisle, 4 altar, 5 pulpit, 6 font, 7 waiting room for christening parties, 8 small hall (stage) 9 near-stores, 10 waiting room, 11 parish clerk, 12 vicar, 13 chapel, 14 lily pond, 15 loggia.
5. The nave is erected in untreated red brick and receives side light from the South. Altar, pulpit and font are of brick, the floor of hard-burned tiles.

3. Die Westseite mit Treppen- und Glockenturm.
4. Grundriß des Erdgeschosses und Schnitt A-A. Legende: 1 Vorhalle, 2 Kirchenraum, 3 Seitenschiff, 4 Altar, 5 Kanzel, 6 Taufbecken, 7 Warteraum für Täuflinge, 8 Kleiner Saal (Bühne), 9 Abstellraum, 10 Warteraum, 11 Küster, 12 Pfarrer, 13 Kapelle, 14 Pflanzenbecken, 15 Loggia.
5. Der Kirchenraum aus unbehandeltem roten Backstein bekommt Seitenlicht von Süden her. Altar, Kanzel und Taufbecken bestehen ebenfalls aus Backstein, der Fußboden aus hartgebrannten Fliesen.

6. The altar wall of the church. The concrete underside of the gallery is visible on the left.
7. Aisle of the church, seen towards the rear wall with the stairs leading up to the gallery.

6. Die Altarwand des Kirchenraumes. Links die schalungsrauhe Beton-Unterseite der Empore.
7. Das Seitenschiff der Kirche mit Blick auf die Rückwand und die zur Empore führende Treppe.

1. The church seen from South-East, with the stairs leading up from the park to the terrace in front of the belfry. ▷
2. The terrace at the foot of the belfry is built of the same yellow brick as the church itself.

1. Die Kirche von Südosten, mit dem Treppenaufgang vom Park zur Terrasse vor dem Glockenturm. ▷
2. Die Terrassenanlage vor dem Glockenturm besteht aus dem gleichen gelben Backstein wie die Kirche selbst.

Inger Exner, Johannes Exner, Knud Erik Larsen

St. Clemens Church at Randers, Jutland, 1963–64
The Lutheran church, situated in the outskirts of Randers, adjoins a residential district in the North and a hillside park in the South, and the nave with its prismatic shape juts out over the steep slope like a ship's stern. This arrangement has also enabled the parish premises on the lower floor to enjoy direct daylight and view. The view over the park and the Gudenå valley is effectively used as a backcloth for the altar table. The church is built in yellow brick; furniture and fittings are of deal. Through a terrace, the church has an attractive second access from the park.

St.-Clemens-Kirche in Randers, Jütland, 1963–64
Die evangelisch-lutherische Kirche, die in einem Vorort von Randers steht, schließt im Norden an ein Villenviertel, im Süden an ein ziemlich hügeliges Parkgelände an, wobei sich das Kirchenschiff mit seiner prismatischen Form wie der Vordersteven eines Schiffes über einen steilen Abhang vorschiebt. Diese Anordnung hat es auch ermöglicht, die Gemeinderäume in einem Untergeschoß mit direkter Beleuchtung und Aussicht unterzubringen. Der Blick über den Park und das Gudenåtal ist im Kirchenraum wirkungsvoll als Hintergrund für den Altartisch ausgenutzt. Die Kirche wurde aus gelbem Backstein errichtet; die Möblierung besteht aus Kiefernholz. Über eine Terrasse hat die Kirche einen schönen zweiten Zugang vom Park her.

3. With its prismatic shape, the church seems to push itself over the South slope. The high windows provide daylight not only for the church but also for the parish premises underneath.
4. The altar is placed in front of the window and panorama wall on the South side, which is divided by narrow brick pillars.

3. Mit ihrer prismatischen Form schiebt sich die Kirche über den Südhang vor. Die hohen Fenster beleuchten nicht nur das Kirchenschiff, sondern auch die darunter liegenden Gemeinderäume.
4. Der Altar vor der durch eng gestellte Backsteinpfeiler aufgeteilten Fenster- und Aussichtswand auf der Südseite.

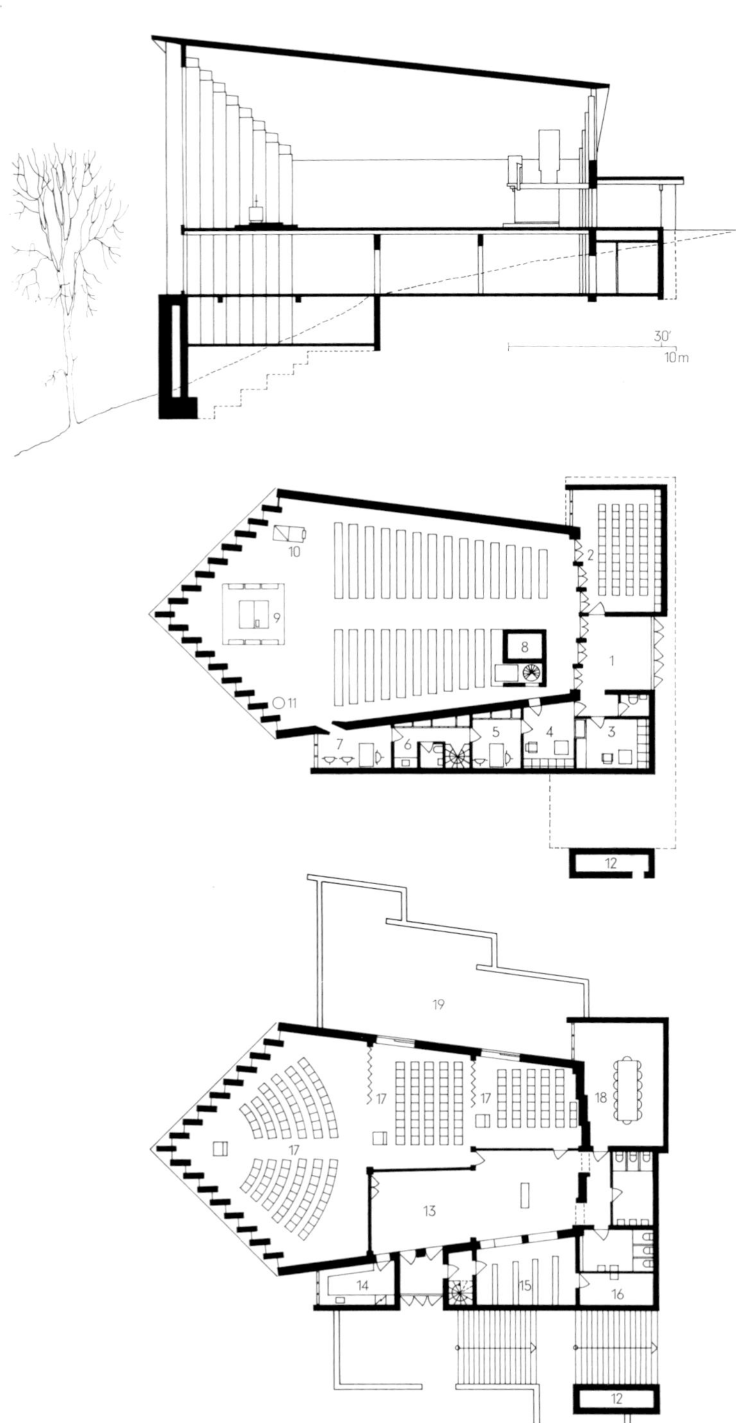

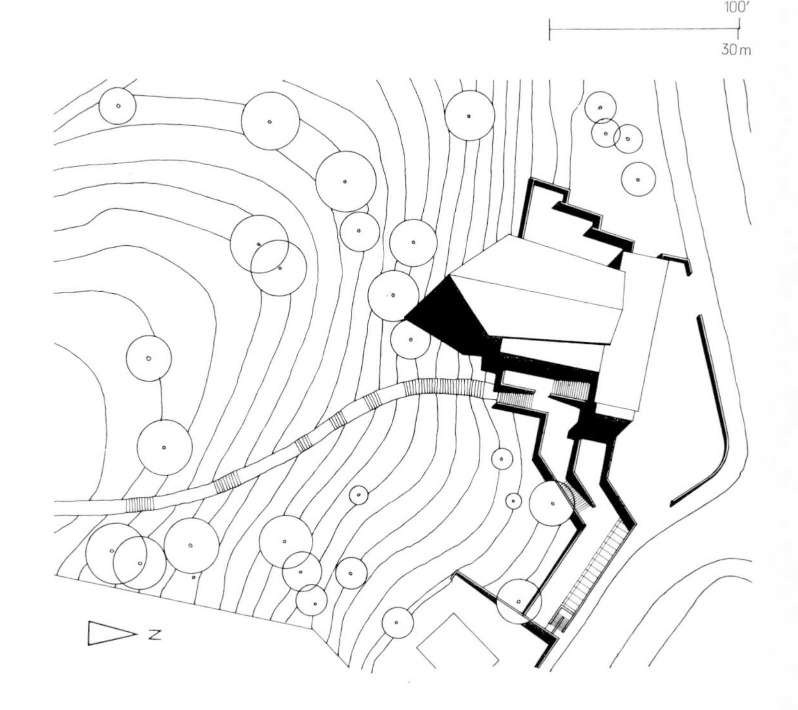

5. Longitudinal section, plans of parish hall and lower church. Key: 1 vestibule, 2 room for confirmees, 3 waiting room, 4 choir practice, 5 office, 6 cupboards, 7 vestry, 8 organ, 9 altar, 10 pulpit, 11 baptismal font, 12 belfry, 13 foyer, 14 kitchen, 15 cloakroom, 16 stores, 17 meeting hall, 18 meeting room, 19 terrace.
6. The altar table is made of Norwegian marble. An old Romanesque baptismal font, originally without feet, has been erected on new feet of chromium plated steel.
7. The organ is made of deal and designed in collaboration with the organ builder Th. Frobenius.
8. Site plan.

5. Längsschnitt, Grundrisse des Hauptgeschosses und des Untergeschosses. Legende: 1 Vorhalle, 2 Raum für den Konfirmandenunterricht, 3 Wartezimmer, 4 Übungsraum des Kirchenchors, 5 Büro, 6 Schränke, 7 Sakristei, 8 Orgel, 9 Altar, 10 Kanzel, 11 Taufbecken, 12 Glockenturm, 13 Vorraum, 14 Küche, 15 Garderobe, 16 Abstellraum, 17 Gemeindesaal, 18 Sitzungszimmer, 19 Terrasse.
6. Der Altartisch besteht aus norwegischem Marmor. Ein altes romanisches Taufbecken, das ursprünglich keine Füße hatte, ist auf einem neuen Untergestell aus verchromtem Stahl aufgestellt.
7. Die Orgel mit ihrem Kiefernholzgehäuse wurde in Zusammenarbeit mit dem Orgelbauer Th. Frobenius entworfen.
8. Lageplan.

Gehrdt Bornebusch, Max Brüel, Jørgen Selchau, Henning Larsen

Crematorium Chapel at Glostrup, near Copenhagen, 1960
The crematorium is situated on level ground at Glostrup, West of Copenhagen. The group of buildings consists of a cubically shaped chapel and a long, low wing with reception room, offices, crematorium proper, etc. The two parts of the group are separated by a long wall on which the names of those buried here will be engraved with bronze lettering. The impressive interior is dominated by a skylight placed above the catafalque where the sun rays are reflected in a composition of wooden boards set at right angles to each other. The patterned walls are of red brick.

Krematoriumskapelle in Glostrup bei Kopenhagen, 1960
Das Krematorium steht auf einem ebenen Gelände bei Glostrup westlich von Kopenhagen. Zu der Anlage gehören eine kubisch gestaltete Kapelle und ein langer, niedriger Anbau mit Empfangsraum, Büros, Krematorium und so weiter. Die beiden Bauteile sind durch eine lange Mauer getrennt, auf der die Namen der dort Beigesetzten in Bronzebuchstaben eingelassen werden sollen. Das eindrucksvolle Innere der Kapelle wird durch das über dem Katafalk angebrachte Oberlicht beherrscht, wo sich das Licht in einer Komposition aus rechtwinklig zueinander gestellten Holzflächen bricht. Das lebhaft gemusterte Mauerwerk besteht aus rotem Backstein.

1. The woodwork of the low West wing is dark-stained.
2. The chapel seen from the South. Behind the wall on the left are all the ancillary rooms.
3. Section and plan.
4. Interior of the chapel with the toplight sculpture of wooden boards above the brick catafalque.

1. Die Holzkonstruktion des niedrigen Westflügels ist dunkel imprägniert.
2. Die Kapelle von Süden gesehen. Hinter der Mauer links liegen alle Nebenräume.
3. Schnitt und Grundriß.
4. Das Innere der Kapelle mit der Oberlichtskulptur aus Holzplatten über dem gemauerten Katafalk.

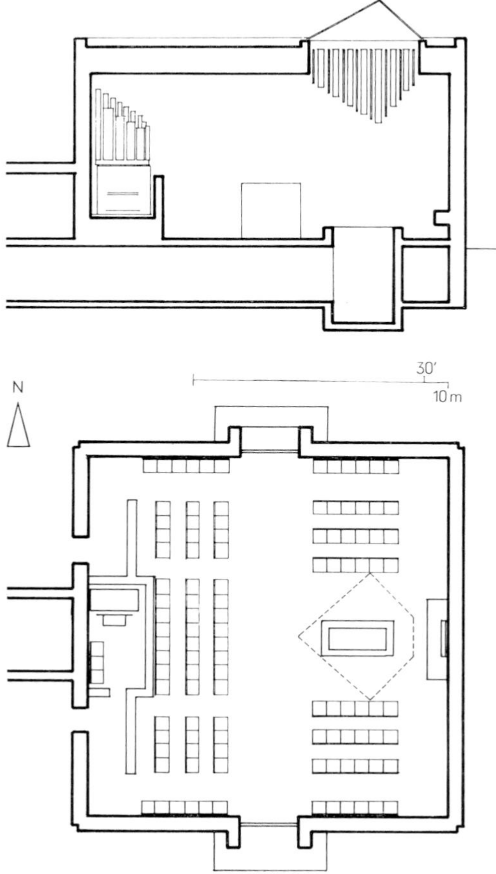

Index

Photographers Credit · Photonachweis

Inga Aistrup, Vedbæk 6 (1, 2), 7 (3), 8 (4)
Brems Foto, Aalborg 150 (2), 151 (3), 152 (5, 6), 153 (7, 8)
Carrebye, København 184 (1), 185 (3)
Henrik Clausen, Roskilde 120 (1)
Hammerschmidt Foto, Århus 90 (1), 91 (4), 129 (3), 131 (1), 132 (2), 133 (4), 134 (6–8)
Erik Hansen, København 17 (15), 92 (1, 2), 93 (4), 96 (1), 97 (2), 135 (9, 10)
Bent Hassing Reklamefoto, København 41 (3, 4)
Hauerslev's Atelier, København 12 (10)
Keld Helmer-Petersen, København 36 (1), 37 (3, 4), 40 (1), 46 (1), 47 (2), 48 (4, 5), 49 (6, 7), 58 (1), 59 (4, 6), 61 (3–5), 65 (1), 66 (2), 67 (5, 6), 68 (1), 69 (3, 4), 70 (6, 7), 71 (10, 11), 85 (4), 86 (2), 87 (3), 168 (1), 169 (4), 170 (5–7), 171 (1), 172 (3, 4), 173 (6, 7), 180 (1), 181 (3–5), 182 (1), 183 (3–5), 194 (2), 195 (3–5), 202 (3, 4), 203 (5–7, 9, 10), 204 (1), 205 (2), 206 (1), 207 (3), 208 (5, 6)
Palle Hestbech, Søborg-København 89 (4, 5)
Jesper Høm / Delta, København 54 (1, 2), 55 (4–6), 56 (1), 57 (3–5), 140 (1), 141 (2), 142 (4–5), 143 (6–8), 176 (1, 2), 177 (3, 4), 209 (1), 210 (3), 211 (5), 212 (6, 7)
Ingemann, København 41 (5)
Axel Jensen 208 (4)
Merete Johansen & Henning Camre, København 59 (3)
Jonals Co., København 10 (6), 11 (8, 9), 130 (4–6)
Birte Palle Jørgensen, Hjallese 106 (1), 107 (2), 108 (3, 4), 109 (6–8), 122 (5–7), 216 (1, 2), 217 (4)
Mogens S. Koch, København 84 (1), 85 (5)
Claus Kœfœd Fotografi, Erik Hansens Eftf., København 34 (1), 35 (3–5)
Maarbjergs Atelier, Gentofte Torv 13 (12)
Leonore Mau, Hamburg-Othmarschen 45 (2–4)
Svend Munk, København 59 (7)
Rigmor Mydtskov & Steen Rønne, København 27 (20, 21), 146 (2, 3)
Nordisk Pressefoto, København 126 (5, 7)
Claus Ørsted / Delta, København 121 (4)
Thomas Pedersen & Poul Pedersen, Århus 50 (1), 51 (3–5), 110 (2, 3), 111 (4), 112 (5, 6, 8), 124 (1), 125 (3), 126 (4, 6), 127 (8), 162 (1), 163 (2, 4), 186 (1, 2), 187 (3), 188 (4), 213 (1), 214 (3, 4), 215 (6, 7)
Rading Reklamefoto, København 38 (1), 39 (3)
Louis Schnakenburg, Reklamefotografi, København 94 (3), 95 (6)
Jan Selzer, København 118 (6), 119 (7)
Poul Erik Skriver, København 10 (7), 70 (9), 128 (1)
Sonnenburg Fotografi, København 136 (1), 137 (4, 5), 138 (6–8)
Stadsarkivets fotografiske atelier 9 (5)
Strüwing Reklamefoto, København 12 (11), 62 (2), 63 (4), 64 (6, 8), 72 (1), 73 (4, 5), 74 (6–8), 75 (9), 76 (2, 3), 77 (5), 78 (2), 79 (3, 4), 80 (3, 4), 81 (5), 82 (1), 83 (4, 5), 98 (1), 99 (2), 100 (3, 4), 101 (6–8), 102 (9, 10), 148 (1), 149 (3–5), 156 (1, 3), 157 (4, 5), 158 (1), 159 (3), 160 (4–6), 161 (7–9), 164 (1), 165 (3, 4), 166 (5), 167 (6, 7), 174 (1), 175 (3, 4), 178 (1), 179 (3–5), 189 (1, 2), 190 (3–5), 191 (6), 196 (1), 197 (2, 4, 5), 198 (6, 7), 199 (9)
Else Tholstrup 42 (1, 2), 43 (3, 5), 67 (7)
Thy, København 39 (2)

Die Gesamtherstellung lag in den Händen der Passavia Druckerei AG Passau. Für die Schrift wurde die Monotype-Grotesk verwendet. Das holzfreie Original-Kunstdruckpapier Artiprint P lieferte die Feldmühle AG, Düsseldorf. Die Klischees wurden angefertigt von den Graphischen Kunstanstalten Brend'Amour, Simhart & Co. und Osiris, beide in München; Scham & Storsberg, Ulm/Donau.